Hubertus Elffers

The Commercial Dutch Grammar

Hubertus Elffers

The Commercial Dutch Grammar

ISBN/EAN: 9783741186998

Manufactured in Europe, USA, Canada, Australia, Japa

Cover: Foto ©Andreas Hilbeck / pixelio.de

Manufactured and distributed by brebook publishing software (www.brebook.com)

Hubertus Elffers

The Commercial Dutch Grammar

THE COMMERCIAL DUTCH GRAMMAR

(SUPERSEDING THE PRACTICAL DUTCH GRAMMAR),

A GRAMMAR FOR PRIVATE STUDENTS, CIVIL SERVANTS, BUSINESS MEN, AND FOR USE IN COLLEGES AND THE HIGHER CLASSES IN SCHOOLS.

BY

HUBERTUS ELFFERS,

AUTHOR OF THE "ELEMENTARY GRAMMAR OF THE DUTCH LANGUAGE," "COURSE OF DUTCH COMPOSITION," "LEESBOEK VOOR ZUID-AFRIKA," ETC.
SWORN TRANSLATOR FOR THE DUTCH, ENGLISH, FRENCH, AND GERMAN LANGUAGES

J. C. JUTA & CO.,
CAPE TOWN. | JOHANNESBURG
PORT ELIZABETH.
1896.

PREFACE.

The Practical Dutch Grammar has had a run of ten years. In that time the author has seen its extended 6th (i.e. 7th) Edition. Its record has all along been so satisfactory and encouraging, that it shall be preserved on the fly-leaf of the book which supersedes it.

The present volume is issued under another name. The disappearance of the word "Practical" from the title, however, does not affect the practical side of the book. On the contrary, this will be found increased to such an extent, as to render comparison between the two a matter of difficulty. The "Practical Grammar" was the writer's first attempt; a further experience of ten years of language teaching in South Africa should to some extent be a warrant for the superiority of the present work above its predecessor.

Not only that,—but Africa's actual wants were not fully revealed to the young author of the "Practical Grammar." While it, however, ran its course, the fairest opportunities were furnished him for using eye and ear,— and the "Commercial Grammar" is issued as the embodiment of hints kindly furnished.

Provision has been made for schools. English children have the "Elementary Dutch Grammar," Dutch children the "Practische Hollandsche Spraakkunst," while one series of Dutch Readers has been issued with English vocabularies annexed. But another class of students must be reached. Young men reading for the Matriculation or the Civil Service examinations, men in business, merchants and agents, those are they for whom this book has been compiled, and to whom the author inscribes it with the fervent hope that they may find it what they need.

H. E.

"THE TRANSLATION OFFICE," CAPE TOWN,
1 *Jan.* 1895.

TABLE OF CONTENTS.

CHAPTER I.

THE ALPHABET . . . . PAGE 1-8
   Vowels, 1; Consonants, 2; Diphthongs, 3; Spelling and Pronunciation, 3-4; Ex. on Pronunciation, 4-6; Division of words in Syllables, 6-7; Syllables open and closed, 7; Ex. on Syllables, 7-8.

CHAPTER II.

SPELLING 9-24
   Final Consonants, 9-10; Single and double *a* and *u*, 10; Single *i* and double *ie*, 11; Single and double *e* and *o*, 11-12; Choice between *ei* and *ij*, 13; Homonyms with *e* and *ee*, 13; Homonyms with *o* and *oo*, 14; Homonyms with *ij* and *ei*, 14; Ex. on the use of single and double vowels, 15-20; Spelling of Compound Nouns, 20-21; Compound forms joining parts by *e* or *en*, 21-22; Ex. on same, 22-24.

CHAPTER III.

PARTS OF SPEECH.—THE ARTICLE 25-34
   Classification of the Article, 25; Forms of the Article, 26; Declension, 26-27; Omission and Repetition, 27-28; Used in Dutch when omitted in English, 28-29; Transl. Ex. and Gr. Ex. on the Article, 29-33; Conversation about Time, 33-34.

CHAPTER IV.

FORMATION OF THE PLURAL 35-50
   Plural in *s*, 35; in *'s*, 35; in *en*, 35-36; either *s* or *en*, 36; Words in *ie*, 36; Plural in *ers* or *eren*, 37; Different meanings of homonyms brought out by their plural, 37-38; Irregular plural forms, 38-39; Words having no plural

forms, 39; List of words having synonymous plural forms, 39–40; Words having no singular forms, 40; Sing. form used with plural meaning, 40; Final consonants with regard to the formation of the plural, 41–42; Gr. Ex. on plural forms of nouns, 42–43 and 48; Transl. Ex. on Present of "*hebben*" and "*zijn*," 43–45; Gr. and Transl. Ex. on formation of Plural, 45–49; Conversation about Meals, 49–50.

CHAPTER V.

THE GENDER OF SUBSTANTIVES 51–73
Rules to ascertain the Gender of Nouns, 51–57; The Common Gender, 57–58; The Gender of Compound Nouns, 58; List of words with different meaning according to their gender, 59; Natural Gender, 59–60; Synopsis of Rules on Genders, 60–62; Gr. Ex. on Genders, 62–64; Conjugation of "*hebben*" and "*zijn*," 64–65; How to translate the Second Person, 65–66; Transl. Ex., 66–68; Gr. Ex. on Genders, 69–71; Conv. about Forms of Greeting and Address, 72–73.

CHAPTER VI.

DECLENSION 74–101
Definition, 74; Nom., Gen., Dat., and Acc. Cases, 74–76; Obs. on Use of Cases, 76–77; Declension of the Attributive Adj. and of the Demonstrative Pron. (*deze*, *die*, etc.) and the Poss. Pron., 77–81; Form of two or more adjectives preceding one noun, 81–82; Adj. not declined when preceded by *een*, *geen*, *eenig*, etc., 82; Obs. on Declension, 82–83; Attrib. Adj. not preceded by defining word, 83–84; Attrib. Adj. in titles, 84; Strong and Weak declension, 84–85; Gr. Ex. on Declension, 87–90; Comparison between Book, Corresp. and Colloq. Dutch, 90–91; Conj. of "*leeren*" and "*stelen*," 91–94; Transl. Ex. 95–99; Conv. about the Weather, Shopping, 99–101.

CHAPTER VII.

THE ADJECTIVE 102–129
Adjectives used attributively and predicatively, 102; Agreement of Attrib. Adj., 103; Difference in meaning between inflected and uninflected form after *een*, *geen*, etc., 103; Adj. not declined, 103–104; Adj. ending in *s* not *sch*, 104;

Degrees of comparison, 105-106; Gr. Ex. and Trans. Ex. on the Adjective, 107-111; Conj. of "*dansen*" and "*lezen*," 111-114; Transl. Ex. 115-117; The Numeral Adjective, Classification, 117-118; Cardinals *één* and *beide*, 118-119; Plural forms of Cardinals (Indef.) and Ordinals, 119; Idiom. renderings of "some" and "any," 120; Idiom. Expressions, 121; Num. Adj. compounded with *voudig*, *lei, hande, maal*, etc. and the compound "*anderhalf*," 122; List of Card. and Ord. Numbers, 123-124; Gr. and Transl. Ex. on Numeral Adj. 124-126; Transl. Ex., 126-128; Conv. about Relations, 128-129.

CHAPTER VIII.

THE PRONOUN 130-155

Classification, 130; Pers. Pron. 130-134; Reflex. Pers. Pron., 132; Declension of *zelf*, 133; The Poss. Case of Pers. Pron., 133-134; Poss. Pron., 134-135; Interrog. Pron., 135-136; Compound forms "*erin*," "*eruit*," etc., 136; Indef. Pron., 136-138; The Pron. "*men*," 137; Transl. of "whoever," etc., 138; Correl. Pron., 138-139; Demonstr. Pron., 140-141; The use of "*er*," 140; Rel. Pron., 141-143; Gr. Ex. and Transl. Ex. on the Pronoun, 143-148; Transl. Ex., 148-153; Conv. about Travelling by Land and Railways, 154-155.

CHAPTER IX.

THE VERB. 156-224

Stem, 156-157; Conjugation, weak and strong, 157; Form of Conj., 158-159; Use of "*hebben*" and "*zijn*," 160; Complete Conj. of "*hebben*," 161-162; of "*zijn*," 162-163; Conj. of "*zullen*," 163; of "*worden*," 164-165; Voice, Comp. between Act. and Pass. voice of "*bijten*," 165-167; Examples illustrating the forms of the simple and compound tenses of the Pass. Voice, 167; Comp. between the same forms of "*zijn*" used as a Copulative and an Auxiliary of the Pass. Voice, 168; Obs. on the Act. and Pass. Voices, 168-169; Transposition of same, 169; Conj. of Aux. Verbs of Mood, 170-171; Moods, 172; Transl. of the Inf. Mood, 172-174; Transl. of Gerund, the Pres. and Past Part., 174-176; Tenses, 176-177; Obs. on Use of Tenses, 177-178; Number and Person, 178-179; Trans. and Intrans. verbs, 179; Reflex. Verbs, 179-182; Mixed Verbs,

b

182–183; Anomalous Verbs, 183–185; Impers. Verbs, 185–186; Caus. Verbs, 187; Frequent. Verbs, 187; Compound Verbs, 187–190; List of Strong Verbs, 191–196; Gr. Ex. and Transl. Ex. on the Verb, 196–215; Transl. Ex., 215–222; Conv. about Travelling by Sea, 222–224.

CHAPTER X.

THE ADVERB 225–241
Some Verbs followed by Adj., not Adv., 226; Classification, 226–227; Examples of the various classes of Adv., 227–229; The ending "*lijk*" not to be affixed to Adj. of manner, 229–230; Comparison of Adv., 230; Note on "*het eerst*" or "*eerst*," etc., 230–231; Obs. on some Adv., 231–233; Use of "*af*" and "*neer*," 233; Gr. Ex. and Transl. Ex. on the Adverb, 234–235; Transl. Ex. on the Adverb, 234–235; Transl. Ex. 235–240; Conv. about Various Artisans, 240–241.

CHAPTER XI.

THE PREPOSITION 242–272
Place of "*halve*" and "*wegen*," 242; Prep. formerly gov. other Cases besides the Acc., 243; Different relations pointed out by Prep., 243–244; Prep. indicating different relations, 244–246; List of Prep. verbs using differ. prep. in Dutch and English, 249–267; Transl. Ex., 268–270; Conv. about Trades and Occupations, 271–272.

CHAPTER XII.

THE CONJUNCTION 273–285
Classification, 273; Subdivisions and Examples, 274–278; Observations, 278–279; Transl. Ex., 279–283; Conv. about Teaching and Schools, 283–285.

CHAPTER XIII.

THE INTERJECTION 286–287

CHAPTER XIV.

ETYMOLOGY 288–305
Classification of words, 288; Words derived from same root, 288–289; Formation of Nouns, 289–290; Fem. names of

TABLE OF CONTENTS. xi

PAGE

Pers., etc., 290; Names of instruments, etc., 291; Diminutives, 291–292; Formation of Abstract Nouns, 293–294; of Verbs, 294–297; of Adverbs, 297; of Compound Words, 297–298; List of Words requiring explanation, 299–301; Where to place the accent, 301–302; Transl. Ex., 303–305.

CHAPTER XV.

CONSTRUCTION 306–317
Construction of Principal Sentence, 306–309; When Predicate consists of more than one word, 306–307; Place of Object, 307; Place of Adverbial extensions, 308–309; Place of "*niet*," 309; Constr. of Sub-ordinate Sentence, 310–311; Place of verbal forms at the end of Sub-ord. Sent., 310–311; Inversion of the Princ. Sent., 311–313; Inversion of the Sub-ord. Sent., 313–314; Transl. Ex., 315–317.

CHAPTER XVI.

PARSING AND ANALYSIS 318–325
List of Abbreviations, 318; Example of Parsing, 319–322; Analysis, 322–325.

CHAPTER XVII.

CORRESPONDENCE 326–336
Ways of beginning and closing letters, 326–332; Notes, 332; List of Terms, etc., 333–336.

CHAPTER XVIII.

OFFICIAL AND DOCUMENTARY LANGUAGE 337–357

CHAPTER XIX.

LIST OF CAPE IDIOMS. 358–383

ENGLISH-DUTCH VOCABULARY 384–390

(xii)

LIST OF EXERCISES ON SPECIAL POINTS OF GRAMMAR AND IDIOM.

		PAGE
On the Present of "*hebben*" and "*zijn*"		43–45
,, First Rule of Construction		66
,, Second ,, ,,		67
,, Third ,, ,,		67–68
On How to transl. the Interrog., Neg., and Neg.-Interrog. Forms		68–69
On the Fourth Rule of Construction		95
,, Transl. of Present Participle		96
,, ,, "to like to" and "to want to"		97
,, ,, "*hij hoopt te zullen,*" etc.		97–98
,, ,, the Progressive Form		98
,, ,, "when"		99
,, ,, "if"		115
,, ,, "then"		115–116
,, Fifth Rule of Construction		116–117
,, Sixth ,, ,,		126
,, Transl. of Pres. Part. II.		127
,, ,, "may," "might," "should"		148–149
,, ,, "will," "would"		149–150
,, ,, "if," "as if"		151
,, ,, "to know"		151–152
,, ,, "used to"		152
,, Seventh Rule of Construction		153
,, Transl. of "to mean"		215–217
,, ,, "I can give it," etc.		217
,, ,, "will he give it to me?" etc.		217–218
,, ,, "should," "ought to"		218–219
,, ,, "to have to," etc.		219–220
,, ,, "we make him say it," etc.		220
,, ,, "I have the floor washed," etc.		221
,, ,, "he likes doing it," etc.		221–222
,, ,, "*na,*" "*nadat,*" "*daarna*"		236–237
,, ,, "to put"		237–239

THE COMMERCIAL DUTCH GRAMMAR.

CHAPTER I.

I.—THE ALPHABET.

(*Het Alfabet.*)

1. THE Dutch alphabet consists of the same letters as the English, but the letters *c*, *q*, *x*, and *y* are not used in words of Dutch origin.

2. The following are the vowels (*klinkers*) in use: A, pron. like in Eng. a*sk* ; E, pron. like in Eng. *convey*; I (written "*ie*" for double "*i*"), pron. like in Eng. *k*nee ; O, pron. like in Eng. *w*oe ; U, pron. like in French *mûr* ; OE, pron. like in Eng. *p*ool*; EU, like in German *öde*.

> NOTE.—For the correct pronunciation of *O*, *OE*, *U*, and *EU*, it is necessary to bring the lips forward. This done, for the *O*-sound leave a larger, and for the *OE*-sound a small round opening ; for the *EU*-sound a broad slit, and for the *U*-sound a narrow slit between the lips.

3. Five vowels, viz. *a*, *e*, *i*, *o*, *u*, have each a double sound. When written with the double sign, *aa*, *ee*, *ie*, *oo*, *uu*, or when occurring (whether double or single) at the end of a syllable, or when forming a syllable by themselves, their sound is full, as indicated in § 2; but when single, and enclosed between consonants, their sound becomes imperfect: *man* (as in Germ. *Mann*); *les* (as in Eng. *test*); *lip*, pr. like English; *hop*, pr. like English ; *rust* (slightly less broad than *u* in Eng. *rust*).

B

NOTE.—The *e* has a third sound, approaching that of the imperfect *u*. It occurs in the article *de*; in the flexion endings of the adjective; in the verbal prefixes *be*, *ge*, and *ver*, and suffix *en*; in the plural ending *en* of nouns, and in unaccented syllables before *m*, *n*, *l*, *p*, *r*, *t*. The sound of this *e* is heard in the second syllable of the English word *bundle*.

4. Of the consonants (*medeklinkers*), B is pronounced as in Eng. bai*liff*; D, as in Eng. dai*nty*; K, as in Eng. ca*price*; P, as in Eng. pa*le*; R, as in Eng. er*ror*; T, as in Eng. ta*ke*; and Z, pron. *zett*, like in French; F, L, M, N, and S, like in English; H, like English ha*!* J, like Eng. *yea*; G, like *ch* in Scotch *nicht* and *loch*; V, like a very soft Eng. *f*; and W, materially like Eng. *v*.

NOTE.—*G* is always a guttural, except when occurring after *n*, when it sounds like in the English word *ring*.

5. The English *Y*, when found in foreign words, used in Dutch, is pronounced like Eng. *ee*. The Dutch *IJ* is originally a double *i*, now written *i* and *j* combined. The sound represented by this combination, which is foreign to the English language, lies close to the sound of *ay* in the Eng. word *pay*, the teeth, when pronouncing the Dutch word "*pij*," being less widely apart than for the pronunciation of Eng. *pay*.

NOTE.—The *ij*-sound changes into Dutch *i* in the word *bijzonder* (particular), and into a toneless *u* in *dikwijls* (often), and in the ending *lijk* (Eng. *ly*).

6. The letters *c*, *q*, and *x* are only met with in words of foreign origin, and are there pronounced like in English; *t*, in such words, occurring before the ending *ie*, is pronounced like *s*, e.g. *natie*, nation, pr. *na-sie*.

7. *C* occurs in Dutch in combination with *H*, *ch* being the representation of a guttural sound, sharper than that of *g*. *SCH*, when found at the beginning of a word, or as the initial letters of a stem after a prefix, should be pronounced as a combination of *s* and the guttural *ch*; when otherwise found, its sound is *s* only.

8. *TH* is pronounced as single *t*, and *PH* like *f*.

NOTE.—The *sch* is sounded in the suffix *schap*.

9. The Dutch language has the following diphthongs: *Ei*, formerly *ai* (*ag*), pron. exactly like *ij*; *Au*, pron. like in Engl. *stout*; *Ou*, pron. softer than *au*, rather more like *o* in *below*; *Ui*, no equivalent in English, softer than German *eu*, pronounced in a line with *u* and *eu* (see Note, par. 2), but with a wider opening of the mouth; *Aai*, like *ay* in Scotch pronunciation of *Mckay*; *Ooi*, full Dutch o-sound with i-sound attached, like *oh-y*; *Eeu*, full sound of Dutch *e*, ending in the sound of *w*; *Ieu*, full sound of Dutch *i*, ending in that of *w*.

NOTE.—Many people make no difference between *Au* and *Ou*, pronouncing them both like the latter of the two.

II.—SPELLING AND PRONUNCIATION.

(Spelling en Uitspraak.).

Broadly speaking, Dutch should be pronounced as it is spelled. The following are the cases in which pronunciation differs from spelling:

1. The sound of *ij* sometimes changes to that of *i*, and at other times to that of *u* (see I, 5, Note).
2. The sound of *sch* is sometimes that of a single *s* (see I, 7).
3. The sound of *th* is that of a single *t* (see I, 8).
4. The *w* is left out in the pronunciation of *erwt* (Eng. pea). It is pronounced *ert*.
5. Final *t* is many times left out before the diminutive ending *je*, as in *nestje* (little nest), pronounced *nesje*.
6. The *t* before final *ie* in words of French origin, is pronounced like *s* (see I, 6).
7. The guttural sound of *g* is lost whenever *n* precedes it (see I, 4, Note).
8. Final *b*, *d*, and *g*, are respectively pronounced like *p*, *t*, and *ch*.
9. The initial *z* of *zestig*, sixty, and *zeventig*, seventy, is pronounced like *s*.

10. The diminutive ending *je* is colloquially pronounced *ie*, except when preceded by *d* or *t*; e.g. *koppie* (for *kopje*), *boekie* (for *boekje*); but *mannetje*, and *handje*.

11. The pronunciation of the endings *de*, *der*, and *den*, is often *je*, *jer*, and *jen* in colloquial speech. *De goede man* (the good man), is pronounced *de goeie man;* likewise does *breeder* (broader) sound *breejer*, and *sleden* (sledges), *slejen*.

This is the case in :—

(ADJECTIVES) *goede, goeie* (good), *breede, breeje* (broad), *roode, rooie* (red), *doode, dooie* (dead), *kwade, kwaaie* (angry), &c.; whereas, *oude* (old), and *koude* (cold) change their *d* into a *w, ouwe, kouwe*.

(NOUNS) *laden, laaien* (drawers), *leden, lejen* (members), *kleeden, kleejen* (carpets), *smeden, smejen* (smiths), *sneden, snejen* (slices), &c.

(VERBS) *laden, laaien* (to load), *snijden, snijen* (to cut), *lijden, lijen* (to suffer), *leiden, leien* (to lead), *rijden, rijen* (to ride), &c.

12. In loose speech the final *n* of the ending *en* of nouns and verbs, and of inflected articles and adjectives, is dropped.

EXERCISE ON PRONUNCIATION.

Pronounce according to the hints in the undermentioned paragraphs of section I.

2.

Paar, taal, haas, maat, va-der, ma-len, ta-fel, za-del; meel, reet, geel, le-pel, ze-dig, le-ven, we-zel; diep, stier, sliep, iets, ieder, vie-ren, bie-len, wie-den; kool, roos, pook, treon, mo-len, wo-nen, ko-per, sto-ven; uur, muur, uw, sluw; vu-ren, ju-bel, du-wen, mu-zick; koek, woest, poel, troep, moe-der, loe-ren, woe-dend, roe-ren; neus, heup, deur, kneu, sleu-ren, leu-zo, steu-nen, kleu-rig.

3.

(FULL VOWELS.) Baat, ba-ten, aap, a-del; zeef, ste-len, eer, e-del, vee; dienst, wie-len, iep, ie-ren, drie; roof, do-ren, oor, o-pen, stroo; stuur, stu-ren, u-ren, ruw.

(IMPERFECT VOWELS.) Kar, slap, plat, man, stam, land, stal, want, plan, lam; vel, mes, wet, test, net, spel, ren, stem, pen, kers; dik, mis, lip, ik, bril, stil, kin, pit, krimp, dirk; mul, hulk, rum, kunst, lust, hurk, muts, dun, ruk, wuft.

§ 3. NOTE.—Bree-de, ka-le, laf-fen, de, ge-loop, ver-haal, be-derf, koo-pen, ee-ren, val-len, rom-mel, de-det, dee-sem, re-ten, loo-pen, wan-de-len, krab-be-len, re-gee-ren.

4.

Baas, bas, buur, bus, boel, boek, bok, beek, bek; daar, dorp, deur, doel, dek, dak, dwaas, dwars, diep, dik, dis-tel; kaal, kap, koor, kor, kwee, kwast, kist, kiel, ko-ren; peer, paard, pronk, proest, pis-tool, pest, pret; raam, ram, roes, rust, rank, rit-se-len, riet; teer, turf, troep, toorn, to-ren, trap-pe-len; zak, zaak, ziek, zink, zulk, zool, zeem, zoet, zwal-ken; haan, hoop, hop, hak, haal, help, hulp, hoed, heup; jaar, jas, jood, jank, joel, jouk, jong; goot, grot, geul, gaas, gas, groef, gist, grim-men; vaas, vroom, voelt, vleug, vlag, vlok, vin-nen; waan, woest, wier, wraak, wrok, worst.

5.

(FOREIGN WORDS.) Synode, tyrannie, hypocriet.

(DUTCH WORDS.) Rijm, vijl, stijf, grijp, wrijven, lijvig, blijken, wijzen.

6.

District, concept, examen, exceptie, promotie, delicaat, garantie, inconsequent (also spelled "*inkonsekwent*").

7.

Lach, kuch, zucht, kracht, licht, ge-zicht, ver-licht, ge-lucht, macht, wacht, ge-dacht, schaap, schip, schut, schop, schom-mel, schim, schat, schol, schram, schrik, schrijn, ge-schaamd, ver-scho-len, her-schapen, ont-schie-ten, blijd-schap; (pronounced like *s*) mensch, men-schen, wasch, was-schen, musch, mus-schen, tus-schen, steedsch, steed-sche.

8.

Thee, thuis, thans, althans; nimph (also spelled *nimf*), philosophen (*filosofen*), photographie, telegraphisch (pr. *telegrafies*).

9.

Lei, wei-de, reis, stei-ge-ren, fontein, lei-den, stei-ler, rein; paus, kous, saus, lauw, flauw, rouw, dauw, vrouw, flauw; huis, rui-ken, tuin, wui-ven, dui-nen, muis, ruim, pruik; taai, zaai-en, haai, maai-en; hooi, mooi-er, strooi-en, tooi-en, dooi; eeu-wig, leeu-wen, sproeuw, geeu-wen; nieuw, nieu-we, krieu-wen.

III.—SYLLABLES.

(Lettergrepen.)

1. The pronunciation of Dutch words is a simple and easy matter, after the sounds have been mastered. On the pronunciation depends the division of words into syllables.

2. This division has no connection with etymology. No matter how a word has been derived, compounded, contracted or abridged, its syllables depend on the way of opening and closing the mouth when it is pronounced.

3. Perfect articulation gives perfect division into syllables. There is no other rule.

4. Foreigners may observe:—

(*a*) That one consonant found between two vowels goes with the vowel which follows it: *hazen = ha-zen, leven = le-ven, ademen = a-de-men.*

(b) That of a combination of two or more consonants, one is retained by the first vowel, whereas the remainder go with the vowel following them: *dampig* = *dam-pig*, *schande* = *schan-de*, *korsten* = *kor-sten*, *dorschen* = *dor-schen*, —unless such division should stand in the way of pronunciation: *ernstig* = *ern-stig*, instead of *er-nstig*, *ambten* = *amb-ten*, and not *am-bten*.

> NOTE 1.—These rules do not include compound words, which naturally keep their parts intact: *plaatskaart* = *plaats-kaart*, *slagaar* = *slag-aar*. Likewise do the suffixes *aard*, *achtig*, and *rijk* retain their own letters; *blauw-achtig*, *gunst-rijk*, *laf-aard*.
>
> NOTE 2.—The compositions *ch*, *sch*, and *ng* are not divided: *lachen* = *la-chen*; *ruischen* = *rui-schen*; *angstig* = *ang-stig*; *koningin* = *ko-ning-in*.

Syllables—open and closed.

In Dutch a syllable is termed a) open (*open*), when it ends in a vowel; b) closed (*gesloten*), when it ends in a consonant.

Examples of a) *vre-de, be-te-ren, ga-de-loo-ze*.

Examples of b) *lan-den, won-der-daad, on-ein-dig-heid*.

EXERCISE ON SYLLABLES.

Break the words of the following exercises into syllables, noticing which of the syllables are open, and which closed:—

1.

Laken, monster, paarden, stallen, dochters, zonen, handen, paneel, kapstok, brandwacht, kapoen, vinger, planten, struiken, boomen, pennen, hazen, eenden, vinden, stokpaard, ketting, wartaal, ganzen, spiegel, vragen, denken, klinken, mengen, marktplaats, slokdarm, waschmand.

2.

Bederven, gedenken, ontvangen, stamelen, regeeren, vergelden, hagelen, hergeven, oorlogen, droefenis, latafel, ouderdom, gestorven, schrijfbureau, schuifgordijn, akelig, inktkoker, plaveien, instrument, onttrekken, uitvinding, overlast, blikslager.

3.

Betooveren, gedachtenis, goedhartigheid, nauwkeurige, bedelende, nadrukkelijk, onloochenbaar, monsterachtig, wellevendheid, anderhalve, onaangenaam, milddadigheid, havelooze, tandenpoeder, horlogekast, overmachtig, voorwereldlijk, ontstentenis, kompagnieën, vergiffenis, dialektiek, professoraat, regulatie, landarbeid, Zaterdag, blijmoedige, bruiloftsdisch, edelmoedigheid.

4.

Keukengereedschap, kousenfabriek, katoenspinnerij, overeenkomstig, houtzaagmolen, koninginnemantel, Israelitisme, spoorwegmaatschappijen, testamentbezorger, philosophieën, genealogie, onderwijzersvereenigingen, horlogemakerswinkel, primitiviteit, invalideninstituut, zeilenmakerswerkplaats.

CHAPTER II.

SPELLING.

(*Spelling.*)

I. Dutch spelling compares very favourably with English spelling. In the pronunciation of Dutch words every letter is sounded. (See the exceptions to this rule in Chap. I, Section II.) A word pronounced, therefore, is a word spelled. This holds good but for the choice of a single or double letter for the representation of full-sounded vowels. In this respect there are obvious discrepancies and striking anomalies, which should, as early as possible, be removed. There is a movement on foot aiming at thorough reform. When such reform shall have reached its object, the present chapter will have lost most of its significance. Then every full-sounded *a* will be written *aa*; every full-sounded *e*, *ee*; every full *i*, either *ii*, or *ie*; *o*, *oo*; and *u*, *uu*; while either *ei* or *ij* will be abolished. That change will render Dutch spelling well-nigh perfect, and remove every difficulty which now remains in it. However, seeing that the said reform is at the present moment little beyond the stage of a strong and healthy wish, and considering how slowly changes in languages are brought about, it is incumbent on the writer to furnish the following rules *pro tem*.

II. Words without inflexion take their final consonant according to pronunciation : *met, zich, noch*.

Note.—*Noch* is *neither, nog* is *yet*. This difference in spelling is likely to be removed by the new rules spoken of under § I.

III. When the final consonant of a word is a hard one, the last but one should be hard also; likewise is a soft final consonant preceded by a soft one: *nacht* has *ch*, because it ends in *t*; *deugd* has *g*, because it ends in *d*.

> NOTE 1.—This rule gives way to etymology, and is therefore not applied in the conjugation of verbs: *hij legt* keeps its *g* before the *t*, seeing the *g* forms a part of the stem of the verb.
>
> NOTE 2.—Exceptions to the rule are: *reeds*, already; *steeds*, always; *sinds*, since; *bereids*, already.

IV. Neither words nor syllables can end in double consonants. The English endings *ff* and *ss*, and the German *tt* and *nn* can, therefore, not be met with at the end of a syllable of any Dutch word.

V. Words or syllables cannot end in either a *v* or a *z*. Where such endings would be demanded by derivation, the *v* is made an *f*, and the *z* an *s*: *vreezen*, to fear; *ik vrees*, I fear; *sterven*, to die; *hij stierf*, he died.

VI. Touching declinable words, the question whether they end in *d* or *t* must be settled by declining them: *paard*, horse, sounds *paart*, but is written with *d* because its plural is *paarden*. *Vraag*, question, sounds *vraach*, but is written with *g* because the plural is *vragen*, in which *g*, not being final (*vra-gen*), is pronounced soft. So also *vreemd*, strange, with *d*, because of *vreem-de*; *groot*, large, with *t*, because of *groo-ter*.

> NOTE.—Further reference to this matter will be found in the chapter on the Plural and that on the Verb.

VII. Rules about single and double *a* and *u*.

1. The double sign *aa* or *uu* is used—

(*a*) When the full sound of the vowel opens a syllable: *aar*, vein; *uur*, hour.

(*b*) When the full sound is closed up between consonants: *daad*, *duur*.

2. The single *a* or *u* is used—

(*a*) When the full sound constitutes a syllable in itself: *a-del*, noble; *u-ren*, hours.

(b) When the full sound is heard in an open syllable: *vra-gen*, to ask; *du-ren*, to last.

(c) Whenever the sound is imperfect: *ar-moe-de*, poverty; *urn*, urn; *dak*, roof; *hut*, hut.

(d) When the full-sounded *u* is followed by *w*: *ruw*, rough; *sluw*, sly.

VIII. Rules about single and double *I*.

1. The double sign (*ie*) is used—

(a) When the full sound occurs between consonants: *dienst*, service; *mier*, ant.

(b) In open syllables, when accented, or final: *mie-ren*, ants; *ver-drie-tig*, sorrowful; *foe-lie*, mace.

(c) When the full sound constitutes a syllable in itself in purely Dutch words: *ie-mand*, some one; *ie-der*, every one.

2. The single sign (*i*) is used—

(a) When the sound is imperfect between consonants: *dik*, thick; *mik-ken*, to aim.

(b) In open syllables, unaccented and not final: *mu-zi-kant*, bandsman; *fa-bri-kant*, manufacturer.

(c) In words taken from foreign languages: *i-de-aal*, ideal; *i-di-oot*, idiot; *i-dee*, idea.

IX. Rules about single and double *e* and *o*.

1. In very many words the question about spelling with double or single *e* or *o* is settled by comparison with corresponding words in English, German, or French, a double vowel in these languages pointing to the use of the double sign in Dutch, and a single vowel to the single sign. In some cases comparison is possible between one Dutch word and another.

EXAMPLES OF DOUBLE VOWELS:

Bleeken, to bleach; *scheede*, sheath; *breede*, broad; *heelen*, to heal.

Gelooven, to believe; *hoopen*, heaps; *droomen*, to dream; *stroomen*, streams; *berooven*, to bereave.

EXAMPLES OF SINGLE VOWELS:

Leven, to live; *peluw,* pillow; *schepen,* ships; *ketel,* kettle; *degen,* dagger.

Blozen, to blush; *hopen,* to hope; *drogen,* to dry; *goten,* gutters.

EXAMPLES OF COMPARING DUTCH WITH DUTCH:

Scheede with *scheiden;* *heelen* with *heilzaam;* *breede* with *verbreiden;* *wegen* with *weg;* *hemel* with *hemd;* *schepen* with *schip;* *degen* with *dagge;* *edel* with *adel;* *blozen* with *blos;* *oorlogen* with *oorlog,* and this again with *uitleggen.*

NOTE 1.—When searching for corresponding words, regard should be had to form and not to meaning, which may be different.
EXAMPLES: *boom,* tree, is compared to Eng. *beam* though different in meaning. On the contrary no comparison is possible between Dutch *vrede* and Eng. *peace.*

NOTE 2.—This rule is difficult of application, because of words now having to be compared to an English cognate, and now to a German one: *weken* is in Eng. *weeks,* but in German *Wochen,* and takes its one *e* from its German cognate.

2. Words of one syllable ending in the *e*-sound or *o*-sound have the double vowels:

Thee, tea; *vee,* cattle; *zee,* sea; *wee,* woe; *kwee,* quince; *twee,* two; *mee,* with; *stroo,* straw; *zoo,* so; *vloo,* flea.

3. In contracted syllables the *e*-sound and *o*-sound are represented by the double sign:

Leeg (*ledig*), empty; *veer* (*veder*), feather; *weer* (*weder*), weather; *preeken* (*prediken*), to preach.

Boom (*bodem*), bottom; *door* (*dojer*), yolk; *vroolijk* (*vrodelijk*), merry.

4. The endings *eelen, eezen, eesche,* and *eeren,* have the double *e;* the endings *loozen* and *genooten* have the double *o:*

Houweelen, pick-axes; *juweelen,* jewels; *Portugeezen,* Portuguese (noun); *Soendaneezen,* Sundanese (noun); *Europeesche,* European; *Japaneesche,* Japanese (adjective); *noteeren,* to note; *braveeren,* to brave; *hanteeren,* to handle.

Boomlooze, treeless; *moederlooze*, motherless; *speelgenooten*, playmates; *reisgenooten*, travelling-companions.

NOTE.—The ending *eeren* forms a number of Dutch verbs from French (Latin) stems. The original Dutch ending *eren*, which has a single *e*, is only found in *teren*, to live on, *verteren*, to consume, *deren*, to hurt, *beweren*, to maintain, *ontberen*, to lack, *verweren*, to defend.

X. Rules as to the choice between *ei* and *ij*.

1. Like in the case of *e* and *o*, a corresponding word in English or German having *two* vowels, points to the use of *ei* in Dutch; likewise, if the foreign cognate has *one* vowel, the *ij* takes its place in Dutch:

Feilen, failings; *fontein*, fountain; *spreiden*, to spread; *meid*, maid; *zeide*, said.

Rijst, rice; *prijs*, price; *lijst*, list; *dozijn*, dozen; *paradijs*, paradise; *wijn*, wine; *rijzen*, to rise.

2. When contraction has taken place, *ei* must be used:
Zeil (*zegel*), sail; *dweil* (*dwegel*), clout; *keil* (*kegel*), wedge.

3. *Ei* is used in the endings *heid*, *teit*, and *lei*:
goedheid, goodness; *majesteit*, majesty; *allerlei*, all kinds of.

4. *IJ* is used in the endings *ij*, *ijn*, *ijs*, and *lijk*:
Bakkerij, bakery; *galerij*, gallery; *dolfijn*, dolfin; *radijs*, radish; *eerlijk*, honest.

XI. The meanings of the following words of like pronunciation should be acquired.

(*a*) Homonyms with *e* and *ee*:

helen, to hide.
keren, to sweep.
lenen, to lean (also pr. *leunen*).
rede, speech.
slepen, to trail along (intrans.).
veren, pl. of *veer*, ferry.
verweren, to defend.

weken, weeks.
wezen, to be.

heelen, to heal, to cure.
keeren, turns, times.
leenen, to lend.
reede, roadstead.
sleepen, to drag (trans.).
veeren, feathers.
verweeren, to become weatherbeaten.
weeken, to soak.
weezen, orphans.

(b) Homonyms with *o* and *oo:*

genoten, enjoyed (infin. genieten).
hopen, to-hope.
horen, horn.
kloven, ravines.
kolen, coals.
koper, copper.
kozen, chose (infin. *kiezen*).
lover, one who praises.
poten, to plant.
roken, smelled (infin. *ruiken*).
roven, scurfs.
schoten, shots.
schoven, shoved (infin. *schuiven*).
sloven, drudges.
slopen, to level, also past tense of *sluipen*.
sloten, locks.
tonen, tones.
tronen, thrones.

genooten, fellows.
hoopen, heaps.
hooren, to hear.
klooven, to cleave.
koolen, cabbages.
kooper, purchaser.
koozen, to caress.
loover, foliage.
pooten, legs.
rooken, to smoke.
rooven, to rob.
schooten, laps.
schooven, sheaves.
slooven, aprons.
sloopen, pillow-cases.

slooten, ditches.
toonen, to show.
troonen, to allure.

(c) Homonyms with *ij* and *ei:*

bij, bee.
berijden, to ride on.
ijk, stamp, assizer's mark.
fijt, whitlow.
hij, he.
lijden, to suffer.
mij, me.
mijt, mite.
pijl, arrow.
rij, row.
rijken, rich people, also king-
doms.
Rijn, Rhine.
rijs, young twigs (collective).
stijl, style, also door-post.
vijl, file.
vlijen, to lay flat.
wij, we.
wijden, to consecrate.
wijten, to impute.
zijde, silk.

bei, berry.
bereiden, to prepare.
eik, oak.
feit, fact.
hei or *heide*, heath.
leiden, to lead.
Mei, May.
meid, servant.
peil, water-mark.
rei, choir.
reiken, to reach.

rein, pure.
reis, voyage.
steil, steep.
veil, for sale.
vleien, to flatter.
wei or *weide*, meadow.
weiden, to graze.
weiten, pl. of wheat.
zeide, said.

Exercise I.

1.

Fill up the blanks with single or double *a*:

V–n w–r kw–m de m–n, dien ik d–r z–g? Hij
From where came the man whom I there saw? He
kw–m v–n den k–nt v–n de st–d. W–t z–l ik hem
came from the side of the town. What shall I him
r–den, –ls hij mij vr–gt? R–d hem zijn–rmen v–der
advise when he me asks? Advise him his poor father
w–t te helpen. Wie k–n dit r–dsel r–den: w–t w–s
a little to help. Who can this riddle guess: what was
w–s, eer w–s w–s w–s? De m–st v–n d–t schip is –f, de
wax, ere wax was wax? The mast of that ship is off, the
kr–cht v–n den storm heeft hem den voorl–tsten n–cht –f
force of the storm has it the previous night down
gesl–gen. Ik z–l u voor uwe str–f v–n –vond
struck. I shall you for your punishment this evening
l–ten w–ter dr–gen. De j–ger is op de j–cht geg–n, en
let water carry. The hunter is on the hunt gone, and
heeft twee h–zen en drie fez–nten thuis gebr–cht.
has two hares and three pheasants home brought.

2.

Fill up the blanks with single or double *u*:

Aan den m–r in zijne st–deerkamer hing een r–w kruis.
On the wall in his study hung a rude crucifix.
Zijn die vr–chten — niet te z–r? O neen, ik houd
Are those fruits (for) you not too sour? O no, I like
van z–re vr–chten, meer dan —. D–w de l–cifersdoos
sour fruits, more than you. Push the match-box
open met –wen vinger, S–zie. St–r –wen knecht om het
open with your finger, Susie. Send your servant the
paard van –wen b–rman te h–ren. Gij z–lt het zelf
horse of your neighbour to hire. You will it yourself

moeten gaan h–ren: ik kan den knecht n– niet st–ren.
must go (and) hire: I can the servant now not send.

Het zal niet veel –ren meer d–ren, of die m–r zal
It will not many hours more last, before that wall will

om liggen. Die vreemde hond, die daar zoo valsch ligt
down lie. That strange dog, which there so false lies

te gl–ren, heeft n– en dan vreemde k–ren.
to lurk, has now and then strange whims.

3.

Fill up the blanks with single or double *e*:

H–ft de kl–fpleister de wond in het b–n van uwen
Has the sticking-plaster the wound in the leg of your

n–f g–n–z–n? Ik h–b h–t br–de papier aan smalle r–p–n
cousin healed? I have the wide paper in narrow strips

g–sn–d–n. Br–ng mij h–t n–t, dat d– kn–cht h–d–n
cut. Bring me the net which the servant to-day

v–rst–ld h–ft; ik zal h–t ov–r d– h–g l–gg–n. D– h–m–ls
mended has; I shall it over the hedge lay. The testers

d–r b–dd–n zijn n–tj–s afg–v–gd. B–rg h–t g–ld in uw
of the beds are neatly dusted. Put the money in your

v–st w–g, and–rs wordt h–t uitg–g–v–n. Br–ng
waistcoat by, or else (will) be it spent. Bring

h–t sch–rp– m–s bij d–n kn–cht, –n z–g h–m, dat hij h–t
the sharp knife to the servant, and tell him, that he the

h–ft moet vastz–tt–n. D– w–t van h–t g–w–t–n van
handle must fix. The law of the conscience of

–lken m–nsch z–gt h–m, dat st–l–n onr–cht is.
every man tells him that to steal wrong is.

4.

Fill up the blanks with single or double *o*:

Ik heb geh–rd, dat de r–ver den k–pman verm–rd
I have heard, that the robber the merchant murdered

heeft. Het kind dr–mde van sp–ken, die in den t–ren
has. The child dreamt of ghosts, which in the tower

w–nden. De t–venaars en g–chelaars k–nden den k–ning
lived. The magicians and conjurors could (to) the king
zijnen dr–m niet uitleggen. –nze v–rouders leefden in
his dream not explain. Our ancestors lived in
b–sschen, en droegen –ssenhuiden met de h–rens –p hunne
woods, and wore ox-hides with the horns on their
h–fden. Hij geh–rzaamt u –p bel–fte dat gij
heads. He obeys you on (the) promise that you
hem zult bel–nen. W–nen er –k menschen –p b–men?
him will reward. Live there any people on trees?
Ja, en er zijn –k s–mmige menschens–rten, die in
Yes, and there are also some kinds of people, who in
h–len en spel–nken w–nen. De vr–lijke z–n t–vert
holes and caves live. The bright sun throws (by
eenen sch–nen b–g tegen de d–nkere w–lken.
magic) a pretty arch against the dark clouds.

5.

Fill up the blanks with *ei* or *ij*:

Z–t g– ber–d m– te leeren r–den? W–s m– de
Are you ready me to teach to ride? Show me the
r– boomen, die g– geplant hebt. Z–ne bl–dschap is
row (of) trees, which you planted have. His mirth is
maar sch–n; h– is niet waarl–k vrool–k. W–n wordt uit
but pretence; he is not really merry. Wine is from
druiven ber–d, en az–n uit w–n. Het m–sje zal
grapes prepared, and vinegar out of wine. The girl will
de r– harer vriendinnen op eene l– schr–ven, en u de
the row of her friends on a slate write, and you the
l–st dan w–zen. Ik ben bl–, dat g– die schilder– kr–gt.
list then show. I am glad, that you that painting get.
De h–ning sch–dt het w–land van m–nen tuin.
The fence separates the pasture-ground from my garden.
Als w– eerl–k en vl–tig z–n, leven w– vr– en bl–.
When we honest and diligent are, live we free and happy.

G— *moet niet te veel t–d aan r–den w–den; dat zou*
You must not too much time to riding devote; that would
niet w–s z–n. De berg is te st–l om af te gl–den.
not wise be. The mountain is too steep to down slide.

1. a.

Fill up the blanks with single or double *a*:

De bekw–me tuinier is bezig, de t–kken v–n de boomen
The skilful gardener is busy, the branches of the trees
te k–ppen. J–n, geef mij mijn regenm–ntel eens –n. In
to chop. John, hand me my waterproof just (on). In
een huis vindt men k–mers, r–men, k–sten, tr–ppen,
a house finds one rooms, windows, presses, staircases,
en op een huis een d–k. Kl–dden m–ken is j–mmerlijk
and on a house a roof. Blots (to) make is exceedingly
slordig. Wij kw–men n– –cht uur des –vonds
untidy. We came after eight o'clock in the evening
–n. W–t een n–cht vol b–nge zorgen! De m–nen
(on). What a night full (of) anxious cares! The manes
onzer p–rden zijn zw–rt. De m–n schijnt th–ns –lle
of our horses are black. The moon shines now all
n–chten en de zon –lle d–gen.
nights and the sun all days.

2. a

Fill up the blanks with single or double *u*:

Ged–rende die paar –ren hadden wij heel wat te verd–ren
During those few hours had we a good deal to endure
van onze b–ren. Het g–re weder heeft ons belet,
from our neighbours. The cold weather has us prevented,
de meid om vr–chten te st–ren. De m–sschen en
the servant for fruit to send. The sparrows and
zwal–wen zijn nooit r–stige nab–ren. H–r mij een rijtuig
swallows are never quiet neighbours. Hire me a vehicle

voor een –r, en vraag hoe d–r het zal komen. D–nne
for an hour, and ask how expensive it will be. Thin
stof is niet zelden d–rzamer dan grove en
material is not seldom more lasting than coarse and
r–we . Gij z–lt —we st–rsche k–ren eenmaal
rough (ones). You will (for) your sour whims once
bez–ren. Geen m–ren verd–ren der –ren geweld.
sorry be. No walls endure of the hours (the) force.

3. a.

Fill up the blanks with single or double *e*:

Niet t– l–v–n om t– –t–n, maar t– –t–n om t– l–v–n, is –n
Not to live for to eat, but to eat for to live, is a
guld–n r–g–l. In d– Midd–l–uw–n l–fd–n d– –d–l–n in
golden rule. In the Middle Ages lived the nobles in
trotsch– kast–l–n. Ond–r h–t sp–l–n bl–k h–t, dat
proud castles. During the playing appeared it that
er v–l ont–vr–d–nen war–n. De sch–p–n der
there many discontented (ones) were. The ships of the
z–var–nd– mog–ndh–d–n –v–nar–n –lkand–r in st–rkt–.
sea-faring powers equal each other in strength.
–cht– witt– b–r–n word–n all–n in koud– str–k–n aang–troff–n.
Real white bears are only in cold regions found.
K–m–l –n kam–l zijn nam–n m–t g–lijk– b–t–k–nis.
Camel and camel are names with like meaning.

4. a.

Fill up the blanks with single or double *o*:

Wie –ren heeft –m te h–ren, die h–re. L–pend –f
Who ears has for to hear, let him hear. Flowing or
str–mend water is het gez–ndst. De vr–lijke spr–ngen
streaming water is (the) wholesomest. The merry bounds
der eekh–rntjes in de h–ge b–men vermaakten –ns allen.
of the squirrels in the high trees amused us all.
Hoe k–mt het, dat de g–ten z– slecht l–pen: wat kan de
How comes it, that the gutters so badly run: what can the

–rzaak zijn van zulk eene d–rl–pende verst–pping? De
cause be of such a regular obstruction? The

d–rn heeft de –pene w–nd –ntst–ken.   Gel–f hem niet
thorn has the open wound inflamed. Believe him not

weer;   –p mijn w–rd gij beh–rt hem niet te gel–ven.
any more; upon my word you ought him not to trust.

Abrik–zen, framb–zen en   st–fperen   zijn –verheerlijke
Apricots, raspberries and stewing pears are delicious

vruchten.
fruits.

5. a.

Fill up the blanks with *ei* or *ij*:

Z–ne r–s langs den R–n heeft h– in v–f weken ten
His trip along the Rhine has he in five weeks to (an)

–nde gebracht. R–ne vreugde en ware bl–dschap kunnen
end brought. Pure joy and true gladness can

b–de in pal–zen en hutten gesmaakt worden. W– ber–kten
both in palaces and huts tasted be. We reached

den top des   bergs   juist b–t–ds, om de zon boven
the top of the mountain just in time, for the sun above

den gezichts–nder te zien r–zen. M–d vl–taal: zij voert
the   horizon to see rise. Shun flattery: it leads

meestent–ds tot v–nzer–. Tot zulke r–melar– is hij
mostly to hypocrisy. Of such bad verses is he

evenmin in staat, als het p–nzend br–n z–ns vaders tot
as little capable, as the pensive brain of his father of

het voortbrengen van dergel–ke zottern–.
the production of such like foolery.

Spelling of Compound Nouns.

XII. Most compounds combine their constituent parts without altering the form of either part, and causing them to appear as one word, no hyphens being used: *stal* en *deur* form *staldeur*, stable-door: *schroef* en *draaier* form *schroefdraaier*, screw-driver.

In some cases, however, slight changes in the first part of the compound may be noticed:

1. If the first part ends in *e*, this *e* is generally dropped; *aarde* and *appel* form *aardappel*, potato.

2. Principally to facilitate pronunciation, some words drop their final *d* when compounded: *rijtoer*, from *rijdtoer*, drive; *zijraam*, from *zijdraam*, side-window; *leiband*, from *leidband*, leading-strings.

3. Words which take the double plural ending *ers* or *eren* (see page 37), drop the additional *s* or *en*, and retain their original plural form in *er* when compounded: *hoenderhok*, fowl-house; *eiermand*, egg-basket.

4. The first part of a compound frequently takes the letter *s* either *a*) as a sign of the genitive case, or *b*) to bring out a plural meaning, or *c*) for the sake of euphony.

EXAMPLES:

   a) *Timmermansgereedschap*, carpenter's tools; *bruidskleed*, bridal dress; *dorpsschool*, village school.

   b) *Meisjesschool*, girls' school; *jongensboek*, book for boys.

   c) *Scheidsrechter*, arbiter; *schutsheer*, protector.

The compound forms which join their two parts together by *e* or *en* require more attention. The letter *e* represents a singular meaning, but changes into *en*, whenever the second word commences with a *vowel* or an *h*. Where this is not the case, *en* represents a plural. Compounds with the word *boom* (tree), or the name of any part of a tree, necessarily have *e*, and not *en* (as they are not uncommonly spelled), except when the second part begins with a *vowel* or an *h*.

EXAMPLES OF SINGULAR FORMS:

Paardestaart, tail of a horse; *lampeglas*, lamp-chimney; *speldeknop*, pin's head; *pereschil*, peel of a pear.

Eikeboom, oak-tree; *eiketak*, branch of an oak-tree; *vijgeblad*, fig-leaf; *tulpebol*, tulip-bulb; *rozestruik*, rose-bush; but *eikenhout*, oak-wood; *hondenhok*, dog's kennel; *ganzenei*, egg of a goose; *brillenhuis*, spectacle-case.

EXAMPLES OF PLURAL FORMS:

Boekenkast, book-case; *vriendenkring*, circle of friends; *lampenmagazijn*, store for lamps; *bijenbrood*, bee-bread.

NOTE.—In a few cases *en* is added to the first part of the word to express: *a*) a masculine name of an animal; *b*) a position in society.

EXAMPLES: *a*) *berenpoot*, bear's paw; *apenkuur*, monkey's tricks; *b*) *boerenknecht*, farm-servant.

EXERCISE II.

1.

Fill up the blanks with *e* or *en*:

Heeft hij boek—planken in zijne kamer, of is er een boek-
Has he book-shelves in his room, or is there a book-
kast? Koopt men lamp—glazen in een kleer—winkel? Ziet
case? Buys one lamp chimneys in a tailor's shop? Sees
men ooit eene paard—krib in eenen koei—stal? De tulp—
one ever a horse-manger in a cow-stable? The tulip-
bollen staan in den grond. Hij heeft de per—schillen en
bulbs are in the ground. He has the pear-peels and
de pruim—pitten in de vuilnismand gegooid. Met
the plum-stones into the waste-basket thrown. With
naald—punten moet men voorzichtig zijn. Hij heeft zijn
needle-points should one careful be. He has his
brill—huis in zijnen zak gestoken. Zijn die brill—
spectacle-case in his pocket put. Are those spectacle
glazen groen of blauw? In de eik—laan staat een jonge
glasses green or blue? In the oak avenue is a young
per—boom, die verplant moet worden. De vriend—
pear-tree, which transplanted should be. The friendly
kring komt van avond bijeen.
circle comes to-night together.

2.

Do the same with:

Die haren zijn van een paard-staart afkomstig. De goeder-
Those hairs are from a horse's tail come. The goods
trein vertrekt een half uur later dan de person- trein.
train leaves a half-hour later than the passengers' train.
Hij heeft zich als een boer-knecht verhuurd. Die
He has himself as a farm-servant hired out. That
soldat-rok past hem goed. Hij draagt een heer-hoed
soldier's frock fits him well. He wears a gentleman's hat
bij zijn jongenspak. Een voss-kop is spits, en een
with his boy's suit. A fox's head is pointed and a
ber-klauw is plat. Eend-eieren zijn duur. Hij gebruikt
bear's paw is flat. Ducks' eggs are expensive. He uses
eenen eend-vleugel bij het teekenen. Hij schrijft met
a duck's wing with the drawing. He writes with
stalen pennen, en zijn vader met ganz-veeren. In het
steel pens, and his father with quills. In the
hond-hok ligt een koei-horen. Mannen behooren geene
dog's kennel lies a cow's horn. Men ought no
vrouw-kleeren te dragen.
women's clothes to wear.

3.

Do the same with:

De roz-struiken moeten in Juni gesnoeid worden. Eik-hout
The rose-bushes must in June cut be. Oak wood
geeft meer hitte dan wilg-hout. Pauw-veeren
gives more heat than willow wood. Peacock's feathers
zijn mooier dan pauw-oogen. Zwan-dons is heer-
are prettier than peacock's eyes. Swan's down is delight-
lijk zacht in kussens. De kerk-muur is vol zwaluw-
fully soft in pillows. The church wall is full swallow's
nesten. Paard-ooren staan op, maar hond-ooren hangen.
nests. Horse's ears stand up, but dog's ears hang.
Konijn-staarten zijn kort en gekruld. De Vrijstaat heeft
Rabbits' tails are short and curled. The Free State has

steenkool–mijnen.   *Het arme kind had drie speld–knoppen*
coal-mines.   The poor child had three pin's-heads
ingeslikt.   *De stippen op dit blad zijn zoo fijn als speld–*
swallowed.   The dots on this leaf are as fine as pins'
punten.   *Die pijp–kop is van meerschuim gemaakt.*   *De*
points.   That pipe-bowl is of meerschaum made.   The
lamp–kap is gebarsten.   *Het mol–rad wordt door water*
lamp-shade is cracked.   The mill-wheel is by water
gedreven.
driven.

CHAPTER III.

PARTS OF SPEECH.

(*Rededeelen.*)

THERE are ten classes of words, called *Rededeelen*, Parts of Speech.

They are: 1. *Het Zelfstandig Naamwoord*, the Noun Substantive; 2. *Het Lidwoord*, the Article; 3. *Het Bijvoegelijk Naamwoord*, the Adjective; 4. *Het Voornaamwoord*, the Pronoun; 5. *Het Telwoord*, the Numeral Adjective; 6. *Het Werkwoord*, the Verb; 7. *Het Bijwoord*, the Adverb; 8. *Het Voegwoord*, the Conjunction; 9. *Het Voorzetsel*, the Preposition; 10. *Het Tusschenwerpsel*, the Interjection.

NOTE.—The above names are for the greater part literally translated from the original Latin.

The Article.

(*Het Lidwoord.*)

I. The Article, *het Lidwoord*, is a word which is placed before a Noun to indicate whether the noun has a definite or an indefinite meaning.

NOTE.—English grammars no longer take the article as a separate part of speech, but call it a "distinguishing adjective." This term, however, is not applicable to the Dutch article, it having a declension which differs from that of the adjective.

II. There are two articles: the definite, *het bepalende lidwoord*, and the indefinite, *het niet-bepalende lidwoord*.

FORMS OF THE ARTICLE.

III. The definite article is: for the Singular Number of the Masculine Gender, "*de*"; for the Singular Number of the Feminine Gender, "*de*"; for the Singular Number of the Neuter Gender, "*het*"; for the Plural Number of every Gender, "*de*."

The indefinite article is: for the Masculine Singular, "*een*"; for the Feminine Singular, "*eene*"; for the Neuter Singular, "*een*."

IV. Articles can never be used without a noun which they qualify. They are declined as follows:—

MASCULINE. *Mannelijk.*

SINGULAR.   PLURAL.
(*Enkelvoud.*)   (*Meervoud.*)

Nom. *de man*, the man.
Gen. *des mans* (or *van den man*), of the man.
Dat. *den man* (or *aan den man*), to the man.
Acc. *den man*, the man.

Nom. *de mannen*, the men.
Gen. *der mannen* (*van de mannen*), of the men.
Dat. *den mannen* (*aan de mannen*), to the men.
Acc. *de mannen*, the men.

SINGULAR.   PLURAL.
(*Enkelvoud.*)   (*Meervoud.*)

Nom. *een man*, a man.
Gen. *eens mans* (*van eenen man*), of a man.
Dat. *eenen man* (*aan eenen man*), to a man.
Acc. *eenen man*, a man.

Nom. *mannen*, men.
Gen. *van mannen*, of men.
Dat. *aan mannen*, to men.
Acc. *mannen*, men.

FEMININE. *Vrouwelijk.*

SINGULAR.   PLURAL.
(*Enkelvoud.*)   (*Meervoud.*)

Nom. *de vrouw*, the woman.
Gen. *der vrouw* (*van de vrouw*), of the woman.
Dat. *der vrouw* (*aan de vrouw*), to the woman.
Acc. *de vrouw*, the woman.

Nom. *de vrouwen*, the women.
Gen. *der vrouwen* (*van de vrouwen*), of the women.
Dat. *den vrouwen* (*aan de vrouwen*), to the women.
Acc. *de vrouwen*, the women.

FEMININE. SINGULAR. (*Enkelvoud.*)	*Vrouwelijk.* PLURAL. (*Meervoud.*)

Nom. *eene vrouw*, a woman.
Gen. *eener vrouw* (*van eene vrouw*), of a woman.
Dat. *eener vrouw* (*aan eene vrouw*), to a woman.
Acc. *eene vrouw*, a woman.

Nom. *vrouwen*, women.
Gen. *van vrouwen*, of women.
Dat. *aan vrouwen*, to women.
Acc. *vrouwen*, women.

NEUTER. SINGULAR. (*Enkelvoud.*)	*Onzijdig.* PLURAL. (*Meervoud.*)

Nom. *het kind*, the child.
Gen. *des kinds* (*van het kind*), of the child.
Dat. *het kind* (*aan het kind*), to the child.
Acc. *het kind*, the child.

Nom. *de kinderen*, the children.
Gen. *der kinderen* (*van de kinderen*), of the children.
Dat. *den kinderen* (*aan de kinderen*), to the children.
Acc. *de kinderen*, the children.

SINGULAR. (*Enkelvoud.*)	PLURAL. (*Meervoud.*)

Nom. *een kind*, a child.
Gen. *eens kinds* (*van een kind*), of a child.
Dat. *een kind* (*aan een kind*), to a child.
Acc. *een kind*, a child.

Nom. *kinderen*, children.
Gen. *van kinderen*, of children.
Dat. *aan kinderen*, to children.
Acc. *kinderen*, children.

V. Nouns may reject the article, when such omission causes no ambiguity : *De koeien, paarden en schapen zijn alle verkocht*, the cows, horses, and sheep have all been sold.

> OBSERVATION 1.—The article may never be omitted when its form is not exactly like that of the article expressed. It is wrong to write: *Ik heb den vader en moeder van onze meid gezien*, I saw the father and mother of our servant-girl; since the masculine form *den* becomes *de* before the feminine *moeder*.
>
> OBS. 2.—The article must always be left out before the second of two nouns which refer to one and the same person; *Hij werd de vriend en verzorger dier arme kinderen*, He became the friend and guardian of those poor children.

OBS. 3.—The definite article is left out after the words *alle*, all, and *beide*, both : *Alle menschen moeten sterven*, all men must die; *Beide vogels zijn ontsnapt*, both the birds have escaped.

OBS. 4.—It is customary to repeat the article, though its form be like that of the first article : (1) if one noun is singular and the other plural: *De moeder en de dochters zijn heden aangekomen*, the mother and the daughters have arrived to-day ; (2) in emphatic expressions : *Beide de goeden en de kwaden zullen er onder lijden*, both the good and the bad will suffer by it.

OBS. 5.—The article is omitted before the names of professions : The boy wants to be a carpenter, *de jongen wil timmerman worden*.

NOTE.—Poets often make use of the abbreviated form *d'* for *de* and even for *den*.

VI. The article is required in Dutch where it is not used in English :

1. With Nouns representing a class :—

    Man is mortal, *de mensch is sterfelijk*.
    The language of animals, *de taal der dieren*.

2. Before the names of :—

    Meals:—We were at breakfast, *wij zaten aan het ontbijt*.
    Diseases :—He has had small-pox, *hij heeft de pokken gehad*.
    Seasons:—Spring is a happy time, *de lente is een vroolijke tijd*.
    Streets :—He lives in Burg street, *hij woont in de Burgstraat*.
    Mountains :—We ascended Table Mountain, *wij klommen den Tafelberg op*.
    Religious sects :—He was converted to Christianity, *hij werd tot het Christendom bekeed*.
    Arts and sciences :—He studies history, *hij bestudeert de geschiedenis*.

3. Before proper nouns preceded by adjectives:—

Little Charles is ill, *de kleine Karel is ziek.*

4. Before abstract nouns when taken in their whole extent:—

Youth, *de jeugd;* old age, *de ouderdom;* life, *het leven;* death, *de dood;* eternity, *de eeuwigheid;* nature, *de natuur;* creation, *de schepping.*

EXERCISES FOR TRANSLATION.—*Vertaaloefeningen.*

NOTE 1.—The gender of the nouns used in the exercises is indicated by *m.* for the masculine, *v.* for the feminine, and *o.* for the neuter gender.

NOTE 2.—After prepositions use the Accusative (Objective) case.

NOTE 3.—The sentences of the Exercises for Translation are meant to be committed to memory after correction.

EXERCISE III.

bird,	*vogel, m.*	cage,	*kooi, v.*	stable,	*stal, m.*
cupboard,	*kast, v.*	pencil,	*potlood, o.*	plate,	*bord, o.*
book,	*boek, o.*	sun,	*zon, v.*	table,	*tafel, v.*
house,	*huis, o.*	garden,	*tuin, m.*	stick,	*stok, m.*
room,	*kamer, v.*	lamb,	*lam, o.*	lion,	*leeuw, m.*
forest,	*woud, o.*	mine,	*van mij,*	sky,	*lucht, v.*
is,	*is.*	in,	*in,*	on,	*op.*
large,	*groot.*	broken,	*stuk,*	small,	*klein.*

The bird is in the cage. The plate is in the cupboard. The pencil is on the table. The book is mine. The sun is in the sky. The house is in the garden. The house is small, the garden is large. The stick is broken. The lamb is in the stable. The lion is in the forest. The pencil is in the cupboard. The lamb is in the garden. The cupboard is in the room. The pencil is in the room. The plate is small; the table is large.

Exercise IV.

horse,	*paard, o.*	carriage,	*rijtuig, o.*	wheel,	*wiel, o.*
bonnet,	*hoed, m.*	cap,	*muts, v.*	hat,	*hoed, m.*
umbrella,	*paraplu, v.*	child,	*kind, o.*	dog,	*hond, m.*
street,	*straat, v.*	summer,	*zomer, m.*	door,	*deur, v.*
not,]	*niet,*	never,	*nooit,*	red,	*rood.*
ill,	*ziek,* *	often,	*dikwijls,*	and,	*en.*
always,	*altijd,*	warm,	*warm,*	round,	*rond.*
expensive,	*duur,*	study,	*studeerkamer, v.*		
		my,	*mijne,*	it,	*het.*

A stable and a horse. A carriage and a wheel. A carriage is expensive. A wheel is round. A bonnet and a cap. A bonnet is not a cap. A hat and a stick. An umbrella is never red. A child is ill. The dog is often in my study. The house is in (the) Humbert-street. It is always warm in (the) summer.

Exercise V.

mother,	*moeder, v.*	boy,	*jongen, m.*	window,	*venster, o.*
town,	*stad, v.*	tree,	*boom, m.*	heat,	*hitte, v.*
long,	*lang.*	great,	*groot.*	high,	*hoog.*

The cage of the bird. The bonnet of the mother. The wheel of the carriage. The child's cap (cap of the child). The door of the stable. The pencil of the boy. The boy's umbrella. The door of the study is small. The window of the room is large. The street of the town is long. The heat of the summer is great. The tree of the forest is high. The wheel of the carriage is round.

Exercise VI.

paw,	*klauw, m.*	page,	*bladzijde, v.*	beam,	*straal, m.*
sore,	*zeer.*	dirty,	*vuil.*	hot,	*heet.*
		winter,	*winter, m.*		

The mother's umbrella (the umbrella of the mother) is broken. The lion's paw is sore. The page of the book is dirty. The sun's beam is long. The boy's cap is dirty.

PARTS OF SPEECH.

tho bird's cage is not round. The mother's child is often ill. The door of the cupboard is small. The sun is hot in (the) summer. The child is always ill in (the) winter. The cap of the boy is on the table. The book is on the table in the study. The horse in the stable is mine.

GRAMMAR EXERCISES.—*Taaloefeningen.*
EXERCISE VII.
1.

Fill up the blanks with the definite article:

— *boer* (m) *beploegt* — *veld* (o). *Zij plukt* — *schoonste*
The farmer ploughs the field. She picks the finest

bloemen (v) *af.* *Leg* — *zadel* (o) *op* — *paard* (o) *en rijd*
flowers off. Put the saddle on the horse and ride

naar — *markt* (v). — *hek* (o) *om* — *huis* (o) *is van*
to the market. The railing round the house is of

— *beste ijzer* (o) *gemaakt.* *Hij heeft moedwillig* — *blad* (o)
the best iron made. He has on purpose the leaf

uit — *boek* (o) *gescheurd.* — *oven* (m) *wil niet branden:*
out (of) the book torn. The oven will not burn:

— *vuur* (o) *gaat gedurig uit.* — *plaag* (v) *breidt zich*
the fire goes continually out. The plague spreads itself

over — *gansche land* (o) *uit.* — *vogels* (m), *welke 's*
over the whole country out. The birds which in

winters naar — *warme zuiden* (o) *vertrekken, zijn talrijk.*
winter to the warm south depart, are numerous.

— *wagen* (m) *is nieuw,* — *wielen* (o) *ervan zijn oud.* —
The waggon is new, the wheels of it are old. The

schoenmaker (m) *heeft* — *rekening* (v) *van* — *vorige*
shoe-maker has the account of the previous

maand (v) *gezonden.*
month sent.

2.

Fill up the blanks with the indefinite article:

— *vogel* (m) *zingt,* — *muis* (v) *piept,* — *koe* (v) *loeit,* —
A bird sings, a mouse squeaks, a cow lows, a

paard (o) *hinnikt*, — *leeuw* (m) *brult*, — *beer* (m) *bromt*, — horse neighs, a lion roars, a bear growls, a
wolf (m) *huilt*, — *hond* (m) *blaft*, — *schaap* (o) *blaat*. *Gis-* wolf howls, a dog barks, a sheep bleats. Yes-
teren schoot ik — *konijn* (o) *en ving* — *rat* (v). *Welk* — terday shot I a rabbit and caught a rat. What a
vreugde (v) *voor* — *armen man* (m). *Wat* — *gewoel* (o), joy for a poor man. What a commotion,
wat — *drukte* (v), *wat* — *gejuich* (o) *op straat*. *Blijf* what a bustle, what a shouting in (the) street. Stay
toch — *oogenblik* (o), *ik moet u nog* — *geschiedenis* (v) just a moment, I must you yet a story
vertellen. — *kikvorsch* (m) *en* — *pad* (v) *behooren tot* — tell. A frog and a toad belong to a
diersoort (v), *die men schuwt*. — *jong* (o) *van* — class of animals which one shuns. A young of a
varken (o) *noemt men* — *big* (v). pig calls one a young pig.

3.

Fill up the blanks with the definite or indefinite article:

— *rad* (o) — *machine* (v) *is stuk*. — *straat* (v) *loopt* The wheel of the machine is broken. The street runs
rechtuit naar — *zee* (v). — *zee* (v) *is* — *deel* (n) *van* — straight to the sea. A sea is a part of an
oceaan (m). — *fabriek* (v) *op* — *hoek* (m) — *markt* (v) *is* ocean. The factory at the corner of the market is
afgebrand. *Heeft u* — *kapitein* (m) *van* — *oorlogschip* (o) burnt down. Have you the captain of the man-of-war
gezien, dat in — *baai* (v) *ligt*. *Neen, maar ik heb eenigen,* seen, that in the bay lies. No, but I have some
— *officieren* (m) *en* — *matrozen* (m) *gezien*. — of the officers and of the sailors seen. (The)
Kaapstad (v) *ligt aan* — *voet* (m) *van* — *Tafelberg*. Cape-Town lies at the foot of (the) Table-mountain.

— *beide torentjes* (n) *van* — *kasteel* (n) *aan* — *overzijde* (v)
The both turrets of the castle at the other side
— *rivier* (v) *zijn afgewaaid. Aan* — *ingang* (m) *van*
of the river are blown down. At the entrance of
— *Tafelbaai* (v) *ligt Robbeneiland.* — *zoon* (m) —
the Table bay lies Robben Island. The son of the
dokters (m) *is naar Schotland gegaan om in* — *medicij-*
doctor has to Scotland gone in order (in the) medi-
nen te studeeren. — *beiden spoorwegbeambten* (m)
cine to study. (To the) both railway officials has
is — *zware boete* (v) *opgelegd, omdat zij bij* —
been a heavy fine imposed, because they at the
naderen (n) *van* — *trein* (m) *niet op hunnen post* (m) *waren.* —
approach of the train not at their post were. (The)
Buddhisme (o) *heeft veel aanhangers* (m) *in* — *Chineesche*
Buddhism has many adherents in the Chinese
rijk (o). — *bewoners* (m) *van vele* — *Zuidzee*
empire. The inhabitants of many of the South Sea
eilanden zijn tot — *Christendom* (o) *bekeerd.* —
Islands are to (the) Christianity converted. The
heer (m), *dien u van morgen in* — *museum* (o)
gentleman whom you this morning in the museum
ontmoet heeft, is leeraar in — *mathesis* (v).
met have, is professor of mathematics.

CONVERSATIE.

Tijd.

1. *Hoe laat is het?*
2. *Het is tien uur.*
3. *Het is kwart voor vijf.*
4. *Het is half zeven.*
5. *Het is tien minuten over acht.*
6. *Hoe laat staat u op?*
7. *Ik ben altijd op tegen zes uur.*
8. *Hoe laat ontbijt u?*

CONVERSATION.

Time.

1. What time is it?
2. It is ten o'clock.
3. It is a quarter to five.
4. It is half past six.
5. It is ten minutes past eight.
6. What time do you rise?
7. I am always up by six o'clock.
8. What time do you take breakfast?

9. *Wij ontbijten nooit na acht uur.*
10. *Tegen twee uur zal ik bij u aankomen.*
11. *De stoomboot vertrekt om twaalf uur vandaag.*
12. *Gaan zij iederen dag naar school?*
13. *Zij gaan dagelijks behalve 's Zaterdags.*
14. *Aanstaande week zal ik vertrokken zijn.*
15. *Mijn verjaardag valt in de eerstkomende maand.*
16. *Wij hebben reeds veertien dagen op u gewacht.*
17. *Kom over drie dagen terug.*
18. *Mijn vader is juist vijftig jaar oud.*
19. *De zon gaat in den winter laat op.*
20. *De zon gaat in den winter vroeg onder.*
21. *Na zonsondergang komen de sterren te voorschijn.*
22. *Wij begonnen onze reis vóór het aanbreken van den dag.*
23. *Toen ik een half uur weg was, kwam mijn broeder thuis.*
24. *De veldslag werd den zeven en twintigsten Maart geleverd.*
25. *Ik verjaar op den laatsten Februari.*
26. *Londen, 2 Mei 1884.*
27. *Na mijnen dood zal u alles duidelijk worden.*
28. *Overmorgen hoop ik u weer te zien.*
29. *Ik ben eergisteren gevallen.*
30. *Is u te laat aan den trein gekomen?*
31. *Ik was juist bijtijds, maar de trein was te vroeg.*

9. We never breakfast later than eight o'clock.
10. I shall come to you about two o'clock.
11. The steamer sails at noon to-day.
12. Do they go to school every day?
13. They go every day but Saturday.
14. Next week I shall be gone.
15. My birthday is next month.
16. We have been waiting for you a fortnight.
17. Come back in three days.
18. My father is just fifty years of age.
19. The sun rises late in winter.
20. The sun sets early in winter.
21. After sunset the stars make their appearance.
22. We started on our journey before daybreak.
23. Half an hour after I had left, my brother came home.
24. The battle was fought on the twenty-seventh of March.
25. My birthday is on the last day of February.
26. London, May 2nd, 1884.
27. After my death everything will become clear to you.
28. The day after to-morrow I hope to see you again.
29. I had a fall the day before yesterday.
30. Were you too late for the train?
31. I was just in time, but the train was too early.

CHAPTER IV.

FORMATION OF THE PLURAL.

(*Meervoudsvorming.*)

I. The endings of the plural in Dutch are, *s*, *'s*, *en*, *n*, *ers*, *eren*.

II. In *s* ends—

1. The plural of all diminutives: *huisjes*, small houses; *boompjes*, small trees; *deurtjes*, small doors.

2. The plural of words ending in *el*, *em*, *en*, *er*, *aar*, *ier*, and *aard*: *eikels*, acorns; *bezems*, brooms; *varkens*, pigs; *blakers*, candlesticks; *handelaars*, merchants; *winkeliers*, shopkeepers; *dronkaards*, drunkards.

3. The plural of foreign words used in Dutch, except when they end in *a*, *o*, or *u*: *bals*, balls (dances); *datums*, dates; *dames*, ladies; *horloges*, watches; *tantes*, aunts.

NOTE.—Those words are regarded as foreign which have not either through long use, or through change of spelling, actually been taken up in the language as Dutch words.

III. In *'s* end the plural forms of all foreign words which have their original spelling, and end in *a*, *o*, or *u*; *massa*, mass, *massa's*; *echo*, echo, *echo's*; *paraplu*, umbrella, *paraplu's*.

IV. In *en* ends the plural of—

1. All Dutch monosyllables, with the exception of the following:
ra, pl. *raas*, yard; *vla*, pl. *vlaas*, custard; *kok*, pl. *koks*, male cook; *oom*, pl. *ooms*, uncle; *maat*,

pl. *maats*, comrade; *man*, pl. *mans* or *mannen*, man; *knecht*, pl. *knechts* or *knechten*, male servant; *zoon*, pl. *zoons* or *zonen*, son. See § IX.

2. Most of the words taken from foreign languages, but Dutchified through long use, which do not end in a vowel:

Avonturen, adventures; *advokaten*, advocates; *presenten*, presents; *figuren*, figures; *rivieren*, rivers.

3. All other words, except those which fall under the rules below.

V. In *n* ends the plural of—
1. All Dutch words ending in *e* : *gedaante*, shape, *gedaanten*; *ziekte*, illness, *ziekten*.

VI. Either in *s* or *en* ends the plural of some words in *el*, *er*, *en*, *em*, and of many derivatives in *aar*, *or*, *eur*, and those in *ier* which express the names of persons.

EXAMPLES: *vogels*, birds; *bezems*, brooms; *dienaars*, servants; *directeurs*, directors; *officiers*, officers; *professor*, professors; or *vogelen*, *bezemen*, etc.

NOTE 1.—Of words which allow of both endings, only the form in *s* is colloquial: *Drie vogels vliegen boven ons huis*, three birds are flying above our house; *'s vogelen des hemels hebben nesten*, the fowls of the air have nests. The latter expression is biblical language.

NOTE 2.—Mark that professional names which end in *or* take the accent on the last syllable but one, both in the singular and the plural: *professor*, plural *professors*, *professóren*.

VII. Words ending in *ie* require special attention. Those which have the accent on the last syllable but one, form their plural in *n* or sometimes *s*: *natie*, nations, *natiën*, or *naties*; *lelie*, lily, *leliën*, or *lelies*; *provincie*, province, *provinciën*; *kanarie*, canary, *kanaries*.

The following, however, which have the accent on the final *ie*, take *en*:

knie,	knee,	*knieën*.
drie,	three,	*drieën*.
copie,	copy,	*copieën*.
genie,	genius,	*genieën*.
theorie,	theory,	*theorieën*.

melodie,	melody,	melodieën.
harmonie,	harmony,	harmonieën.
menagerie,	menagery,	menagerieën.
profetie,	prophecy,	profetieën.
philosophie,	philosophy,	philosophieën.
photographie,	photography,	photographieën.
galanterie,	fancy article,	galanterieën.

Mark the diæresis on the last *e*, which these words have in common with those ending in *ee* : *zee*, sea, *zeeën* ; *wee*, woe, *weeën*.

VIII. The double plural ending *ers* or *eren*, is adopted by the following nouns of the neuter gender:

blad,	leaf,	*bladen* or *bladeren*. See § IX.
ei,	egg,	*eiers* or *eieren*.
gelid,	rank,	*gelederen*.
gemoed,	mind,	*gemoederen*.
goed,	goods,	*goederen*.
hoen,	fowl,	*hoenders*.
kalf,	calf,	*kalvers* or *kalveren*.
kind,	child,	*kinders* or *kinderen*.
lam,	lamb,	*lammers* or *lammeren*.
lied,	song,	*liederen*.
rad,	wheel,	*raderen*.
rund,	cow or ox,	*runders* or *runderen*.
spaan,	chip,	*spaanders*.
volk,	nation,	*volken* or *volkeren*.

NOTE.—This double ending is not an original one. As in German, so also in Dutch, the plural of neuter nouns was formerly formed by *er*. To this plural ending it has become customary to add the endings used for the other genders, viz., *s* and *en*, which custom has created the double forms *ers* and *eren* now in use. In compound words the old ending *er* still expresses a real plural : *kinderkamer*, nursery ; *hoenderhok*, fowl-house ; *eiermand*, egg-basket.
The old plural is used with a singular meaning in *spaander*, chip, and in the Cape Dutch forms *een hoender*, *een eier*.

IX. Some homonymous words bring out their different meanings in the plural. Such are—

SINGULAR.	FIRST PLURAL.	MEANING.	SECOND PLURAL.	MEANING.
been,	*beenen*,	legs.	*beenderen*,	bones.
blad,	*bladen*,	leaves of books.	*bladeren*,	leaves of trees.
deken,	*dekens*,	blankets.	*dekenen*,	deacons.
heiden,	*heidens*,	gipsies.	*heidenen*,	heathen.
hemel,	*hemels*,	canopies.	*hemelen*,	heavens.
kleed,	*kleeden*,	carpets.	*kleederen*,	clothes.

SINGULAR.	FIRST PLURAL.	MEANING.	SECOND PLURAL.	MEANING.
knecht,	knechts,	men-servants.	knechten,*	slaves.
letter,	letters,	letters.	letteren,	literature.
man,	mans,	husbands.	mannen,	men.
middel,	middels,	waists.	middelen,	means.
reden,	redens,	ratios.	redenen,	reasons.
spel,	spellen,	booths.	spelen,	games.
studie,	studies,	sketches.	studiën,	studies.
tafel,	tafels,	tables.	tafelen,	tables (of the law)
vader,	vaders,	fathers.	vaderen,	ancestors.
teeken,	teekens,	signs.	teekenen,	miracles.
wortel,	wortels,	roots.	wortelen,	carrots.
zoon,	zoons,	children of one family.	zonen,	natives of the same country.

* NOTE.—In composition *knechten* only should be used: *krijgsknechten*, soldiers; *dienstknechten*, male servants.

X. A few words have an irregular plural form:

smid,	smith,	smeden.	lid,	limb and member,	leden.
split,	slit,	spleten.	schip,	ship,	schepen.
stad,	town,	steden.	koe,	cow,	koeien.
vloo,	flea,	vlooien.	zoo,	sod,	zooien.
rede,	speech,	redenen.	vleesch,	meat, flesh,	vleezen,

(old Dutch *vlees*, *vleys*.)

NOTE 1.—*Smids*, smiths, and *zoden*, sods, are likewise used.
NOTE 2.—The *i* in the plural forms of *koe* and *vloo* is the *h* of their German cognates.

2. Words ending in *heid* (old D. *hede*) take *heden*: *waarheid*, *waarheden*, truth; *zaligheid*, *zaligheden*, bliss.

NOTE.—This ending corresponds to the old English *head*: Godhead, *Godheid*; and the modern *hood*: childhood, *kindsheid*.

3. Words compounded with *man* commonly take the plural *lieden*, the colloquial form of which is *lui*: *timmerman*, carpenter, *timmerlieden* (*timmerlui*); *jonkman*, bachelor, *jongelieden* (*lui*). The plural *mans* or *mannen*, is, however, used as well. *Engelschman*, Englishman, has *Engelschen*; likewise *Franschman*, Frenchman, *Franschen*. *Buurman*, neighbour, takes *buren*.

4. The plural of *armvol*, armful, and *handvol*, handful, is

FORMATION OF THE PLURAL. 39

arnwollen and *handvollen*. The English "spoonful" has no equivalent in Dutch: two spoonfuls = *twee lepels vol*.

The words *asch*, ashes, *leven*, life, and *bod*, bid, are always used in the singular: He has had two bids for his house, *hij heeft tweemaal een bod voor zijn huis gehad*. Notice also: They have lost their lives in it, *zij hebben er het leven bij verloren*.

NOTE.—Observe, however—It has cost many lives, *Het heeft veel menschenlevens gekost*

XI. The following words have no plural form:

1. PROPER NOUNS, except when they designate different individuals of the same family names: *de Hugo's*, members of the Hugo family.
2. NAMES OF MATERIALS, except when they express particular kinds, or certain specified quantities or pieces: *wateren*, rivers or seas; *brooden*, loaves; *zouten*, chemicals; *wijnen*, wines.
3. ABSTRACT NOUNS, except when they express a variety: *deugden*, virtues; *schoonheden*, beauties; *bevalligheden*, graces.
4. The following, which, having no plural form of their own, borrow that of synonymous words:

WORDS.	SYNONYMS.	MEANINGS.	PLURAL FORMS.
aanbod,	aanbieding,	offer,	aanbiedingen.
bedrog,	bedriegerij,	deceit,	bedriegerijen.
beleg,	belegering,	siege,	belegeringen.
doel,	doeleinde,	purpose,	doeleinden.
genot,	genieting,	pleasure,	genietingen.
gevoel,	gevoelen,	feeling,	gevoelens.
hoop,	verwachting,	hope,	verwachtingen.
inleg,	inlage,	deposit,	inlagen.
kunde,	kundigheid,	knowledge,	kundigheden.
leer,	leering,	doctrine,	leeringen.
oordeel,	oordeelvelling,	judgment,	oordeelvellingen.
raad,	raadgeving,	advice,	raadgevingen.
roof,	rooverij,	robbery,	rooverijen.
troost,	vertroosting,	consolation,	vertroostingen.
twijfel,	twijfeling,	doubt,	twijfelingen.
verdriet,	verdrietelijkheid,	sorrow,	verdrietelijkheden.
zege,	zegepraal,	victory,	zegepralen.
zegen,	zegening,	blessing,	zegeningen.

XII. The following words have no singular:

gebroeders,	brothers (in a commercial firm).	*manieren,*	manners.
hersenen,	brains.	*mazelen,*	measles.
inkomsten,	revenue.	*onkosten,*	expense.
kolen,	coal.	*ouders,*	parents.
kosten,	cost.	*pokken,*	small-pox.
ledematen,	limbs (of the body).	*toebereidselen,*	preparations.
lieden,	people.	*voorouders,*	ancestors.
manen,	mane.	*zeden,*	customs.
		zemelen,	bran.

And the names of several mountain ranges and groups of islands:

de Pyreneeën, the Pyrenees; *de Apennijnen,* the Apennines.

NOTE.—There are in Dutch no such combinations as "*a pair of scissors,*" "*a pair of compasses,*" by which one object only is meant. A "pair of scissors" is simply *eene schaar,* plural *scharen.* A "pair of spectacles" is *eene bril,* plural *brillen.* Naturally, "a pair of boots" is *een paar schoenen.*

XIII. Of some words the singular form is used with a plural meaning:

(a) To express measure, weight or number:

de voet,	the foot;	*vier voet lang,*	four feet long.
het pond,	the pound;	*vijftig pond zwaar,*	weighing fifty pounds.
het paar,	the pair;	*twee paar schoenen,*	two pairs of shoes.
het dozijn,	the dozen;	*tien dozijn pennen,*	ten dozen nibs.

(b) In the following idioms:

op de been (for *beenen*) *brengen,*	to raise (of an army).
onder de voet (for *voeten*) *geraken,*	to be trampled over.
slaag (for *slagen*) *krijgen,*	to be thrashed.

OBS.—The following should be noticed: *drie guldens,* three florins, means three coins, each a florin—whereas *drie gulden* means any number of coins which together represent the value of three florins; *vijf ellen laken,* five yards of cloth, means five different pieces of cloth each measuring one yard—whereas *vijf el laken* means one piece of cloth measuring five yards.

XIV.—Final Consonants with regard to the Formation of the Plural.

Rules for changing final *f* and *s* into *v* and *z*.

1. A final consonant, occurring after a full vowel or a diphthong, is not doubled before a plural ending: *boek*, book, *boeken; ruit*, pane, *ruiten*. The same rule applies when an imperfect vowel becomes full in the plural, as in the following 27:

bad,	bath,	*baden*.	*verdrag*,	treaty,	*verdragen*.
blad,	leaf,	*bladen*.	*bevel*,	command,	*bevelen*.
dag,	day,	*dagen*.	*gebed*,	prayer,	*gebeden*.
dak,	roof,	*daken*.	*gebrek*,	fault,	*gebreken*.
dal,	valley,	*dalen*.	*spel*,	game,	*spelen*.
gat,	hole,	*gaten*.	*tred*,	step,	*treden*.
glas,	glass,	*glazen*.	*weg*,	way,	*wegen*.
graf,	grave,	*graven*.	*god*,	god,	*goden*.
pad,	path,	*paden*.	*hof*,	court,	*hoven*.
rad,	wheel,	*raderen*.	*hol*,	den,	*holen*.
slag,	blow,	*slagen*.	*lot*,	lot,	*loten*.
staf,	staff,	*staven*.	*oorlog*,	war,	*oorlogen*.
vat,	barrel,	*vaten*.	*schot*,	shot,	*schoten*.
		slot,	lock,	*sloten*.	

2. Nouns ending in a consonant, preceded by a short vowel, which retains its imperfect sound in the plural, double their final consonant: *bok*, goat, *bokken; hak*, heel, *hakken; blok*, block, *blokken; kat*, cat, *katten*. This doubling of the consonant serves to close the first syllable and to open the second, thereby preserving the imperfect vowel-sound.

EXCEPTIONS:

1. *Ch* (final) is never doubled, and *sch* only doubles its *s*: *glimlach*, smile, *glimlachen; musch*, sparrow, *musschen*.
2. When the final consonant is preceded by an unaccented *i* or *e*, it is not doubled, so as not to change the accent: *pérzik*, peach, *pérziken* (not *perzikken*); *monnik*, monk, *monniken* (nor *monnikken*); *dréumes*, dwarf, *dréumesen* (not *dreuméssen*); *havik*, hawk, *haviken* (not *havikken*). The ending *is*, however, does not fall under this rule: *secretáris*, secretary, *secretárissen; vónnis*, sentence, *vonnissen*.

OBS.—Rules 1 and 2 apply to the formation of the infinitive forms of verbs, whose stem has a short vowel: *bakken,* to bake (stem *bak*); also to the flexion-forms of adjectives: *dom,* stupid, *domme.*

3. Nouns ending in *f* or *s*, change *f* and *s* into *v* and *z*:

(*a*) When preceded either by a diphthong, a full vowel, or one which becomes full in the plural, *e.g. duif,* pigeon, *duiven; haas,* hare, *hazen.* Except—*philosofen,* philosophers, *photografen,* photographers, *kousen,* stockings, *kruisen,* crosses, *struisen,* ostriches, *pausen,* popes, *spiesen,* spears.

(*b*) When preceded by a consonant, *f* changes into *v*, except in the two foreign words *triomfen,* triumphs, and *ninfen,* nymphs.

The *s* only changes into *z* when preceded by *l, m,* and *r*: *halzen,* necks; *gemzen,* chamois; *laarzen,* boots;—and in the following words in *ns*:

Bonzen, bounces; *ganzen,* geese; *trenzen,* snaffles; *grenzen,* boundaries; *grijnzen,* grins; *cijnzen,* tributes; *donzen,* downs (feathers); likewise the verb *glanzen,* to shine.

Walsen, walses; *polsen,* pulses; *kaarsen,* candles; *kersen,* cherries; *koersen,* courses; *persen,* presses; *schorsen,* barks (of trees); *floersen,* veils (figurative), are exceptions.

Note.—The cause of this change of final letters must be found in the original form of these words. They formerly ended in *ve* and *ze* but dropped their final *e*: *duive, roze* (the plural of which was naturally *duiven, rozen*), became *duiv, rooz,* and afterwards *duif, roos,* the hardening of final *v* and *z* tending to facilitate the pronunciation.

GRAMMAR EXERCISES.—*Taaloefeningen.*

Exercise VIII.

Write the plural forms of:

1.

Paard, horse; *merrie,* mare; *kalf,* calf; *kuiken,* chicken; *hoen,* fowl; *haan,* cock; *hen,* hen; *schaap,* sheep; *ooi,* ewe; *ram,* ram; *volk,* nation; *man,* man; *wind,* wind; *storm,* storm; *schip,* ship; *ei,* egg; *mand,* basket; *zoon,* son; *vader,* father; *last,* burden; *lepel,* spoon; *vork,* fork; *mes,* knife; *lade,* drawer; *bord,* plate; *inktpot,* inkpot; *pen,* pen; *papier,* paper; *vloeipapier,* blotting-paper; *boek,* book; *bladzijde,* page; *kalender,* calendar; *maand,* month; *week,* week; *jaar,* year; *dag,* day; *minuut,* minute;

FORMATION OF THE PLURAL.

kwartier, quarter; *klok*, clock; *wijzer*, hand; *slinger*, pendulum; *muur*, wall; *kamer*, room; *tafel*, table; *stoel*, chair; *lamp*, lamp.

2.

Paal, pole; *draad*, wire; *schroef*, screw; *spijker*, nail; *hamer*, hammer; *boor*, gimlet; *beitel*, chisel; *zaag*, saw; *timmerman*, carpenter; *metselaar*, mason; *troffel*, trowel; *schietlood*, plummet; *haak*, square; *waterpas*, water-level; *kruiwagen*, wheelbarrow; *schop*, shovel; *graaf*, spade; *hark*, rake; *schoffel*, hoe; *bloem*, flower; *struik*, bush; *heester*, shrub; *grond*, soil; *perk*, plot; *bed*, bed; *pad*, path; *boom*, tree; *blad*, leaf; *knop*, bud; *twijg*, twig; *tak*, branch; *wortel*, root; *huis*, house; *dak*, roof; *raam*, window; *kamer*, room; *waranda*, verandah; *keuken*, kitchen; *stal*, stable; *bad*, bath; *gang*, passage; *portaal*, lobby; *trap*, staircase; *leuning*, rail; *trede*, step; *zolder*, loft; *plafond*, ceiling.

EXERCISES FOR TRANSLATION.—*Vertaaloefeningen.*

ik ben, I am.
gij zijt, thou art.
hij is, he is.
zij is, she is.
het is, it is.
u is (form of address), you are.
wij zijn, we are.
gij zijt, you are.
zij zijn, they are.

ik heb, I have.
gij hebt, thou hast.
hij heeft, he has.
zij heeft, she has.
het heeft, it has.
u heeft (in address), you have.
wij hebben, we have.
gij hebt, you have.
zij hebben, they have.

NOTE.—Words, if not given above the exercises, will be found in the foregoing Gr. Ex., or in the Transl. Ex. pp. 29-31.

EXERCISE IX.

My, *mijn* (m and o), *mijne* (v); his, *zijn* (m and o), *zijne* (v); her, *haar* (m and o), *hare* (v); your, *uw* (m and o), *uwe* (v); our, *onze* (m and v), *ons* (o); their, *hun* (m and o), *hunne* (v).

I have a pencil. You have a carriage and a horse. We have a house. The study has a door and a window. The child has a book and an umbrella. The horse has a stable. You have a cupboard in your house. He is in the room. You are in your study. Are they in the carriage? They have a table in their room. The lion has a cage in the garden. His stick is on his back. Our horse is in the street. The sun has heat in (the) summer.

Exercise X.

Lady, *dame, f*; this, *deze* (*m* and *v*), *dit* (*o*); that, *die* (*m* and *v*), *dat* (*o*); or, *of*.

Is this carriage mine? Have you her bonnet or her cap? We have his pencil and his book. Are you in her room? He is in his room. Is mother in her room? That lady is in her study. Child, you are dirty. He has the wheel of our carriage in the stable. The dog is in their garden: it (he) is mine. The lady and the child are in their room. The mother and the boy have a bird in a cage. The door of our stable is broken. A door of a cupboard is never large. We have a child: it is often ill. In (the) summer the days are long.

Exercise XI.

school,	*school, v.*	longer,	*langer.*	yes,	*ja.*
slate,	*lei, v.*	many,	*veel.*	also,	*ook.*
two,	*twee.*	on,	*aan.*	there,	*er.*
five,	*vijf.*	hundred,	*honderd.*	thousand,	*duizend.*
than,	*dan.*	those,	*die.*		

NOTE.—Words in square brackets [ ] are not to be translated.

The chickens are in the garden. Two of our hens have chickens. In the school we have inkpots, books, and slates. On the table there are forks and knives. Have you [got] blotting-paper in your books? Years are longer than months, and months are longer than days. Are there leaves on the trees, and buds on the shrubs? These books have many pages. We have two windows in our kitchen. The lobbies in those houses are large, and the staircases high. The boy has many eggs in his basket.

His father has [a] thousand sheep, and my uncle has five hundred ewes. Have you [any] screws or nails for me? Yes, and also a hammer, and a gimlet.

Exercise XII.

sister,	*zuster, v.*	why,	*waarom.*	me,	*mij.*
brother,	*broeder, m.*	only,	*maar.*	no,	*neen.*
bedroom,	*slaapkamer, v.*	good,	*goed.*	more,	*meer.*
parents,	*ouders, m.*	very,	*zeer, heel.*	but,	*maar.*
one,	*een, eene, een.*	all,	*al.*	for,	*voor.*
where,	*waar.*	these,	*deze.*		

You have two horses in your stables. Why only two? Staircases have steps and railings. We have more flowers in our garden than you. Yes, but I have more shrubs in mine. How many (*hoeveel*) bedrooms are there in your house? One for my sister, two for my brothers, one for my parents, and one for me. Have the children [got] rakes and hoes? No, but the boys have spades. Carpenters use (*gebruiken*) chisels, saws, and hammers, and masons use trowels, squares, and a plummet. The buds on the trees are large. I am on the roof of our house. Where are you, mother? I am in the kitchen, my boy. Is the soil in his garden good? Yes, the soil in all these gardens is very good.

GRAMMAR EXERCISES.—*Taaloefeningen.*

Exercise XIII.

Fill up the blanks, using nouns in the plural:

Onz– koe– en onz– schaap– loopen in de wei–.
Our cows and our sheep run in the meadows.

Waar zijn d– mensch–, die gisteren hier waren? Eend–
Where are the people, who yesterday here were? Ducks

en gans– zijn zwemvogel–. Leeuw–, beer–, tijger–,
and geese are swimming birds. Lions, bears, tigers,

wolf–, vos–, en kat– zijn alle dieren, die vleesch eten.
wolves, foxes, and cats are all animals that flesh eat.
Olifant–, kameel–, os–, bok– en schaap– eten geen
Elephants, camels, oxen, goats and sheep eat no
vleesch, maar plant–. Op onz– reis– hebben wij stad–,
flesh, but plants. On our journeys have we towns,
dorp–, rivier–, beek–, sluis–, brug–, markt–, kerk—,
villages, rivers, brooks, sluices, bridges, markets, churches,
toren–, schip–, en zoo voorts (enz.) gezien. De voornaamste
towers, ships, and so forth (etc.) seen. The principal
deel– van huis– zijn de fondament–, de muur–, de
parts of houses are the foundations, the walls, the
venster–, de deur–, de schoorsteen–, en de dak–. Schip–
windows, the doors, the chimneys, and the roofs. Ships
hebben kiel–, roer–, mast–, anker–, zeil–, vlag–, ra–.
have keels, helms, masts, anchors, sails, flags, yards.

Exercise XIV.

Dez– visch– wonen in de noordelijke zee–. Op punt–
These fishes live in the northern seas. On points
waar de golf– van twee oceaan– elkander ontmoeten,
where the waves of two oceans each other meet,
zijn die golf– zeer hoog. Hebt gij muis– of rat– in
are those waves very high. Have you mice or rats in
de val– gezien? De bosch– zijn vol eekhorentje– en
the traps seen? The woods are full (of) squirrels and
aap–. De eekhoren– stelen de ei– uit de nest–
monkeys. The squirrels steal the eggs out (of) the nests
der vogel– in de hooge boom–. Meerkat– leven in gat–
of the birds in the high trees. Marmosets live in holes
in het veld. Wij ontdekten gisteren drie echo– in de
in the field. We discovered yesterday three echoes in the
berg–. De dal– zijn vol bloem–, en al de
mountains. The valleys are full (of) flowers, and all the
struik– hebben knop–. De land– zijn in provincie–
shrubs have buds. The countries are in provinces

FORMATION OF THE PLURAL.

verdeeld, en die weder in wijk–. De dame– hebben de
divided, and those again in wards. The ladies have the
photographie– in album– gezet. Dez– kind– zijn in
photographs in albums put. These children are in
hunne hoop– teleurgesteld. Ik kan uw– aanbod– niet
their hopes disappointed. I can your offers not
aannemen. Drie stoomboot– zijn vergaan, en honderden
accept. Three steamers are wrecked, and hundreds
mensch– omgekomen.
(of) people perished.

TRANSLATION EXERCISES.—*Vertaaloefeningen.*

Exercise XV.

sugar,	*suiker, v.*	tea,	*thee, v.*	coffee,	*koffie, v.*
oats,	*haver, v.*	journey,	*reis, v.*	tie,	*das, v.*
glove,	*handschoen, m.*	shirt,	*hemd, o.*	hat,	*hoed, m.*
one,	*één,*	taller,	*grooter,*	give,	*geef.*
		for sale,	*te koop.*		

NOTE.—Words given as examples to special rules are n t repeated.

How many loaves have you [got]? I have five loaves. Have you [got] two spoonfuls of sugar for me? A handful, if you like (*als gij wilt*). Those Englishmen are taller than these Frenchmen. My neighbours are carpenters and masons. Our horses have oats, and our cows bran and water. Give me five pounds [of] tea, and two pounds [of] coffee. The boys have two dozen nibs. These walls are [a] hundred feet high. One child ha (the) small pox, and two children have (the) measles. There are great (*groote*) preparations for his journey. Shirts, stockings, ties, gloves, and hats are for sale at Scott brothers (*bij de Gebroeders Scott*) in (the) Plein Street.

Exercise XVI.

woman,	*vrouw, v.*	land,	*land, o.*	carpet,	*tapijt, o.*
shop,	*winkel, m.*	key,	*sleutel, m.*	mouse,	*muis, v.*
girl,	*meisje, o.*	boot,	*schoen, m.*	outside,	*buiten.*
sea,	*zee, v.*	rat,	*rat, v.*	new,	*nieuw.*
rabbit,	*konijn, o.*	mole,	*mol, m.*	on,	*in.*
tooth,	*tand, m.*	strong,	*sterk.*	along,	*langs.*
		broken,	*gebroken.*		

We have two uncles, two aunts, and five nephews. The women are in the shop, and their husbands are outside. The roots of the trees are long and strong. The tree has [a] thousand leaves, and my book has only [a] hundred leaves. The bones of his legs are broken. All the rooms have new carpets, and the girls have new clothes. The songs of your children are new to me (*mij nieuw*). The watch has many wheels. We have [a] hundred lambs, and many fowls also. The ships are on the sea, and the towns are on (*op*) the land. There are two kinds of meat (two meats) on [the] table. We have sods along the paths in our garden. These doors have locks and keys. Children have many faults. There are holes in those walls. The heels of my boots are high. Cats, rats, mice, rabbits, and moles have sharp teeth.

GRAMMAR EXERCISES.—*Taaloefeningen.*

Exercise XVII.

1.

Write out the plural forms of:

Toestel, apparatus; *schop*, spade; *haard*, hearth; *kachel*, stove; *blaker*, candlestick; *kandelaar*, candlestick; *tropee*, trophy; *evangelie*, gospel; *knie*, knee; *zee*, sea; *lijf*, body; *corset*, corset; *leus*, motto; *ei*, egg; *blad*, leaf; *dak*, roof;

bol, globe; *les*, lesson; *mombakkes*, mask; *vonnis*, sentence; *schijf*, disk; *laars*, boot; *slof*, slipper; *pantoffel*, slipper; *zool*, sole; *dans*, dance; *krans*, wreath; *varken*, pig; *koe*, cow; *kalf*, calf; *big*, young pig; *os*, ox; *giraffe*, giraffe; *tobbe*, tub; *schans*, trench; *duif*, dove; *doffer*, male pigeon; *staatsman*, policeman; *ambachtsman*, artisan; *perzik*, peach; *druif*, grape; *peer*, pear; *havik*, hawk; *musch*, sparrow; *kolibri*, colibri; *raad*, advice or council; *genot*, pleasure; *zege*, victory; *bedrog*, deceit; *goedheid*, goodness; *gebergte*, mountain range; *studie*, study; *lidmaat*, member or limb; *rif*, reef, carcass; *vleesch*, meat; *tin*, tin; *ijzer*, iron; *smid*, blacksmith; *wortel*, root, carrot; *hemel*, heaven, tester (of a bed); *genie*, genius; *tournooi*, tournament; *dame*, lady; *dokter*, physician; *doctor*, doctor; *horloge*, watch; *gelid*, rank; *berin*, she-bear; *vla*, custard; *kanarie*, canary; *oom*, uncle; *been*, leg, bone; *papegaai*, parrot; *spel*, game; *philosoof*, philosopher; *struis*, ostrich; *nimf*, fairy; *neus*, nose; *els*, awl; *hertog*, duke; *graaf*, count; *koningin*, queen; *zoon*, son; *domoor*, dunce; *vlag*, flag; *glas*, glass; *teen*, toe, osier; *warande*, verandah; *bies*, rush; *menagerie*, menagery; *hypotheek*, bond; *mikroskoop*, microscope; *idée*, idea; *telegram*, telegram; *piano*, piano; *harmonium*, harmonium; *twee*, two; *drie*, three; *zes*, six; *negen*, nine; *vijf*, five; *zeven*, seven; *nul*, zero; *opstel*, composition; *dictaat*, dictation; *preek*, sermon; *reden*, reason.

<table>
<tr><td>CONVERSATIE.</td><td>CONVERSATION.</td></tr>
</table>

Maaltijden.   Meals.

1. *Heeft u ontbeten?* — 1. Have you had breakfast?
2. *Nog niet; wij onbijten gewoonlijk om 9 uur.* — 2. Not yet, we usually breakfast at 9 o'clock.
3. *Wil u nu een kop koffie gebruiken?* — 3. Will you take a cup of coffee now?
4. *Dank u; ik wacht liever tot het ontbijt.* — 4. No, thanks; I prefer waiting till breakfast time.
5. *Wil u bij mij komen dineeren?* — 5. Will you come and dine with me?

6. Dank u; ik ben reeds uitgevraagd.
7. Kom dan morgen toch koffie drinken om 1 uur, of soupeeren om 9 uur.
8. Geef mij een bord soep.
9. Geef mij een stukje gebraden vleesch en wat radijs.
10. Is de biefstuk malsch?
11. Kan ik u dienen met wat gestoofd schapenvleesch?
12. Mag ik u een stukje gebraden beestenvleesch geven?
13. Ik wil graag iets van dien gebraden eend en wat groene erwten nemen.
14. Wat groente mag ik u aanbieden?
15. Gestoofde aardappelen en bloemkool, als 't u blieft.
16. Zal u wijn of bier gebruiken?
17. Geef mij een glas stout.
18. Er zijn poddingen, taarten en pastijen; wat mag ik u zenden?
19. Wat appeltaart en vla.
20. Voor dessert zijn er rozijnen en amandelen, gember, appelen, sinaasappelen, ananassen en vijgen.
21. Blieft u thee of koffie na den eten?
22. Een klein kopje sterke koffie, als 't u blieft.
23. Verkiest u het zonder melk en suiker?
24. Chocolade gebruik ik zonder suiker, maar nooit thee of koffie.
25. Geef mij het brood eens aan, als 't u blieft.
26. Ik houd van ham met eieren voor ontbijt.
27. Zou u mij de kaas willen passeeren?
28. Met genoegen.

6. I am invited out, thanks very much.
7. Well, then come to luncheon to-morrow at 1 o'clock, or to supper at 9 o'clock.
8. Give me a plate of soup.
9. Give me some roast beef and some radish.
10. Is the beefsteak tender.
11. Can I help you to some mutton stew?
12. May I give you some roast beef?
13. I should like some roast duck and green peas, please.
14. What vegetables can I offer you?
15. Boiled potatoes and cauliflower, please.
16. Will you take wine or beer?
17. Give me a glass of stout.
18. There are puddings, tarts and pies; which shall I send you?
19. Some apple-tart and custard.
20. For dessert there are raisins and almonds, preserved ginger, apples, oranges, pineapples and figs.
21. Will you take tea or coffee after dinner?
22. A small cup of strong coffee, please.
23. Do you prefer it without milk and sugar?
24. I take chocolate without sugar, but never tea or coffee.
25. Pass me the bread, please.
26. I like ham and eggs for breakfast.
27. May I trouble you for the cheese?
28. With pleasure.

CHAPTER V.

THE GENDER OF SUBSTANTIVES.

(*Het Geslacht der Zelfstandige Naamwoorden.*)

I. The gender of a noun is the way in which it is declined. There being three different ways of declining a noun, there are accordingly three genders, called the Masculine, the Feminine, and the Neuter gender (*het Mannelijk, Vrouwelijk en Onzijdig geslacht*). It should be apparent from this definition, that the names of inanimate objects must be treated like the names of persons and animals, and are therefore *not Neuter* on account of things having *no sex*, but are Masculine, Feminine, or Neuter, according as they are declined.

> NOTE TO THE STUDENT.—To foreigners there is perhaps nothing more difficult in the Dutch language than the genders. Even to born Dutchmen they are a great drawback to correct writing. In speaking only two genders are observed, Neuter nouns being by instinct felt to be neuter, while all other substantives, even those that are most obviously feminine, are used with the masculine gender. The rules below are indispensable for correct writing. However, after having acquired them, the student will find that he is by no means able to determine the gender of every Dutch word. More rules might be added, but the difficulty would remain. The only way to acquire the genders is to make it a practice to observe them with the nouns as often as they occur. A good reliable dictionary, besides, is indispensable for reference.

II. RULES TO ASCERTAIN THE GENDER OF NOUNS.

1. Names of male persons and male animals are Masculine, as: *koning*, king; *broeder*, brother; *leeuw*, lion; *stier*, bull.

2. Names of female persons and female animals are Feminine, as: *keizerin*, empress; *waschvrouw*, washerwoman; *berin*, she-bear; *koe*, cow.

> EXCEPTIONS: *het wijf*, the woman (term of contempt), is Neut. *Het arme mensch*, the poor creature, is heard of women, though *mensch* is Masc.

3. When the male and the female animal have only one name, that name is Masculine for the larger animals, and Feminine for the smaller, as (Masculine): *struis*, ostrich; *kameel*, camel; and (Feminine): *kat*, cat; *muis*, mouse.

> EXCEPTIONS: *mol*, mole; *spreeuw*, starling; *nachtegaal*, nightingale; *vink*, finch; *kikvorsch*, frog, are Masc. *Giraffe*, giraffe, is Fem.

4. When the male and the female animal have each a separate name, but there is a third name for the two together, this third name is Neuter, as: *ram*, ram, Masculine; *ooi*, ewe, Feminine; *schaap*, sheep, Neuter; *Haan*, cock, Masculine; *hen*, hen, Feminine; and *hoen*, fowl, Neuter.

> EXCEPTION: *hond*, dog, is Masc., though it has *reu* for the male and *teef* for the female animal.

5. Names of trees are Masculine, as: *eik*, oak; *wilg*, willow.

> EXCEPTIONS: *linde*, lime-tree, *tamarisk*, and *tamarinde*, tamarind-tree, are Fem.

6. Names of shrubs, plants, and flowers are Feminine, as: *jasmijn*, jessamine; *geranium*, geranium; *rogge*, rye; *perzik*, peach; *peer*, pear.

The word *struik*, shrub, is Masculine.

> EXCEPTIONS: The names of plants and fruits ending in *oen, ier, ing, er,* and *el* are Masc.: *meloen*, melon; *anjelier*, pink; *zuring*, sorrel; *eikel*, (*aker*), acorn; *komkommer*, cucumber; *mispel*, medlar; *klaver*, clover.

7. Names of the parts of trees and plants are Feminine, as: *schors*, bark; *schil*, peel; *twijg*, twig.

> EXCEPTIONS: *tronk*, trunk; *stam*, stem; *tak*, branch; *wortel*, root; and *bast*, bark, are Masc.; *blad*, leaf, is Neut.

8. Names of mountains and large rivers are Masculine, as: *de Mont Blanc*, the Mont Blanc; *de Nijl*, the Nile.

9. Names of small rivers and brooks are Feminine, as: *de Jordaan*, Jordan; *de Kidron*, Kidron.

10. Names of seasons, months and days are Masculine, as: *herfst*, autumn; *Maart*, March; *Zaterdag*, Saturday.

> EXCEPTION: *lente*, spring, is Fem.
>
> NOTE.—*Dag*, day, is Masc.; *eeuw*, century, *maand*, month, and *week*, week, are Fem.; *jaar*, year, *seizoen*, season, and *uur*, hour, are Neut.

11. Names of ships are Masculine, when they end in *er*, as: *driemaster*, three-masted ship.

12. Names of ships are Feminine, when they do not end in *er*, as: *sloep*, sloop; *boot*, boat.

> EXCEPTIONS: *fregat*, frigate, and *jacht*, yacht, are Neut.
>
> NOTE.—The word *schip*, ship, is Neut. Proper names of ships are Feminine.

13. Monosyllabic names of the parts of ships are Feminine, as: *ra*, yard; *stang*, bar; *kiel*, keel.

> EXCEPTIONS: *boeg*, bow, and *mast*, mast, are Masc. *Roer*, helm; *zeil*, sail; *ruim*, hold; *dek*, deck, are Neut.

14. Names of coins are Masculine: *stuiver*, penny; *gulden*, florin.

> EXCEPTION: *het pond*, the sovereign.

15. Names of precious stones are Masculine, when they indicate single pieces, as: *De diamant in dezen ring*, the diamond in this ring; but when they have a collective meaning, they are Neuter: *Het diamant van Zuid-Afrika*, the diamond of South Africa.

16. Stems of verbs expressing an action are Masculine, as: *slaap*, sleep; *glimlach*, smile; *val*, fall.

> NOTE.—Many words derived from verbal stems are Feminine because they used to have the ending *e*. Such are: *eer*, honour; *wraak*, revenge; *spraak*, speech; *maat*, measure; *praal*, splendour; *vraag*, question; *vrees*, fear; *leer*, doctrine; *straf*, punishment; *reis*, journey; *hoop*, hope; *zorg*, care; *huur*, ren'; *spijt*, sorrow; *hulp*, help; *breuk*, breach; *keus*, choice; *teug* (fem. *tijgen* = to draw), draught.

17. Stems of verbs meaning an instrument or tool are Feminine, as: *val*, trap; *zaag*, saw; *boor*, gimlet.

> EXCEPTION: *ploeg*, plough, is Masc.

18. Stems of verbs ending in *st*, in which *st* cannot be removed, are Masculine, as: *twist*, quarrel; *oogst*, harvest; *dorst*, thirst; *troost*, consolation; *last*, burden.

> EXCEPTION: *rust*, rest, is Fem.

19. Stems of verbs to which *st* is added, and from which it can be separated, are Feminine, as: *kunst*, art; *komst*, coming.

> EXCEPTIONS: *dienst*, service; *angst*, anxiety; *ernst*, seriousness, are Masc.

20. Stems of verbs with the unaccented verbal prefixes, *be, ge, ver,* and *ont,* are Neuter, as: *bedrag*, amount; *verlof*, leave; *ontbijt*, breakfast.

> EXCEPTION: *verkoop*, sale, is Masc.

21. Names of the letters of the alphabet, of the figures, and of musical notes, are Feminine, as: *eene o*, an o; *eene vijf*, a five; *eene do*, a do.

22. Monosyllabic names of the parts of the human body are Feminine, as: *heup*, hip; *long*, lung; *kin*, chin; *maag*, stomach.

> EXCEPTIONS: *arm*, arm; *neus*, nose; *rug*, back; *voet*, foot; *hiel*, heel; *teen*, toe; *nek*, neck; *hals*, neck; *tand*, tooth; *mond*, mouth; *baard*, beard, are Masc.
>
> *Oor*, ear; *oog*, eye; *vel*, skin; *been*, leg; *hoofd*, head; *hart*, heart; *lijf*, body, are Neuter.

23. Names of musical instruments are Feminine, as: *trompet*, trumpet; *harp*, harp; *viool*, violin.

> EXCEPTIONS: *triangel*, triangle, is Masc.; *klavier*, piano, and *orgel*, organ, are Neuter.

24. All diminutives are Neuter, as: *kindje*, little child; *raampje*, small window.

25. Names of materials, especially metals, are Neuter, as: *goud*, gold; *katoen*, cotton.

> EXCEPTIONS: *zijde*, silk; *franje*, fringe; *kant*, lace; *watten*, wadding; *melk*, milk; *boter*, butter; *kaas*, cheese; *siroop*, syrup; *snuif*, snuff; *suiker*, sugar; *kool*, coal; *thee*, tea; *wol*, wool; *zeep*, soap; *zwavel*, sulphur; *kamfer*, camphor; *gom*, gum; *hars*, resin, etc., are Fem.
>
> *Aluin*, alum; *azijn*, vinegar; *wijn*, wine; *kalk*, lime; *mosterd*, mustard; *tabak*, tobacco; *room*, cream; *honing*, honey, etc., are Masc.

26. Words expressing a collection of objects are Neuter, as: *leger*, army; *dozijn*, dozen; *geld*, money; *bosch*, bosch.

> EXCEPTIONS: *zwerm*, swarm; *stoet*, train; *troep*, troop, are Masc. *Bende*, band; *vloot*, fleet; *kudde*, flock; *schaar*, crowd, are Fem.

27. Words which begin with *ge* and end in *te* are Neuter, when they express a collection, as: *gevogelte*, all the birds; *gebeente*, all the bones belonging to a skeleton.

28. Names of countries, towns and villages are Neuter, as: *het oude Rome*, old Rome; *het machtige Engeland*, mighty England.

> NOTE.—*Stad*, town, is Fem.; *land*, country, and *dorp*, village, are Neut.

29. The names of the young of animals are Neuter, as; *kuiken*, chicken; *veulen*, colt; *lam*, lamb; *kalf*, calf; *welp*, whelp.

> EXCEPTION: *big*, young pig, is Fem.

30. Infinitive verbs, and further all parts of speech used as nouns, are Neuter, as: *het leven*, life, *het voornemen*, the intention; *het voor en tegen*, the pro and con.

31. Names of instruments ending in *el*, *er*, and *aar*, are Masculine, as: *sleutel*, key; *hamer*, hammer; *lessenaar*, desk.

> EXCEPTIONS: *griffel*, slate-pencil; *schoffel*, hoe; *sikkel*, sickle; *gaffel*, pitchfork; *ladder*, ladder; and *kluister*, fetter, are Fem.

> NOTE.—The endings *er* and *el* mark the Masc. gender for essentially Dutch words. Words of foreign origin having these endings are Neut., as: *artikel*, article; *orgel*, organ; *offer*, sacrifice; *venster*, window; *cijfer*, figure; *klooster*, convent; *meubel*, piece of furniture.

32. Words in *m*, *em*, *rm*, *lm*, *end*, and *ond*, are Masculine, as: *riem*, thong; *bezem*, broom; *worm*, worm; *zalm*, salmon; *ochtend*, morning; *avond*, evening.

> EXCEPTIONS: *bloem*, flower; *kiem*, germ; and *uniform*, uniform, are Fem. *Raam*, window; *scherm*, screen, are Neut.

33. Words in *dom*, when expressing a *state*, or *condition*, as; *wasdom*, growth; *adeldom*, nobility (also as a collective); *rijkdom*, riches; *ouderdom*, old age, are Masculine.

All the others are Neuter, as: *Christendom*, Christianity; *menschdom*, human race; *hertogdom*, dukedom.

Notice that *Christendom*, Christianity, means the creed of Christians, while Eng. Christendom (the collective body of Christians) is Dutch *Christenheid*.
Heidendom, means both "heathenism" and "heathen" in a collective sense.

§ 34. Words in *schap*, indicating a *profession* or an *estate*, as *priesterschap*, priesthood; *graafschap*, earldom; *landschap*, province—and the words: *gezantschap*, embassy; *genootschap*, society; *gereedschap*, tools; and *gezelschap*, company, are Neuter.

All the others are Feminine, as; *blijdschap*, joy; *boodschap*, message; *buurtschap*, neighbourhood; *rekenschap*, (rendering of) account; *manschap*, crew.

35. Words in *ing*, not derived from verbs, are Masculine, as: *ketting*, chain; *rotting*, cane; *ring*, ring.

36. Words in *ing*, derived from verbs, are Feminine, as: *teekening*, drawing; *bedoeling*, meaning.

37. Words ending in *d, cht, t, e, ij, ie, uw, nis, heid, teit, uur, ier*, are Fem., as: *deugd*, virtue; *kracht*, strength; *markt*, market; *vreugde*, joy; *heerschappij*, dominion; *knie*, knee; *schaduw*, shadow; *begrafenis*, funeral; *waarheid*, truth; *majesteit*, majesty; *natuur*, nature; *rivier*, river.

EXCEPTIONS: in *d—vloed*, flood; *eed*, oath; *rand*, border; *draad*, thread; *raad*, advice; *gloed*, glow; *hoed*, hat, are Masc. *Hemd*, shirt; *zwaard*, sword; *leed*, grief; *lid*, member (limb); and *land*, country, are Neut.
In *cht* and *t—echt*, matrimony: *plicht*, duty; *nacht*, night; *tocht*, journey; *geest*, spirit, are Masc. *Licht*, light; *wicht*, babe; *recht*, right; *ambt*, profession; *ambacht*, trade; *schrift*, writing, are Neut.
In *de—vrede*, peace, is Masc. *Geleide*, escort; *getij(de)*, tide; *eind(e)*, end; and *webbe*, web, are Neut.
In *ie—concilie*, council; *evangelie*, gospel; and *genie*, genius, and *land*, country, are Neut.
In *nis—vonnis*, sentence; and *vuilnis* (*vullis*), dirt, are Neut.

38. All words ending in *sel* and derived from Verbs are Neuter, as: *deksel*, lid; *handvatsel*, handle.

39. Foreign words in *aan, ant* (and), *aard* and *ont,* are Masc., as: *orkaan,* hurricane; *oceaan,* ocean; *foliant,* book in folio; *tulband,* turban; *standaard,* standard; *tabbaard,* gown; *horizont,* horizon.

40. Foreign words ending in *as, eet, ot, iek, ier, teit, uut,* and *uur,* are Fem., as: *matras,* mattress; *komeet,* comet; *kalot,* cap; *republiek,* commonwealth; *rivier,* river; *majesteit,* majesty; *natuur,* nature; *minuut,* minute.

    EXCEPTIONS: *schavot,* scaffold; *koliek,* colic; *harnas,* armour; *kompas,* compass; *moeras,* swamp; *formulier,* formulary, *kwartier,* quarter; *papier,* paper; *avontuur,* adventure, and *figuur,* shape, are Neuter.

41. Foreign words in *aal, aat, eel, ent, et, oen, oor,* are Neut., as: *portaal,* portal; *kanaal,* canal; *klimaat,* climate; *karaat,* carat; *kasteel,* castle; *priëel,* summer-house; *parlement,* parliament; *talent,* talent; *korset,* corset; *harpoen,* harpoon; *kantoor,* office; *plantsoen,* plantation; *seizoen,* season; *musket,* musket; *bekkeneel,* skull.

    EXCEPTION: *kaneel,* cinnamon, is Fem.

III. RULES FOR THE COMMON GENDER.—Words which according to their signification, may either be Masculine or Feminine, are said to have a common gender (*Gemeen geslacht*). They are:

1. Names of persons and animals ending in *ling:* *lieveling,* darling; *vreemdeling,* stranger; *nesteling,* nestling.

2. Names of persons ending in *noot* or *genoot: echtgenoot,* consort; *landgenoot,* fellow-countryman; *speelgenoot,* playfellow.

3. The following words: *bode,* messenger; *dienstbode,* servant; *gids,* guide; *getuige,* witness; *wees,* orphan; *lidmaat,* member of a congregation; *erfgenaam,* heir.

Besides these names of persons, a few other words have a double gender. They are:

1. Words, metaphorically used to indicate persons; *ondeugd*, Fem. with the meaning " vice "; Masc. with the meaning " a naughty boy "; and Fem. again, with the meaning " a naughty girl ": *bloed*, Neut., means " blood," Masc. " wretch."

2. Names of fruits which apply also to trees producing the fruit. In that case the word is Fem. when it indicates the fruit, and Masc. when it is used for the tree: *kers*, Fem. cherry, *kers*, Masc. cherry-tree.

3. Names of materials which at the same time may indicate a separate piece. When the word is used for the material as such, it is either Neut. or Fem.; when it indicates a piece, it is either Masc. or Fem.:

Diamant, diamond, may be either Neut. or Masc.;
Turf, peat, is Fem. or Masc.;
Kurk, cork, is Neut. or Fem.

In like manner *visch*, fish, is Masc. and Fem.: *Ik heb eenen visch* (Masc.) *gevangen*, I caught a fish; and *Wij zullen visch* (Fem.) *voor ons middagmaal hebben*, we shall have fish for dinner.

IV. RULES FOR THE GENDER OF COMPOUND NOUNS.—All compound nouns follow the gender of their last part. Examples: *huis* is Neut., and *deur* is Fem., therefore *huisdeur* Fem.; *tafel* is Fem., and *kleed* is Neut., therefore *tafelkleed* Neuter.

There are a few words, however, whose gender changes in composition: *blik* is Masc., but *oogenblik*, moment, is Neut.; *stip* is Fem., but *tijdstip*, date, is Neut.; *kant* is Masc., but *vierkant*, square, is Neut.; *hof* is Masc., but *kerkhof*, churchyard, is Neut.

THE GENDER OF SUBSTANTIVES. 59

V. WORDS WHICH HAVE CHANGED THEIR GENDER.—*Tijd* is now Masc.; *nacht* is now Masc.; *feest* is now Neut.; *oog* is now Neut.; *hart* is now Neut.; *oor* is now Neut., whereas all these words were once Feminine.

VI. Mark the following list of words:

Bal, ball, globe, Masc.
Blik, look, Masc.
Das, badger, Masc.
Deken, deacon, Masc.
Gang, passage, Fem.
Graaf, count, Masc.
Hof, court, Neut.
Hoop, heap, Masc.
Kant, edge or side, Masc.
Loods, pilot, Masc.
Maal, time, Fem.
Morgen, acre, Neut.
Palm, palm-tree, Masc.
Patroon, cartridge, Fem.
Post, post-office, Fem.
Punt, subject, Neut.
Slag, blow, Masc.
Stof, material, Fem.
Traan, tear, Masc.
Trap, kick, Masc.
Val, fall, Masc.
Vlek, stain, Fem.
Vorst, prince, Masc.
Zucht, sigh, Masc.

Bal, dance, ball, Neut.
Blik, tin, Neut.
Das, neck-tie, Fem.
Deken, blanket, Fem.
Gang, gait, Masc.
Graaf, spade, Fem.
Hof, garden, Masc.
Hoop, hope, Fem.
Kant, lace, Fem.
Loods, barn, Fem.
Maal, meal, Neut.
Morgen, morning, Masc.
Palm, palm of the hand, Fem.
Patroon, pattern, Neut.
Post, situation, Masc.
Punt, point and full-stop, Fem.
Slag, trap and kind, Neut.
Stof, dust, Neut.
Traan, whale-oil, Fem.
Trap, staircase, Fem.
Val, trap, Fem.
Vlek, hamlet, Neut.
Vorst, frost and roof-ridge, Fem.
Zucht, strong desire, or disease, Fem.

VII. NATURAL GENDER. — *Natuurlijk Geslacht.* — The Natural Gender of persons and animals is indicated by their names.

The ending *es* makes Feminine names of persons of Masculine ones: *dichter*, poet; *dichteres*, poetess; *zanger*, singer; *zangeres*, lady singer; *dienaar*, servant; *dienares*, (female) servant.

The ending *in* does the same: *koning*, king; *koningin*, queen; *keizer*, emperor; *keizerin*, empress; *gemaal*, consort, (Fem.) *gemalin*.

It also derives names of female animals from those of

male: *leeuw*, lion, *leeuwin; wolf*, wolf, *wolfin; beer*, boar, *berin*.

The ending *ster* makes Feminine names of the stems of verbs, where the male appellation is *er* : *bakker*, baker, *bakster; naaister*, needle-woman; *schoonmaakster*, char-woman.

The same ending *ster* is added to male appellations ending in *aar* : *toovenaar*, magician, *toovenaarster; bedelaar*, beggar, *bedelaarster*. The Feminine of *dief*, thief, is *dievegge*.

Notice further the following distinctions :

Masculine.	Feminine.	Masculine.	Feminine.
man, man.	*vrouw*, woman.	*knecht*, man-servant.	*meid*, maid.
man, husband.	*vrouw*, wife.		
vader, father.	*moeder*, mother.	*hengst*, stallion.	*merrie*, mare.
zoon, son.	*dochter*, daughter.	*kater*, he-cat.	*kat*, she-cat.
		haan, cock.	*hen*, hen.
bruigom, bridegroom.	*bruid*, bride.	*ram*, ram.	*ooi*, ewe.
		doffer, cock-pigeon.	*duif*, hen-pigeon.
oom, uncle.	*tante*, aunt.		
neef, nephew, cousin.	*nicht*, niece, cousin.	*bul(stier)*, bull.	*koe*, cow.
		bok, buck.	*hinde*, doe.
monnik, monk.	*non*, nun.	*bok*, he-goat.	*geit*, she-goat.
heer, gentleman.	*dame*, lady.	*woerd*, drake.	*eend*, duck.
		beer, male pig.	*zeug*, sow.

The animals are further distinguished as *mannetje*, male, *wijfje*, female, as :

Mannetjes olifant, male elephant; *wijfjes kameel*, female camel.

VIII. Synopsis of Rules on the Gender.

1. *Animals.*

Special names of males are Masculine.
Special names of females are Feminine.
Names common to either sex, each having a special name besides, are Neuter. One exception.
Names common to either sex, when no special names are used, are Masculine for large, and Feminine for small animals. Six exceptions.

2. *Ships.*

Names ending in *er* are Masculine.
Names not ending in *er* are Feminine. Two exceptions.

3. *Stems of Verbs.*

Masculine when indicating an action.
Feminine, when indicating an instrument. One exception.

4. *Words in* dom.

Masculine when indicating a state or condition.
Neuter, all the others.

5. *Words in* schap.

Neuter when indicating profession, or estate.
Feminine, all the others. Three exceptions.

6. *Words in* st.

Masculine when inseparable from stem. One exception.
Feminine when separable from stem. One exception.

7. *Masculine only.*

Names of trees. Three exceptions.
Names of mountains and large rivers.
Names of seasons, months, and days. One exception.
Names of coins. One exception.
Names of precious stones.

8. *Feminine only.*

Names of shrubs, plants, and flowers. Exceptions.
Names of small rivers, and brooks.
Names of letters, and figures in arithmetic.
Names of parts of trees. Six exceptions.
Names of parts of the human body. Eighteen exceptions.
Names of the parts of ships. Six exceptions.
Names of musical instruments. Three exceptions.

9. *Neuter only.*

Names of countries, and towns.
Names of collections. Seven exceptions.
Names of materials. Exceptions.
All diminutives.
Names of collections with prefix *ge*, and suffix *te*.

Names of the young of animals. One exception.
Stems of verbs, with inseparable accented particles.
Stems of verbs, with unaccented prefixes. One exception.
Infinitive forms of verbs and other parts of speech used as nouns.

10. Masculine Endings.

El, er, aar, (instruments; six exceptions, and Neuter rule); *ing* (not derived from verbs); *oen, ier, ing, er, el* (fruits); *m, lm, rm, ond, end.*
Aan, ant, (and), aard, ont (foreign words).

11. Feminine Endings.

D (eleven exceptions), *cht* (eleven exceptions), *e* (five exceptions), *ie* (three exceptions), *nis* (two exceptions), *ing* (derived from verbs).
As, eet, ot, iek, ier, teit, uut uur (foreign words, ten exceptions).

12. Neuter Endings.

Je, tje, pje and other diminutive endings.
Sel (derived from verbs).
Aal, aat, eel, ent, et, oen, oor (foreign words, one exception).

GRAMMAR EXERCISES.—*Taaloefeningen.*

Exercise XVIII.

1.

State the genders of the following words:

Duif, pigeon; *muis,* mouse; *walvisch,* whale; *tijger,* tiger; *hutje,* little hut; *noot,* nut; *karavaan,* caravan; *ochtend,* morning; *loop,* course; *wedren,* race; *Woensdag,* Wednesday; *Maart,* March; *zwaluw,* swallow; *blijdschap,* gladness; *goedheid,* goodness; *geweer,* gun; *meisje,* girl; *jongen,* boy; *koningin,* queen; *hoest,* cough; *schaaf,* plane; *lade,* drawer; *hamer,* hammer; *dorp,* village.

2.

Haan, cock; *kuiken,* chicken; *stier,* bull; *kalf,* calf; *ladder,* ladder; *sleutel,* key; *vreugde,* joy; *slag,* blow or trap; *val,* fall or trap; *spinnekop,* spider; *bark,* barque;

trap, kick or staircase; *toevoegsel*, addition; *menschdom*, human race; *hyena*, hyena; *plooisel*, frilling; *vriend*, friend; *gevangenis*, prison; *paard*, horse; *gros*, gross; *last*, burden; *geboomte*, collection of trees.

3.

Hoop, hope; *bal*, ball; *rijst*, rice; *visch*, fish; *lente*, spring; *aap*, ape; *zes*, six; *herfst*, autumn; *schacht*, shaft; *leven*, life; *ouderdom*, old age; *dienst*, service; *schoffel*, hoe; *getuigenis*, testimony; *vriendschap*, friendship; *koliek*, colic; *gedans*, dancing; *gewicht*, weight; *ontvangst*, reception.

4.

Vierkant, square; *hart*, heart; *maal*, meal; *tooneel*, scene; *smeersel*, unguent; *minuut*, minute; *kurk*, cork; *fregat*, frigate; *morgen*, morning; *rust*, rest; *horizont*, horizon; *zalm*, salmon; *kaneel*, cinnamon; *Oostenrijk*, Austria; *droom*, dream; *gebed*, prayer; *vlek*, stain; *watten*, wadding; *gids*, guide; *landschap*, landscape; *schavot*, scaffold.

5.

Express the Feminine form of the following Masculine words:

Vijand, enemy; *onderwijzer*, teacher; *vink*, cock-finch; *kameel*, male camel; *bruigom*, bridegroom; *raadsman*, counsellor; *meester*, master; *dienaar*, servant; *haan*, cock; *boekhouder*, book-keeper; *monnik*, monk; *beschermer*, protector; *spreker*, speaker; *ram*, ram; *leugenaar*, liar; *das*, male badger; *slaaf*, slave; *vriend*, friend; *metgezel*, companion; *oom*, uncle; *hengst*, stallion; *woerd*, drake; *bok*, he-goat; *aap*, male monkey.

6.

Voogd, guardian; *wandelaar*, walker; *voetganger*, pedestrian; *beer*, boar; *beer*, he-bear; *broeder*, brother; *bakker*, baker; *graaf*, count; *doffer*, male pigeon; *meerkat*, male marmoset; *tijger*, male tiger; *bedrieger*, deceiver; *zanger*, singer; *wolf*, wolf; *musch*, cock-sparrow; *keizer*, emperor; *neef*, nephew; *reiziger*, traveller; *knecht*, man-servant; *peetoom*, godfather; *gemaal*, consort; *bok*, buck; *stier*, bull; *heer*, gentleman; *schrijver*, author; *dichter*, poet.

CONJUGATION OF THE VERBS "*hebben*," to have, and "*zijn*" to be.

AANTOONENDE WIJS. INDICATIVE MOOD.

Onvolmaakt Tegenwoordige Tijd. Present Tense.

Ik heb, I have.
Gij hebt, thou hast.
Hij (zij, het) heeft, he (she, it) has.
Wij hebben, we have.
Gij hebt, you have.
Zij hebben, they have.

Ik ben, I am.
Gij zijt, thou art.
Hij (zij, het) is, he (she, it) is.
Wij zijn, we are.
Gij zijt, you are.
Zij zijn, they are.

NOTE.—Each of these verbs 's its own auxiliary. See next tense.

Volmaakt Tegenwoordige Tijd. Perfect Tense.

Ik heb gehad, I have had.
Gij hebt gehad, thou hast had.
Hij heeft gehad, he has had.
Wij hebben gehad, we have had.
Gij hebt gehad, you have had.
Zij hebben gehad, they have had.

Ik ben geweest, I have been.
Gij zijt geweest, thou hast been.
Hij is geweest, he has been.
Wij zijn geweest, we have been.
Gij zijt geweest, you have been.
Zij zijn geweest, they have been.

Onvolmaakt Verleden Tijd. Imperfect Tense.

Ik had, I had.
Gij hadt, thou hadst.
Hij had, he had.
Wij hadden, we had.
Gij hadt, you had.
Zij hadden, they had.

Ik was, I was.
Gij waart, thou wast.
Hij was, he was.
Wij waren, we were.
Gij waart, you were.
Zij waren, they were.

Volmaakt Verleden Tijd. Pluperfect Tense.

Ik had gehad, I had had.
Gij hadt gehad, thou hadst had.
Hij had gehad, he had had.
Wij hadden gehad, we had had.
Gij hadt gehad, you had had.
Zij hadden gehad, they had had.

Ik was geweest, I had been.
Gij waart geweest, thou hadst been.
Hij was geweest, he had been.
Wij waren geweest, we had been.
Gij waart geweest, you had been.
Zij waren geweest, they had been.

AANTOONENDE WIJS.   INDICATIVE MOOD.
Onvolmaakt Toekomende Tijd.   Future Tense.

Ik zal hebben, I shall have.	*Ik zal zijn,* I shall be.
Gij zult hebben, thou wilt have.	*Gij zult zijn,* thou wilt be.
Hij zal hebben, he will have.	*Hij zal zijn,* he will be.
Wij zullen hebben, we shall have.	*Wij zullen zijn,* we shall be.
Gij zult hebben, you will have.	*Gij zult zijn,* you will be.
Zij zullen hebben, they will have.	*Zij zullen zijn,* they will be.

Volmaakt Toekomende Tijd.   Future Perfect Tense.

Ik zal gehad hebben, I shall have had.	*Ik zal geweest zijn,* I shall have been.
Gij zult gehad hebben, thou wilt have had.	*Gij zult geweest zijn,* thou wilt have been.
Hij zal gehad hebben, he will have had.	*Hij zal geweest zijn,* he will have been.
Wij zullen gehad hebben, we shall have had.	*Wij zullen geweest zijn,* we shall have been.
Gij zult gehad hebben, you will have had.	*Gij zult geweest zijn,* you will have been.
Zij zullen gehhebbad en, they will have had.	*Zij zullen geweest zijn,* they will have been.

GEBIEDENDE WIJS.   IMPERATIVE MOOD.

Enkelvoud.	*Singular.*	*Enkelvoud.*	*Singular.*
Laat mij hebben,	let me have.	*Laat mij zijn,*	let me be.
Heb,	have (thou).	*Wees,*	be (thou).
Laat hem hebben,	let him have.	*Laat hem zijn,*	let him be.

Meervoud.	*Plural.*	*Meervoud.*	*Plural.*
Laat ons hebben,	let us have.	*Laat ons zijn,*	let us be.
Hebt,	have (ye).	*Weest, zijt,*	be (ye).
Laat hen hebben,	let them have.	*Laat hen zijn,*	let them be.

HOW TO TRANSLATE THE SECOND PERSON.

In correspondence and public speaking "*gij hebt, gij zijt,*" etc., are u ed with both singular and plural meaning.

In prayer, also, "*gij hebt, gij zijt,*" etc., are the only forms in vogue.

In conversation "*u heeft, u is,*" etc., should be used, though the forms "*u hebt, u zijt,*" etc., are heard as well, especially when a plural meaning is to be conveyed.

D

In loose and familiar talk "*je hebt, je zijt*" are the singular, and "*jullie hebt, jullie zijt,*" the plural forms in use.

Parents to children, close friends to friends, children to children, masters to servants, use the pronoun "*je*" and "*jullie.*"

Foreigners should use "*u*" throughout, except when speaking to small children, or servants.

NOTE.—These observations apply to the conjugation of all verbs.

TRANSLATION EXERCISES.*—*Vertaaloefeningen.*

EXERCISE XIX.

FIRST RULE OF CONSTRUCTION.—When in a principal sentence the verb consists of two parts (auxiliary and past participle), the auxiliary is retained in the position occupied by the English verb, and the past participle forms the last word of the sentence.

This rule may only be broken when various extensions, or a subordinate sentence intervening, the distance between the two parts of the verb is rendered greater than is consistent with clearness.

NOTE.—For the words of these and all the following translation exercises the student is referred to the English-Dutch Vocabulary.

I have a friend. I have [had] a friend (had). I had a friend. I had [had] a friend (had). I shall [have] a friend (have). I shall [have had] a friend (have had). You are my friend. You have [been] my friend (been). You were my friend. You had [been] my friend (been). You will [be] my friend (be). You will [have been] my friend (have been). Let us [be] friends (be). Be (sing.) my friend. Be (plur.) my friends. Let him [have] a book (have). Let me [have] a hat (have). Let us [have] courage (have). Thou hadst [had] a sister (had). You had [been] to (*naar*) Cape-Town (been). They will

---

* In these and all further translation exercises words given in square [ ] brackest are meant to be left out, whereas those in common ( ) brackets are supplied for translation.

[have] the pleasure (have). She had [had] a message from her uncle (had). My aunt had [been] to Wynberg (been). Be quiet, children.

Exercise XX.

SECOND RULE OF CONSTRUCTION.—In infinitive phrases the verb stands last.

[To be] young (to be). [To have] parents (to have). [To have been] in the street (been to have). [To have had] a horse (had to have). To be obedient, is good. It is good [to be] obedient (to be). To have brothers, is pleasant. It is pleasant [to have] brothers (to have). To be obedient is to be good. To have parents is to be rich. To have a friend is to have a treasure. To have been rich is to have had friends. To be sickly is to be much at home. To have been ill was painful to (*voor*) him. To have health and to be diligent is to be rich. It was difficult for the boy to be obedient. It was good of you to be in the street. It was kind of him to have bread and tea for us.

Exercise XXI.

THIRD RULE OF CONSTRUCTION.—In subordinate sentences the verb stands last. When such a sentence has a lengthy extension, the verb *may* be placed in front of it, but may *never* be in front of the direct object.

The child is happy, because it [is] obedient (is). One (*Men*) has friends, if one [is] rich (is). I asked (*vroeg*) the girl why she [had] so little work (had). The boy would (*zou*) work in the garden, if he [had] a spade (had). I am rich, because I [have] parents (have). The girl was poor, because she [had been] ill (had been). I should have gone out (*uitgegaan zijn*), if I [had had] a horse (had had). He would be tired, if he [had been] at (*op*) school (had been). I asked the man where he was going (*heen ging*). He answered (*antwoordde*) me that he [was going] to Cape Town (was going = *ging*). The harvest is small, as the weather [has been] bad (has been). Ask (*Vraag*) the boy, whether he [had] a ₂horse ₁yesterday (had). She told (*zeide*) me that she [was] ₂very (*erg*) tired ₁last night (was). I told my brother that the cows [were] very thin (were). He asked me if I [had had] a message from my uncle (had had). She told me that she [had been] ₂sickly ₁[for] a long time (had been). My brother told me that the poor man [could] not work (could = *kon*), because he [had] no (*geen*) tools (had).

How to translate the Interrogative, Negative, and Negative-Interrogative Forms.

No auxiliary being used for the rendering of these forms, they are for all verbs as simple, as in English they are with the verb "to be."

  Do I have? = have I? = *heb ik?*
  I do not have = I have not = *ik heb niet.*
  Do I not have? = have I not? = *heb ik niet?*
  Are you?   = *zijt gij?* or, *is u?*
  You are not ·= *gij zijt niet*, or, *u is niet*.
  Are you not? = *zijt gij niet?* or, *is u niet?*

The same rule applies to all verbs.

NOTE.—The Interrogative '*did*' followed by an infinitive is frequently translated by the perfect tense; *e.g.*, Did you see him? = have you seen him? See p. 177, OBSERVATIONS.

Exercise XXII.

Have you an uncle? Yes, I have two uncles and two aunts. Are you young, my boy? Yes, sir, quite young. How old are you? I am twelve. Are you not older, John? No, sir, I am just twelve. Have you had breakfast afterwards? Did you have a horse yesterday? No, I had a bicycle. Were you not tired last night? A little, yes, but not much (*erg*). Did his uncle have (the) fever? His uncle had (the) fever, and his aunt too. Will he not (yet) have had a (not a=*geen*) message [yet]? He will not have had a message before twelve o'clock. Did she not have much pain? No, not very much Are you obedient to your parents? I am always obedient to my parents and teachers. Will you be in school to-morrow? I shall be in school at nine o'clock.

GRAMMAR EXERCISES.—*Taaloefeningen.*

EXERCISE XXIII.

Fill up the blanks in the following exercises, assigning genders to all nouns.

1.

— *koper van Zuid-Afrika wordt in Wales gesmolten.* —
The copper of South Africa is in Wales smelted. The
Vrijstaat is — republiek. — *haver zal in — midden (o)*
Free State is a republic. The oats will in the middle
van — zomer rijp zijn. Deze man klaagt altijd over
of the summer ripe be. This man complains always of
— *gebreken van — ouderdom. Lukas, — schrijver van*
the infirmities of (the) old age. St. Luke, the author of
— *derde evangelie, was — dokter. Ik kan u — juiste*
the third Gospel, was a physician. I can you the exact
tijdstip van — gebeurtenis niet zeggen. — *genootschap van*
date of the event not tell. The association of
schoone kunsten heeft — prijs voor — beste teekening
fine arts has a price for the best drawing
uitgeloofd. — *kerkhof ligt aan — voet van — berg.*
offered. The churchyard lies at the foot of the mountain.
Bij — tijding van — aankomst harer moeder straalde
At the news of the arrival of her mother streamed (to)
— *kleine meisje — blijdschap uit — oogen.*
the little girl the joy out of the eyes.

Na — dood van Koning Willem — derde werd —
After the death of King William the Third was the
Groot-Hertogdom Luxemburg van — kroon van Holland
Grand-Duchy of Luxembourg from the crown of Holland
gescheiden. Er is — groote zwerm sprinkhanen over
separated. There has a large swarm of locusts over
— eigendom van — magistraat getrokken; ze hebben al
the property of the magistrate passed; they have all
— gras (o) en — mielies afgevreten, zoo dat — vee
the grass and the mealies eaten off, so that the cattle
nu geen voedsel heeft. Toen — Melrose gisteren middag
now no food has. As the Melrose yesterday afternoon
— haven van Liverpool uitstoomde, is — tegen
the harbour of Liverpool was steaming out, has she with
— Australische boot aangevaren, die daar voor anker
the Australian boat collided, which there at anchor was
lag; het is aan — tegenwoordigheid van geest van —
riding; it is to the presence of mind of the
eersten stuurman te danken, dat — beide schepen er zonder
first officer owing, that (the) both ships without
groote schade afgekomen zijn.
great injury come off have.

2.

Deze schrijf- heeft met haar eerste boek grooten opgang
This authoress has with her first book great success
gemaakt. — opera-zanger- zal zichzelve op — piano
had. The opera-singer will herself on the piano
begeleiden. Door — val uit — boom heeft —
accompany. Through the fall out (of) the tree has the
man zich aan — been verwond. Hagar, — dienst- van
man himself on the leg wounded. Hagar, the servant of
Sara, trok met haren zoon — woestijn van Arabië in. Ik
Sarah, went with her son the desert of Arabia in. I
heb met — zwarten draad — patroon van — kant op —
have with a black thread the pattern of the lace on the

witte zijde aangegeven. Door — omvallen van --
white silk indicated. Through the capsizing of the
olielamp (v) is er — groote vlek op— marmeren vloer (m)
oil-lamp is a large stain on the marble floor
van — gang gekomen. — schip is onder geleide van —
of the passage come. The ship is under guidance of an
ervaren loods veilig in — haven aangeland. Er
experienced pilot safely in the harbour arrived. There
bestaat — groote overeenkomst tusschen — klimaat en —
exists a great similarity between the climate and the
voortbrengselen van — Kaap Kolonie en — Zuiden (o) van
productions of the Cape Colony and the South of
Europa. Bij -- onlangs gehouden schietwedstrijd heeft —
Europe. At the recently held shooting-match has the
zoon — oude baron- — palm — overwinning
son of the old baroness the palm of the victory
weggedragen. — —, die men van St. Helena
carried off. The servants, which one from St. Helena
invoert, zijn niet altijd van — beste slag. — — van
imports, are not always of the best sort. The Queen of
Groot Britannië draagt tevens — titel (m) van
Great Britain bears at the same time the title of
— van Indië. — bedelaar- die van morgen
Empress of India. The beggar-woman who this morning
aan — deur (v) was, deed zulk — roerend verhaal van —
at the door was, did such a touching account of the
dood van haren —, dat mijne — — tranen in —
death of her husband, that (to) my mother the tears in the
oogen sprongen. — glas voor — ramen (n) is met —
eyes came. The glass for the windows is with a
diamant gesneden.
diamond cut.

Conversatie.
Wijze van groeten en aanspreken.

1. *Goeden morgen, mijnheer.*
2. *Goeden avond, mevrouw.*
3. *Hoe gaat het u?*
4. *Hoe vaart u?*
5. *Zeer wel, dank u.*
6. *Zoo tusschenbeide, dank u.*
7. *Ik ben vandaag niet zoo heel wel.*
8. *Ik voel mij heel onwel.*
9. *Ik voel mij erg ziek.*
10. *Wat scheelt u?*
11. *Ik heb zware hoofdpijn.*
12. *Dat spijt me.*
13. *Adieu; tot weerziens.*
14. *Mag ik het genoegen hebben, u te vergezellen?*
15. *Hoe heerlijk zijn de avonden dezer dagen, vindt u niet?*
16. *Zullen we niet nog een eindje verder wandelen?*
17. *Met genoegen: de wandeling doet mij goed.*
18. *Is u van plan, naar den schouwburg te gaan van avond?*
19. *Neen, mij dunkt, het stuk zal niet amusant zijn.*
20. *Waar zullen we dan heengaan?*
21. *Naar de opera; hoe kan u nog twijfelen?*
22. *Heeft u van den dood van mevrouw B. gehoord?*
23. *Ja, ik ben daar vandaag gaan condoleeren.*
24. *Heeft u een prettigen dag gehad bij mijnheer A.?*
25. *Hoe zou het anders kunnen?*
26. *Ik féliciteer u wel met uw geboortedag!*
27. *Veel heil met het nieuwe jaar!*

Conversation.
Forms of greeting and address.

1. Good morning, sir.
2. Good evening, madam.
3. How are you?
4. How do you do?
5. Quite well, thank you.
6. Middling, thank you.
7. I am not so well to-day.
8. I feel very unwell.
9. I feel quite ill.
10. What is the matter?
11. I have a bad headache.
12. I am sorry for you.
13. Good-bye; I hope I shall see you again.
14. May I have the pleasure of accompanying you?
15. We are having delightful evenings, don't you think so?
16. Shall we not go a little farther?
17. With pleasure: the walk is doing me good.
18. Do you intend going to the theatre to-night?
19. No, I don't think the play will be an amusing one.
20. Where shall we go then?
21. To the opera, how can you be in doubt?
22. Did you hear of the death of Mrs. B.?
23. Yes, I called there to-day to express my sympathy.
24. Did you spend a pleasant day with Mr. A.?
25. How could it be otherwise?
26. I wish you many happy returns of your birthday!
27. A happy new year to you!

28. Hartelijk dank.
29. Ik ben u zeer verplicht.
30. Zeer verplicht.
31. Zou u mij eene gunst willen bewijzen?
32. Van harte gaarne, als ik het kan.
33. Doe het toch vooral niet!
34. Heeft u mijnheer C. eene visite gemaakt?
35. Ik heb mijn naamkaartje achtergelaten, want hij was niet thuis.

28. Many thanks.
29. I am much obliged to you.
30. Much obliged.
31. Would you do me a favour?
32. I shall be most happy if I can.
33. Pray, don't do it!
34. Have you called upon Mr. C.?
35. I left my card, he was not at home.

CHAPTER VI.

DECLENSION.

(*Verbuiging.*)

I. The changes of form to which Articles, Nouns, Adjectives and Pronouns are subject, are together called their declension.

Declension expresses gender, *geslacht;* number, *getal;* and case, *naamval.*

There are three genders : masculine, *mannelijk;* feminine, *vrouwelijk;* and neuter, *onzijdig.*

There are two numbers : singular, *enkelvoud*, and plural, *meervoud.*

There are four cases : nominative, *nominatief;* genitive, *genitief;* dative, *datief;* and accusative, *accusatief*—more commonly called : *eerste, tweede, derde, en vierde naamval,* first, second, third, and fourth case.

II. Nominative Case.

1. The subject of a sentence is in the nominative case :

De hond *blaft*, the dog barks.

2. The name of a person or thing addressed, *de aangesproken persoon*—Latin vocative—is in the nominative case :

Jongens, *let op !* Boys, pay attention !

3. The verbs *zijn*, to be, *worden*, to become, *heeten*, to be called, *blijven*, to remain, *schijnen*, to seem, *lijken*, to

soem, and *blijken*, to appear to be, take the nominative case before and after them.

Hij *is mijn* **vriend**=he is my friend.
Hij *lijkt een* **vreemdeling**=he seems a stranger.
Hij *wordt* **soldaat**=he becomes a soldier.

NOTE.—The student should notice that the subject and the person named by the predicate of which these verbs form part, are the very same.

4. A noun in apposition to a Nominative case is likewise in the Nominative case: **Jakob, de oude tuinier,** *is gekomen,* Jacob, the old gardener, has come; **Hij** *woont bij mij als* **vriend,** he lives in my house as a friend.

III. GENITIVE CASE.

The genitive case expresses possession, relation, descent, or part of some whole.

EXAMPLE :—

Possession : *Mijns vaders huis,* my father's house.
Relation : *De stralen der zon,* the sun's rays.
Descent : *De kinderen onzer tante,* our aunt's children.
Part of a whole : *Eene bete broods,* a bit of bread.

IV. DATIVE CASE.

1. The person or thing profiting or losing by an action, is in the dative case: *Geef* **mij** *dat mes,* give me that knife; *Gij doet* **mij** *verdriet aan,* you cause me grief.

2. The personal pronoun when used instead of a possessive pronoun, is in the dative case : *Hij wascht* **zich** *de handen,* he washes his hands, for: *hij wascht zijne handen.*

V. ACCUSATIVE CASE.

1. The direct object of a transitive verb is in the accusative case: *De metselaar bouwde* **een huis,** the mason built a house.

2. The verbs : *noemen,* to call, *heeten* (trans.), to call, *schelden,* to call (names), *maken,* to make, *prijzen,* to praise, *bevinden,* to find to be, *achten,* to consider, *zich betoonen,* to

show one's self, *zich gevoelen*, to feel one's self, *zich teekenen*, to sign one's self, are followed by two accusative cases. *Ik teeken* mij *uwen* dienaar, I sign myself your servant; *Hij noemt* mij *zijnen* vriend, he calls me his friend.

> NOTE.—Observe that the personal pronoun and the following noun are in apposition.

3. Every noun governed by any preposition is in the Accusative case.

> OBS.—In old Dutch some prepositions governed the genitive and others the dative case. This fact is traceable in the following expressions:—
>
> Genitive: *binnenshuis*, inside the house,
> *buitenstijds*, unseasonably;
> Dative: *mettertijd (met der tijd)*, in time.
> *ter oore komen (te der oore)*, to come to one's ears, to hear.

4. Nouns expressing time, *tijd*, weight, *gewicht*, measure, *maat*, or value, *waarde*, are in the Accusative case: *De appel kost eenen* stuiver, the apple costs a penny. *Het pakje weegt een* pond, the parcel weighs one pound.

5. A noun in apposition to an Accusative case is likewise in the Accusative case: *Ik roep* Willem, den koetsier, I am calling William, the driver. *De naam van* Alexander den Grooten, *als* veroveraar *is alom bekend*, the name of Alexander the Great, as a conqueror, is universally known.

IMPORTANT OBSERVATIONS ON THE USE OF THE CASES.

1. The Possessive and Dative cases are being discarded more and more. Their places are supplied by the objective (Accusative) case with prepositions. This is indicated in Chapter III., where the first forms of declension are shown. Thus:

> Of the father, *des vaders*, is now *van den vader*.
> To the father, *den vader*, is now *aan den vader*, or *voor den vader*.

The reason why the Possessive and Dative cases are retained, is, because they are met with in books. In correspondence, however, they are becoming rare, so that the student, while writing correct Dutch, may dispense with them, though for reading purposes he must be acquainted with them.

2. In speaking there is practically no case but the first (Nominative). Conversationally, the declensions of p. 26 would be: *de man*, the man; *van de man*, of the man; *aan de man*, to the man; *de man*, the man. And again, *een man*, a man; *van een man*, of a man; *aan een man*, to a man; *een man*, a man;—and so on through the three genders.

3. The student will have noticed before this, and will here observe again the disparity which exists between Dutch spoken and Dutch written. The reason may be looked for in the gradual wearing away of grammatical forms, which by some is hailed as the only natural compromise between the speech of the learned and that of the uneducated, while others deplore it as tending to rob the language of its beauty. It is almost needless to say that the absence of declension-forms in the Cape *patois* makes it desirable to have as few in the correct medium-Dutch of South Africa as is consistent with the elements of grammar generally, which, as far as the subject of the present chapter is concerned, means, that the Possessive and Dative cases should only be used where they are found to be unavoidable. See here p. 82, IX.

VI. The Demonstrative Pronouns *deze* (Neuter *dit*), this, and *die* (Neuter *dat*) that, and the Possessive Pronoun *onze* (Neuter *ons*), our, follow the declension of the definite article *de* (Neuter *het*), the.

The Attributive Adjective is declined according to the changes in the word by which it is preceded. The following examples will indicate these changes:

MANNELIJK.

Enkelvoud.

1 nv. De, deze, die, onze goede vader.
2 nv. Des, dezes, diens, onzes goeden vaders.
   or Van den, dezen, dien, onzen goeden vader.
3 nv. Den, dezen, dien, onzen goeden vader.
   or Aan den, dezen, dien, onzen goeden vader.
4 nv. Den, dezen, dien, onzen goeden vader.

Meervoud.

1 nv. De, deze, die, onze goede vaders.
2 nv. Der, dezer, dier, onzer goede vaders.
   or Van de, deze, die, onze goede vaders.
3 nv. Den, dezen, dien, onzen goeden vaders.
   or Aan de, deze, die, onze goede vaders.
4 nv. De, deze, die, onze goede vaders.

VROUWELIJK.

Enkelvoud.

1 nv. De, deze, die, onze oude tante.
2 nv. Der, dezer, dier, onzer oude tante.
   or Van de, deze, die, onze oude tante.
3 nv. Der, dezer, dier, onzer oude tante.
   or Aan de, deze, die, onze oude tante.
4 nv. De, deze, die, onze oude tante.

MASCULINE.

Singular.

Nom. The, this, that, our good father.
Gen. Of the, this, that, our good father.

Dat. To the, this, that, our good father.

Acc. The, this, that, our good father.

Plural.

Nom. The, these, those, our good fathers.
Gen. Of the, these, those, our good fathers.

Dat. To the, these, those, our good fathers.

Acc. The, these, those, our good fathers.

FEMININE.

Singular.

Nom. The, this, that, our old aunt.
Gen. Of the, this, that, our old aunt.

Dat. To the, this, that, our old aunt.

Acc. The, this, that, our old aunt.

VROUWELIJK.	FEMININE.
Meervoud.	*Plural.*

1 nv.	De, deze, die, onze oude tantes.	*Nom.* The, these, those, our old aunts.
2 nv.	Der, dezer, dier, onzer oude tantes.	*Gen.* Of the, these, those, our old aunts.
	or Van de, deze, die, onze oude tantes.	
3 nv.	Den, dezen, dien, onzen ouden tantes.	*Dat.* To the, these, those, our old aunts.
	or Aan de, deze, die, onze oude tantes.	
4 nv.	De, deze, die, onze oude tantes.	*Acc.* The, these, those, our old aunts.

ONZIJDIG.	NEUTER.
Enkelvoud.	*Singular.*

1 nv.	Het, dit, dat, ons, kleine kind.	*Nom.* The, this, that, our small child.
2 nv.	Des, dezes, diens, onzes kleinen kinds.	*Gen.* Of the, this, that, our small child.
	or Van het, dit, dat, ons kleine kind.	
3 nv.	Den, dezen, dien, onzen kleinen kinde (obsolete).	*Dat.* To the, this, that, our small child.
	or Aan het, dit, dat, ons kleine kind.	
4 nv.	Het, dit, dat, ons kleine kind.	*Acc.* The, this, that, our small child.

Meervoud.	*Plural.*

1 nv.	De, deze, die, onze kleine kinderen.	*Nom.* The, these, those, our small children.
2 nv.	Der, dezer, dier, onzer kleine kinderen.	*Gen.* Of the, these, those, our small children.
	or Van de, deze, die, onze kleine kinderen.	
3 nv.	Den, dezen, dien, onzen kleinen kinderen.	*Dat.* To the, these, those, our small children.
	or Aan de, deze, die, onze kleine kinderen.	
4 nv.	De, deze, die, onze kleine kinderen.	*Acc.* The, these, those, our small children.

VII. The Possessive Pronouns *mijn*, my, *uw*, your, *zijn*, his, *haar*, her, *zijn*, its, *hun*, their, have, in the singular, the declension of the indefinite article *een*, a (an), while in the plural they go according to the plural forms of par. VI.

MANNELIJK.
Enkelvoud.

1 nv. *Een, mijn, uw, zijn, haar, hun groote hond.*
2 nv. *Eens, mijns, uws, zijns, haars, huns grooten honds.*
 or *Van eenen, mijnen, uwen, zijnen, haren, hunnen grooten hond.*
3 nv. *Eenen, mijnen, uwen, zijnen, haren, hunnen grooten hond.*
 or *Aan eenen, mijnen, uwen, zijnen, haren, hunnen grooten hond.*
4 nv. *Eenen, mijnen, uwen, zijnen, haren, hunnen grooten hond.*

MASCULINE.
Singular.

Nom. A, my, your, his, her, their large dog.
Gen. Of a, my, your, his, her, their large dog.

Dat. To a, my, your, his, her, their large dog.

Acc. A, my, your, his, her, their large dog.

VROUWELIJK.
Enkelvoud.

1 nv. *Eene, mijne, uwe, zijne, hare, hunne witte muts.*
2 nv. *Eener, mijner, uwer, zijner, harer, hunner witte muts.*
 or *Van eene, mijne, uwe, zijne, hare, hunne witte muts.*
3 nv. *Eener, mijner, uwer, zijner, harer, hunner witte muts.*
 or *Aan eene, mijne, uwe, zijne, hare, hunne witte muts.*
4 nv. *Eene, mijne, uwe, zijne, hare, hunne witte muts.*

FEMININE.
Singular.

Nom. A, my, your, his, her, their white cap.
Gen. Of a, my, your, his, her, their white cap.

Dat. To a, my, your, his, her, their white cap.

Acc. A, my, your, his, her, their white cap.

DECLENSION.

ONZIJDIG.	NEUTER.
Enkelvoud.	*Singular.*

1 nv. *Een, mijn, uw, zijn, haar, hun oud(e) huis.* — Nom. A, my, your, his, her, their old house.

2 nv. *Eens, mijns, uws, zijns, haars, huns ouden huizes.* — Gen. Of a, my, your, his, her, their old house.

or *Van een, mijn, uw, zijn, haar, hun oud(e) huis.*

3 nv. *Eenen, mijnen, uwen, zijnen, haren, hunnen ouden huize* (obsolete). — Dat. To a, my, your, his, her, their old house.

or *Aan een, mijn, uw, zijn, haar, hun, oud(e) huis.*

4 nv. *Een, mijn, uw, zijn, haar, hun oud(e) huis.* (see § VIII.) — Acc. A, my, your, his, her, their old house.

MEERVOUD.	PLURAL.
Mannelijk.	*Masculine.*

1 nv. —, *mijne, uwe, zijne, hare, hunne, groote honden, enz.* — Nom. —, my, your, his, her, their large dogs, etc.

Vrouwelijk. — *Feminine.*

1 nv. —, *mijne, uwe, zijne, hare, hunne witte mutsen, enz.* — Nom. —, my, your, his, her, their white caps, etc.

Onzijdig. — *Neuter.*

1 nv. —, *mijne, uwe, zijne, hare, hunne oude huizen, enz.* — Nom. —, my, your, his, her, their old houses, etc.

Exactly like the plural forms of par. VI.

OBS.—When two or more attributive adjectives are joined to a noun, each one is declined separately like the first (as shown above). Such adjectives should be separated by commas:

1 nv. *Deze oude, trouwe hond,* this old and faithful dog.
2 nv. *Dezes ouden, trouwen honds*—and so on.

When, however, the adjectives together convey one idea only' the last one alone is declined:

Eene rood, wit en blauwe vlag, a red, white, and blue flag; plural—*rood, wit en blauwe vlaggen,* red, white, and blue flags.

VIII. The Adjective has no *e* (i.e. it is not declined) in the Neuter gender, Singular number, when preceded by one of the following eight words:—*een,* a (an); *geen,* no; *eenig,* some; *elk,* each; *ieder,* every; *zeker,* a certain; *menig,* many a; *welk,* which.

NOTE.—This is likewise the case after the Numeral Adjective *veel, wat,* and *sommig.*

EXAMPLE.

1 nv. *Een, geen, elk, ieder,*   *Nom.* A, no, each, every, many
     menig, welk klein   a, which small child,
     kind, enz.   etc.
1 nv. *Wat frisch water.*   Some fresh water.

IX. The following observations may be a guide to correct declension.

1. The Masculine Singular is distinguished by an *n* in three cases out of four. Besides, the 4th case is like the 3rd.
2. The distinguishing letter of the Feminine Singular is *e*; the 1st case is like the 4th; the 2nd case like the 3rd; it bears great resemblance to the plural.
3. The Neuter Singular has no declension of its own; its 1st, 3rd, and 4th cases are equal, and its 2nd case is a borrowed Masculine Genitive.
4. The distinguishing letter of the Plural is *e* again; its 1st case is like the 4th.
5. In Plural forms there is no distinction of gender; all Plural forms are equal.
6. When the Article or other *first* word ends in *e* or *r*, the Adjective must end in *e*; when the first word ends in *s* or *en*, the Adjective must end in *en*.
7. For correspondence purposes, discarding the 2nd and 3rd cases, we may note:—
    that the Masculine Obj. has *n*;
    that in the Feminine Singular there are no changes;
    that in the Neuter Singular there are no changes;
    that in the Plural forms there are no changes.

8. The Adjective, whenever placed before a noun, ends in *e*, whether it be used in the Masculine, Feminine or Neuter gender, Singular or Plural; the only case of absence of this *e* being in the Neuter Singular, after the words enumerated in § VIII.

9. Nouns take *s* in the 2nd case Masculine and Neuter Singular. It should be observed that *no apostrophe* may there be used. The only use of the apostrophe in Dutch is in the Plural forms of a few words (see p. 35, § III.) and for indicating the Possessive case of proper nouns ending in *s*, e.g., *Paulus' zendbrieven*, St. Paul's Epistles.

10. When Masculine and Neuter Nouns end in *s* or *sch*, their 2nd case is expressed by means of the Preposition *van*, of: e.g., *de os*, the ox, *van den os* (not *des osses*); *de wensch*, the wish, *van den wensch* (not *des wensches*); *het glas*, the glass, *van het glas* (not *des glasses*). The Possessive cases of *huis*, house (*des huizes*), and *vleesch*, flesh (*des vleesches*), are occasionally met with.

X. Nouns may take an adjective which is not preceded by any defining word. In this case the adjective, being the first word, should take the declension of the article. The following examples will show that this does take place, but in a modified form.

MANNELIJK.	MASCULINE.
Enkelvoud.	*Singular.*
1 nv. *Oude wijn.*	Nom. Old wine.
2 nv. *Ouden wijns* (or *van ouden wijn*).	Gen. Of old wine.
3 nv. *Ouden* (or *aan ouden*) *wijn.*	Dat. To old wine.
4 nv. *Ouden wijn.*	Acc. Old wine.
Meervoud.	*Plural.*
1 nv. *Oude wijnen.*	Nom. Old wines.
2 nv. *Ouder* (or *van oude*) *wijnen.*	Gen. Of old wines.
3 nv. *Ouden* (or *aan oude*) *wijnen.*	Dat. To old wines.
4 nv. *Oude wijnen.*	Acc. Old wines.

	VROUWELIJK.	FEMININE.
	Enkelvoud.	*Singular.*
1 nv.	*Fijne kant.*	*Nom.* Fine lace.
2 nv.	*Van fijne kant.*	*Gen.* Of fine lace.
3 nv.	*Aan fijne kant.*	*Dat.* To fine lace.
4 nv.	*Fijne kant.*	*Acc.* Fine lace.
	Meervoud.	*Plural.*
1 nv.	*Fijne kanten.*	*Nom.* Fine laces.
2 nv.	*Fijner kanten,* or *van fijne kanten.*	*Gen.* Of fine laces.
3 nv.	*Fijnen kanten,* or *aan fijne kanten.*	*Dat.* To fine laces.
4 nv.	*Fijne kanten.*	*Acc.* Fine laces.

	ONZIJDIG.	NEUTER.
	Enkelvoud.	*Singular.*
1 nv.	*Helder licht.*	*Nom.* Bright light.
2 nv.	*Van helder licht.*	*Gen.* Of bright light.
3 nv.	*Aan helder licht.*	*Dat.* To bright light.
4 nv.	*Helder licht.*	*Acc.* Bright light.
	Meervoud.	*Plural.*
1 nv.	*Heldere lichten.*	*Nom.* Bright lights.
2 nv.	*Helderer lichten,* or *van heldere lichten.*	*Gen.* Of bright lights.
3 nv.	*Helderen lichten,* or *aan heldere lichten.*	*Dat.* To bright lights.
4 nv.	*Heldere lichten.*	*Acc.* Bright lights.

XI. In titles, Attributive Adjectives are placed after the nouns which they qualify. Their declension, however, is not affected thereby, e.g. :—

	MANNELIJK.	MASCULINE.
	Enkelvoud.	*Singular.*
1 nv.	*Peter de Groote.*	*Nom.* Peter the Great.
2 nv.	*Peters des Grooten.*	*Gen.* Of Peter the Great.
3 nv.	*Peter den Grooten.*	*Dat.* To Peter the Great.
4 nv.	*Peter den Grooten.*	*Acc.* Peter the Great.

XII. By far the most Masculine and Neuter nouns take *s* as a sign of the Possessive (Genitive) case, as assorted

DECLENSION. 85

above. These are said to belong to the Strong Declension (*Sterke Verbuiging*). Of some few, however, the Possessive case ends in *en*. Such are:—

1. The masculine words: *mensch*, man; *heer*, gentleman; *vorst*, sovereign; *graaf*, count; *prins*, prince; *hertog*, duke; *profeet*, prophet; and *nar*, clown.
2. The Neuter word: *hart*, heart.
3. All Adjectives, and Adjective Pronouns, when used as Nouns: *de wijze*, the wise man; *de goede*, the good man; *de mijne*, mine.

Their declension is as follows:—

MANNELIJK.   MASCULINE.

Enkelvoud.   *Singular.*

1 nv.	*De vorst.*	*Nom.* The sovereign.
2 nv.	*Des vorsten.*	*Gen.* Of the sovereign.
3 nv.	*Den vorst.*	*Dat.* To the sovereign.
4 nv.	*Den vorst.*	*Acc.* The sovereign.
1 nv.	*De goede.*	*Nom.* The good one.
2 nv.	*Des goeden.*	*Gen.* Of the good one.
3 nv.	*Den goede.*	*Dat.* To the good one.
4 nv.	*Den goede.*	*Acc.* The good one.

Meervoud.   *Plural.*

1 nv.	*De vorsten.*	*Nom.* The sovereigns.
2 nv.	*Der vorsten.*	*Gen.* Of the sovereigns.
3 nv.	*Den vorsten*	*Dat.* To the sovereigns.
4 nv.	*De vorsten.*	*Acc.* The sovereigns.
1 nv.	*De goeden.*	*Nom.* The good.
2 nv.	*Der goeden.*	*Gen.* Of the good.
3 nv.	*Den goeden.*	*Dat.* To the good.
4 nv.	*De goeden.*	*Acc.* The good.

De mijne, mine, or mine own; *de uwe*, yours, or your

own; *de onze*, ours, or our own, etc., are declined as follows:

MANNELIJK.	VROUWELIJK.	ONZIJDIG.
Enkelvoud.	*Enkelvoud.*	*Enkelvoud.*
1 nv. *De mijne.*	1 nv. *De mijne.*	1 nv. *Het mijne.*
2 nv. *Des mijnen.*	2 nv. *Der mijne.*	2 nv. *Van het mijne.*
3 nv. *Den mijne.*	3 nv. *Der* (or *de mijne*).	3 nv. *Het mijne.*
4 nv. *Den mijne.*	4 nv. *De Mijne.*	4 nv. *Het mijne.*

Meervoud voor alle geslachten.
(Plural for the three genders.)

(Meaning Persons.)	(Meaning Things.)
1 nv. *De mijnen.*	1 nv. *De mijne.*
2 nv. *Der mijnen.*	2 nv. *Der mijne.*
3 nv. *Den mijnen.*	3 nv. *Den mijnen.*
4 nv. *De mijnen.*	4 nv. *De mijne.*

OBS.—The above difference in the plural forms the student should mark. Other words—like *de anderen*, the others; *sommigen*, some; *eenigen*, some; *dezen*, these; *genen*, the others; *velen*, many; *weinigen*, few, etc.,—take *n* when they refer to persons, and drop it whenever they refer to things.
De mijnen, de uwen, etc., are used in the peculiar sense of my (your) people (or family).

XIII. Compound Pronouns (*i.e.* pronouns, the first part of which is the definite article) likewise follow the weak declension. They are: *degene*, he, or whoever; *dezelfde*, the same; *dezulke*, such an one. Example:—

MANNELIJK.	VROUWELIJK.	ONZIJDIG.
Enkelvoud.	*Enkelvoud.*	*Enkelvoud.*
1 nv. *Dezelfde.*	1 nv. *Dezelfde.*	1 nv. *Hetzelfde.*
2 nv. *Deszelfden.*	2 nv. *Derzelfde.*	2 nv. *Deszelfden.*
3 nv. *Denzelfde.*	3 nv. *Derzelfde.*	3 nv. *Hetzelfde.*
4 nv. *Denzelfde.*	4 nv. *Dezelfde.*	4 nv. *Hetzelfde.*

Meervoud voor alle geslachten.

(Meaning Persons.)	(Meaning Things.)
1 nv. *Dezelfden.*	1 nv. *Dezelfde.*
2 nv. *Derzelfden.*	2 nv. *Derzelfde.*
3 nv. *Denzelfden.*	3 nv. *Denzelfden.*
4 nv. *Dezelfden.*	4 nv. *Dezelfde.*

GRAMMAR EXERCISES.—*Taaloefeningen.*
Exercise XXIV.

NOTE.—In the declension of adjectives the rule holds good that when the last syllable contains an imperfect vowel which is to be preserved, the final consonant must be doubled: *stil*, quiet, *stille; dik*, thick, *dikke.*
It should be understood that dashes are sometimes placed where there is no omission, to test the pupil's knowledge of the rules of declension.

Fill up the blanks in the following sentences:

Ik heb een– lang– brief (m) van mijn– trouw– vriend
I have a long letter from my faithful friend
ontvangen. Op d– eerst– avond na d– slag,
received. On the first evening after the battle,
bezochten wij — tooneel van di– vreeselijk– strijd.
visited we the scene of that terrible conflict.
In — dicht– bosch onder d– dor– bladeren (o) verborgen,
In the dense bush under the dry leaves hidden,
lag een– giftig– adder (v). D– hoog–, prachtig– huis (o) is
lay a poisonous adder. This high, beautiful house, is
door d– beroemd– Engelsch– architect gebouwd. Er
by that famous English architect built. There
liep een arm– kind (o) langs d– stil– straten (v); d– rijk–
went a poor child along the quiet streets; the rich
dame gaf het geld. In — schoon– klimaat d–
lady gave it money. In the beautiful climate of the
zuidelijk– landen is het gemakkelijk, gezond te zijn. —
southern countries is it easy, healthy to be. The
fraai– rijtuig (o) van d– koning was met zes prachtig–
fine carriage of the king was by six splendid
paarden bespannen. Ik wil u dez– schrikkelijk– afgrond (m)
horses drawn. I want you this terrible abyss,
dez– ontzaglijk– kloven (v), dez– snel– stroom (m), en
these tremendous gorges, this quick stream, and
dez– trotsch– bergspitsen (v) toonen. Menig– onschuldig–
these proud mountain peaks show. Many innocent
hart is verleid geworden door slecht– gezelschap.
heart has seduced been by bad company.

Exercise XXV.

Decline in full (singular and plural):—

1. Masculine:
   De oude tuinman, the old gardener.
   Die groote boom, that large tree.
   Een slimme jongen, a sharp boy.
   Willem de derde, William the Third.
   Mijn trouwe, lieve hond, my faithful and dear dog.
   De brave, the honest one.
   Dezelfde jonge knecht, the same young servant.
   Een mooie, vette os, a pretty fat ox.
   Deze geel en zwarte tijger, this yellow and black tiger.
   Alexander de Groote, Alexander the Great.
   Onze alom beminde hertog, our universally beloved duke.
   Lekkere, zoete wijn, nice and sweet wine.
   Haar pas aangestelde secretaris, her newly-appointed secretary.

2. Feminine:
   De oude bank, the old bench.
   Deze kleine kamer, this small room.
   Eene nieuwe japon, a new dress.
   Die goede, brave vrouw, that good and honest woman.
   Mijne arme, oude vriendin, my poor old friend.
   Eerlijke verdeeling, honest division.
   Eene zeer groote weide, a very large meadow.
   Deze uitstekend goede koffie, this exceedingly good coffee.
   Maria de Katholieke, Mary the Catholic.
   Die oude, rood bonte koe, that old red-and-white cow.
   Dezelfde trotsche zwaan, the same proud swan.
   De met klimop bedekte warande, the ivy-roofed verandah.

3. Neuter:
   Het speelsche dier, the playful animal.
   Dit heidensche gebruik, this heathen custom.
   Dat heete vuur, that hot fire.
   Een oud en vervallen huis, an old and decaying house.
   Sterk bier, strong beer.
   Hetzelfde lange gesprek, the same lengthy conversation.
   Dat jonge, sterke paard, that young and strong horse.
   Haar zwarte, doordringende oog, her black and penetrating eye.
   Dit lange, groene gras, this long green grass.
   Een fraai geslepen glas, a beautifully-cut tumbler.
   Menig nu vergeten spreekwoord, many a now-forgotten proverb.
   Een zeker vergelegen gebergte, a certain far-distant range of mountains.

Exercise XXVI.

Fill up the blanks in the following exercises, assigning genders and cases to nouns.

1.

Om d– inhoud (m) van e– lichaam (o) te berekenen, is het
For the contents of a body to calculate, is it
noodig d– lengte, d– breedte, en d– hoogte ervan
necessary the length, the breadth, and the height of it
te kennen. In welk– landen vindt men d– hoogst–
to know. In which countries finds one the highest
bergen, d– snelst– rivieren, en d– grootst–
mountains, the most rapid rivers, and the largest
meren? Hoe oud was d– man, die gisteren door zulk
lakes? How old was the man, who yesterday by such
ee– groot– stoet (m) van menschen ten grave gedragen werd?
a large crowd of people to the grave borne was?
Hij was d– oudst– man uit d– gansch– stad (v), en moet ver
He was the oldest man of the whole town, and must far
in d– negentig geweest zijn. Als gij u– koeien naar d–
in the nineties been have. If you your cows to the
weide zendt, zal ik d– mijne– ook zenden. Eenig– jaren
field send, shall I mine also send. Some years
geleden hebben d– Franschen ee– vreeselijk– oorlog (m)
ago have the French a terrible war
gevoerd tegen d– Duitschers, doch d– laatst– hebben ee–
carried on against the Germans, but the latter have a
schitterend– overwinning behaald.
brilliant victory gained.

2.

D– tempel (m) van Salomo, di– groot–, wijz– koning, is
The temple of Solomon, that great and wise king, has
door ee– van d– koningen van — Babylonische rijk (o)
by one of the kings of the Babylonian empire
verwoest geworden. D– kameel wordt in — noordelijk– deel (o)
destroyed been. The camel is in the northern part

van Afrika, en in vel- landen van Azië gevonden; hij is
of Africa, and in many countries of Asia found; he is
ee- van d- nuttigst- huisdieren. D- hard-,
one of the most useful domestic animals. The hard,
drog- stammen d- boomen zijn met frisch-, week-, groen-
dry trunks of the trees are with fresh, soft, green
mos (o) bedekt. Zal ik u opnoemen, wat ik op
moss covered. Shall I for you enumerate what I on
di- lang- reis (v) gezien heb? Groot- steden, prachtig-
that long journey soon have? Large towns, beautiful
dorpen, veel- wild- dieren (o) opgesloten in eng- kooien (v),
villages, many wild animals locked up in narrow cages,
breed-, snel stroomend- rivieren, waar rijk versierd-
broad, rapidly flowing rivers, where richly decorated
bootjes op ronddreven, tallooz- groen- weivelden (o),
boats on floated about, numberless green meadows,
heerlijk schoon- kerken, ee- stalen brug (v) van meer
delightfully beautiful churches, a steel bridge of more
dan ee- mijl (v) lang, en meer dergelijk- wonderlijk- dingen (o),
than a mile long, and more such wonderful things,
waarvan men zoo menig- verhaal in d- schoolboeken (o)
of which one so many an account in the schoolbooks

leest.
reads.

The student is recommended to study the following examples:—

English . . . The water of the river trickles through the hard ground.
Book Dutch . . Het water der rivier zijpelt door den harden grond.
Corresp. Dutch . Het water van de rivier zijpelt door den harden grond.
Colloq. Dutch . Het water van de rivier zijpelt door de harde grond.
English . . . No one has ever trodden the bottom of this terrible abyss.
Book Dutch . . Niemand heeft ooit den bodem dezes vreeselijken afgronds betreden.

Corresp. Dutch	.	*Niemand heeft ooit den bodem van dezen vreese-lijken afgrond betreden.*
Colloq. Dutch	.	*Niemand heeft ooit de bodem van deze vreese-lijke afgrond betreden.*
English	. . .	Have you considered the action of the sun's heat on the leaves of this tree?
Book Dutch	. .	*Hebt gij de werking der zonnewarmte op de bladeren dezes booms nagegaan?*
Corresp. Dutch	.	*Hebt gij de werking van de zonnewarmte op de bladeren van dezen boom nagegaan?*
Colloq. Dutch	.	*Heeft u de werking van de zonnewarmte op de blaren van deze boom nagegaan?*
English	. . .	I have intimated the king's pleasure to your old father.
Book Dutch	. .	*Ik heb uwen ouden vader den wil des konings bekend gemaakt.*
Corresp. Dutch	.	*Ik heb den wil van den koning aan uwen ouden vader bekend gemaakt.*
Colloq. Dutch	.	*Ik heb uw oude vader de wil van de koning bekend gemaakt.*

NOTE 1.—The last example will show that the dative case is in colloquial language indicated not by endings, but by position, which is more effective, and corresponds to the way in which the dative case of the personal pronoun is used.

NOTE 2.—The indication of differences between Correspondence and Colloquial Dutch should not lead the student to suppose that the exercises of this book might be translated into the latter. Colloquial Dutch serves merely for speaking purposes, and should not be made a written language of, seeing that even the easiest and loosest correspondence between educated people adheres to grammatical forms on the lines of the present chapter.

CONJUGATION OF THE WEAK VERB "*leeren,*" to learn, and the STRONG VERB "*stelen,*" to steal.

INDICATIVE MOOD.   AANTOONENDE WIJS.

Present Tense.   Onvolmaakt Tegenwoordige Tijd.

Ik leer, I learn.	*Ik steel,* I steal.
Gij leert, thou learnest.	*Gij steelt,* thou stealest.
Hij leert, he learns.	*Hij steelt,* he steals.
Wij leeren, we learn.	*Wij stelen,* we steal.
Gij leert, you learn.	*Gij steelt,* you steal.
Zij leeren, they learn.	*Zij stelen,* they steal.

Indicative Mood. Aantoonende Wijs.

Perfect Tense. Volmaakt Tegenwoordige Tijd.

Ik heb geleerd, I have learned.
Gij hebt geleerd, thou hast learned.
Hij heeft geleerd, he has learned.
Wij hebben geleerd, we have learned.
Gij hebt geleerd, you have learned.
Zij hebben geleerd, they have learned.

Ik heb gestolen, I have stolen.
Gij hebt gestolen, thou hast stolen.
Hij heeft gestolen, he has stolen.
Wij hebben gestolen, we have stolen.
Gij hebt gestolen, you have stolen.
Zij hebben gestolen, they have stolen.

Imperfect Tense. Onvolmaakt Verleden Tijd.

Ik leerde, I learned.
Gij leerdet, thou learnedst.
Hij leerde, he learned.
Wij leerden, we learned.
Gij leerdet, you learned.
Zij leerden, they learned.

Ik stal, I stole.
Gij staalt, thou stolest.
Hij stal, he stole.
Wij stalen, we stole.
Gij staalt, you stole.
Zij stalen, they stole.

Pluperfect Tense. Volmaakt Verleden Tijd.

Ik had geleerd, I had learned.
Gij hadt geleerd, thou hadst learned.
Hij had geleerd, he had learned.
Wij hadden geleerd, we had learned.
Gij hadt geleerd, you had learned.
Zij hadden geleerd, they had learned.

Ik had gestolen, I had stolen.
Gij hadt gestolen, thou hadst stolen.
Hij had gestolen, he had stolen.
Wij hadden gestolen, we had stolen.
Gij hadt gestolen, you had stolen.
Zij hadden gestolen, they had stolen.

Future Tense. Onvolmaakt Toekomende Tijd.

Ik zal leeren, I shall learn.
Gij zult leeren, thou wilt learn.
Hij zal leeren, he will learn.
Wij zullen leeren, we shall learn.
Gij zult leeren, you will learn.
Zij zullen leeren, they will learn.

Ik zal stelen, I shall steal.
Gij zult stelen, thou wilt steal.
Hij zal stelen, he will steal.
Wij zullen stelen, we shall steal.
Gij zult stelen, you will steal.
Zij zullen stelen, they will steal.

INDICATIVE MOOD.   AANTOONENDE WIJS.
Future Perfect Tense.   Volmaakt Toekomende Tijd.

Ik zal geleerd hebben, I shall have learned.
Gij zult geleerd hebben, thou wilt have learned.
Hij zal geleerd hebben, he will have learned.
Wij zullen geleerd hebben, we shall have learned.
Gij zult geleerd hebben, you will have learned.
Zij zullen geleerd hebben, they will have learned.

Ik zal gestolen hebben, I shall have stolen.
Gij zult gestolen hebben, thou wilt have stolen.
Hij zal gestolen hebben, he will have stolen.
Wij zullen gestolen hebben, we shall have stolen.
Gij zult gestolen hebben, you will have stolen.
Zij zullen gestolen hebben, they will have stolen.

SUBJUNCTIVE MOOD.   AANVOEGENDE WIJS.
Future Tense.   Onvolm. Toek. Tijd.

Ik zou leeren, I should learn.
Gij zoudt leeren, thou wouldst learn.
Hij zou leeren, he would learn.
Wij zouden leeren, we should learn.
Gij zoudt leeren, you would learn.
Zij zouden leeren, they would learn.

Ik zou stelen, I should steal.
Gij zoud stelen, thou wouldst steal.
Hij zou stelen, he would steal.
Wij zouden stelen, we should steal.
Gij zoudt stelen, you would steal.
Zij zouden stelen, they would steal.

Future Perfect Tense.   Volm. Toek. Tijd.

Ik zou geleerd hebben, I should have learned.
Gij zoudt geleerd hebben, thou wouldst have learned.
Hij zou geleerd hebben, he would have learned.
Wij zouden geleerd hebben, we should have learned.
Gij zoudt geleerd hebben, you would have learned.
Zij zouden geleerd hebben, they would have learned.

Ik zou gestolen hebben, I should have stolen.
Gij zoudt gestolen hebben, thou wouldst have stolen.
Hij zou gestolen hebben, he would have stolen.
Wij zouden gestolen hebben, we should have stolen.
Gij zoudt gestolen hebben, you would have stolen.
Zij zouden gestolen hebben, they would have stolen.

IMPERATIVE MOOD. GEBIEDENDE WIJS.

Singular. *Enkelvoud.*

Laat *mij leeren*, let me learn.   Laat *mij stelen*, let me steal.
Leer, learn (thou).   *Steel*, steal (thou).
Laat *hem leeren*, let him learn.   Laat *hem stelen*, let him steal.

Plural. *Meervoud.*

Laat *ons leeren* (*leeren wij*), let us learn.   Laat *ons stelen* (*stelen wij*), let us steal.
Leert, learn (ye).   *Steelt*, steal (ye).
Laat *hen leeren* (*leeren zij*), let them learn.   Laat *hen stelen* (*stelen zij*), let them steal.

INFINITIVE MOOD. ONBEPAALDE WIJS.

Present Tense. *Onvolmaakt Tegenwoordige Tijd.*
(*Te*) *leeren*, to learn.   (*Te*) *stelen*, to steal.

Perfect Tense. *Volmaakt Tegenwoordige Tijd.*
Geleerd (*te*) *hebben*, to have learned.   *Gestolen* (*te*) *hebben*, to have stolen.

Future Tense. *Onvolmaakt Toekmende Tijd.*
(*Te*) *zullen leeren* (no equivalent; see EXERCISE XXXI).   (*Te*) *zullen stelen* (no equivalent; see EXERCISE XXXI).

Future Perfect Tense. *Volmaakt Toekomende Tijd.*
(*Te*) *zullen geleerd hebben* (no equivalent).   (*Te*) *zullen gestolen hebben* (no equivalent).

Present Participle. *Tegenwoordig Deelwoord.*
Leerende, learning.   *Stelende*, stealing.

Past Participle. *Verleden Deelwoord.*
Geleerd, learned.   *Gestolen*, stolen.

Like "*leeren*" conjugate the weak verbs: *spelen, speelde, gespeeld*, to play; *deelen, deelde, gedeeld*, to divide, to share; *leven, leefde, geleefd*, to live; *bouwen, bouwde, gebouwd*, to build; *vertellen, vertelde, verteld*, to tell; *vragen, vraagde, gevraagd*, to ask.

DECLENSION.

Like "*stelen*" conjugate the strong verbs: *slapen, sliep, geslapen*, to sleep; *nemen, nam, genomen*, to take; *roepen, riep, geroepen*, to call; *geven, gaf, gegeven*, to give; *meten, mat, gemeten*, to measure; *wegen, woog, gewogen*, to weigh.

TRANSLATION EXERCISES.—*Vertaaloefeningen.*

Exercise XXVII.

Fourth Rule of Construction.—When a subordinate sentence precedes the principal one, the construction of the latter is inverted, *i.e.*, the verb is placed before its subject. If the verb consists of two parts, the auxiliary only precedes the subject, and the principal verb closes the sentence (see First Rule).

Notice here the need of the comma, for separating two verbs which belong to different sentences.

If you [have learned] that long lesson (have learned), (can = *kan*) you [can] go. If he had a book, (would) he [would] learn the alphabet. When I asked your uncle to tell that story, (said) he [said] that he had told it (*ze*) already. When dogs [are] young (are), (are) they [are] ively. If the man has stolen the money, (is) he [is] a thief. After (*nadat*) he weighed the parcel, (gave) he [gave] it to the boy. If my sister has no pain, (sleeps) she [sleeps] very well. Because the man was ill and poor, (was) he [was] miserable. When I was rich, (had) I [had] many friends. As I had no horse, (could = *kon*) I [could] not go. If I had had a garden behind the house, (would) I [would] [have been] glad (*blij*) (have been). As the boy had a spade, (worked) he [worked] in the garden. When my uncle's horses (the horses of my uncle) had much grass, (were) they [were] fat. If the child had been at (*op*) school, (would) it [would] have been tired (have been). If he asks for (*om*) the inkpot, (will) my mother [will] give it (him) (give). When the child has played [for] an hour, (will) it will [be] satisfied (be).

Exercise XXVIII.

TRANSLATION OF PRESENT PARTICIPLE.—Present part'ciples are rarely used. They are translated in various ways. The following rendering should be noted first:

Having a book, the boy is happy = as the boy has a book, he is happy = *daar de jongen een boek heeft, is hij gelukkig.*
Being ill, the child was at home = as the child was ill, it was at home = *daar het kind ziek was, was het thuis.*

Having parents, (is) the child [is] happy. Having books, (was) the boy [was] contented. Being small, the girl had little work. Having a spade, the boy worked (*werkte*) in the garden. Being obedient, the child was happy. Having been ill (as he had been sick), the man was poor. The poor man being ill, was (he) miserable. The boy, having tools, was (he) happy. The child having been (as the child had been) at (*op*) school, was (it) tired. The weather having been bad, the harvest was small. Having had rain, the trees had leaves. Having no bread, the children were hungry. The cat having had milk, was (she) contented. My horses were fat, having had much grass. Your cows were thin, having had no forage.

Exercise XXIX.

Let us build three houses here. Why three? There is room for four. There is no room for four houses on this small bit of ground. Would he have stolen the old horse if there (*er*) had been a young [one]? If you tell me this, I shall not ask you again. What will he ask me? He will ask you to give up the key which he gave (has given) you. This is the little bird that built its pretty nest among the green twigs. How long did the dog live? It (he) lived five years. I had a horse once which was twenty years old. If your uncle built (has built) on the new piece of ground, I will build on the old [one]. He has not built yet; but he will build on the large new piece of ground next to the old inn. Because he wanted to (*wilde*) play in the afternoon, he learned his lessons in the morning. You have had the money in your pocket; why did you play (played you) with it (*ermee*)?

Exercise XXX.

NOTE.—" To like to," and " to want to," are both rendered by "*willen, wilde, gewild.*"

The boy wants to learn those difficult words. Yes, but he does not want to (*wil* . . . . *niet*) [learn] his lesson for his teacher (not learn). I should like to (*zou* . . . . *willen*) ask you for (*om*) the paper. The old man did not want to ask for money. Would you like to have a large house and a pretty garden? I should like to have many good books. He wants to give all his money to the poor. Give me those roses! No, I do [not] want to (*wil* . . . . *niet*) [give] you those roses (not give); they are too pretty and too fresh. Do you want to have more ink? Who would not [like to be] rich and happy (like to be)? I should not [like to build] in this street (like to build); there are already too many large houses. He wanted to call his father, but he was not in his room. The carpenter wants to measure the table. Let him first measure the height of the door.

Exercise XXXI.

Observe:

Hij hoopt te zullen slapen = he hopes that he will sleep.
Hij verwacht te zullen bouwen = he expects that he will build.
Hij denkt te zullen komen = he thinks that he will come.
Hij gelooft morgen beter te zullen zijn = he believes that he will be better to-morrow.
Hij zegt om één uur daar geweest te zullen zijn = he says that at one o'clock he will have been there.
Hij belooft zijne lessen dan geleerd te zullen hebben = he promises that then he will have learned his lessons.

NOTE.—The latter part of these sentences may also be literally translated from the English.

She hopes that she will live. I expect that I shall call you. They think that they will come to-morrow. He

promises that he will have given the money. She believes
that she will be ill to-morrow. Having slept, the child
was much better. Let the bird live, boys! Having built
a strong castle, the king was safe. John and Henry, share
the marbles! Let them also share the money! Let us
tell the story of that fearful fire to our parents. The
carpenter expects that he will build three large houses.
The girl believes that she [will] once [be] very rich (will
be). Let us measure these sticks; they are long and
strong. Do not always play, children! Let them play
now; they will (the next hour) learn their spelling
(*spelles, v.*) [the next hour]. Charles, call the servant, I
want to [ask] him something (ask). Yes, father, I shall
call him.

THE PROGRESSIVE FORM.

The Dutch language has no Progressive Form. Phrases in
that form are therefore expressed in the corresponding tense of the
verb, without indicating continuance of action.

> He is writing a letter = He writes a letter = *Hij schrijft eenen
> brief.*
> He was reading the paper = He read the paper = *Hij las de
> courant.*
> I shall be going to-morrow = I shall go to-morrow = *Ik zal
> morgen gaan.*

When it is necessary to give prominence to the continuous
character of an action, another kind of expression is used:

> He is always writing = *Hij is altijd aan het schrijven.*
> Do not speak to him, he is reading = *Spreek niet tot hem, hij
> is aan het lezen.*

EXERCISE XXXII.

The woman is weighing the meat. He was calling his
father. The child was sleeping all (the whole) day. He
was telling me about (*van*) his mother, who [is] dead (is).
We have been learning our spelling, and we have been
playing in the room. The thief has been stealing again.
The good dog was still living. Did you call me? No, I
was calling your brother. How long did your sister

sleep? She slept [for] three hours. She is always sleeping when (*als*) I want to go out (*uitgaan*). Will you be measuring the carpet? I have measured it already, but I shall measure it again. Was the mason building the house? He has been building two houses on the main road, and [now] he is building (now) a third. Were you telling him about that crow with the large wings? Tell me that too. I shall tell you by and by.

Exercise XXXIII.

Note.—The word "when" is translated by "*toen*," when an action is expressed in the Past Tense, purporting to name a fact which has occurred *once*.

In sentences, the verb of which is in the Present or Future Tense, or in the Past Tense, when a habit or regularly occurring event is expressed, the word "when" is rendered by "*wanneer*," or "*als*."

You were sleeping when (*toen*) I called. My father was measuring the door when (*toen*) I gave him the letter. You play when (*wanneer*) you must learn (must = *moet*). He had the letter in his hand when (*toen*) he was playing. When (*wanneer*) will you call the cat? I called the cat when I was in the passage. When you divide the marbles, you must (*moet*) call me. When the postman had weighed the book, he gave it to me. Were you building the wall when I [saw] you (saw, *zag*)? Yes, I was building the wall when you called me to (*om te*) measure the door. When did the thief steal the money? He stole the money at (*om*) 5 o'clock. Were you sleeping when he stole it? He took it when we were in [the] house, but we were all sleeping. Was he dividing the marbles when you asked him to play? He always gives me his books when he plays.

Conversatie.	Conversation.
Het Weder.	**The Weather.**
Boodschappen doen.	**Shopping.**
1. *De lucht is bewolkt.*	1. The sky is cloudy.
2. *We zullen donderweer krijgen.*	2. We shall have a thunderstorm.

3. De donder ratelt; het onweert.
4. Het licht; heeft u den bliksem gezien?
5. Die bliksemstraal was heel fel.
6. Het weer klaart op; het zal morgen mooi weer zijn.
7. Wat een prachtige regenboog!
8. Welk weer heeft u op uwe reis gehad?
9. Guur, stormachtig weer.
10. Er heeft een harde, doordringende wind gewaaid.
11. De wind heeft een aantal schoorsteenen afgewaaid.
12. De wind is gaan liggen.
13. Het regent hard.
14. Het is erg koud; het hagelt, sneeuwt, vriest.
15. De sneeuw smelt.
16. De rivier is bevroren.
17. Het vriest dat het kraakt.
18. Het is buitengewoon koud.
19. De vorige winter was bijzonder streng.
20. Het is nu zacht weer.
21. De zon schijnt.
22. De maan gaat van avond om acht uur op.
23. We hebben heerlijk, bekoorlijk, mooi weer.
24. Gisteren was het triestig, somber, onaangenaam, veranderlijk.
25. Het is hier vochtig en naar in den winter.
26. De hitte in den zomer is vreeselijk op de vlakten.

3. The thunder rolls; it thunders.
4. There is lightning; did you see the lightning?
5. That flash of lightning was very vivid.
6. The weather is clearing up; it will be fine to-morrow.
7. What a splendid rainbow!
8. What sort of weather did you have on your journey?
9. Rough, stormy weather.
10. There has been a strong piercing wind.
11. The wind has blown a number of chimneys down.
12. The wind has abated.
13. It rains hard.
14. It is very cold; it hails, snows, freezes.
15. The snow is melting.
16. The river is frozen.
17. It freezes very hard.
18. It is extremely cold.
19. Last winter was particularly severe.
20. This is mild weather.
21. The sun shines.
22. The moon rises at eight to-night.
23. We have delightful, charming, fine weather.
24. Yesterday it was gloomy, dull, disagreeable, changeable.
25. It is damp and dismal here in winter.
26. The heat is terrible in the plains in summer.

---

27. Laat ons dien winkel binnengaan—ik heb verscheidene dingen noodig.
28. Ik zou graag wat hoeden willen zien.

27. Let us go into that shop—there are several things I want.
28. I should like to see some hats.

DECLENSION.

29. Deze zijn naar den laatsten smaak, mijnheer.
30. Laat ons wat zwart laken zien, als 't u blieft.
31. Dit is niet fijn genoeg.
32. Wat kost het?
33. U heeft geene keus.
34. De prijs is te hoog.
35. Ik moet een paar glacé handschoenen hebben.
36. Dit paar is te groot: ik draag nummer 7.
37. Heeft u sterke leeren schoenen?
38. Die zijn te lang, te nauw, te kort.
39. Ik houd van lage hakken.
40. Het fatsoen bevalt me niet.
41. Laat me eens wat zakdoeken en dassen zien.
42. Wil u mij uwe beste zijden paraplu's wijzen?
43. Wat kost deze?
44. Vijftien shilling, mijnheer.
45. Ik zou graag witte linnen boorden en manchetten zien.
46. Zoo is het genoeg; dank u.

29. These are the newest style, sir.
30. Show us some black cloth, please.
31. This is not fine enough.
32. What is the price?
33. You have no choice.
34. The price is too high.
35. I want a pair of kid gloves.
36. This pair is too large: I wear no. 7.
37. Have you strong leather boots?
38. Those are too long, too narrow, too short.
39. I like low heels.
40. I don't like the shape.
41. Show me some handkerchiefs and some ties.
42. Can I see some of your best silk umbrellas?
43. What is the price of this one?
44. Fifteen shillings, sir.
45. I wish to see some white linen collars and cuffs.
46. That is enough; thank you.

CHAPTER VII.

THE ADJECTIVE.

(*Het Bijvoegelijke Naamwoord.*)

I. ADJECTIVES denote distinguishing attributes or qualities of persons and things: De *trouwe* vriend, the faithful friend; Het *witte* papier, the white paper.

II. Adjectives may be used attributively and predicatively. An adjective used attributively, *Attributief Bijvoegelijk naamwoord*, is connected directly with its Noun: de *warme* koffie, the warm coffee.

An adjective used predicatively, *Predicatief Bijvoegelijk naamwoord*, is connected with its noun by means of some form of one of the Copulative Verbs: *zijn*, to be; *worden*, to become; *blijven*, to remain; *heeten*, to be called; *schijnen*, to seem; *blijken*, to appear: *Hij is goed*, he is good; *Zij blijft trouw*, she appears faithful; *Dat heet mooi*, that is called pretty.

> OBS. 1.—The adjective, when used predicatively, is not declined, but it may be inflected to express the degrees of comparison: *Die boom is hoog, maar deze is hooger*, that tree is high, but this one is higher.
>
> OBS. 2.—Other verbs besides those mentioned above may be accompanied by an adjective used predicatively, when, namely, such adjective refers to a noun, and not to the action expressed by the verb: *e.g., De deur is bruin geschilderd*, the door has been painted brown. Here obviously, "*brown*" does not refer to the action of painting, but qualifies "*door*"; it is therefore, not an adverb, but an adjective.

III. The Attributive Adjective agrees with the noun

to which it is attached in gender, number, and case. (See Chapter on Declension.)

In a few particular cases, however, it remains unaltered:

> *Case* 1.—When it **follows** its noun directly, instead of directly **preceding** it. This was often the case in older Dutch, but rarely occurs now. *Vaderlief* = dear father; *kindlief* = dear child; *Staten-Generaal* = General States (House of Assembly), are surviving examples.
>
> *Case* 2.—When the Indefinite Article "*een*" stands between the noun and its adjective: *Hoe wijs een man*, how wise a man; *Te groot een verlies*, too great a loss; *Zoo vroom eene vrouw*, so pious a woman.

IV. After the words *een*, a; *geen*, no; *eenig*, any; *elk*, every; *ieder*, each; *menig*, many; *zeker*, certain, and *welk*, when, occurring before the name of a male person, the adjective, by its being either declined or retaining its original form, applies the same quality with a different meaning to the person, to whose name it is attached.

The uninflected adjective in such a case refers to those qualities which pertain to the **state** or **title** of the person; the inflected adjective refers to his **inner qualities** as a man, irrespective of the name he bears: *een goed koning*, a good king; *een goede koning*, a good-hearted king; *een knap schoenmaker*, an able shoemaker; *een knappe schoenmaker*, a good-looking shoemaker; *een groot koopman*, a merchant who has a large business; *een groote koopman*, a tall merchant; *een oud soldaat*, a soldier who has been long in the service; *een oude soldaat*, an old man who is a soldier.

> NOTE.—*Een oudsoldaat* means a former soldier; likewise does *een oudleerling* mean a former pupil.

V. The following kinds of Attributive Adjectives are not declined:

1. Adjectives denoting a material, and which end in *en*; e.g. *eene zijden japon*, a silk dress; *gouden horloges*, gold watches.

2. Adjectives of three or more syllables, when they end in *en*; e.g. *eene afgelegen plaats*, a lonely place.

3. Adjectives which by means of the ending *er* are derived from the names of places, villages or towns; e.g. *de Kamper boot*, a steamer plying between Kampen and some other town; *de Rotterdammer markt*, the market of Rotterdam.

NOTE.—The ending *er* is not the usual ending for Adjectives derived from names of places. The common ending is *sch*: *Beaufortsche schapen*, Beaufort sheep; *Wellingtonsche wijn*, Wellington wine.

4. The comparative degree of adjectives, because in it they take the ending *er*: *Nooit had ik schooner kans*, I never had a better chance; *Ik heb meer bloemen dan gij*, I have more flowers than you.

5. Adjectives which end in *lei* or *hande*: *allerlei vee*, all kinds of cattle; *allerhande boeken*, all kinds of books.

6. The two adjectives *rechter*, right, and *linker*, left, because they never stand alone, but always form part of the noun which they qualify: *mijne rechterhand*, my right hand; *zijn linkerbeen*, his left leg.

7. The adjective "*eigen*," when it is taken in the meaning of *dezelfde*, the same: *Hij stierf op den eigen dag, waarop zijn broeder geboren werd*, he died on the same day on which his brother was born.

NOTE.—If *eigen* is taken in the usual meaning of "own," it is declined in the ordinary way: *mijne eigene zuster*, my own sister.

NOTE 2.—If two or more adjectives are attached to one noun, together expressing but *one* quality, the last of these adjectives is declined and the others remain unchanged: *Holland heeft eene rood, wit en blauwe vlag*, Holland has a red, white and blue flag.

OBS.—Adjectives ending in *sch* may for the greater part be used as adverbs, but then they drop the *ch*: *Ik zie hem dagelijks*, I see him daily; *Voorwaarts komen*, to come to the front. There are a few adjectives, however, which claim special attention, because though ending in a hissing sound, they simply take *s* and not *sch*. These are: *dwars*, across; *wars*, averse; *bits*, tart; *flets*, faded; *paars*, violet; *sits*, chintz; *vuns*, musty; *vies*, dirty; *dras*, marshy; *voos*, spongy; *spits*, pointed; *kras*, strong; *los*, loose; *bros*, brittle; *ros*, ruddy; *wis*, sure, and *gewis*, certain. Examples: *een gewisse dood*, a certain death; *een drasse grond*, a marshy ground; *vooze radijs*, spongy radishes; *rasse schreden*, quick steps.

THE ADJECTIVE.

VI. DEGREES OF COMPARISON (*Trappen van Vergelijking*). Objects may possess a quality absolutely or comparatively. Absolute possession is expressed by the Positive degree, *Stellende trap*, i.e., the unchanged form of the adjective: *Mijne les is lang*, my lesson is long.

Comparative possession, *i.e.*, possession in comparison with other objects having the same quality, is expressed in two ways:

1. By the Comparative degree, *Vergrootende trap*, which indicates that an object possesses the like quality with another, only in a higher degree: *Het paard is grooter dan de koe*, the horse is taller than the cow.

2. By the Superlative degree, *Overtreffende trap*, which indicates that one object possesses some quality in a higher degree than any other object to which it is compared; *Onder alle bloemen is deze de mooiste*, among all flowers this is the prettiest one.

The Comparative degree is formed by adding *er* to the unchanged form of the adjective: *groot, grooter*, great, greater.

The Superlative degree is formed by adding *st* to the unchanged form of the adjective: *groot, grootst*, great, greatest.

NOTE.—In forming the comparative of adjectives ending in *f* or *s*, take note of the rules for the formation of the plural of nouns ending in those letters.

OBS. 1.—Adjectives ending in *r* form their comparative by adding *der*, instead of *er*. The comparative of *na*, near, is likewise *nader*, and of *moe*, tired, *moeder*.

OBS. 2.—Adjectives in *s* or *sch* form their superlative by adding *t*, instead of *st*: *wijs*, wise, *wijzer, wijst* (not *wijsst*).

OBS. 3.—*Meer*, more, and *meest*, most, may not, as a rule, be used in Dutch for the formation of the degrees of comparison. The endings *er* and *st* are added, irrespective of the number of syllables. In one special case, however, the ending *st* of the superlative stands in the way of easy pronunciation, namely in *woestst*, most desolate, which should therefore be *meest woest*.

OBS. 4.—There is a case in which the word *meer* must invariably be used to indicate the Comparative degree, viz., when two qualities attributed to one and the same object are compared, e.g., *Deze tafel is meer eenig dan mooi*, this table is more unique than pretty; *Eene koe is meer nuttig dan gezellig*, a cow is more useful than sociable.

NOTE.—*Meer* and *meest* must also be employed in the comparison of Past Participles used as predicative adjectives: *Zij is meer vermoeid dan haar broeder*, she is more tired than her brother; *Mijne schoenen zijn het meest versleten van alle*, my boots are the most worn-out ones of all.

OBS. 5.—In using superlatives, the student should be careful about the article that precedes the adjective. When we speak of different objects among which one stands prominent, the article must be chosen according to the gender of the noun employed, and the superlative ends in *ste*: *De mooiste stad van den ganschen omtrek*, the finest town of the whole neighbourhood; *Het nieuwste boek, dat ik bezit*, the newest book I possess. When, however, parts of the same thing are compared, the superlative ends in *st*, and the article preceding it is "*het*" in all cases: *Aan de zuidzijde is de stad het mooist*, the town is prettiest on the south side; *De zieke is 's morgens het zwakst*, the patient is weakest in the morning.

OBS. 6.—Some adjectives from their nature can have no degrees of comparison. Such are:

(a) Adjectives which indicate a material: *eene zijden japon*, a silk dress.

(b) Adjectives whose meaning is complete in the positive degree: *dood*, dead; *stom*, dumb; *ledig*, empty; *luchtdicht*, air-tight; *splinternieuw*, brand-new; *gitzwart*, jet-black; *ontelbaar*, innumerable; *overaltegenwoordig*, omnipresent; *drieëenig*, triune; *bloedrood*, blood-red; *almachtig*, almighty; *aardsch*, earthy; *Engelsch*, English, *Fransch*, French, etc.

(c) Adjectives derived from adverbs: *voormalig*, former; *dadelijksch*, daily; *trapsgewijze*, gradual; *schriftelijk*, in writing; *mondeling*, verbal.

OBS. 7.—A few adjectives have an irregular comparison:

POSITIVE.		COMPARATIVE.	SUPERLATIVE.
goed,[*]	good,	*beter*,	*best*.
kwaad,	bad,	*erger*,	*ergst*.
veel,	much,	*meer*,	*meest*.
weinig,	little,	*minder*,	*minst*.
vroeg,	early,	*vroeger* (*eerder*),	*vroegst* (*eerst*).

[*] NOTE.—The old positive degree is *bet* or *bat* = *goed*, which is still found in the word *Betuwe* (*bat ouwe*, good soil), a part of Gelderland; also in *betovergrootvader*, grandfather's grandfather, and in *beweter*, wiseacre.

THE ADJECTIVE.

OBS. 8.—After comparatives "*dan*," than, must be used, and never "*als*," the latter being a Germanism: *Hij is rijker dan ik*, he is richer than I.

GRAMMAR EXERCISES.—*Taaloefeningen.*

EXERCISE XXXIV.

Write out the degrees of comparison of the following Adjectives.

1.

Groot, great; *zwart*, black; *glad*, slippery; *klein*, small; *hoog*, high; *laag*, low; *rond*, round; *dik*, thick; *lang*, long; *diep*, deep; *bont*, gaudy; *vlak*, level; *krom*, crooked; *vuil*, dirty; *bleek*, pale; *droog*, dry; *mooi*, fine; *breed*, broad; *steil*, steep; *dicht*, close; *druk*, busy; *vroeg*, early; *dun*, thin; *laf*, insipid; *wit*, white; *heet*, hot; *koel*, cool; *echt*, real; *dood*, dead; *vroom*, pious; *koud*, cold; *flink*, thorough.

2.

Boos, angry; *gelijk*, even; *grof*, coarse; *geleerd*, learned; *vies*, dirty; *dor*, dry; *stevig*, firm; *valsch*, false; *gouden*, gold; *lief*, dear; *broos*, frail; *gek*, mad; *bekend*, known; *duur*, expensive; *beroemd*, celebrated; *doof*, deaf; *levend*, alive; *kostbaar*, costly; *dwars*, cross; *wijs*, wise; *fraai*, pretty; *erg*, bad; *schuinsch*, oblique; *glanzig*, glossy; *scheef*, awry; *moe*, tired; *lui*, lazy; *bemind*, loved; *pikzwart*, pitchblack; *vlijtig*, diligent; *kras*, firm; *angstig*, anxious; *schuw*, shy; *spits*, pointed; *mager*, thin; *braaf*, good.

3.

Versleten, worn out; *landelijk*, rural; *zijden*, silken; *aardsch*, earthly; *aangenaam*, agreeable; *verteerbaar*, digestive; *naar*, disagreeable; *bloo*, timid; *levenloos*, lifeless; *doornat*, wet through; *behaard*, hairy; *blozend*, blooming; *geëerd*, honoured; *klaar*, clear; *vroolijk*, merry; *ijselijk*, frightful; *sneeuwwit*, snow-white; *laat*, late;

getand, indented; *levenslustig*, merry; *na*, near; *oppassend*, respectable; *bekwaam*, clever; *woest*, wild; *almachtig*, almighty; *veerkrachtig*, elastic; *verlept*, faded; *stuk*, broken; *oprecht*, sincere; *menschelijk*, human; *begrensd*, bounded; *gemeten*, measured; *beproefd*, tried; *schitterend*, brilliant; *akelig*, dismal; *glooiend*, sloping; *verheven*, raised; *breedgerand*, broad-brimmed.

EXERCISE XXXV.

Fill up the blanks in the following exercises.

1.

— *paars- lint (o) van mijn- hoed (m) ziet er flet- uit.*
The violet ribbon of my hat looks faded.
Toen ik te Aliwal-Noord was, nam ik dagelijks een-
When I at Aliwal North was, took I daily a
bad (o) in — warm- bron-. D- taal (v) van —
bath in the hot springs. The language of the
dagelijk- leven noemt men — omgangstaal. —
everyday life calls one the colloquial language. The
wit- en zwart- paard van — postrijder heeft zijn-
white and black horse of the postrider has its
poot (m) gebroken. Amsterdam is op paal- gebouwd, die
leg broken. Amsterdam is on piles built which
door d- dras- grond (m) tot op d- onderliggend- vast-
through the marshy soil on to the underlying firm
laag (v) heengedreven zijn. Ik kan niet zooveel in d- man
layer driven down are. I can not so much in the man
zien, mij lijkt hij - zeer alledaag- mensch (m). Bij d-
see, to me looks he a very common person. In the
ros- gloed (m) dien d- brand verspreidde, liep d-
ruddy glow which the fire cast, ran (about) the
arm- man wanhopig naar de zijn- te zoeken.
poor man in despair for his wife and children to look.
Mijn- vader is- kras- man; ofschoon hij- tijdgenoot
My father is a vigorous man, though he a contemporary

THE ADJECTIVE.

van Willem — Tweed- is, wandelt hij nog elk- dag
of William the Second is, walks he still every day (for)
een- uur. Als — jong- mensch— zich op —
an hour. When these young people (themselves) on the
bros- ijs(o) wagen, gaan zij een- gewis- dood(m)
brittle ice venture, go they a certain death
tegemoet.
to meet.

2.

D- woorden — wijz- zijn als goud- appel- op
The words of the wise are like golden apples on
zilver- schaal-. Van — plafond(o) hingen groot-
silver dishes. From the ceiling were hanging large
kristal- kroonlampen af, die d- zaal(v) met —
crystal candelabra down, which the hall with a
tooverachtig- licht vervulden. D- vreemdeling droeg - zwaar-
fairy-like light filled. The stranger wore a heavy
goud- ring aan d- middelvinger zijn- recht- hand.
gold ring on the middle finger of his right hand.
Zet d- beid- raam- wijd open, er is een vuns-
Throw (the) both windows wide open, there is a stuffy
lucht in d- kamer(v). D- groot- steen- vaas- op d-
smell in the room. The large stone vases on the
stoep(v) vóór ons- huis(o) zijn van — fijnst-
verandah in front of our house are of the finest
aardewerk. Sinds uw- neef naar d- universiteit gegaan
earthenware. Since your cousin to the university gone
is, is hij een- verwaand- -weter geworden, met wien ik
is, has he a conceited wiseacre become, with whom I
lief- niets meer te doen wil hebben.
rather nothing more to do will have.

3.

— paard behoort tot een- edeler- diersoort(v) dan
The horse belongs to a nobler kind of animals than
d- koe. D- vroeg- bezitter van — landgoed(o)
the cow. The former owner of this estate

stamde in d– recht– lijn (v) van Lodewijk d– Eerst– af
descended in the direct line from Lewis the First.
D– jong– boer ontving ons met d– eigen– gastvrijheid,
The young farmer received us with the same hospitality
die zijn– vader gekenmerkt had. Bij — onderzoek
which his father characterised had. At the investigation
bleek, dat d– Compagnie — schip aan een–
(it) appeared, that the Company the vessel to an
onervaren– kapitein had toevertrouwd. Bij — flauw–
inexperienced captain had entrusted. By the faint
schijnsel mijn– lantaarn (v) zag ik een– man met ras–
glimmer of my lantern saw I a man with quick
schreden dwars– — veld (o) oversteken; en toen hij naderbij
steps athwart the field cross; and when he nearer
kwam, herkende ik d– stap van mijn– eigen– vader.
came, recognised I the step of my own father.

TRANSLATION EXERCISES.—*Vertaaloefeningen.*

Exercise XXXVI.

(*On § IV.*)

The good-looking son of our schoolmaster has become an able carpenter. Louis the Sixteenth of France was a good man, but not a good king. The blacksmith in the village is a former soldier. There is a very old soldier in the hospital. The captain who called (*eene visite maakte*) last night, is a soldier of long standing. There is not a good doctor in the town. Any good-hearted doctor would have had pity on that poor woman. No bad clerk ever makes a good manager. Many [a] great man is not duly appreciated until (*dan*) after his death. My uncle Henri is such a tall man that he goes by the name of Goliath. This poor man was a great merchant once, but he failed in business and since then has never been able (*heeft . . . kunnen*) to get on. Of late years Austria has been a faithful ally to (*voor*) Germany. This young man is but (*nog maar*) a young mason.

EXERCISE XXXVII.

(On § VI.)

The soap-manufactory is the highest house in the town. Your brother is more diligent than mine (*de mijne*). The river was deepest where we attempted to cross it (*ze*). Colonial coal is not so dear as foreign coal. In many parts of South Africa the scenery is more grand than pretty. The almond-tree blossoms first of all the trees in our garden. This bread is the least palatable which (*dat*) I have tasted for a long time (*in langen tijd*). A more faithful dog than mine I have never seen. Your dress looks more worn than your cloak. This young barrister is the most learned of all his colleagues. Our dog barked loudest as (*toen*) we neared the gorge. King Solomon was the wisest man of his time. The horse is liveliest when it has been in the stable (*op stal gestaan heeft*) [for] a few days. The wildest (*woest*) parts of the country are the least fertile (sup. of *onvruchtbaar*). Figs are among (*behooren tot*) the most wholesome [of] fruits. Of all these lamps this [one] is the least expensive. [A] cheaper cloth than the one (*hetgeen*) you have, is no good (*deugt niet*). A more terrific thunderstorm than yesterday's (*die van*) I have never witnessed.

CONJUGATION of the WEAK VERB "*dansen,*" to dance, and the STRONG VERB "*lezen,*" to read.

INDICATIVE MOOD.   AANTOONENDE WIJS.

Present Tense.   *Onvolmaakt Tegenwoordige Tijd.*

Ik dans, I dance.   *Ik lees*, I read.
Gij danst, thou dancest.   *Gij leest*, thou readest.
Hij danst, he dances.   *Hij leest*, he reads.
Wij dansen, we dance.   *Wij lezen*, we read.
Gij danst, you dance.   *Gij leest*, you read.
Zij dansen, they dance.   *Zij lezen*, they read.

INDICATIVE MOOD.   AANTOONENDE WIJS.

Perfect Tense.   Volmaakt Tegenwoordige Tijd.

Ik heb gedanst, I have danced.
Gij hebt gedanst, thou hast danced.
Hij heeft gedanst, he has danced.
Wij hebben gedanst, we have danced.
Gij hebt gedanst, you have danced.
Zij hebben gedanst, they have danced.

Ik heb gelezen, I have read.
Gij hebt gelezen, thou hast read.
Hij heeft gelezen, he has read.
Wij hebben gelezen, we have read.
Gij hebt gelezen, you have read.
Zij hebben gelezen, they have read.

Imperfect Tense.   Onvolmaakt Verleden Tijd.

Ik danste, I danced.
Gij danstet, thou dancedst.
Hij danste, he danced.
Wij dansten, we danced.
Gij danstet, you danced.
Zij dansten, they danced.

Ik las, I read.
Gij laast, thou readest.
Hij las, he read.
Wij lazen, we read.
Gij laast, you read.
Zij lazen, they read.

Pluperfect Tense.   Volmaakt Verleden Tijd.

Ik had gedanst, I had danced.
Gij hadt gedanst, thou hadst danced.
Hij had gedanst, he had danced.
Wij hadden gedanst, we had danced.
Gij hadt gedanst, you had danced.
Zij hadden gedanst, they had danced.

Ik had gelezen, I had read.
Gij hadt gelezen, thou hadst read.
Hij had gelezen, he had read.
Wij hadden gelezen, we had read.
Gij hadt gelezen, you had read.
Zij hadden gelezen, they had read.

Future Tense.   Onvolmaakt Toekomende Tijd.

Ik zal dansen, I shall dance.
Gij zult dansen, thou wilt dance.
Hij zal dansen, he will dance.
Wij zullen dansen, we shall dance.
Gij zult dansen, you will dance.
Zij zullen dansen, they will dance.

Ik zal lezen, I shall read.
Gij zult lezen, thou wilt read.
Hij zal lezen, he will read.
Wij zullen lezen, we shall read.
Gij zult lezen, you will read.
Zij zullen lezen, they will read.

THE ADJECTIVE.

INDICATIVE MOOD.   AANTOONENDE WIJS.

Future Perfect Tense.   *Volmaakt Toekomende Tijd.*

Ik zal gedanst hebben, I shall have danced.
Gij zult gedanst hebben, thou wilt have danced.
Hij zal gedanst hebben, he will have danced.
Wij zullen gedanst hebben, we shall have danced.
Gij zult gedanst hebben, you will have danced.
Zij zullen gedanst hebben, they will have danced.

Ik zal gelezen hebben, I shall have read.
Gij zult gelezen hebben, thou wilt have read.
Hij zal gelezen hebben, he will have read.
Wij zullen gelezen hebben, we shall have read.
Gij zult gelezen hebben, you will have read.
Zij zullen gelezen hebben, they will have read.

SUBJUNCTIVE MOOD.   AANVOEGENDE WIJS.

Future Tense.   *Onv. Toek. Tijd.*

Ik zou dansen, I should dance.
Gij zoudt dansen, thou wouldst dance.
Hij zou dansen, he would dance.
Wij zouden dansen, we should dance.
Gij zoudt dansen, you would dance.
Zij zouden dansen, they would dance.

Ik zou lezen, I should read.
Gij zoudt lezen, thou wouldst read.
Hij zou lezen, he would read.
Wij zouden lezen, we should read.
Gij zoudt lezen, you would read.
Zij zouden lezen, they would read.

Future Perf. Tense.   *Volm. Toek. Tijd.*

Ik zou gedanst hebben, I should have danced.
Gij zoudt gedanst hebben, thou wouldst have danced.
Hij zou gedanst hebben, he would have danced.
Wij zouden gedanst hebben, we should have danced.
Gij zoudt gedanst hebben, you would have danced.
Zij zouden gedanst hebben, they would have danced.

Ik zou gelezen hebben, I should have read.
Gij zoudt gelezen hebben, thou wouldst have read.
Hij zou gelezen hebben, he would have read.
Wij zouden gelezen hebben, we should have read.
Gij zoudt gelezen hebben, you would have read.
Zij zouden gelezen hebben, they would have read.

IMPERATIVE MOOD. GEBIEDENDE WIJS.

Singular.   *Enkelvoud.*

Laat mij dansen, let me dance.   *Laat mij lezen,* let me read.
Dans, dance (thou).   *Lees,* read (thou).
Laat hem dansen, let him dance.   *Laat hem lezen,* let him read.

Plural.   *Meervoud.*

Laat ons dansen, let us dance.   *Laat ons lezen,* let us read.
Danst, dance (ye).   *Leest,* read (ye).
Laat hen dansen, let them dance.   *Laat hen lezen,* let them read.

INFINITIVE MOOD. ONBEPAALDE WIJS.

Present Tense.   *Onvolmaakt Tegenwoordige Tijd.*

(Te) dansen, to dance.   *(Te) lezen,* to read.

Perfect Tense.   *Volmaakt Tegenwoordige Tijd.*

Gedanst (te) hebben, to have danced.   *Gelezen (te) hebben,* to have read.

Future Tense.   *Onvolmaakt Toekomende Tijd.*

(Te) zullen dansen (no equivalent, see Exercise XXXI)   *(Te) zullen lezen* (no equivalent, see Exercise XXXI)

Future Perfect Tense.   *Volmaakt Toekomende Tijd.*

(Te) zullen gedanst hebben (no equivalent).   *(Te) zullen gelezen hebben* (no equivalent).

Present Participle.   *Tegenwoordig Deelwoord.*

Dansende, dancing.   *Lezende,* reading.

Past Participle.   *Verleden Deelwoord.*

Gedanst, danced.   *Gelezen,* read.

Like "*dansen*" conjugate the weak verbs: *kloppen, klopte, geklopt,* to knock; *straffen, strafte, gestraft,* to punish; *gissen, giste, gegist,* to guess; *blaffen, blafte, geblaft,* to bark; *hakken, hakte, gehakt,* to chop; *missen, miste, gemist,* to miss, to spare.

THE ADJECTIVE.

Like "*lezen*" conjugate the strong Verbs: *wijzen, wees, gewezen,* to show, to point out; *verliezen, verloor, verloren,* to lose; *genezen, genas, genezen,* to cure; *prijzen, prees, geprezen,* to praise; *vriezen, vroor, gevroren,* to freeze; *rijzen, rees, gerezen,* to rise.

Exercise XXXVIII.

Note.—Translate "if" by "*indien*," or "*als*," the shorter word being sometimes preferred.

Can you spare [me] one of these new pencils? Yes, I shall give you one (*er ... een*), because you ask me for it (*er ... om*). If these girls dance in their room, they will be punished. Did you call (Have ... called) your own dog or (the) mine? I have called mine three times, but he does not hear, for he is barking at (*tegen*) another dog. If you lose your books, will the teacher punish you? He praised the little boy when he had learned that long verse. If the man had chopped the wood, I should have asked him nothing. Can you guess why he called me? Would she lose all these plants if it should freeze (froze)? Read, children, and tell me what is (*staat*) in the letter. Let us knock at (*aan*) the door. If you give me the medicine, it (she) will cure me. If they had shown the money, the thief would have stolen it. If you had guessed the contents of the letter, would you have read (*voorgelezen*) it to your friend? Do not bark so, old dog, your voice is hoarse with it (*er van*).

Exercise XXXIX.

Note.—" Then " is translated by "*dan*," when introducing a conclusive sentence, following a conditional one:

If he goes, then I must stay, *als hij gaat, dan moet ik blijven.*
Suppose he had said so, then you would have answered, *veronderstel dat hij dit gezegd had, dan zoudt gij geantwoord hebben.*

"Then," when an adverb of time, is translated by "*dan*" for the Present and Future tenses, and by "*toen*" for the Past tense.

I go to the baker, and then to the butcher, *ik ga naar den bakker en dan naar den slager.*

He will come, and then I shall hear it, *hij zal komen, en dan zal ik het hooren.*

She ran to her mother and then fainted, *zij liep naar hare moeder toe, en viel toen flauw.*

In the latter meaning it may usually be translated by "*daarna*" as well, especially when there is a clear succession of events in point of time.

The boy asked his friends (*om*) to play with him, and then they ran about in the field. I shall miss you when you are gone (*weg*), for then I shall have no one to (*om . . . te*) play with me. Were they all praising the girl that night (*avond*)? They praised her very [much], and showed me her beautiful prizes. When the shopkeeper weighed the sugar, he found out his mistake. He will measure the ground first, and then he will build a large dwelling-house on it (*er op*). Were the children sleeping when you called them? No, they were not sleeping any more, they were playing; the girls had dolls, and the boys had marbles. One boy was chopping wood for his mother in the yard, and the eldest boy was sitting reading (*te lezen*) in a corner of the dining-room. Would you like to go to the post-office first (*eerst*), and then to the station? I would rather (*liever*) go to the station first. You want to show me the pictures, my little boy? Having lost her money, the poor woman was in great distress.

Exercise XL.

FIFTH RULE OF CONSTRUCTION.—When the object (direct or indirect), or an adverbial extension stands first in a principal sentence, the subject is placed after the predicate.

Yesterday (showed) my brother [showed] me the new house. Five pounds (gave) the man [gave] for the old donkey. Him (called) he [called], not you. To dance

(Rule 2) [on] that night (*avond*), would have been [a] shame. (It) to have missed [it], would have been to have lost it. Now that my mother is gone (*weg*), my all (*alles*) is gone. The passage (would) you [would] not measure for me, (said) you [said]; why not? (The) life on earth is pleasant to (*voor*) some people, but miserable to many. In the school I learn, in my bed I sleep; when I am at table, I eat, and when (I am) in the garden, I play. That you must (*moet*) not ask me, for how can (*kan*) I tell it you? Would the thief have stolen the money, if you had given him some bread? Work [you] must (you) whether (*of*) you are rich or (*of*) poor; all people must work. After the battle the soldiers divided the spoil amongst (*onder*) them (*zich*). Behind the house is a large garden with many precious fruit-trees.

VII. THE NUMERAL ADJECTIVE.—*Het Telwoord.*

NUMERAL ADJECTIVES, though taken in Dutch as a separate part of speech, are real adjectives expressing a quantity. That quantity may be defined or not, hence the distinction between *Bepaalde Telwoorden*, Definite Numeral Adjectives, and *Onbepaalde Telwoorden*, Indefinite Numeral Adjectives. Besides expressing a quantity, these Adjectives may also point out the place a certain object takes in a series, hence the distinction between *Hoofdgetallen*, Cardinal Numbers, and *Ranggetallen*, Ordinal Numbers. The place or order may again be defined or not. The distinctions are shown in the following table:—

TELWOORDEN.	*Numeral Adjectives.*
1. *Hoofdgetallen* (Cardinals).	a. *Bepaalde* (definite).
	b. *Onbepaalde* (indefinite).
2. *Ranggetallen* (Ordinals).	a. *Bepaalde* (definite).
	b. *Onbepaalde* (indefinite).

EXAMPLES :

1. a. *een*, one ; *twee*, two ; *twintig*, twenty ; *beide*, both ; etc.

1. b. *Veel*, much, many; *alle*, all; *eenige*, some, any; *wat*, some; *weinig*, little, few; *sommige*, some; *geen*, no, etc.
2. a. *eerste*, first; *derde*, third; *vijftigste*, fiftieth, etc.
2. b. *hoeveelste*, which (in the order); *zooveelste*, such an one (in the order); *laatste*, last; *middelste*, the middle one.

Sentences on 1. b.

Deze man heeft eenige huizen te koop, this man has some houses for sale.
Hij heeft veel nieuwe boeken, he has many new books.
Sommige dagen heb ik te veel werk, on some days I have too much work.
Er zijn geene appelen aan den boom, there are no apples on the tree.
Heeft u alle (al de) eieren in die mand? have you got all the eggs in that basket?

NOTE.—If the word *alle* is followed by the definite article or a demonstrative pronoun, its form is undeclined, i.e. *al* (not *alle*), e.g., *ik heb al de huizen geteld*, I have counted all the houses.

Sentences on 2. b.

De hoeveelste plaats heeft uw broeder in de klas, which place has your brother got in class?
U zegt, dat dit het twintigste boek is? ik wist niet dat het al het zooveelste was, you say that this is the twentieth book? I did not know we had had so many.
Het middelste huis in de straat is het mijne, the middle one of the houses of this street is mine.

OBS.—Num. Adj. both definite and indefinite, like all adjectives, may be used as nouns of the weak declension (see p. 85): *Vele eersten zullen de laatsten zijn*, many (that are) first shall be last; *Sommigen raden dit aan, anderen wat anders*, some advise this, others something else.

VIII. Cardinals are not declined except *één*, one (written with a double accent to distinguish it from the indefinite article *een*), and *beide*.

Één, moreover, is not declined when it occurs in combination with another cardinal: *een en twintig jaren*, twenty-one years. In this case some write *eenentwintig*.

Één, used by itself, is declined like the indefinite article, except that it has no form for the genitive case. When preceded by the definite article or a demonstrative pronoun, it is declined like an adjective, and even has a plural: *Aan den eenen kant zou ik er wel lust in hebben,* on the one hand I should rather like it; *De eenen zeggen dit, de anderen dat,* some say this and others that.

> NOTE.—All Cardinals have a plural form when used as the names of arithmetical figures: *Schrijf vier vijven op uwe lei,* put down four fives on your slate.

> OBS.—*Honderden* and *duizenden,* real substantives, though treated as adjectives, never change their form: *Honderden uren ver,* hundreds of hours distant.

Beide, meaning "both," has of course only a plural form, and is declined: *beide, beider, beiden, beide.* Used by itself and referring to persons, the nom. and acc. case of it is *beiden: Ik heb van beiden evenveel vriendelijkheid ondervonden,* I have experienced equal kindness from both. But when referring to things, or when used to qualify a noun, these cases (not the dative) are *beide: Licht en duisternis zijn mij beide even welkom op hunne beurt,* light and darkness are both equally welcome to me in their turn; *Mijne beide broeders zijn dood,* both my brothers are dead.

IX. The indefinite Cardinals, as well as the definite and indefinite Ordinals, are all declined like common adjectives. When used separately, and referring to persons, they all take *n* in every case of the plural, like nouns of the weak declension, but they drop this *n,* when they refer to things.

Veel and *weinig,* when occurring before plural nouns, convey the idea of quantity, whereas *vele* and *weinige* mean different kinds:

> *Mijn vriend heeft veel boeken, en ik heb er weinig,* my friend has many books, and I have few.
> *Er groeien vele appelen in onzen tuin, hoewel het getal onzer boomen niet groot is,* we have many kinds of apples growing in our garden, though the number of trees is not large.

> NOTE.—Usually the word *soorten,* kinds, is added, to facilitate comprehension.

X. Notice the following idiomatic renderings:—

(a) Of the word "Some."

1. Before names of materials, or collective nouns: some tea, *wat thee*; some fuel, *wat brandhout*; some money, *wat geld*;—likewise before plural nouns (in colloquial style): some apples, *wat appelen*.

NOTE.—*Een beetje*, literally "a little bit," is likewise used before materials: some (a little) water, *een beetje water*; some cake, *een beetje koek*;—and *een paar*, a few, or *een stuk of wat*, before plurals: some (a few) stones, *een stuk of wat steenen*.

2. Before plural words: some houses, *eenige (een paar) huizen*; some cows, *eenige (een paar) koeien*.
3. With the meaning of "a little": May I give you some (a little) of this? *mag ik u hiervan iets (wat) geven?*
4. With the meaning of "a few": Some (a few) of these birds are green, *enkele van deze vogels zijn groen*.
5. To bring out "kind" or "sort": Some flour is good, and some is not, *sommig meel is goed en ander niet;* Some (kinds of) people can do that, and others not, *sommige menschen kunnen dat, en anderen niet.*

NOTE.—The principal idea of *eenige* is number, and of *sommige*, various kinds.

6. Signifying "several": We tarried there some days, *wij vertoefden daar verscheidene dagen*.
7. In its most indefinite signification: I should like to give him some (kind of) reward, *ik zou hem graag de eene of andere belooning geven;* Some day I hope to see you again, *den eenen of anderen dag hoop ik u weer te zien*.

(b) Of the word "Any."

1. In questions: Have you any books? *heeft u ook boeken?* Are there any children in the lane? *zijn er ook kinderen in de laan?*
2. In negations: Have you got these pears? No, not any, *Heeft u die peren? Neen, geen enkele;* He had not any money with him, *hij had volstrekt geen geld bij zich*.
3. With emphasis, before a singular noun: You must come in any case, *gij moet in elk geval komen*.
With emphasis, before a plural noun: I expect you under any circumstances, *ik zal u onder alle omstandigheden verwachten;* the safe is proof against any attacks by thieves, *de brandkast is bestand tegen alle aanvallen van dieven*.

4. In a general sense: He did as well as any boy could have done, *hij deed het zoo goed als een jongen het maar kan.*
5. Before an Adjective: Any other horse would have kicked, *ieder ander paard zou geschopt hebben.*

XI. Mark further the following expressions:
1. At one o'clock, *om één uur.*
2. At half-past two, *om half-drie* (remember the hyphen).
3. At about five o'clock, *omstreeks vijf uur.*
4. Some six pounds, *een pond of zes* (*een* unaccented).
5. Some twenty years, *een jaar of twintig* (this way of expression is not customary for sums higher than twenty).
6. Some hundred books, *een honderd boeken.*
7. Some few sheep, *een schaap of wat.*
8. Some fifteen young trees, *een stuk of vijftien jonge boomen.* (Use "*ongeveer*" before large quantities.)
9. About a fortnight, *een veertien dagen* (*een dag of veertien*).
10. About four weeks, *een vier weken* (*eene week of vier*).
11. About fifty bags of rice, *een vijftig zakken rijst.*
12. Some eight days, *een acht dagen* (*een dag of acht*).
13. Chapter fourth, *hoofdstuk vier,* or *het vierde hoofdstuk.*
14. The tenth verse, *vers tien,* or *het tiende vers.*
15. London, the twelfth of May, *Londen, twaalf Mei* (no other form is used).
16. Manchester, December 31st, 1821, *Manchester,* 31 *December,* 1821.
17. William the Third, *Willem de Derde* (no other form is used).
18. This paper is sold at ten shillings a ream, *dit papier wordt verkocht tegen tien shillings per* (or *den*) *riem.*
19. Pens for sale, four a penny, *pennen te koop, vier voor een stuiver.*
20. The two of us, *wij tweeën.*
21. The whole of us, *wij allen.*
22. I saw all four of them, *ik zag hen alle vier.*
23. Only the three of them are going, *zij gaan maar met hen drieeën.*
24. We four were alone, *wij vieren waren alleen.*
25. Twenty of them will climb the mountain, *zij gaan met hen twintigen den berg op.*

XII. Common adjectives are formed from Cardinal Numbers by the addition of *voudig* or *vuldig,* meaning "fold." Such adjectives are called *Verdubbelgetallen* (multiplicatives): *tweevoudig,* twofold; *viervoudig,* fourfold;

menigvuldig, manifold; *veelvoudig*, manifold. They are declined like ordinary adjectives.

XIII. By means of the endings *lei* and *hande* (both obsolete Dutch words, meaning "kind" or "sort"), Adjectives are formed from Cardinal Numbers; these, however, are indeclinable. On account of their meaning they are called *Soortgetallen* (variatives): *eenerlei*, of the same kind; *velerlei*, of various kinds; *allerlei*, all sorts of; *tweerlei*, of two kinds; *zesderlei*, of six different kinds; *honderderlei*, *duizenderlei*, etc.

> OBS.—Since the endings *lei* and *hande* mean "kind" or "sort," it is obviously incorrect to speak of *velerlei soorten* (literally many kinds of kinds). Every grammar warns against this pleonasm, but colloquial language defies grammar in not only sometimes adding the word *soort* to a *soortgetal*, but even making it a rule to do so.

XIV. There are also a few Adverbs derived from Cardinal Numbers by means of the endings *maal*, *werf*, and *keer*, all meaning "time" or "turn." In Dutch they are called *Herhalingsgetallen*; in English, Adverbs of Number: *driemaal*, *driewerf*, *driekeer*, three times; *eenmaal*, once, etc.

> NOTE 1.—*Maal* and *keer* are also used as Substantives: *Ik zie hem drie malen op één dag*, I see him three times in one day; *Ik heb hem voor den derden keer gewaarschuwd*, I have warned him for the third time.

> NOTE 2.—Like *maal* and *keer*, the word *reis* was formerly used to express time or turn. It is very seldom heard now but in one contraction, which the student must needs be acquainted with, viz., *ereis*, pronounced *erus*, a contraction of *een reis*, once. It is often heard in children's tales.

XV. "One and a half" is translated *anderhalf* (not, as in Cape Dutch, *een en een half*). The meaning of this is "one whole (not expressed) and the other half." In the same manner *derdehalf*, two and a half; *vierdehalf*, three and a half; *vijfdehalf*, four and a half; and *zesdehalf*, five and a half, are made use of, though seldom.

XVI. List of Cardinal and Ordinal Numbers.

CARDINALS.	MEANING.	ORDINALS.
één,	one,	de of het eerste.
twee,	two,	,, ,, tweede.
drie,	three,	,, ,, derde.
vier,	four,	,, ,, vierde.
vijf,	five,	,, ,, vijfde.
zes,	six,	,, ,, zesde.
zeven,	seven,	,, ,, zevende.
acht,	eight,	,, ,, achtste.
negen,	nine,	,, ,, negende.
tien,	ten,	,, ,, tiende.
elf,	eleven,	,, ,, elfde.
twaalf,	twelve,	,, ,, twaalfde.
dertien,	thirteen,	,, ,, dertiende.
veertien,	fourteen,	,, ,, veertiende.
vijftien,	fifteen,	,, ,, vijftiende.
zestien,	sixteen,	,, ,, zestiende.
zeventien,	seventeen,	,, ,, zeventiende.
achttien,	eighteen,	,, ,, achttiende.
negentien,	nineteen,	,, ,, negentiende.
twintig,	twenty,	,, ,, twintigste.
een en twintig,	twenty-one,	,, ,, een en twintigste.
twee en twintig,	twenty-two,	,, ,, twee en twintigste.
drie en twintig,	twenty-three,	,, ,, drie en twintigste.
dertig,	thirty,	,, ,, dertigste.
veertig,	forty,	,, ,, veertigste.
vijftig,	fifty,	,, ,, vijftigste.
zestig,	sixty,	,, ,, zestigste.
zeventig,	seventy,	,, ,, zeventigste.
tachtig,	eighty,	,, ,, tachtigste.
negentig,	ninety,	,, ,, negentigste.
honderd,	a hundred,	,, ,, honderdste.
honderd een,	a hundred and one,	,, ,, honderd en eerste.
honderd twee,	a hundred and two,	,, ,, honderd en tweede.
honderd tien,	a hundred and ten,	,, ,, honderd en tiende.
twee honderd,	two hundred,	,, ,, twee honderdste.
twee honderd een,	two hundred and one,	,, ,, tweehonderd en eerste.
twee honderd tien,	two hundred and ten,	,, ,, tweehonderd en tiende.
drie honderd,	three hundred,	,, ,, driehonderdste.
vier honderd,	four hundred,	,, ,, vierhonderdste.

CARDINALS.	MEANING.	ORDINALS.
duizend,	a thousand,	de or het duizendste.
duizend en een,	a thousand and one,	,, ,, duizend en eerste.
duizend en twee,	a thousand and two,	,, ,, duizend en tweede.
duizend en tien,	a thousand and ten,	,, ,, duizende en tiende.
duizend één honderd,	one thousand one hundred,	,, ,, duizend één honderdste.
twee duizend,	two thousand,	,, ,, twee duizendste.
tien duizend,	ten thousand,	,, ,, tien duizendste.
een millioen,	a million,	,, ,, millioenste.

NOTE 1.—*Millioen* is a noun of the neuter gender: *een millioen sterren*, a million of stars.

NOTE 2.—Be careful not to write *achttien* with one *t*. Its composition demands a double *t*.

NOTE 3.—Mark *acht, achttien,* and *tachtig*. The *t* in this latter word is prefixed.

NOTE 4.—A (or one) hundred, and a (or one) thousand should simply be translated *honderd* (not *een honderd*), and *duizend* (not *een duizend*).

NOTE 5.—In summing up, translate first, second, third, fourth, fifth, sixth, etc., only by *ten eerste, ten tweede, ten derde, ten vierde, ten vijfde, ten zesde*.
The Cape custom of writing *eerstens, tweedens, derdens, vierdens,* etc., is a Germanism, and not to be encouraged.

EXERCISE XLI.

(On Writing out Numbers.)

Write out in words the numbers given below, noticing specially the following points:

Unlike the English:
(a) *Vijf honderd twee; drie honderd twintig* = five hundred and two; three hundred and twenty.
(b) *Vijf en twintig* = twenty-five.
(c) *Duizend* = one thousand; *honderd* = one hundred.

Like the English:
(a) *Duizend en één, duizend en twintig* = a thousand and one, a thousand and twenty,

(b) *De honderd en eerste, de honderd en twintigste* = the one hundred and first, the one hundred and twentieth.
(c) *Een millioen en één* = a million and one.

5340; 3003; 525; 1,000,001; 720,540; 4400; 505; 8808; 7,070,070; 6,006,006; 9,900,099; 1,001,100.

Write out the Ordinal forms of the Cardinal Numbers above.

TRANSLATION EXERCISES.—*Vertaaloefeningen.*

Exercise XLII.

Some ten of our young rose-trees are frostbitten (*doodgerijpt*). Give the child some hot milk to drink. The battle of Waterloo was fought on the eighteenth of June, eighteen hundred and fifteen. A party of twenty young men went up the mountain together. Some few sheep among the lot were poor, but all the rest were in splendid condition (*zagen er bijzonder goed uit*). I would like to give this poor boy some reward for his honesty. The merchant showed me a few samples [of] Java coffee, the best of which (*waarvan*) is (*wordt*) sold at (*voor*) eighteen pence a (the) pound. After we had spent about a fortnight at (*aan*) the strand, my mother was taken (became) so ill that all of us had to (must) return home (*naar huis*). I did not have any mistakes in my dictation to-day. The last house in the street is my brother's (that of—). There are two kinds of seed in this bag. This man has received a fourfold reward.

Exercise XLIII.

This parcel weighs a pound and a half. The child has been punished twice to-day. There are various kinds of books in our school library. The painter painted the wall three times. For some reason or other the child had not done her work. May I give you some of this meat? Yes, thank you (if you please = *als 't u belieft*). In less than ten minutes there were hundreds [of] people on the scene of the fire. What day of the month was (it) yesterday? It was the twenty-fifth. The letter was dated: Rotterdam, June 22nd, 1894. Are there any children that have got no pens? Some of the fowls had their wings clipped (*werden gekortwiekt*). Some of the sugar (which) we have had from that shop has been very bad. I gave the child some cake and sent her home. Some advise me to go by rail (*per spoor*), others to take the steamer, and being a stranger (as I am —) I do not know what will be best.

Exercise XLIV.

Sixth Rule of Construction.—If a negative sentence contains an object, whether direct or indirect, the adverb "*niet*" is placed after such object. For the rest the position of "*niet*" in negative sentences does not materially differ in Dutch from the one it holds in English, and is scarcely definable by rules.

Did he not tell you a story? He did not take the money from my eldest brother. We did not play in the garden, but in the dining-room. Lions do not live longer than elephants. When we travel in the mountains, we do not sleep in tents, but in caves. Did the medicine cure your poor mother? Did the children learn all their lessons in an hour and a half? Did he have any stories to tell? He told (*er*) some (*een paar*) but not many. Did you not ask him to weigh the meat? The boys did not play (with) marbles, when they were in the field. Did not your grandfather live till (*tot*) the house was built? The teachers did not praise the children when they had done (*gedaan*) their work, but they punished them whenever it was not done. I should not have taken the books, if I had not asked him. The dogs would not have barked at (*tegen*) the boys, if they had not played in the street.

Exercise XLV.

TRANSLATION OF PRESENT PARTICIPLE. II.—Present Participles (see Ex. XXVIII., p. 96) are secondly translated by means of the conjunction "*terwijl*" while:—Take care, she said, laying her hand on his shoulder, *pas op, zei zij, terwijl zij hare hand op zijnen schouder legde.* (See p. 175, Obs. 3, c.)

Do not make a mistake in telling him (while you tell him) the story. The dog barked at (*tegen*) me, showing (while he showed) (*liet zien*) his teeth in between (*tusschen in*). Asking the shop-keeper to show him some boots, he stole the laces. Dividing the apples amongst (*onder*) her children, the mother lost (*er*) one. She walked ₂up and down ₁her room, learning her lesson. Coming up to me (*naar mij toe*), the stranger handed me this letter. Reading over the sentence, I discovered my mistake. Playing with the hatchet, the little boy hurt his hand. Looking for shells on the beach, I found this pretty gold ring. Oh, my brother, she cried (*riep*) (she), running towards him and embracing him. Taking up her bundle of sticks, the old woman walked off.

Exercise XLVI.

An Irishman was in (had once) want of money. He thought he would go [and] steal. Looking about in his house, he found an old rusty pistol. He took the weapon and went to a spot where (the) farmers used to (*plachten*) pass on [their] way (*naar*) home from (the) market. Placing himself behind a large tree, he waited (transl. he placed . . . and waited) till someone came past. After half an hour a cart appeared, in which [there] sat an old farmer. The thief jumped [from] out his hiding-place (*te voorschijn*), and made for (ran towards) the horse. Grasping the reins, he levelled the pistol at the farmer's head, and cried, "Your money or your life!" The farmer replied, "Do not kill me; let us rather make an agreement. I give you my money, and you give me that pistol." Hereupon the thief handed over his weapon, and the farmer handed over his purse. The thief ran off with his prize, but the farmer jumped down from his cart and ran after him (*hem achterna*). He soon overtook him, and seizing him by his collar, exclaimed (he), "Now my money, or your life!" "Oh," cried the Irishman, "shoot away (*schiet maar toe*), there is no powder in my pistol!"

Conversatie.
Familiebetrekkingen.

1. *Deze oude heer is het hoofd der familie.*
2. *Leven uwe ouders nog?*
3. *Mijn vader leeft nog, maar mijne moeder is reeds eenige jaren dood.*
4. *Heeft u veel familiebetrekkingen?*
5. *Zeer weinig nabestaanden.*
6. *Ik heb een oom in Amerika en verscheidene neven in Indië.*
7. *Hoe is die jonge man aan u verwant?*
8. *Hij is mijn neef, en dit jonge meisje is mijne nicht.*
9. *Mijne tante en nichten komen vandaag.*
10. *Onze dochter en schoonzoon zijn gisteren aangekomen.*
11. *Mijn oom schrijft iedere week aan zijne kinderen.*
12. *Mijn schoonvader gaf mij dit boek, en mijne schoonmoeder zond mij een horloge.*
13. *Wanneer zullen mijnheer M. en mejuffrouw K. trouwen.*

Conversation.
Relations.

1. This old gentleman is head of the family.
2. Are your parents still living?
3. My father is living, but my mother died some years ago.
4. Have you many relations?
5. Very few near relatives.
6. I have an uncle in America and several cousins in India.
7. How is that young man related to you?
8. He is my nephew and this young girl is my niece.
9. My aunt and cousins come to-day.
10. Our daughter and son-in-law arrived yesterday.
11. My uncle writes to his children every week.
12. My father-in-law gave me this book, and my mother-in-law sent me a watch.
13. When are Mr. M. and Miss K. to be married?

14. De geboden zijn verleden Zondag afgelezen.
15. Hare grootouders hebben kostbare geschenken gezonden.
16. Mijne overgrootouders leven nog.
17. Is die heer familie van u?
18. Hij is een verre bloedverwant van mij.
19. Met wien is uwe tante getrouwd?
20. Met kapitein Innes, haar achterneef.
21. Is u op de bruiloft geweest?
22. Neen, maar mijn schoonzuster is er geweest.
23. Zij zal eene uitstekende vrouw zijn.
24. Mijne broeders en zusters zijn allen getrouwd, en wonen in Londen.
25. Hebben zij kinderen?
26. Mijn oudste broeder heeft vijf zoons en twee tweelingdochters.
27. Mijne moeder houdt heel veel van hare kleinkinderen.
28. Is mijnheer H. weduwnaar?
29. Ja, zijne vrouw is verleden jaar gestorven, en heeft een dochtertje van vier jaar en een kindje van pas een paar maanden nagelaten.

14. The banns were published last Sunday.
15. Her grandfather and grandmother have sent valuable presents.
16. My great-grandparents are still living.
17. Is that gentleman a relation of yours?
18. He is distantly related to me.
19. Whom has your aunt married?
20. Captain Innes, her second cousin.
21. Were you at the wedding?
22. No, but my sister-in-law was there.
23. She will make an excellent wife.
24. My brothers and sisters are all married and live in London.
25. Have they any children?
26. My eldest brother has five sons and two twin daughters.
27. My mother is very fond of her grand-children.
28. Is Mr. H. a widower?
29. Yes, his wife died last year, and left one little girl of four years and a baby of only a few months old.

CHAPTER VIII.

THE PRONOUN.

(*Het Voornaamwoord.*)

I. A PRONOUN, *Voornaamwoord*, as the name indicates, stands for a noun, that is, takes the place of a noun.

II. The kinds of Pronouns are—

Persoonlijke (Personal).
Betrekkelijke (Relative).
Vragende (Interrogative).
Onbepaalde (Indefinite).
Bepaling aankondigende (Correlative).
Aanwijzende (Demonstrative).
Bezittelijke (Possessive).

III. PERSONAL PRONOUNS. The Personal Pronouns are—

1st Person.		2nd Person.	
Singular.	Plural.	Singular.	Plural.
Ik, I.	*Wij*, we.	*Gij, jij*, thou.	*Gij, jullie*, you.

3rd Person.

Singular.	Plural.
Hij, zij, het, he, she, it.	*Zij*, they.

IV. The pronouns of the first and second persons have no distinction of gender, but those of the third person have. Their declension is accordingly as follows:

PERSOON.	GESLACHT.	ENKELVOUD.	MEERVOUD.
Eerste	{ Mann., Vr. or Onz.	1 nv. I, *ik*.	We, *wij*.
		2 nv. Mine, *mijner*, *mijn*.	Ours, *onzer, ons*.
		3 nv. Me, *mij, me*.	Us, *ons*.
		4 nv. Me, *mij, me*,	Us, *ons*.

Persoon.	Geslacht.	Enkelvoud.	Meervoud.
Tweede.	Mann., Vr. or Onz.	1 nv. Thou, *gij, ge; jij, je*.	You, *gij, ge; jullie*.
		2 nv. Thine, *uwer, uw; van jou*.	Yours, *uwer-van jullie*.
		3 nv. Thee, *u; jou, je*.	You, *u; jullie*.
		4 nv. Thee, *u; jou, je*.	You, *u; jullie*.
Derde.	Mannelijk.	1 nv. He, *hij*.	They, *zij, ze*.
		2 nv. His, *zijner, zijn*.	Theirs, *hunner, hun*.
		3 nv. Him, *hem*.	Them, *hun, ze*.
		4 nv. Him, *hem*.	Them, *hen, ze*.
Derde.	Vrouwelijk.	1 nv. She, *zij, ze*.	Like the Singular.
		2 nv. Hers, *harer, haar*.	
		3 nv. Her, *haar, ze*.	
		4 nv. Her, *haar, ze*.	
Derde.	Onzijdig.	1 nv. It, *het*.	Like the Masculine Plural.
		2 nv. Its, *zijns, zijn*.	
		3 nv. It, *het*.	
		4 nv. It, *het*.	

Obs. 1.—The old form of the 2nd Person Singular, *du* (thou), possessive case *dijn* (thine), is obsolete. The apparent difficulty resulting therefrom has been hinted at before. The following rules should be adopted:—

(*a*) In books, correspondence, and public speaking use *gij*, or *ge*, singular and plural, with verb in 2nd person;

(*b*) In polite speaking use *u*, singular and plural, with verb in 3rd person (sometimes the 2nd).

(*c*) In familiar talk to children, brothers, sisters, and close friends, use *je* (with emphasis *jij*) singular, and *jullie* plural, with verb in 2nd person. (See p. 65.)

Obs. 2.—*Ik* is usually pronounced *'k*, and often written so. *Hij* is often pronounced *i*, especially after words ending in *t*, but in writing remains *hij*. *Ge, je*, and *we* are soft forms for *gij, jij*, and *wij*, and are very commonly used, both in speaking and writing, when no emphasis is required.

Obs. 3.—Personal Pronouns agree with the natural and not with the grammatical gender of the nouns to which they refer: *Dat meisje heeft haar* (not *zijn*) *boek verloren*, that girl has lost her book.

Obs. 4.—Personal Pronouns also agree in number with the nouns for which they stand, and this is the case even with collective nouns : *Toen de menigte dit hoorde, ging zij* (singular) *uiteen,* when the crowd heard this, they dispersed.

Obs. 5.—*Elkander* or *elkaar, mekander* or *mekaar,* meaning "each other" or "one another," are called Reciprocal Pronouns, *wederkeerige persoonlijke voornaamwoorden,* because their meaning indicates that the action of the verb with which they stand passes continually from one person to another : *Zij slaan elkander,* they beat each other; *Zij bedriegen elkander,* they deceive one another.

Note.—When used as above, these pronouns have neither nominative nor possessive case. They may, however, be used as adjective pronouns indicating possession, in which case they take a genitive form : *Wij verheugen ons in elkanders gezelschap,* we are glad of each other's company.

Obs. 6.—*Zich,* one's self, is the Reflexive Pronoun, *terugwerkend voornaamwoord,* of the 3rd person, masculine, feminine, and neuter, only used in the 3rd and 4th cases, while for the Reflexive Pronouns of the 1st and 2nd persons the objective cases of these pronouns are used.

Examples:

Ik . .		. . *mij,* I myself.
Gij . .		. . *u,* you yourself.
Hij . .	With verb in between.	. . *zich,* he himself.
Zij . .		. . *zich,* she herself.
Het . .		. . *zich,* it itself.
Men .		. . *zich,* one oneself.
Wij. .		. . *ons,* we ourselves.
Gij . .		. . *u,* you yourselves.
Zij . .		. . *zich,* they themselves.

Note 1.—Notice particularly that "I myself" is translated by *ik zelf,* and not *ik mijzelf,* e.g. I go myself, *ik ga zelf;* She will do it herself, *zij zal het zelve doen.* The addition of the pronoun *zelf* serves only to accentuate the meaning, so that in the use of reflexive verbs it should only be added where emphasis is required. "Must I go and wash myself?" should therefore be rendered, *Moet ik mij gaan wasschen ?* unless there is question of 'not washing some one else,' in which case alone it should be : *Moet ik mijzelf gaan wasschen ?*

Note 2.—When the reflexive pronoun forms the preposition-object of the verb, the Dutch expression corresponds with the English one :

He said to himself, *hij zeide bij zichzelf;*
I thought to myself, *ik dacht bij mijzelf.*

Obs. 7.—Declension of the Personal Pronoun with the word "*zelf*":

    Mannelijk.   *Vrouwelijk.*

1 nv. *Ik, gij, hij zelf*, I myself, etc.   *Ik, gij, zij zelve.*
2 nv. *Van mijzelven*, or *mijzelf*, etc.   *Van mijzelve*, etc.
3 nv. *Mijzelven, uzelven, hemzelven,*   *Mijzelve, uzelve, haarzelve.*
      or   or   or
4 nv. *Mijzelf,*   *uzelf,*   *hemzelf.*   *Mijzelve, uzelve, haarzelve.*

          Onzijdig.

1 nv. *Ik, gij, hetzelf.*
2 nv. *Van mijzelf, van hetzelf*, etc.
3 nv. *Mijzelven, uzelven, hetzelf.*
       or   or   or
4 nv. *Mijzelf,*   *uzelf,*   *hetzelf.*

    Meervoud voor de drie Geslachten.

1 nv. *Wij, gij, zijzelven* (of persons)—*zijzelve* (of things).
2 nv. *Van onszelven*, etc.
3 nv. *Ons, u, hunzelven,*   „   „
4 nv. *Ons, u, henzelven,*   „   „   —*zezelve.*

Not only personal pronouns, but also nouns may take this word *zelf* to render their meaning more emphatic:

    Mannelijk.   *Vrouwelijk.*   *Onzijdig.*

1 nv. *De broeder zelf,*   *De zuster zelve,*   *Het kind zelf.*
2 nv. *Des broeders zelven,*   *Der zuster zelve,*   *Des kinds zelven.*
3 nv. *Den broeder zelven,*   *Der (of de) zuster*   *Het kind zelf.*
       or   *zelve.*
4 nv. *Den broeder zelf.*   *De zuster zelve.*   *Het kind zelf.*

    Meervoud voor de drie Geslachten.

1 nv. *De broeders, zusters, kinderen zelven,*   *zelve.*
2 nv. *Der broeders, zusters, kinderen zelven,*   for things   *zelve,*
3 nv. *Den broeders, zusters, kinderen zelven,*   *zelven,*
4 nv. *De broeders, zusters, kinderen zelven,*   *zelve.*

Note.—Mark the difference between this word and the word *zelfs*, meaning "even," which is often confused with it.

Obs. 8.—The Possessive case of personal pronouns is now rarely used, but is met with in some time-established expressions (*geijkte termen*), such as: *gedenk mijner*, think of me; *erbarm u zijner*, have pity on him; *de meesten hunner*, most of them; *velen uwer, weinigen uwer*, many of you, few of you.

Sometimes the Possessive case of personal pronouns is found compounded with another word, so as to form an Adverbial phrase: *Ik doe het uwentwege, om uwentwil, uwenthalve*, I do it for your sake. The *t* in these compositions is inserted for the sake of facilitating pronunciation.

NOTE.—Write: *Ik ben u beider vriend*, I am a friend of both of you, (not—**uwer** *beider vriend*, nor—**uw** *beider vriend*): *Hun aller broeder*, a brother of them all (not: **hunner** *aller broeder*).

NOTE 2.—The English double possessive is not used in Dutch. "A friend of mine" is translated *een vriend van mij*, or *een mijner vrienden*.

"At my aunt's" should be rendered: *bij mijne tante aan huis*.

V. POSSESSIVE PRONOUNS, *Bezittelijke Voornaamwoorden.*— For the possessive case of personal pronouns, two different forms have been given (see IV). The second of those forms is that of the possessive pronoun, with a slight modification in the ending of *ons* (1st pers. plur.). Hence we have:

Possessive Pronoun of the First Person before a—

	Masc. N.	Fem. N.	Neut. N.
Singular (of *ik*)	mijn,	mijne,	mijn.
Plural (of *wij*)	onze,	onze,	ons.

Possessive Pronoun of the Second Person:

Singular (of *gij*)	uw,	uwe,	uw.
Singular (of *gij*)	uw,	uwe,	uw.
Plural (of *jij*)	jouw,	jouwe,	jouw.
Plural (of *jullie*)	jullie,	jullie,	jullie.

Possessive Pronoun of the third Person, Masc. and Neut.:

Singular (of *hij* and *het*)	zijn,	zijne,	zijn.
Plural (of *zij*)	hun,	hunne,	hun.

Possessive Pronoun of the third Person, Fem.:

Singular (of *zij*)	haar,	hare,	haar.
Plural (of *zij*)	haar,	hare,	haar.

NOTE 1.—For the declension of the possessive pronouns, see p. 78, and following.

NOTE 2.—The possessive pronouns may be used as nouns, and then follow the weak declension (see pp. 85, 86.) When so used they take the definite article: *de mijne*, mine; *de uwe*, yours; *de zijne*, his.

OBS. 1.—Possessive Pronouns may be used as adverbial phrases of place in connection with the preposition *te* (*ten*): *Zal ik u ten mijnent of ten uwent ontmoeten?* shall I meet you at my house or at yours?

NOTE.—Considering that the preposition here mentioned is a contraction of *te den*, and that this *den* is the old 3rd case, neut. gend., of the definite article, it is obvious that in expressions like the above the possessive pronouns were once used as nouns of the neuter gender. These expressions are not used in colloquial language.

OBS. 2.—Possessive Pronouns referring to more than one person, must be in the plural: *Mijn broeder en mijne zuster doen hun jaarlijksch reisje*, my brother and sister are making their yearly trip; *Gij en ik hebben ons werk klaar*, you and I have finished our work. *Gij en hij hebt beiden uw zin*, you and he have both what you wanted.

It will be seen from these examples that in such cases the 1st person is preferred before the 2nd, and the 2nd before the 3rd; likewise the masculine gender over the feminine.

VI. INTERROGATIVE PRONOUNS, *Vragende Voornaamwoorden.*—These are: *wie, wat, welk, hoedanig een, wat voor een.*

Wie, who, enquires after persons;

Wat, what, enquires after things;

Welk, translates 'which' in the expression "which of";

Welk, which, or what, is an Adjective Pronoun enquiring into the nature of its noun;

Hoedanig een, (plur. *hoedanige*) and *wat voor een* (plur. *wat voor*) translate "what kind of," "what sort of."

EXAMPLES:

Wie is daar? who is there?

Wat valt daar? what falls there?

Welk van de boeken wil u hebben? which of the books will you have?

Welke boomen worden omgehakt? which trees are being cut down?

Wat voor een (hoedanig een) mensch is hij? what kind of a man is he?

OBS. 1.—DECLENSION OF INTERROGATIVE PRONOUNS:—

MANNELIJK.	VROUWELIJK.	ONZIJDIG.	MEERVOUD DER DRIE GESLACHTEN
Enkelvoud.	*Enkelvoud.*	*Enkelvoud.*	
1 nv. *wie,*	*wie,*	*wat,*	*wie.*
2 nv. *wiens, van wien,*	*van wie,*	*waarvan,*	*wier, van wie.*
3 nv. *wien,*	*aan wie,*	*waaraan,*	*wien.*
4 nv. *wien,*	*wie,*	*wat,*	*wie.*
1 nv. *welke, welk,*	*welke,*	*welk,*	*welke.*
2 nv. *van welken,*	*van welke,*	*van welk,*	*van welke.*
3 nv. *welken,*	*welke, aan welke,*	*welk,*	*welken.*
4 nv. *welken,*	*welke,*	*welk,*	*welke.*

MANNELIJK.

Enkelvoud.	*Meervoud.*
1 nv. *wat voor een man,*	1 nv. *wat voor mannen.*
2 nv. *van wat voor eenen man,*	2 nv. *van wat voor mannen.*
3 nv. *aan wat voor cenen man,*	3 nv. *aan wat voor mannen.*
4 nv. *wat voor eenen man,*	4 nv. *wat voor mannen.*

OBS. 2.—Notice that *het* (Pers.), *dit* and *dat* (Demon.), and *wat* (Interr.) can never be used after Prepositions. New compositions are therefore formed as follows :

With *het*, the word becomes *er* and the Preposition annexed: *erin, eruit,* etc.
With *dit*, the word becomes *hier* and the Preposition annexed: *hierin, hieruit,* etc.
Likewise those with *dat* become *daarin, daaruit,* etc.
And those with *wat* become *waarin, waaruit,* etc.

Whenever things, and even animals, are referred to, these compound forms are used rather than the separate pronouns, as : *Het paard, waarover,* etc. (not *over hetwelk*) *ik sprak,* the horse of which I spoke; *De bloemen, waarvan* (not *van welke*) *ik zooveel houd,* the flowers, of which I am so fond.

VI. INDEFINITE PRONOUNS, *Onbepaalde Voornamwoorden.*— Indefinite Pronouns give a name to what is either unknown or too little defined to receive any special name. They refer to persons as well as to things, to names of objects as well as to names of materials. Most of them stand alone, and one requires a noun after it. To the former belong: *men*, one, *iemand*, somebody, *niemand*, nobody, *sommigen*, some people, *iets*, anything, *niets*, nothing, *een*, one, someone, *geen*, no one, *alwie*, any one, and, *alwat*, anything;—the latter is *zeker*, a certain. Notice also the following:

Deze en gene, one and another (some people);
Deze of gene, some one or other;
De een of ander, some one or other;
De een of de ander, one or the other;
Het een of ander, something or other;
Het een of het ander, (the) one thing or the other (another);
Het een en ander, some things.

In the following examples, the different translations of "*men*" should be specially noticed:

Men moet daar altijd lang wachten, one has always to wait a long time there;
Men moet oppassen voor natte voeten, you should beware of damp feet;
Men spreekt gewoonlijk te veel, people usually speak too much;
Men zegt wel eens, dat oorlog goed is, they say sometimes that war is a good thing;
Men heeft mij tweemaal bedrogen, I have been twice deceived;
Men zegt, it is said.

Obs. 1.—The pronoun "*men*" can only be used in the nom. case, and is consequently the subject of the sentence in which it is found. Being a pronoun of the 3rd person, the Possessive and Reflexive Pronouns referring to it must be those of the same person, as:

Door zich te veel aan koude en nattigheid bloot te stellen, benadeelt men zijne gezondheid, by exposing oneself too much to cold and damp weather, one injures one's health.

OBS. 2.—Notice that the pronoun *one*, occurring after an adjective, is not translated:

I have a dog, and a good one, *ik heb een hond, en een goeden ;*
Here are two books, both new ones, *hier zijn twee boeken, beide nieuw.*

OBS. 3.—"Whoever" and "whatever" are translated by *wie ook* and *wat ook*, likewise "which(so)ever" by *welke ook*, "how(so)ever" by *hoe ook*, and "where(so)ever" by *waar ook*, the place of the word "*ook*" being after the subject and object of the sentence:

Wat hij ook doet, whatever he does ;
Wie hem dat ook zegt, whoever tells him that.

OBS. 4.—The Indefinite Pronouns *iemand, niemand, iets, niets,* and *wat,* together with the Adjectives *weinig, veel, eenig, geen,* and *heel wat,* when followed by an adjective of quality, cause this adjective to end in *s* (genitive), as:

Iemand vreemds, any strangers ?
Niemand vreemds, no strangers ;
Iets goeds, anything good ?
Niets bijzonders, nothing particular ;
Weinig nieuws, little news ;
Veel kwaads, much evil ;
Eenig nieuws, anything new ?
Geen goeds, nothing good ;
Heel wat slechts, a good deal of bad (things).

VIII. CORRELATIVE PRONOUNS, *Bepaling aankondigende Voornaamwoorden,* which are distinguished from all other pronouns by the necessity of their being followed by a complement in the form of an Adjective Sentence, in order to render their meaning complete.

1. They are collected from among the Personal, Indefinite, and Demonstrative Pronouns, but applied to perform a distinctly different function.

Hij, die tevreden is, is gelukkig, he, who is content, is happy. Here the person represented by the pronoun *hij* only becomes known to the hearer, after the adjective sentence defining that person has been added. *Hij* is here no Personal, but a Correlative Pronoun.

THE PRONOUN.

The pronouns belonging to this class are: *hij, die, deze, dat, degene, hetgene, diegene, datgene, dezelfde, hetzelfde, zulken* and *zoodanigen* (the latter two are only used in the plural).

EXAMPLES:

Degenen, die schuldig bevonden werden, zijn allen gestraft, those that were found guilty, have all been punished.

Dezelfden, die we gisteren ontmoetten, zijn daareven voorbij gekomen, the same people whom we met yesterday, have just come past.

Laat degenen onder u, die zien willen, achter blijven, let those among you, who wish to see, stay behind.

Die kunnen allen rustig zijn, die er geen deel aan genomen hebben, all those may feel at ease, who have taken no part in it.

Dezen zijn het, die ons verleid hebben, these are they who have seduced us.

OBS.—Declension of the pronouns *degene* and *dezelfde*:

ENKELVOUD.

Mannelijk. *Vrouwelijk.*

1 nv. degene, dezelfde ; degene, dezelfde ;
2 nv. desgenen, deszelfden ; dergene, derzelfde ;
3 nv. dengene, denzelfde ; dergene, derzelfde ;
4 nv. dengene, denzelfde ; degene, dezelfde ;

Onzijdig.

1 nv. hetgeen, hetzelfde.
2 nv. desgenen, deszelfden.
3 nv. hetgeen, hetzelfde.
4 nv. hetgeen, hetzelfde.

MEERVOUD voor de drie Geslachten.

1 nv. degenen, dezelfden.
2 nv. dergenen, derzelfden.
3 nv. dengenen, denzelfden.
4 nv. degenen, dezelfden.

NOTE.—*Degene* (sing. & plur.) is only used for persons. *Dezelfden* (plur.) loses its *n* when used for things.

IX. Demonstrative Pronouns, *Aanwijzende Voornaamwoorden.* These define the place of persons and objects spoken about, indicating whether the distance between them and the speaker is greater or smaller. They are: *deze,* (neut.) *dit,* this; *die,* (neut.) *dat,* that; *gene,* (also) *gindsche,* (neut.) *gindsch,* yonder.

Obs. 1.—For the declension of these Pronouns, see pp. 78, 79.

Obs. 2.—In the Genitive singular, masculine and neuter of *die,* an *n* is inserted. This was formerly not the case, the 2nd case being *dies,* as may be seen from the expression "*wat dies meer zij*" (what there be more of it) for "et cetera."

Obs. 3.—There are other old forms of the second case singular of *die,* in the masculine and feminine, viz., *des* and *der,* which are now principally found in compound words: *een deskundige,* a person knowing about it (an expert); *desgelijks,* likewise; *deswege,* on account of; *desniettemin,* yet; *desniettegenstaande,* notwithstanding; *derhalve,* therefore; *dergelijke,* such.

Obs. 4.—Both of these forms (*des* and *der*) may occur as separate words: *Wij zijn des gewis,* we are certain of it; *Hoeveel uwer kinderen hebt gij verloren? Wij hebben er (der) reeds vier verloren,* How many of your children have you lost? We have already lost four (of them). This *er* (uneducated people will make it *der*) stands for a noun understood after a numeral adjective.

Note.—On the use of *er :*

Er (pronoun) takes the place of the logical subject in sentences which have an intransitive verb, thereby rendering such sentences more fluent: *Er gebeurde heel wat dien avond,* many things happened that evening.

It occurs before numerals, when the noun by which they should be followed is understood: *Heeft u veel boeken? Ik heb er tien.* Have you many books? I have ten (books).

As an adverb of place, it is the translation of Eng. "there" : *Is u in de kerk geweest? Ja, ik ben er geweest.* Have you been in church? Yes, I have been there. When emphasis is necessary, this "there" is translated by *daar.*

Er is used in the verb *er uitzien,* to look, and in expressions like the following :

Er is mij gezegd, I have been told ;
Er wordt geschoten, there is shooting going on ;
Er wordt daar goed gewerkt, there is some good work done there.

OBS. 5.—The 2nd case of *deze* occurs in two expressions: *schrijver dezes*, the author (of this); *brenger dezes*, the bearer (of this).

OBS. 6.—The 'old 3rd case of *die* and *deze*, neuter gender (*i.e.*, of *dat* and *dit*) is found before many nouns of the neuter gender governed by those prepositions which in old Dutch required the dative: *te dien opzichte*, in that respect; *van dezen huize*, of this family; *te dien einde*, to that end (for that reason); *uit dien hoofde*, on that account.

OBS. 7.—The dative case of *die* and *deze*, feminine gender, is found in: *te dier (dezer) ure*, at that (this) time; *in dier voege*, after that fashion.

OBS. 8.—Whenever the demonstrative pronouns and the personal pronoun of the 3rd person, used as such, are not immediately followed by their noun, but separated from it by one of the Copulative Verbs (*zijn, worden, heeten, blijven, schijnen, lijken, blijken*), they take the form of the neuter gender singular, irrespective of the gender and number of the noun they point out: That was a pleasant meeting, *dat* (not) *die*) *was eene aangename vergadering*; This is my own father, *dit* (not *die*) *is mijn eigen vader*; Those were hard words, *dat* (not *die*) *waren harde woorden*; They were bad trees, *het waren slechte boomen*.

This rule applies equally in the inverted construction: Are these all the books, *zijn dit* (not *deze*) *alle boeken ?*
The Cape language overlooks this important rule.

X. RELATIVE PRONOUNS, *Betrekkelijke Voornaamwoorden*.—Adjective sentences which define or extend the meaning of nouns or pronouns, are introduced by pronouns, which, because they refer to a noun or pronoun already mentioned in the principal sentence, are called Relative Pronouns.

They are: *wie, wat, welke, hetwelk*, and *hetgeen*.

OBS. 1.—Touching the declension of the relative pronouns, it must be remarked that none of them has its forms of declension complete, but that one helps to complete the cases of the other. The following is the declension:

ENKELVOUD.

Mannelijk.	*Vrouwelijk.*
1 nv. *die, welke,*	*die, welke.*
2 nv. *wiens,*	*wier, welker.*
3 nv. *wien, welken,*	(*aan wie, aan welke*).
4 nv. *dien (wien), welken,*	*die (wie), welke.*

Enkelvoud.	Meervoud.
Onzijdig.	*Voor alle Geslachten.*
1 nv. *dat, wat, hetwelk,*	*die, welke.*
2 nv. — *waarvan, welks,*	*wier, welker,*
3 nv. — *waaraan,*	*wien, welken.*
4 nv. *dat, wat, hetwelk,*	*die (wie), welke.*

Obs. 2.—*Die* and *welke* (neuter, *dat* and *hetwelk*) are used indiscriminately for persons and things, though *die* (*dat*) is most commonly used.

Wie is used to make up the missing case of *die*, and after prepositions.

Wie likewise translates "he who."

Wat is used as a relative after *alles* and *al*, and in compounds with prepositions (see p. 136, Obs. 2).

Wat also translates "what" (that which), which, however, may likewise be rendered by *hetgeen*.

The specific use of *hetgeen* is to translate the relative pronoun "which," referring back to a sentence, and not to a noun.

Notice the following examples:

1. *Hij, die dat gedaan heeft, is een kwade jongen,* he who has done this thing, is a bad boy.
2. *De boomen, welke in dat bosch groeien, zijn alle hoog,* the trees which grow in that forest, are all of them high.
3. *De man, wiens vrouw onlangs overleden is,* the man whose wife died a short while ago.
4. *Elk dier* (neut.) *welks hoeven gespleten zijn, herkauwt,* every animal whose hoofs are divided, ruminates.
5. *Dat is eene lamp* (fem.), *wier licht u de oogen bederven zal,* that is a lamp whose light will spoil your eyes.
6. *Toon mij den man, wien zij die beleediging hebben aangedaan,* show me the man, whom they have insulted in that manner.
7. *Mijne jongste zuster is het, aan wie ik dat geschenk gegeven heb,* it is my youngest sister, to whom I have given that present.
8. *Breng mij naar het plekje* (neut.) *waaraan zoovele herinneringen verbonden zijn,* take me to the spot, to which so many memories cling.
9. *Hier is de jongen, naar wien gij gevraagd hebt,* here is the boy for whom you have enquired.
10. *Zij is eene vrouw, die men vertrouwen kan,* she is a woman whom one can trust.
11. *Was het een oud schaap, dat* (*hetwelk*) *de slager vandaag geslacht heeft?* was it an old sheep the butcher killed to-day.
12. *Wie steelt, is een dief,* he who steals is a thief.
13. *Dit is alles* (or *al*) *wat ik te zeggen heb,* this is all I have to say.

14. *Denk aan de zaak, waarvan ik gesproken heb,* think of the matter I spoke of.
15. *Gij behoort niet te aarzelen om te zeggen wat (hetgeen) waar is,* you should not hesitate to say what (that which) is true.
16. *Zij zijn niet gekomen, hetgeen beteekent dat zij ziek zijn,* they have not come, which means that they must be ill.

> OBS. 3. Relative Pronouns must be used, whether expressed or not in English: This is the man he spoke of, *dit is de man, van wien hij sprak;* There stands the house I want, *daar staat het huis, dat ik hebben wil.*
>
> OBS. 4. The Relative Pronoun must agree with its antecedent both in number and gender (not in case). In number it always does agree, but with regard to gender, the Pronoun follows the natural and not the grammatical one: *Mijn arm nichtje, wier* (not *welks*) *arm gebroken is,* my poor little niece whose arm is broken.

GRAMMAR EXERCISES.—*Taaloefeningen.*

EXERCISE XLVII.

In the following sentences substitute pronouns of the third person for those of the first.

Toen ik jong was, nam mijn vader mij dikwijls mede, als hij uit rijden ging. In het gras onder het raam mijner kamer heb ik dezen steen gevonden. Waarom heb ik niet naar den raad mijner ouders geluisterd. Had ik het gedaan, dan bevond ik mij nu niet in deze moeielijkheid. Ik kan mij niet herinneren, dat ik dezen man ooit gezien heb. Ik ben mij niet bewust deze uitdrukking gebruikt te hebben. Ik maak mij zeer bekommerd over den toestand van mijnen vader. Ik heb mijne bezigheid verkocht en wil mijne laatste dagen nu stil op mijn landgoed gaan doorbrengen. Ik ben van morgen mijne plaats rondgereden om te zien, of mijne veewachters mijn bevel nagekomen zijn. Mijn vader antwoordde mij, dat ik mij niet verbeelden moest, dat ik mijzelf rechtvaardigen kon. Ik ben er van overtuigd, dat mijn vriend zich mijner ontfermen zal, als ik mij in mijnen nood tot hem wend.

Exercise XLVIII.

In the above change the pronouns of the first person singular into (1) the first person plural, and (2) the third person plural.

Exercise XLIX.

Fill up the blanks in the following exercise:

Zijn — al d- peer-, — u gekocht heeft? Met
Are those all the pears, which you bought have? With
— sprak u daareven? Met — heer,
whom spoke you just now? With the same gentleman,
over — wij deze- morgen spraken. — die
about whom we this morning were speaking. Those who
— werk (o) af hebben, kunnen heen gaan. Waar
their work finished have, can away go. Where
woont d- vrouw, — kind gisteren gestorven is?
lives the woman, whose child yesterday died has?
Er gaat een- lijst (v) rond voor d- man, —
There goes a subscription-list round for the man, whose
huis afgebrand is. Onthoud al — ik — gezegd
house burnt down is. Remember all that I you told
heb. Zijn — — kinderen — er vroeger zoo
have. Are those the same children that formerly so
gezond uitzagen? De knecht heeft — paard —
healthy looked? The servant has the horse whose
hoefijzer los is, naar d- hoefsmid gebracht. Zoover ik
shoe loose is, to the farrier taken. As far as I
— herinneren kan, gebeurde er die- avond
myself remember can, happened there that evening
niets bijzonder-. Weet gij nog — gij — geld (o)
nothing particular. Know you still whom you the money
gegeven hebt? De dame met — ik van avond zat
given have? The lady with whom I this evening sat
te praten, is de dochter van een oud vriend — —. Weet
talking, is the daughter of an old friend of mine. Know

THE PRONOUN.

gij — linnen gemaakt wordt? Ja, — onderwijzer
you of what linen made is? Yes, my teacher
heeft — — verteld. — is een — boeren, —
has it me told. This is one of the farmers, whose
landerijen door d— overstrooming verwoest zijn.
lands by the flood devastated have been.
— jonge man behoort tot — — onwillekeurig ver-
This young man belongs to those who involuntarily con-
trouwen inboezemen.
fidence inspire.

Exercise L.

Bij — lezing gaf — gehoor (o) door luid applaudiseeren
At the lecture gave the audience by loud applause
— tevredenheid te kennen. — twee honden hebben zoo
their satisfaction to know. Your two dogs have so
met — — gevochten, dat — bloed — langs —
with each other fought, that the blood (to) them along the
kop liep. — buur— doen niets ander— dan
head ran. My neighbours do nothing else but one
— goed— naam belasteren. Ik heb —jongen gezegd
another's reputation run down. I have the boy told
— te gaan wasschen. — honden zijn — —
himself to go (and) wash. What dogs are they about
— u spreekt? — zijn — — — wij van
which you speak? They are the same that we this
morgen gezien hebben. Gij en uw vader kunt morgen
morning seen have. You and your father can to-morrow
— geld komen halen. — der meisjes hebben
your money come (and) fetch. Which of the girls have
— les— gekend? Ik heb van deze— en gene—
their lessons known? I have from one and another
gehoord, dat er veel goed— van het nieuw— ministerie te
heard, that much good of the new ministry to (be)
verwachten is. — — zal gedaan moeten
expected is. Something or other will have to be

worden voor — arme vrouw — — omgekomen
done for this poor woman whose husband killed has
is bij — spoorweg ongeluk, — gisteren bericht
been in the railway accident, of which yesterday news
ontvangen is. — zaak- moesten in — raad
received has been. Such cases should in the council
liever met gesloten- deuren behandeld worden. — beid-
rather with closed doors discussed be. The parents
ouders zijn dood.
of both of them are dead.

Exercise LI.

Translate into English (no reference to vocabulary).

Hij heeft mij het een en ander gezegd.
Hij heeft mij een en ander laten zien.
Gij zult wel (you are sure to) *den een of ander vinden.*
Zal u niet het een of ander gebruiken (take)?
De een of de ander moet vertrekken.
Het een of het ander moet waar zijn.
Deze en gene heeft mij opgezocht (come to see. . . . . .)
Deze of gene zal zich wel over het kind ontfermen (to have pity on).
Er wordt in dit land veel gerookt (*rooken* = to smoke).
Men vermoedt (*vermoeden* = to suppose) *dat de man gek* (insane) *is.*
Deze koeien zien er beter uit dan de mijne.
Dergelijke zaken komen altijd aan het licht (to light).
Waaraan dacht u, toen ik u stoorde (disturbed)?
Een deskundige zou nooit zulk eenen raad gegeven hebben.
De beide meisjes zijn met hare gouvernante (governess) *gaan wandelen.*
Welken weg ik ook insloeg (turned into), *ik kon geenen uitweg* (way out) *vinden.*
Al wat mijn vriend onderneemt (undertakes), *gelukt hem* (he is successful in).

TRANSLATION EXERCISES.—*Vertaaloefeningen.*

EXERCISE LII.

This young girl has her hat full [of] fresh roses. Those that have told you so (*dit*), have misled you. These are the books which I returned to you last night. Which of the two sisters is to sing (*zal* . . .) to-night? What kind of a flower is this? It is a flower that grows wild (*in het wild*) in the Tulbagh (*Tulbagsche*) district, but of which I do not know the name. That must be the same gentleman I met at my uncle's this (*van*) morning. (About) what were these ladies talking [about]? They were talking about what had been discussed at the meeting. Those men are always sober and at their work, it is (*zijn*) such that never lack employment (*zonder werk zijn*). These pears are the same (which) I have had at Mrs. Johnson's (*bij Mevrouw J.*). We met an old friend of ours yesterday, and asked him to have dinner with us (*bij ons te komen dineeren*) this (*van*) evening. Some one or other must have used my scissors. Either the one or the other must go. Please, give bearer the parcel I left at your house (*bij u*). Your father and yourself have both been mistaken. If you will call this evening, I will tell you some things that will interest you.

EXERCISE LIII.

Being afraid (see Ex. XXVIII, p. 96) to be late (*te laat*) for breakfast, I dressed myself ₂in a quarter of an hour ₁this morning. Not having a nurse, my little nieces are accustomed to dress themselves. Being ashamed of his dirty hands, the boy would not come in. It is said that (*er*) a ₃railway accident (has) occurred in the Hex River Pass ₂early ₁this morning. Any one hearing (hears) my case will say that I am right (*gelijk heb*). Whoever comes this way (*hierheen*) must beware of the dogs; they are very fierce [ones]. Whatever you do, you will never get (*er toe krijgen*) that child to apologise (*excuus te vragen*). As long as one is not faultless oneself, one should (*behoorde*) not find fault with one's neighbour. How many fowls do you have? I have twenty-five, and some of them are very good [ones]. There was a good deal of heavy betting at the races yesterday. My vines look so sickly that I will have to (*moeten*) consult an expert about them. I myself told the man that unless he applied himself (*zich aanpakken*) better, I would dismiss him.

EXERCISE LIV.

"May" and "might" are translated by "*mogen*," and its past tense "*mocht*" when they imply **permission.**

You may come to me now, *U mag nu bij mij komen.*
You said, I might go with you, *U zeide, dat ik met u meegaan mocht.*

If they imply **possibility**, they are translated by "*kunnen*" and its past form "*zou kunnen (kon)*"; or by the colloquial phrases: "*het kan (zou kunnen) dat,*" it may (might be) that, especially to bring out the idea of **probability**, as:

He might have done the work, if etc., *hij had het werk kunnen doen (zou ... hebben kunnen doen) als*, etc.
He may come yet, *hij mag nog komen*, or *het mag zijn, dat hij nog komt.*
They might see you from there, *zij zouden u van daar kunnen zien.*
The rain may have come down, *het kan zijn dat de regen neergekomen is*, or *de regen mag neergekomen zijn.*

1. "Should" is translated by "*zou*" if futurity is implied.
2. "Should" „ „ „ "*zou*" if dependent on a condition.
3. "Should" „ „ „ "*behoorde*" or "*moest*" if equivalent to "ought to."
4. "Should" „ „ „ "*mocht*" (*had moeten*), if equivalent to "might."

1. I told him that I should go into town, *ik zeide hem, dat ik naar de stad zou gaan.*
2. I should go to see her, if she were at home, *ik zou haar gaan zien, als zij thuis was.*

THE PRONOUN. 149

3. You should have learned your lessons, *gij hadt uwe lessen moeten (behooren te) leeren.*
4. If you should meet the man, tell him, etc., *als gij den man ontmoeten mocht, zeg hem, enz.*

May I go out when my work is finished? I cannot give you permission, you should have asked your father, before he went out. The boy might finish his lessons in time, if he would only come in (*binnen*) earlier. My uncle told me this morning that I might buy that fine dog. That accident might have been prevented, if the driver had been more careful. I may have seen that man before, but I do not recollect his face. If there were a doctor at hand, the child's life might be saved. I was always of opinion that they might have shown that young man some kindness. These plants should be planted before the sun gets hot. Should you see my brother when he comes home, tell him we may (permission) go to the concert this evening. You might have saved yourself all this trouble if you had heeded your uncle's warnings. We should not have left our friend alone, if we had known he was in trouble. My aunt felt sure (*was er zeker van*) that I should not like those people (would not please me); she may have been right, at all events I am glad she told me I should not accept the situation. You should have taken better care of the little girl, could you not see she was ill? If Mr. B. should call while I am gone, ask him to wait till my return (I return), I shall not be long (be = *uitblijven*). These children should be (do) more careful [about] their work, every one of these words might have been translated correctly, if they had turned to the vocabulary (if they had looked them up in, etc.).

Exercise LV.

"Will" and "would" are frequently used in English by way of idiom. In sentences as "Boys will always do mischief," and "The bird would sometimes come and eat from her hand," the forms "will" and "would" express neither futurity, nor determination. When thus used, they are not translated, but the tenses of the principal Verbs, which they help to express, are used instead. "Boys will always do mischief," becomes, "Boys always do mischief," *jongens doen (maar) altijd kattenkwaad;* and "The bird would sometimes come and eat from her hand," *De vogel kwam somtijds uit hare hand eten.*

A little girl had a bird that she kept locked up (*opgesloten hield*) in a cage. Now and then, however, she would let it out. It would then fly about, and would sit on her shoulder. How is (*komt*) it, that this child will always take so much? The boy would say, Basket, Tiny (*naar je mand, Tiny*), and then the little lap-dog would steal away to her basket (with the) tail between her hind legs. This horse will always put his nose into one's (*iemands*) face, if one (*men*) goes near him. You may (*kunt*) do what you like, these children will always boast.

"Will" and "would," expressing wish, are translated by the verb *willen, wilde, gewild.*

Will you help me, Charles? Yes, certainly. He would (wanted to) say something, but he could (*kon*) not get it out. Will you come (*meekomen*) with me? This way (*kant*), please. The boy said (that) he would not do it. Did he say that he would not (*geene*) have [any] milk in his coffee? He said (that) he wanted (would) no sugar (have). Does he not want to (will) answer you, or can (*kan*) he not answer you? The girl said positively that she did not want to (would not) come. And what did you answer? I said "Very well (*heel goed*), if you do not want to (will not) come, you may (can) stay away."

"Will" and "would," expressing futurity or determination, are translated by the future tenses (Ind. and Subj.) of the verb, (see Conjugation).

He won't go, unless you speak to (*met*) him. The girl would have read it, if her eyes had been good. Will he meet you at the office? He would meet me, if he knew that I would be there. I shan't take the medicine, said the naughty boy.

Exercise LVI.

The conjunction "if," when equivalent to "whether," is translated by "*of*," and not by "*indien*" or "*als*."

Tell me, if you will write. He asked if his father would come. He doubted (*het*) whether it would not be in vain. If you have the courage for it (*er...toe*), it is still the question if you have the required ability. If a man should come with a revolver in his hand, would you open the door to (*voor*) him?

"As if" is rendered by "*als of*," or sometimes "*of*."

He looked as if he was hungry (had hunger). He spoke to me as if he were (was) my master. The lion licked Androcles' hands as if to thank him (as if he would thank him). The robber did as if he wanted to kill me. If you want the doctor to cure (that the doctor cures) you, you must not speak as if you were quite well. The boy knelt down, as if he were going to (would go) pray. The sun rose (*kwam op*) with such splendour, as if there had never been a storm. If the boy had not thrown (*gegooid*) the stone with so much force, as if he wanted to kill the pig, I should ask his father if he would not forgive him this time.

Exercise LVII.

The verb "to know" is translated by *weten* and *kennen*. *Weten* implies the being aware of a fact. *Kennen* implies acquaintance with, or knowledge as the result of learning.

Examples: I know when he came, *ik weet, wanneer hij kwam*.
He did not know, that I was ill, *hij wist niet, da ik ziek was*.
Do you know that man? *Kent gij dien man?*
I know my tables by heart, *ik ken mijne tafels van buiten*.

Whither I go, you know, and the way you know. We do ₂not ₁even know the man; how should we know his whereabouts (where he lives)? It is a thing (*iets*) (that) we all know, that winter is the cold, and summer the hot time of the year. When do you think you will know the result[s] of your examination? We shall know them in a fortnight, I believe. There is a difference between knowing (*te kennen*) the road, and knowing something about (*van*) the road. Have you learned your poetry, Charles? Yes, sir, but I cannot say that I know it. How long will it be before you know French, John? Oh, father, a long time yet. My teacher says I am beginning to know something about it, but that is not knowing it. Did your sister know that you were here? Whether you have heard it or not, you must know it. The soldiers knew that the enemy was behind the hill. Know yourself, I said to someone, but he could (*kon*) not, for he was nobody. To know oneself (*zich*) leads to great humility. If I had only (*maar*) known that you had done the work, I should (it) have let (*laten*) him know. I knew yesterday that he would not live. The last fortnight the boy has known all his lessons.

Exercise LVIII.

"Used to" followed by an Infinitive Verb, is either translated by "was (were) accustomed to," or by the Past Tense of the following verb, strengthened by an adverb of time.

Examples: The boy used to sit there, *de jongen was gewoon daar te zitten*, or, *de jongen zat gewoonlijk*, or *altijd*, or *dikwijls daar*.

The man always used to say that he was very poor. He used to go round to (*bij*) his friends, and tell them of his misery. We used to see him often, but he does not visit us any (*in het geheel niet*) more now. The old man used to tell me about this daughter, when I took (*deed*) a walk with him. When we were in Paris, we used to go to a concert nearly every night. If the boy were used to speak the truth, he would not have said this. Why not? Because this is decidedly a falsehood. And he knew that!

"To be used to" is translated by "*gewoon zijn aan*."

THE PRONOUN.

I am used to his bad temper. She is used to being ill (*aan ziek zijn*). Are you used to that kind of treatment? I have been used to hard words all my (my whole) life. The donkey is used to drawing (*het trekken van*) that heavy load. Poor beast! and to beating (*slaan*) too.

EXERCISE LIX.

SEVENTH RULE OF CONSTRUCTION.—Amongst the extensions of the predicate, that of time takes the first place in the sentence, as: I saw him with his sister in church yesterday, *ik zag hem gisteren met zijne zuster in de kerk*.

When you were in London yesterday you (have) missed Mr. Bran, did you not (*niet waar*)? Yes, I missed him, that is to (*wil*) say, I did not wait for him. I should have (*had...moeten*) seen him at (*aan*) his house last night, but I was afraid to go out in the cold so late. I received a letter from my father yesterday. Where is he now? He was at Paris two days ago, and must now be at Lyons according to (*naar*) what he writes. Has there been any (*nog een*) great war in Europe since the year eighteen hundred and seventy? No, there have been rumours of wars many times, but it has never come to an open breach of the peace. He was (*is*) born at Baarn, a village in the province [of] Utrecht, Holland, on the sixth of March, eighteen hundred and fifty one. At Smithfield in the Orange Free State, a rumbling noise underground frightened some of the inhabitants yesterday. There was (has been) an explosion in the mine last week, whereby twenty-six workmen lost their lives (*het leven*). It is not so easy to be faithful to one's (*zijnen*) duty, whatever (*wat ook*) happens, and at all times (*te allen tijde*).

CONVERSATIE.
Reizen op het Land en per Spoortrein.

1. Waar gaat gij heen?
2. Ik ben op reis naar Londen, Brussel en Venetië.
3. Wanneer vertrekt uwe zuster?
4. Zij vertrekt de volgende week naar Europa.
5. Op welke wijze reist zij?
6. Per trein van Port-Elizabeth naar Kaapstad, en van daar per boot.
7. Mijn vriend heeft per diligence gereisd.
8. Hij heeft plan te paard terug te komen.
9. Welken weg heeft hij genomen?
10. Na het tolhek te zijn doorgegaan, is hij rechts afgedraaid, en heeft den grooten weg naar Beaufort genomen.
11. Dat was een groote omweg.
12. Welken weg zal u nemen?
13. Ik zal den eersten weg aan de linkerhand nemen.
14. Hoe ver is het naar het spoorwegstation?
15. Een kwartier per tram.
16. Ik zal eene vigilante nemen.
17. Waar is uwe bagage?
18. Ik heb het grootste deel er van in het goederenkantoor gelaten.
19. Mijn handkoffertje is in de wagon.
20. Zal ik den portier vragen, uwe zware bagage per goederentrein te laten zenden?

CONVERSATION.
Travelling by Land and Railways.

1. Where are you going?
2. I am on my way to London, Brussels, and Venice.
3. When does your sister leave?
4. She departs for Europe next week.
5. How does she travel?
6. By rail from Port-Elizabeth to Cape-Town, and from there by steamer.
7. My friend has travelled by coach.
8. He intends returning on horse-back.
9. Which road did he take?
10. After passing the toll-gate, he turned to the right, and took the high-road to Beaufort.
11. That was a very round-about-way.
12. Which road will you take?
13. I shall take the first road to the left.
14. How far is it to the railway-station?
15. A quarter of an hour by tram.
16. I shall take a cab.
17. Where is your luggage?
18. I left most of it in the cloak-room.
19. My small portmanteau is in the carriage.
20. Shall I ask the porter to have your heavy luggage sent on by goods-train?

21. Neen, zie er naar, dat het in den goederenwagen komt, als 't u blieft.
22. Wenk even om eene vigilante.
23. Wat kost het van hier naar Woodstock?
24. Eene halve kroon de enkele rit.
25. Houdt deze trein op bij alle tusschenliggende stations?
26. Neen, het is de sneltrein van Londen naar Edenburg; hij houdt alleen bij de voornaamste stations op.
27. Houdt u van reizen per trein?
28. Ik verkies het boven diligence, kar of ossenwagen.
29. Heeft u uw kaartje?
30. Neen, ik wil er nu om gaan.
31. Geef mij één biljet eerste klasse, enkele reis naar Victoria-West.
32. De trein vertrekt om vier uur.
33. Geef mij retour tweede klasse naar Wellington.
34. Dat is een extra trein.

21. No, see it put in the van, please.
22. Just hail a cab.
23. What is the fare from here to Woodstock?
24. Single fare half-a-crown.
25. Does this train stop at all intermediate stations?
26. No, this is the express from London to Edinburgh; it only stops at the principal stations.
27. Do you like travelling by rail?
28. I prefer it to coach, cart, or bullock-waggon.
29. Have you got your ticket?
30. No, I'll go and get it now.
31. Give me one first-class single fare to Victoria-West.
32. The train starts at four o'clock.
33. Give me a return second-class to Wellington.
34. That is a special train.

CHAPTER IX.

THE VERB.

(*Het Werkwoord.*)

I. DEFINITION :—An action may be expressed in two different ways : 1. By a real Verb ; 2. By a Verbal Noun.

EXAMPLES :—

1. I saw the enemy besiege the fort, *ik zag den vijand de stad belegeren.*
2. I read about the siege of the city, *ik las over het beleg (de belegering, het belegeren) der stad.* The verbal Noun *belegeren* has the very same form as the Infinitive Present of the Verb *belegeren*. Hence the necessity arises of marking how the action is expressed, before a correct translation can be given.

II. STEM :—The Infinitive form of Dutch verbs ends in *en* (in six cases *n*). These six are the irregular monosyllabic verbs: *doen, gaan, slaan, staan, zien,* and *zijn.*

The stem of a verb is found by removing this ending *en*. To determine the stem is a matter of importance, as will be seen from the conjugation-form in the next paragraph. Many times the stem, so found, is different from what may be termed the working-stem, the latter receiving its shape (spelling) from pronunciation. To determine this spelling, the following rules should be observed.

1. Of the six monosyllabic verbs mentioned above, the stems are respectively *doe, ga, sla, sta, zie,* and *zij* (or *wees*).

2. If the ending *en* is preceded by a single consonant, before which there occurs a single vowel, this vowel is doubled so as to preserve its full sound: *huren*, stem *huur*, to hire.

3. If the ending *en* is preceded by a double consonant, the stem takes a single consonant: *straffen*, stem *straf*, to punish.

4. If the ending *en* is preceded by *v* or *z*, the stem takes *f* or *s : leven*, stem; *leef*, to live; *vreezen*, stem *vrees*, to fear.

NOTE.—This *f* of the stem changes back into the *v* of the Inf. form, and likewise *s* into *z*, whenever the stem takes one of the endings *e, et*, or *en* in the course of the conjugation, in which cases also the double vowel assumed under Rule 2, is changed back into the single one of the Infinitive.

III. CONJUGATION, WEAK AND STRONG:—Two different ways of conjugation are distinguished :

(a) The WEAK CONJUGATION, marked by
1. Unchanged vowel-sound throughout;
2. Formation of past tense by adding to the stem *te*, when the last letter of such stem is one of the sharp consonants *t, k, f, s, ch*, and *p* (all of which are found in the composition, *'t kofschip*), and *de* in all other cases;
3. Formation of the past participle by prefixing *ge* to the stem, and adding *t* or *d* to it according to the particulars of No. 2.

(b.) The STRONG CONJUGATION, marked by
1. Change of vowel-sound in Past Tense, or sometimes there and in Past Participle;
2. Formation of Past Participle by prefixing *ge* to the stem (original or modified), and adding *en*.

The full list of Strong Verbs is given on p. 191.

NOTE.—In (a) 2 and 3, the letters *f* and *s* of the working stems, which are *v* and *z* in the Infinitive forms, are followed by *de* and *d*, and not by *te* and *t*.

III. — A COMPLETE FORM OF CONJUGATION, *Vorm van Vervoeging*:

INDICATIVE MOOD. SUBJUNCTIVE MOOD.
(*Aantoonende Wijs.*) (*Aanvoegende Wijs.*)
Present Tense. Onvolmaakt Tegenwoordige Tijd.

1 p. stem.   1 p. (Inf. less final *n*).
2 „ — *t*.   2 „ („   „   „   )*t*.
3 „ — *t*.   3 „ („   „   „   ). .

1 „ — *en*.   1 „ (full Inf. form).
2 „ — *t*.   2 „ (like 2nd pers. sing.).
3 „ — *en*.   3 „ (like 1st pers. plur.).

OBS.—The 3rd pers. sing. pres. tense ends in *t* in every verb, the ending being *dt* when the verb-stem ends in *d*.

Perfect Tense. Volmaakt Tegenwoordige Tijd.

1 p. *heb*   or *ben* ⎫   1 p. *hebbe*   or *zij* ⎫
2 „ *hebt*   „ *zijt* ⎬ with Past Part. 2 „ *hebbet* „ *zijt* ⎬ with Past Part.
3 „ *heeft*   „ *is*   ⎭   3 „ *hebbe*   „ *zij* ⎭

1 „ *hebben* „ *zijn* ⎫   1 „ *hebben* „ *zijn* ⎫
2 „ *hebt*   „ *zijt* ⎬   2 „ *hebbet* „ *zijt* ⎬
3 „ *hebben* „ *zijn* ⎭   3 „ *hebben* „ *zijn* ⎭

Past Tense. Onvolmaakt Verleden Tijd.
For Weak Verbs.

1 p. stem with *te* or *de*.   1 p. stem with *te* or *de*.
2 „   „   „   *tet* „ *det*.   2 „   „   „   *tet* „ *det*.
3 „   „   „   *te* „ *de*.   3 „   „   „   *te* „ *de*.

1 „   „   „   *ten* „ *den*.   1 „   „   „   *ten* „ *den*.
2 „   „   „   *tet* „ *det*.   2 „   „   „   *tet* „ *det*.
3 „   „   „   *ten* „ *den*.   3 „   „   „   *ten* „ *den*.

For Strong Verbs.

1 p. modified stem.   1 p. modified stem *e*.
2 „   „   „   *t*.   2 „   „   „   *et*.
3 „   „   „   3 „   „   „   *e*.

1 „   „   „   *en*.   1 „   „   „   *en*.
2 „   „   „   *t*.   2 „   „   „   *et*.
3 „   „   „   *en*.   3 „   „   „   *en*.

OBS.—The 3rd pers. sing. Past Tense does not end in a *t*.

THE VERB.

INDICATIVE MOOD.	SUBJUNCTIVE MOOD.
Pluperfect Tense.	*Volmaakt Verleden Tijd.*

<table>
<tr><td colspan="3">1 p. had or was</td><td rowspan="6">With Past Part.</td><td colspan="3">1 p. hadde or ware</td><td rowspan="6">With Past Part.</td></tr>
<tr><td colspan="3">2 „ hadt „ waart</td><td colspan="3">2 „ haddet „ waret</td></tr>
<tr><td colspan="3">3 „ had „ was</td><td colspan="3">3 „ hadde „ ware</td></tr>
<tr><td colspan="3">1 „ hadden „ ware</td><td colspan="3">1 „ hadden „ waren</td></tr>
<tr><td colspan="3">2 „ hadt „ waart</td><td colspan="3">2 „ haddet „ waret</td></tr>
<tr><td colspan="3">3 „ hadden „ waren</td><td colspan="3">3 „ hadden „ waren</td></tr>
</table>

Future Tense.   *Onvolmaakt Toekomende Tijd.*

1 p. *zal*	with Infinitive Pres.	1 p. *zou*	with Infinitive Pres.
2 „ *zult*	„ „ „	2 „ *zoudt*	„ „ „
3 „ *zal*	„ „ „	3 „ *zou*	„ „ „
1 „ *zullen*	„ „ „	1 „ *zouden*	„ „ „
2 „ *zult*	„ „ „	2 „ *zoudt*	„ „ „
3 „ *zullen*	„ „ „	3 „ *zouden*	„ „ „

Future Perfect Tense.   *Volmaakt Toekomende Tijd.*

<table>
<tr><td>1 p. zal</td><td>hebben or zijn.</td><td>1 p. zou</td><td>hebben or zijn.</td></tr>
<tr><td>2 „ zult</td><td>„   „   „</td><td>2 „ zoudt</td><td>„   „   „</td></tr>
<tr><td>3 „ zal</td><td>„   „   „</td><td>3 „ zou</td><td>„   „   „</td></tr>
<tr><td>1 „ zullen</td><td>„   „   „</td><td>1 „ zouden</td><td>„   „   „</td></tr>
<tr><td>2 „ zult</td><td>„   „   „</td><td>2 „ zoudt</td><td>„   „   „</td></tr>
<tr><td>3 „ zullen</td><td>„   „   „</td><td>3 „ zouden</td><td>„   „   „</td></tr>
</table>

(with *Past Part.*)

IMPERATIVE MOOD.	GEBIEDENDE WIJS.
Singular (*Enkelvoud*)—stem.	Plural (*Meervoud*)—stem with *t*.

INFINITIVE MOOD.	ONBEPAALDE WIJS.
Present.	*Perfect.*
Name of the Verb.	Past Participle with *hebben* or *zijn*.
Future.	*Future Perfect.*
(*Te*) *zullen* with Infinitive Present.	(*Te*) *zullen* with Participle and *hebben* or *zijn*.

PARTICIPLES.   DEELWOORDEN.

Present (*Tegenwoordig*): Infinitive form with ending *de* or *d*.
Past (*Verleden*):

    For weak Verbs—prefix *ge*, stem, and ending *t* or *d*.
    For strong Verbs—prefix *ge*, stem, and ending *en*.

IV. AUXILIARIES. USE OF "HEBBEN" AND "ZIJN":—
All verbs require the aid of auxiliary verbs to complete their conjugation.

Auxiliaries (*hulpwerkwoorden*) are of three different kinds:

1. Of Tense: *hebben*, to have, *zijn*, to be, *zullen*, shall or will.
2. Of Voice: *worden*, to become, used for Eng. "to be" as auxiliary of the Passive Voice.
3. Of Mood: *kunnen*, can; *moeten*, must; *laten*, let; *mogen*, may; *willen*, to be willing to; *durven*, to dare to.

The Auxiliaries of Tense (*Hulpwerkwoorden van den Tijd*), help to form the Perfect, Pluperfect, and Future Perfect tenses in the various moods.

In Dutch a verb is conjugated with "*zijn*," "to be":

1. When Intransitive, and indicating change of place or condition:

> *De kat is van het dak gevallen*, the cat has fallen from the roof.
> *De sneeuw is gesmolten*, the snow has melted.

2. The following verbs: *zijn*, to be; *blijven*, to remain; *worden*, to become; *ontstaan*, to originate; *gebeuren*, to happen, *geschieden*, to happen; *voorvallen*, to take place.

> NOTE ON (1).—Some intransitive verbs may or may not indicate an actual change. If they do not, they take the auxiliary *hebben*:
>
> *Ik ben de kamer uitgeloopen*, I have walked out of the room (change of place).
> *Ik heb in de kamer rondgeloopen*, I have walked about in the room (motion confined to the space of a room—no actual change).
>
> NOTE ON (2).—It is worthy of note that the verbs *bestaan*, to exist; *plaats hebben*, to take place; and *plaats vinden*, to take place, are conjugated with *hebben*.

V. COMPLETE CONJUGATION of the "AUXILIARY VERB OF TENSE," "*hebben*," "to have."

THE VERB.

INDICATIVE MOOD.	SUBJUNCTIVE MOOD.
(*Aantoonende Wijs.*)	(*Aanvoegende Wijs.*)

Present Tense.   *Onvolmaakt Tegenwoordige Tijd.*

Ik heb, I have.	*Ik hebbe*, if I have.
Gij hebt, thou hast.	*Gij hebbet*, if thou have.
Hij heeft, he has.	*Hij hebbe*, if he have.
Wij hebben, we have.	*Wij hebben*, if we have.
Gij hebt, you have.	*Gij hebbet*, if you have.
Zij hebben, they have.	*Zij hebben*, if they have.

Perfect Tense.   *Volmaakt Tegenw. Tijd.*

Ik heb gehad, I have had, etc.   *Ik hebbe gehad*, if I have had, etc.

Past Tense.   *Onvolmaakt Verleden Tijd.*

Ik had, I had.	*Ik hadde*, if I had.
Gij hadt, thou hadst.	*Gij haddet*, if thou had.
Hij had, he had.	*Hij hadde*, if he had.
Wij hadden, we had.	*Wij hadden*, if we had.
Gij hadt, you had.	*Gij haddet*, if you had.
Zij hadden, they had.	*Zij hadden*, if they had.

Pluperfect Tense.   *Volmaakt Verleden Tijd.*

Ik had gehad, I had had, etc.   *Ik hadde gehad*, if I had had, etc.

Future Tense.   *Onvolmaakt Toekomende Tijd.*

Ik zal hebben, I shall have.	*Ik zou hebben*, I should have.
Gij zult hebben, thou wilt have.	*Gij zoudt hebben*, thou wouldst have.
Hij zal hebben, he will have.	*Hij zou hebben*, he would have.
Wij zullen hebben, we shall have.	*Wij zouden hebben*, we should have.
Gij zult hebben, you will have.	*Gij zoudt hebben*, you would have.
Zij zullen hebben, they will have.	*Zij zouden hebben*, they would have.

Future Perfect Tense.   *Volmaakt Toekomende Tijd.*

Ik zal gehad hebben, I shall have had, etc.   *Ik zou gehad hebben*, I should have had, etc.

IMPERATIVE MOOD.	GEBIEDENDE WIJS.
Singular (*Enkelvoud*), *heb*, have (thou).	Plural (*Meervoud*), *hebt*, have (ye).

G

INFINITIVE MOOD.	ONBEPAALDE WIJS.
Present Tense.	*Perfect Tense.*
Hebben, to have.	Gehad hebben, to have had.
Future Tense.	*Future Perfect Tense.*
Te zullen hebben, (no equivalent).	Te zullen gehad hebben, (no equivalent).
PARTICIPLES.	DEELWOORDEN.
Hebbende, having.	Gehad, had.

VI. COMPLETE CONJUGATION of the AUXILIARY VERB of TENSE, "*zijn*," "to be."

INDICATIVE MOOD.	SUBJUNCTIVE MOOD.
(*Aantoonende Wijs.*)	(*Aanvoegende Wijs.*)

Present Tense. Onvolmaakt Tegenwoordige Tijd.

Ik ben, I am.	Ik zij, if I be.
Gij zijt, thou art.	Gij zijt, if thou be.
Hij is, he is.	Hij zij, if he be.
Wij zijn, we are.	Wij zijn, if we be.
Gij zijt, you are.	Gij zijt, if you be.
Zij zijn, they are.	Zij zijn, if they be.

Perfect Tense. Volmaakt Tegenw. Tijd.

Ik ben geweest, I have been, etc.   Ik zij geweest, if I have been, etc.

Past Tense. Onvolm. Verleden Tijd.

Ik was, I was.	Ik ware, if I were.
Gij waart, thou wast.	Gij waret, if thou were.
Hij was, he was.	Hij ware, if he were.
Wij waren, we were.	Wij waren, if we were.
Gij waart, you were.	Gij waret, if you were.
Zij waren, they were.	Zij waren, if they were.

Pluperfect Tense. Volmaakt Verleden Tijd.

Ik was geweest, I had been, etc.   Ik ware geweest, if I had been, etc.

THE VERB.

Future Tense.   *Onvolm. Toekomende Tijd.*

Ik zal zijn, I shall be.	*Ik zou zijn,* I should be.
Gij zult zijn, thou wilt be.	*Gij zoudt zijn,* thou wouldst be.
Hij zal zijn, he will be.	*Hij zou zijn,* he would be.
Wij zullen zijn, we shall be.	*Wij zouden zijn,* we should be.
Gij zult zijn, you will be.	*Gij zoudt zijn,* you would be.
Zij zullen zijn, they will be.	*Zij zouden zijn,* they would be.

Future Perfect Tense.   *Volmaakt Toek. Tijd.*

Ik zal geweest zijn, I shall have been, etc.   *Ik zou geweest zijn,* I should have been, etc.

IMPERATIVE MOOD.   GEBIEDENDE WIJS.

Singular (*Enkelvoud*), *wees,* be (thou).   Plural (*Meervoud*), *weest* or *zijt* be (ye).

INFINITIVE MOOD.   ONBEPAALDE WIJS.

Present Tense.   *Perfect Tense.*

Zijn, to be.   *Geweest zijn,* to have been.

Future Tense.   *Future Perfect Tense.*

Te zullen zijn, (no equivalent).   *Te zullen geweest zijn,* (no equivalent).

PARTICIPLES.   DEELWOORDEN.

Zijnde, being.   *Geweest,* been.

VII. CONJUGATION of the AUXILIARY VERB of TENSE, "*zullen*," "shall" or "will."

INDICATIVE MOOD.   AANTOONENDE WIJS.

Present Tense. Onvolm. Teg. Tijd.   *Past Tense. Onvolm. Verl. Tijd.*

Ik zal, I shall.	*Ik zou,* I should.
Gij zult, thou wilt.	*Gij zoudt,* thou wouldst.
Hij zal, he will.	*Hij zou,* he would.
Wij zullen, we shall.	*Wij zouden,* we should.
Gij zult, you will.	*Gij zoudt,* you would.
Zij zullen, they will.	*Zij zouden,* they would.

G 2

VIII. Conjugation of the verb "*worden*," to become.

Indicative Mood.	Subjunctive Mood.
(*Aantoonende Wijs.*)	(*Aanvoegende Wijs.*)

Present Tense. Onvolm. Tegenwoordige Tijd.

Ik word, I become.	*Ik worde*, if I become.
Gij wordt, thou becomest.	*Gij wordet*, if thou become.
Hij wordt, he becomes.	*Hij worde*, if he become.
Wij worden, we become.	*Wij worden*, if we become.
Gij wordt, you become.	*Gij wordet*, if you become.
Zij worden, they become.	*Zij worden*, if they become.

Perfect Tense. Volmaakt Tegenw. Tijd.

Ik ben geworden, I have become, etc.	*Ik zij geworden*, if I have become, etc.

Past Tense. Onvolm. Verl. Tijd.

Ik werd, I became.	*Ik werde*, if I became.
Gij werdt, thou becamest.	*Gij werdet*, if thou becamest.
Hij werd, he became.	*Hij werde*, if he became.
Wij werden, we became.	*Wij werden*, if we became.
Gij werdt, you became.	*Gij werdet*, if you became.
Zij werden, they became.	*Zij werden*, if they became.

Pluperfect Tense. Volmaakt Verl. Tijd.

Ik was geworden, I had become, etc.	*Ik ware geworden*, if I had become, etc.

Future Tense. Onvolmaakt Toekomende Tijd.

Ik zal worden, I shall become.	*Ik zou worden*, I should become.
Gij zult worden, thou wilt become.	*Gij zoudt worden*, thou wouldst become.
Hij zal worden, he will become.	*Hij zou worden*, he would become.
Wij zullen worden, we shall become.	*Wij zouden worden*, we should become.
Gij zult worden, you will become.	*Gij zoudt worden*, you would become.
Zij zullen worden, they will become.	*Zij zouden worden*, they would become.

Future Perfect Tense. Volmaakt Toekomende Tijd.

Ik zal geworden zijn, I shall have become, etc.	*Ik zou geworden zijn*, I should have become, etc.

THE VERB.

IMPERATIVE MOOD.	GEBIEDENDE WIJS.
Singular (*Enkelvoud*), *word*, become (thou).	Plural (*Meervoud*), *wordt*, become (ye).

INFINITIVE MOOD. ONBEPAALDE WIJS.

Present Tense.	*Perfect Tense.*
Worden, to become.	*Geworden zijn*, to have become.
Future Tense.	*Future Perfect Tense.*
Te zullen worden, (no equivalent).	*Te zullen geworden zijn*, (no equivalent).

PARTICIPLES. DEELWOORDEN.

Teg.: *wordende*—Pres.: becoming.	*Verl.*: *geworden*—Past: become.

IX. VOICE:—The Dutch verb, like the English one, has two voices, the Active Voice (*Actieve* or *Bedrijvende Vorm*), and the Passive Voice (*Passieve* or *Lijdende Vorm*). The form of the Passive Voice is more pronounced, for the reason that its Auxiliary verb is "*worden*," to become, and not "*zijn*," to be, like in English.

X. COMPARISON between the ACTIVE and PASSIVE VOICES of the verb "*bijten*," to bite.

INFINITIVE MOOD.
Present Tense.

ACTIVE VOICE.	PASSIVE VOICE.
Bijten, to bite.	*Gebeten worden*, to be bitten.

Perfect Tense.

Gebeten hebben, to have bitten.	*Gebeten (geworden) zijn*, to have been bitten.

Future Tense.

Te zullen bijten.	*Te zullen gebeten worden.*

Future Perfect Tense.

Gebeten te zullen hebben.	*Gebeten te zullen (geworden) zijn.*

Indicative Mood.

Present Tense.

Active Voice.	Passive Voice.
Ik bijt, I bite.	*Ik word gebeten,* I am bitten.

Imperfect Tense.

Ik beet, I bit.	*Ik werd gebeten,* I was bitten.

Perfect Tense.

Ik heb gebeten, I have bitten.	*Ik ben gebeten (geworden),* I have been bitten.

Pluperfect Tense.

Ik had gebeten, I had bitten.	*Ik was gebeten (geworden),* I had been bitten.

Future Tense.

Ik zal bijten, I shall bite.	*Ik zal gebeten worden,* I shall be bitten.

Future Perfect Tense.

Ik zal gebeten hebben, I shall have bitten.	*Ik zal gebeten (geworden) zijn,* I shall have been bitten.

Subjunctive Mood.

Present Tense.

Ik bijte, if I bite.	*Ik worde gebeten,* if I bo bitten.

Imperfect Tense.

Ik bete, if I bit.	*Ik werde gebeten,* if I were bitten.

Perfect Tense.

Ik hebbe gebeten, if I have bitten.	*Ik zij gebeten (geworden),* if I have been bitten.

Pluperfect Tense.

Ik hadde gebeten, if I had bitten.	*Ik ware gebeten (geworden),* if I had been bitten.

Future Tense.

Ik zou bijten, if I should bite.	*Ik zou gebeten worden,* I should be bitten.

THE VERB.

SUBJUNCTIVE MOOD.

Future Perfect Tense.

ACTIVE VOICE.   PASSIVE VOICE.
Ik zou gebeten hebben, if I should have bitten.   *Ik zou gebeten (geworden) zijn*, I should have been bitten.

IMPERATIVE MOOD.

Present Tense.

Sing. *bijt*, bite (thou).   *Word gebeten*, be (thou) bitten.
Plur. *bijt*, bite (ye).   *Wordt gebeten*, be (ye) bitten.

PARTICIPLES.

Present.

Bijtende, biting.   *Gebeten wordende*, being bitten.

Past.

Gebeten, bitten.   *Gebeten (geworden)*, having been bitten.

X. A. Notice carefully the following examples:

Het paard wordt vandaag verkocht, the horse is being sold to-day.

Het paard is vandaag verkocht, the horse has been sold to-day.

De bloemen werden gisteren geplant, the flowers were planted yesterday.

De bloemen waren gisteren geplant, the flowers had been planted yesterday.

De schapen zullen morgen geschoren worden, the sheep will be shorn to-morrow.

De schapen zullen morgen geschoren zijn, the sheep will have been shorn to-morrow.

De kamers zouden veranderd worden, the rooms would be altered.

De kamers zouden veranderd zijn, the rooms would have been altered.

X. B. COMPARISON between the same forms of the verb "zijn" used as a COPULATIVE and as an AUXILIARY of the PASSIVE VOICE.

COP. *Het brood is gaar gebakken,* the bread is thoroughly baked.

PAS. *Het brood is gisteren niet gebakken maar vandaag,* the bread has not been baked yesterday but to-day.

PAS. & COP. *De tuin was wel aangelegd, maar was geheel verwilderd,* the garden had been laid out, but had grown completely wild.

COP. *Ik ben verwonderd geweest over uw antwoord,* I have been surprised at your answer.

PAS. *Ik ben bedrogen (geworden) door mijnen tuinman,* I have been deceived by my gardener.

COP. *De sneeuw zal gauw gesmolten zijn,* the snow will soon be melted.

PAS. *Het orgel zal goed bespeeld worden,* the organ will be played well.

COP. *Het water zou bevroren geweest zijn, als, enz.,* the water would have been frozen over, if, etc.

PAS. *Het geheele bosch zou verbrand (geworden) zijn, als, enz.,* the whole wood would have been burned down, if, etc.

COP. *Deze oefening was verbeterd, toen ik ze terugkreeg,* this exercise was corrected when I got it back.

PAS. *De oefeningen waren door den onderwijzer verbeterd,* the exercises had been corrected by the teacher.

X. C. OBSERVATIONS ON THE ACTIVE AND PASSIVE VOICES.

The fact that in English the verb " to be " is used both as a copulative verb to express "state or condition," and as the aux. verb of the Passive Voice, whereas in Dutch there are two separate verbs, viz., "*zijn*" as the COPULATIVE, and "*worden*" as the AUXILIARY of the PASSIVE VOICE, makes it difficult to English students to acquire the use of the correct Passive forms, which should therefore be made a subject of thorough enquiry and practice. The following observations should receive special attention.

1. "Am," "was," "have been," etc., are translated by "*ben*," "*was*," "*ben geweest*," etc., when Copulatives; and by "*word*," "*werd*," "*ben geworden*," etc., when Auxiliaries of the Passive Voice.

2. Where in a Perfect, Pluperfect, or Future Perfect Tense the word "*geworden*" is given in brackets, it is commonly left out. This omission leads to the following comparison:

Present: *Ik word gebeten*, I am bitten.
Past: *Ik werd gebeten*, I was bitten.
Perfect: *Ik ben gebeten*, I have been bitten.
Pluperfect: *Ik was gebeten*, I had been bitten.

from which it will be noticed that the Dutch Perfect Tense is like the English Present, and the Dutch Pluperfect like the English Past.

3. It follows, then, that in the Passive Voice the English "*is*" and "*was*" are rendered by the Dutch "*wordt*" and "*werd*," and the Dutch "*is*" and "*was*" are rendered by the English "has been" and "had been."

4. Notice the peculiar use of the Passive form in Dutch in connection with the pronoun *er* (see Ch. VIII., p. 140).

5. (*a*.) **Transposition** of an **Active** sentence into the **Passive** Voice is only possible when such Active sentence has a Direct Object.
   (*b*.) This Direct Object (Active) is taken as the Subject of the Passive sentence; the verb agrees with the new subject, and the Subject of the Active sentence furnishes an Indirect Object to the Passive sentence:

Active: *De hond beet den man*, the dog bit the man.
Passive: *De man werd door den hond gebeten*, the man was bitten by the dog.

   (*c*.) Active sentences, having as their Subject the indefinite pers. pron. "*men*," lose this pronoun when they are made Passive:

Active: *Men heeft mij eene boodschap gebracht*, they brought me a message.
Passive: *Eene boodschap is mij gebracht (geworden)*, a message has been brought to me; (or rather) *er is mij eene boodschap gebracht (geworden)*.

(*d.*) On the contrary, in bringing back a Passive sentence to its Active form, the Indirect Object (Passive) becomes the Active Subject, and the Passive Subject the Direct Object (Active):

Passive: *De vos is door den boer gevangen (geworden)*, the fox was caught by the farmer.
Active: *De boer heeft den vos gevangen*, the farmer has caught the fox.

(*e.*) In Passive sentences, where the action is not assigned to any particular agent, and consequently no Indirect Object is expressed, the indefinite pers. pron. "*men*" becomes the Subject of the Active sentence:

Passive: *Het boek is gisteren gevonden (geworden)*, the book was found yesterday.
Active: *Men heeft gisteren het boek gevonden*, they found the book yesterday.

(*f.*) The same rule holds for sentences as referred to in Obs. 4:

Passive: *Er is mij gezegd*, I have been told.
Active: *Men heeft mij gezegd*, they have told me.
Passive: *Er wordt hier geschoten*, there is shooting going on here.
Active: *Men schiet hier*, they are shooting here.

XI. CONJUGATION of the AUXILIARY VERBS of MOOD "*mogen*," may, "*kunnen*," can, "*moeten*," must, "*laten*," let, "*durven*," to dare, "*willen*," to be willing to.

AANTOONENDE WIJS. INDICATIVE MOOD.
Onvolmaakt Tegenw. Tijd. Present Tense.

Ik mag, kan, moet, laat, durf, wil, I may, can, must, let, dare, will.
Gij moogt, kunt, moet, laat, durft, wilt, thou mayest, canst, must, etc.
Hij mag, kan, moet, laat, durft, wil, he may, can, must, etc.
Wij mogen, kunnen, moeten, laten, durven, willen.
Gij moogt, kunt, moet, laat, durft, wilt.
Zij mogen, kunnen, moeten, laten, durven, willen.

Volmaakt Tegenw. Tijd. Perfect Tense.

Ik heb ———, I have been allowed to.
Gij hebt gekund, thou hast been able to.
Hij heeft gemoeten, he has been obliged to.
Wij hebben ———, we have let (allowed).
Gij hebt gedurfd, you have dared.
Zij hebben gewild, they have been willing to.

THE VERB.

Onvolmaakt Verleden Tijd. Imperfect Tense.

Ik mocht, kon, moest, liet, dorst, wou, I might, could, had to, let, dared, wanted to.
Gij mocht, kondt, moest, liet, dorst, woudt, thou mightest, couldst, hadst to, etc.
Hij mocht, kon, moest, liet, dorst, wou.
Wij mochten, konden, moesten, lieten, dorsten, wilden.
Gij mocht, kondt, moest, liet, dorst, woudt.
Zij mochten, konden, moesten, lieten, dorsten, wilden.

Volmaakt Verleden Tijd. Pluperfect Tense.

Ik had ——, gekund, gemoeten, ——, gedurfd, gewild, enz., I had been allowed to, had been able to, etc.
  (See Perfect Tense.)

Onvolmaakt Toekomende Tijd. Simple Future Tense.

  Ik zal mogen, I shall be allowed to.
  Gij zult kunnen, thou wilt be able to.
  Hij zal moeten, he will be obliged to.
  Wij zullen laten, we shall let (allow).
  Gij zult durven, you will dare.
  Zij zullen willen, they will be willing to.

Volmaakt Toekomende Tijd. Future Tense.

Ik zal hebben ——, gekund, gemoeten, ——, gedurfd, gewild, enz., I shall have been allowed to, been able to, been obliged to, etc.

  OBS.—The above verbs, it will be seen, are to a far larger degree complete than their English equivalents. The use, however, of their compound tenses in the above form is limited to the cases in which they are not followed by an Infinitive verb. Example:

  Ik heb het niet gedurfd, I did not have the courage (to do) it
  Zij hebben niet gewild, they have not been willing.
  Hij zal niet kunnen, he won't be able to.

  In most cases an Infinitive verb is made to follow, and then the Past Participles of these verbs themselves assume the Infinitive form, as:

  Zij hebben niet willen hooren, they did not want to hear.
  Hij heeft niet kunnen komen, he has not been able to come.
  Zij heeft niet mogen gaan, she was not allowed to go.
  Wij hebben hem niet laten spelen, we have not let him play.

XII. MOOD.—Mood is the form of a verb by which is expressed in what *manner* the action is done.

There are four moods: *a.* Indicative, *Aantoonende wijs;* *b.* Subjunctive, *Aanvoegende wijs;* *c.* Imperative, *Gebiedende wijs;* *d.* Infinitive, *Onbepaalde wijs.*

(*a.*) The Indicative Mood represents an action as a fact, a reality, a truth. The use of it is alike in English and Dutch. Examples: *Dit papier is wit,* this paper is white; *De aarde wentelt om hare as,* the earth rotates round its axis.

(*b.*) The Subjunctive Mood represents an action as a wish, a possibility, or as depending on something else: *Kwame hij slechts,* if he would only come; *Haddet gij uwen plicht gedaan, gij, enz.,* if you had only done your duty, you, etc.

> NOTE.—The use of the Subjunctive Mood is now very limited in the Dutch language. It is never heard of in speaking, and may be taken as confined to pulpit oratory and poetry. A very few time-honoured expressions form exceptions to this rule, as:
> *Hoe dat zij,* however that be.
> *Het ga zooals het wil,* let it go as it may.

(*c.*) The Imperative Mood expresses a command, but at the same time a request or advice.

Command: *Jan, breng mij wat water,* Waiter, bring me some water.

Request: *Kom eens bij mij,* do come to me.

Advice: *Gedraag u goed, mijn kind,* behave yourself, my child.

> NOTE.—The form of request here indicated is intensified by the use of the adverb "*toch*": *Kom toch eens bij mij, kleintje,* do come to me, little one.

XIII. TRANSLATION of the INFINITIVE MOOD:—The Infinitive Mood does not express any action, but merely gives the name of the verb. For the correct translation of it the following rules should be observed:

RULE 1.—The English Infinitive preceded by "to" is rendered in Dutch in like manner:

Sta mij toe, u te vragen, permit me to ask you;

Zij waren niet in staat te komen, they were unable to come;
Ik beveel u, het te doen, I order you to do it;
Denk eraan, het mij te laten zien, remember to let me see it.

RULE 2.—This "*te*" is strengthened by "*om*" (Eng. "for"):

(*a.*) When "purpose" is expressed:

Ik zond hem om te vragen, I sent him (for) to ask.

(*b.*) After Nouns or Pronouns naming or indicating an object which serves a purpose:

Hier is een hamer om dien spijker in te slaan, here is a hammer for knocking (to knock) in that nail;
Geef mij iets om erbij te klimmen, hand me something to reach it.

(*c.*) After the word "*genoeg*" (enough):

Ik heb niet genoeg om te betalen, I have not enough to pay.

(*d.*) After predicative Nouns and Adjectives, implying fitness:

Heeft hij kracht om dat werk te doen? has he strength to do that work?
Is die melk goed om te drinken? is that milk good for drinking (to drink)?

(*e.*) After "*te*" (too) followed by a predicative Adjective:

Hij is te lui om te werken, he is too lazy to work.

RULE 3.—The Dutch Infinitive rejects both "*om*" and "*te*":

(*a.*) When it forms the subject, object, or predicate of a sentence:

Wandelen is gezond, walking (to walk) is pleasant;

Niet antwoorden beteekent hem beleedigen, not to answer means to offend him;
Liegen is bedriegen, to tell lies means to deceive.

(*b.*) After the Auxiliary Verbs of Mood. (See § IV. 3):

Ik mag u niet alleen laten, I may not leave you alone;
Ik durf het hem niet vragen, I dare not ask it of him.

(*c.*) After the verbs: *doen* (to do), *helpen* (to help), *gaan* (to go), *hooren* (to hear), *voelen* (to feel), *komen* (to come), *zien* (to see), *leeren* (to learn and to teach):

Ik leer hem schrijven, I teach him to write;
Ik kom het huis zien, I come to see the house;
Hij gaat baden, he goes to bathe.

XIV. TRANSLATION of the GERUND, the PRESENT PARTICIPLE, and the PAST PARTICIPLE:—

OBS. 1.—Besides the Infinitive form pure and simple, the following are taken as forming parts of the Infinitive Mood: the Gerund, the Present Participle, the Past Participle.

OBS. 2.—The English Gerund is in every case translated by the Dutch Infinitive form. It occurs

(*a.*) As a Noun, when likewise in Dutch it is a noun of the neut. gender:

Riding is pleasant, *rijden is prettig;*
The regular bathing did it, *het geregeld baden heeft het gedaan;*
That screaming is annoying, *dat schreeuwen is vervelend;*

and (*b*) as a Gerundial Infinitive after a Preposition, when it is rendered by the Dutch Infinitive with "*te*":

Bread is good for eating (to eat), *brood is goed om te eten.*
By working hard, *door hard te werken.*

Obs. 3.—Present Participles, with a common ending *de* or *d*, are of rare occurrence in Dutch. Their frequent and varied use in English renders translation a difficult matter.

(*a.*) Occurring in an adjectival enlargement it is translated by the rel. pron. with whatever tense of the verb fits in with the context:

> Do you know of anyone going that way? *Weet u van iemand, die dien kant uitgaat ?*
> I saw a man holding a child by the hand, *Ik zag eenen man, die een kind bij de hand hield.*

(*b.*) In sentences like the following, " I saw the king sitting on his throne," where it takes the place of the Infinitive, e.g., *Ik zag den koning op zijnen troon zitten.*

Of these three forms the first] only is common, the second being antiquated, and the third used in poetical language only.

(*c.*) In case a finite verb, preceded by "as," "while," or "when," can take the place of the Present Participle, this rendering is preferred to the use of the Pres. Part, as being more colloquial: (See pp. 96, 127.)

> Having a garden (as he has a garden), the man is content, *daar hij eenen tuin heeft, is de man tevreden;*
> He got giddy crossing (while he crossed) the bridge, *hij werd duizelig, terwijl hij de brug overging;*
> Seeing (when he saw) his master, the dog ran up to him, *toen de hond zijnen meester zag, liep hij naar hem toe.*

In other cases (*e.g.* where " because " is understood) the Pres. Part. is more common:

> He spoke about it, thinking I did not know it, *hij sprak erover, denkende dat ik het niet wist.*

The same custom prevails for short phrases:

> Saying this, he left the room, *dit zeggende, verliet hij de kamer;*
> On hearing this, she cried, *dit hoorende, schreide zij.*

Obs. 4.—The formation of Past Participles is explained on p. 157. In their use, they do not differ from their English equivalents. It should, however, be observed as a rule of great importance, that a Past Participle, followed by an Infinitive, assumes the form of the Infinitive, without altering its nature, as:

> He is *gone* to work in the garden, *hij is in den tuin* gaan *werken;*
> He has come to see me, *hij is mij* komen *bezoeken.*

(See § XI. Obs.)

XV. Tenses.—Tense is a change in the form of a verb by which time is expressed.

An action may be represented to be performed in the *Present,* to have been performed in the *Past,* or to be going to be performed in the *Future.* Hence there are three principal tenses: a Present, a Past, and a Future tense. Each of these three may represent the action as complete, *done,* or as incomplete, *still being done,* from which it follows that there is:

1. A tense which represents the action as *being done* at the present time: I read and my brother writes, *ik lees en mijn broeder schrijft.* This tense is called the **Present Tense, de onvolmaakt tegenwoordige tijd.**

2. A tense which represents the action as *done, completed* at the present moment: I have read and my brother has written, *ik heb gelezen en mijn broeder heeft geschreven.* This tense is called the **Perfect Tense, de volmaakt tegenwoordige tijd.**

3. A tense which represents the action as being done in a time which is past: When I visited him, he read (was reading), etc., *toen ik hem bezocht, las hij, enz.* This tense is called the **Imperfect (Past) Tense, de onvolmaakt verleden tijd.**

4. A tense which represents the action as *done, completed* before another action took place: He had departed

before I arrived, *hij was vertrokken vóór ik aankwam.* This tense is called the **Pluperfect Tense, de volmaakt verleden tijd.**

5. A tense which represents an action as *going to take place* at a future time: The small tree will some time be large, *de kleine boom zal eenmaal groot zijn.* This tense is called the **Future tense, de onvolmaakt toekomende tijd.**

6. A tense which represents the action as *completed* at a certain future time: When you return, we shall have written our letters, *bij uwe terugkomst zullen wij onze brieven geschreven hebben.* This tense is called the **Future Perfect Tense, de volmaakt toekomende tijd.**

OBSERVATIONS.—The English Imperfect (Past) Tense is translated by the Dutch Imperfect only:

1. When two simultaneous actions or conditions are expressed:

   He saw me as soon as I entered the house, *hij zag mij, zoodra ik het huis inkwam.*
   He seemed an old man when I was yet young, *hij scheen een oude man, toen ik nog jong was.*

2. In all narratives and history:

   Once there lived a king, *er leefde eens een koning.*
   The Zulus defeated the English at Isandula, but were soon afterwards subjected, *de Zulus versloegen de Engelschen bij Isandula, maar werden spoedig daarna onderworpen.*

3. In all other cases, and especially in easy colloquial style, it is preferable to translate the English Past Tense by the Dutch Perfect:

   This morning I gathered fresh roses, *van morgen heb ik versche rozen geplukt.*
   Last summer we travelled in France, *verleden zomer hebben wij in Frankrijk gereisd.*

4. The Present Tense is idiomatically used for the Future Tense:

   Over eenigen tijd zien wij elkander weer om nooit weer te scheiden, after some time we shall meet again never to part any more.

5. In describing an event, when the speaker wants to place the scene vividly before the mind of his hearer, he suddenly changes the Past Tense he was using into the Present:

Toen wij op deze wijze het einde des wouds bereikt hadden, hoorden wij plotseling een luid geraas achter ons. Vóór wij ons konden omkeeren om te onderzoeken wat het was, vliegt er een koningstijger op uit het dichte struikgewas aan onze linkerzijde, grijpt een der paarden bij de keel en werpt het met zijnen ruiter ter aarde. When we had thus come to the end of the forest, all at once we heard a loud noise from behind. Before we could turn round to ascertain what it was, a royal tiger *darts* out from the dense brush-wood on our left, *seizes* one of the horses by the throat and *flings* it to the ground together with its rider.

This change of tenses is very common among the Dutch, who as a rule are more emphatic in their speech than the English.

6. The Perfect Tense, *Volmaakt tegenwoordige tijd*, represents the action as complete at the present moment:

Ik heb mijnen brief geschreven, laat ons hem nu op de post doen, I have written my letter, now let us post it.

7. In the same way as the Present Tense sometimes takes the place of the Future Tense, so may the Perfect Tense take the place of the Future Perfect Tense:

De volgende week om dezen tijd heb ik het zwaarste al gehad, next week about this time I shall have had the worst (the worst will be over for me).

XVI. NUMBER.—Verbs have two numbers: the Singular, *het Enkelvoud*, and the Plural, *het Meervoud*.

A Verb must agree in number with its Nominative. Notice the following differences in idiom:

It *is* I.	*Ik ben het.*
It *is* we.	*Wij zijn het.*
Is it you?	*Zijt gij het?* (*Is u het?*)
The council *have* decided.	*De raad heeft uitgemaakt.*
It *is* the cows that did the mischief.	*Het zijn de koeien, die dat kwaad hebben gedaan.*

OBS. 1.—After two words joined by "and" the verb must be in the *Plural*; after two words joined by "or" or "nor" the verb must be in the *Singular*. Examples:

Gij en *ik* moeten *vaarwel zeggen*, you and I must say good-bye.
Gij of *ik* moet *het doen*, you or I must do it.
Hij noch *ik* kan *gaan*, he nor I can go.

OBS. 2.—When a verb has two subjects in different persons, the verb agrees with the 1st person in preference to the 2nd, and with the 2nd in preference to the 3rd:

Hij of ik heb het gedaan, he or I did it.
Gij en hij kunt beiden gaan, you and he may both go.

XVII. PERSON.—The Dutch verb has three persons, called the first, second, and third person, *de eerste, de tweede, de derde persoon*, each with a singular and a plural form. The endings which mark them may be seen from the Conjugation Form (p. 158).

XVIII. TRANSITIVE and INTRANSITIVE Verbs.—For completing the meaning of a verb, an Object is often added, such Object indicating the person or thing which is either created or changed by the action of the verb. The sentence, "The man builds," cannot be regarded as complete, until the object of his building, the creation of it—a house, church, bridge, shed, etc.—has been added. In the complete sentence, "The man builds a house (*de man bouwt een huis*), "*huis*" is the Direct Object of the verb "*bouwen*," and "*bouwen*" figures as a **Transitive** (**Overgankelijk**, or **Transitief**) verb.

2. All other verbs, *i.e.*, all those whose meaning is not completed by the addition of a Direct Object, are called Intransitive (**Onovergankelijk**, or **Intransitief**).

XIX. 1. REFLEXIVE (TERUGWERKENDE, or REFLEXIEVE) VERBS, whose action returns to the agent, or whose Subject and Direct Object are one and the same person, are manifestly Transitive. In conjugation they take the Reflexive Pronouns, mentioned under Chap. VIII, p. 132.

The particulars of this conjugation are as follows:

Infinitive Present: *Zich (te) wonden*, to wound oneself.

Infinitive Perfect: *Zich gewond (te) hebben*, to have wounded oneself.

Indicative Present: *Ik wond mij*, I wound myself.
Gij wondt u, thou woundest thyself.
Hij wondt zich, he wounds himself.
Wij wonden ons, we wound ourselves.
Gij wondt u, you wound yourselves.
Zij wonden zich, they wound themselves.

2. Reflexive Verbs are subdivided into:

   a. Those which are **of necessity reflexive**, *noodwendig terugwerkende werkw.* Ex. *zich schamen*, to be ashamed; *zich vergissen*, to be mistaken; *zich inbeelden*, to fancy; *zich erbarmen*, to have pity. From these the reflex. pron. is inseparable.

   b. Those which may be **either reflexive or not**, *toevallig terugwerkende werkw.* Ex. *zich bezeeren*, to hurt oneself; *zich wasschen*, to wash oneself; *zich beproeven*, to try oneself. With these the reflex. pron. is only used when required.

3. The following verbs are Reflexive in Dutch, and not so in English:

Zich aanmatigen,	*Hij matigt zich te veel vrijheid aan,* he takes too much liberty.
Zich baden,	*De jongens baadden zich in de rivier,* the boys bathed in the river.
Zich bedenken,	*Bedenk u wel,* consider (the matter) well; *Ik heb mij bedacht,* I have changed my mind.

Zich bedienen van,	Men bedient zich van dynamiet om dit hout te splijten, dynamite is used for splitting this wood.
Zich bedroeven over,	Wij bedroeven ons over uw slecht gedrag, we are grieved at your bad conduct.
Zich begeven naar,	Hij heeft zich naar Afrika begeven, he has gone to Africa.
Zich begrijpen,	Ik kan mij die zaak niet begrijpen, I cannot understand that matter.
Zich beklagen,	Hij zal zich niet over mij te beklagen hebben, he won't have to complain about me.
Zich belasten met,	Hij heeft zich met de uitvoering van mijnen wensch belast, he has taken upon himself to carry out my wish.
Zich beroemen op,	De man beroemt zich op zijne daad, the man boasts of his deed.
Zich beroepen op,	Ik beroep mij op uw gezond verstand, I appeal to your common sense.
Zich bewegen,	De man beweegt zich moeielijk, the man has difficulty in moving about.
Zich beijveren,	De jongen beijvert zich om knap te worden, the boy tries his best to become clever.
Zich erbarmen,	Erbarm u mijner, have mercy on me.
Zich ergeren over,	De onderwijzer ergert zich over de onverschilligheid der leerlingen, the teacher is vexed at the indifference of the pupils.
Zich getroosten,	Ik moet mij die uitgave getroosten, I must put up with the expense.
Zich haasten,	Haast u, anders komen wij te laat, hurry up, else we shall be too late.
Zich herinneren,	Ik herinner mij dat hij mij dat zei, I remember him having told me.
Zich hoeden voor,	Hoed u voor de vriendschap van dien man, beware of the friendship of that man.
Zich keeren,	Hij keerde zich naar mij, en sprak, he turned to me, and said.
Zich neerzetten,	De advokaat zal zich te Pretoria neerzetten, the barrister will settle down at Pretoria.
Zich onderhouden met,	Wij hebben ons aangenaam met haar onderhouden, we had a pleasant conversation with her.
Zich ontfermen over,	Ontferm u over den armen man, have pity on the poor man.
Zich ontzien,	Ik ontzie mij dien man te vragen, I hesitate asking that man.
Zich schamen over,	De vader schaamde zich over het gedrag van zijnen zoon, the father was asham d of the conduct of his son.

Zich storen aan,	Zij stoort zich niet aan de waarschuwingen harer vrienden, she does not mind the warnings of her friends.
Zich verbeelden,	Hij verbeeldt zich heel knap te zijn, he fancies that he is very clever.
Zich verblijden over,	Verblijdt gij u niet over zijn geluk? are you not glad of his good fortune?
Zich vergewissen van,	Hij heeft zich van hare vriendschap vergewist, he has made sure of her friendship.
Zich vergissen,	Vergeef mij, ik heb mij vergist, pardon me, I have made a mistake.
Zich verheugen over,	Wij verheugen ons over die tijding, we rejoice at those tidings.
Zich vermeten,	Wie zou zich vermeten, dien man te beschuldigen, who would be bold enough to accuse that man?
Zich verslikken,	Het kind heeft zich verslikt, daarom hoest het, the child is choking, that's why it coughs.
Zich verspreiden,	De ziekte verspreidt zich over het land, the disease is spreading in the country.
Zich vestigen,	Mijne ouders zullen zich te Kaapstad vestigen, my parents are going to live at Cape Town.
Zich voeden met,	Tijgers voeden zich met vleesch, tigers live on flesh.
Zich voelen,	Hij voelt zich beter van morgen, he feels better this morning.
Zich voorbereiden voor,	Ik bereid mij voor twee examens voor, I am preparing for two examinations.

XX. 1. MIXED VERBS:—Midway between the two kinds of conjugations enumerated under par. III, we find a small number (27) of verbs which half partake of the nature of the Weak conjugation, and half of that of the Strong. These are called **Mixed (Gemengd)**.

2. They are the following:

Infinitive.		Past Tense.	Past Participle.
Bakken,	to bake,	bakte,	gebakken.
Bannen,	to banish,	bande,	gebannen.
Barsten,	to burst,	barstte,	gebarsten.
Braden,	to roast,	braadde,	gebraden.
Brouwen,	to brew,	brouwde,	gebrouwen.
Durven,	to dare,	dorst (durfde),	gedurfd.

Infinitive.		Past tense.	Past Participle.
Heeten,	to be called,	*heette,*	*geheeten.*
Jagen,	to hunt,	*joeg (jaagde),*	*gejaagd.*
Kunnen,	can (to be able),	*kon,*	*gekund.*
Lachen,	to laugh,	*lachte,*	*gelachen.*
Laden,	to load,	*laadde,*	*geladen.*
Leggen,	to lay,	*lei (legde),*	*gelegd.*
Malen,	to grind,	*maalde,*	*gemalen.*
Ontvouwen,	to unfold,	*ontvouwde,*	{ *ontvouwd* (explained). *ontvouwen* (proper sense).
Raden,	to advise,	*raadde,*	*geraden.*
Scheiden,	to separate,	*scheidde,*	*gescheiden.*
Spannen,	to stretch,	*spande,*	*gespannen.*
Spouwen,	to split,	*spouwde,*	*gespouwen.*
Stooten,	to push,	*stootte,*	*gestooten.*
Vouwen,	to fold,	*vouwde,*	*gevouwen.*
Vragen,	to ask,	*vroeg (vraagde),*	*gevraagd.*
Waaien,	to blow,	*woei (waaide),*	*gewaaid.*
Wasschen,	to wash,	*(waschte),*	*gewasschen.*
Weven,	to weave,	*weefde,*	*geweven.*
Wreken,	to revenge,	*wreekte,*	*gewroken.*
Zeggen,	to say,	*zei,*	*gezegd.*
Zouten,	to salt,	*zoutte,*	*gezouten.*

NOTE.—Of these twenty-seven verbs, twenty have a weak past tense and a strong past participle, whereas seven have a strong past tense and a weak past participle.

XXI. 1. ANOMALOUS VERBS:—Where the irregularity of conjugation extends to the **consonants** of the stem, a verb becomes out and out Irregular, and hence is no longer called **Sterk**, but **Onregelmatig (Anomalous).**

The number of these being small (20), and that of the pure Strong verbs considerable (170), the former will be given here, and the "List of Strong Verbs" at the end of the present chapter.

2. List of **Anomalous (Onregelmatige)** verbs:

Infinitive.	Past Tense.	Past Part.	Points of Irregularity.
Brengen, to bring,	bracht (old D. brangede),	gebracht.	Syncope of n from stem; t in 3rd Pers. Sing. Past Tense.
Denken, to think,	dacht (old D. dankede),	gedacht.	Syncope of n from stem; t in 3rd Pers. Sing. Past Tense.
Dunken, to seem, to imagine,	docht,	gedocht.	Syncope of n from stem; t in 3rd Pers. Sing. Past Tense.
Koopen, to buy,	kocht (old D. koopede),	gekocht.	Change of p into ch; t in 3rd Pers. Sing. Past Tense.
Zoeken, to seek,	zocht (old D. zoekede),	gezocht.	Change k into ch; 3rd Pers. Sing. Past Tense.
Plegen, to be accustomed.	placht (old D. plag),	(wanting).	Change of g into ch; t in 3rd Pers. Sing. Past Tense.
Hebben, to have (old D. haven),	had (old D. havede),	gehad (old D. gehaved).	Syncope of v in Past Tense and Past Part.
Weten, to know,	wist (old D. witte, witste),	geweten.	Change of t into s in Imp. Tense.
Moeten, to be obliged,	moest (old D. moette, moetste),	gemoeten.	Change of t into s; t in 3rd Pers. Sing. Past Tense.
Houden, to hold,	hield,	gehouden.	Insertion of l before ending of Past Tense.
Mogen, to be allowed,	mocht (old D. mag),	(wanting).	Change of g into ch; former Imp. now Pres. (see observ.).
Zullen, shall, will, (old D. zollen),	zou (contr. of zolde) (old D. zal),	(wanting).	Former Imp. now Present (see observ.).
Willen, to be willing (old D. wollen),	wilde, (colloquial wou).	gewild.	Former Pres. Subj. now Pres. Ind. (see observ.).
Doen, to do (old D. daden),	deed,	gedaan (old D. gedaden).	Irregular form of Inf.; contracted Past Part.
Gaan, to go, (old D. gangen),	ging,	gegaan (old D. gegangen).	Contracted Infin. and Past Part.

Infinitive.	Past Tense.	Past Part.	Points of Irregularity.
Slaan, to beat, (old D. slagen),	sloeg,	geslagen.	Contracted form of Inf.
Staan, to stand, (old D. standen),	stond,	gestaan (old D. gestanden).	Contracted forms of Inf. and Past Part.
Zien, to see, (old D. zegen),	zag,	gezien (old D. gezegen).	Contracted forms of Inf. and Past Part.
Komen, to come, (old D. kwemen),	kwam,	gekomen (old D. gekwemen).	Altered forms of Inf. and Past Part.
Zijn, or wezen, to be.	was,	geweest (old D. gewezen and geweesd).	Mixture of different roots (see observ.).

OBS.—Besides the irregularities referred to in these lists, notice that *zijn, kunnen, mogen, zullen, en willen* omit the *t* of the third pers. sing. ind. pres.: *Hij is, kan, mag, zal, wil.*

NOTE.—A few of the above verbs have an incomplete conjugation, and may hence be called **Gebrekkige Werkwoorden**, **Defective Verbs**, viz.:

Plegen, kunnen, mogen, zullen have no form for the imperative.
Plegen, zullen have no past participle.
Zijn and *wezen*, both defective, together make up one complete verb, viz. *to be.*

XXII. 1. IMPERSONAL VERBS:—Most verbs have their first, second, and third persons sing. as well as plural, complete in every tense, and are called PERSONAL, *Persoonlijk*; there are a few, however, viz., those which indicate an action that cannot be ascribed to any particular person or thing, which are called IMPERSONAL (*Onpersoonlijk*), and are only used in the third person singular (of every tense): *het regent, sneeuwt, vriest, enz.*, it rains, snows, freezes, etc.

2. The name "Impersonal" is extended to certain expressions, which are only met with in the third person singular. Such are:

Het is koud, it is cold.
Het was winderig, it was windy.
Het zal drukkend zijn, it will be close.

Bedroeven,	*Het bedroeft mij, u zoo te zien,* I am sorry to see you like this.
Behagen,	*Het heeft den koning behaagd,* it has pleased the king.
Believen,	*Geef mij dat boek, als het u blieft,* give me that book, if you please.
Berouwen,	*Het berouwt hem, dat hij het gezegd heeft,* he is sorry that he said so.
Betamen,	*Het betaamt u niet zoo te spreken,* you have no right to speak like that.
Bevreemden,	*Het zal u zeker bevreemden mij hier te zien,* you will no doubt be astonished to see me here.
Dunken,	*Mij dunkt (het dunkt mij) dat het goed is,* I think it is all right.
Heugen,	*Het heugt mij niet u tevoren gezien te hebben,* I do not recollect having seen you before.
Opvallen,	*Het valt mij op, dat hij bleek ziet,* it strikes me that he looks pale.
Schelen,*	*Het kan mij niet schelen,* I don't care.
Smarten,	*Het smart hem, u verdriet te doen,* it pains him to grieve you.
Spijten,	*Het spijt ons, dat gij ziek zijt,* we are sorry that you are ill.
Verdrieten,	*Laat het u niet verdrieten, dat ik weg moet,* don't let it trouble you that I must leave.
Verwonderen,	*Het verwondert mij zeer, dat te hooren,* I am very much surprised to hear it.
Vrijstaan,	*Het staat u vrij, haar uit te noodigen,* you are at liberty to invite her.

3. Likewise are brought under this head certain expressions in the Passive Voice, by which an action is ascribed to an agent or agents, whose name is not mentioned (see pp. 140, 169):

Er wordt daar gedanst, they are dancing there;
Er werd goed geschoten, the shooting was good;
Er zal heel wat over gesproken worden, the matter will be much talked about.

---

* NOTE.—Observe the different meanings of the verb "*schelen*":
Niets kan hem schelen, he does not care about anything.
Wat scheelt er aan? what is the matter?
Het scheelde weinig of ik was gevallen, I very nearly fell.
Het scheelt heel wat dat deze weg korter is, this way is shorter by a good deal.
Het zal mij veel schelen als ik een paard heb, it will make a great difference to me, when I have a horse.

In the two latter sentences the idea of "difference" underlies the meaning of the verb '*schelen,*' and with this meaning it also occurs as a personal verb: *Mijn horloge scheelt weinig bij het uwe,* my watch differs little from yours.

XXIII. CAUSATIVE VERBS:—Some verbs, derived from existing ones by a change in their radical vowel, indicate that their *subject* is the cause of an action performed by the *object*. They are called CAUSATIVE VERBS (*Causatieve, Oorzakelijke Werkwoorden*). Among them the following are some of the most common:

Original Verbs.	Derivatives.
Drinken, to drink.	*Drenken*, to cause to drink.
Liggen, to lie.	*Leggen*, to cause to lie.
Vallen, to fall.	*Vellen*, to cause to fall.
Waken, to be awake.	*Wekken*, to cause to wake up.
Zitten, to sit.	*Zetten*, to cause to sit.

XXIV. FREQUENTATIVE VERBS:—Another kind of Verbs, called FREQUENTATIVE (*Frequentatieve, Herhalings-Werkwoorden*), because they indicate a constant repetition of the action, are formed from existing ones by adding the ending *elen* or *eren* to their verbal stems, with an occasional change of the stem-vowel:

Original Verbs.	Derivatives.
Bidden, to pray, ask.	*Bedelen*, to ask continually, to beg.
Druipen, to drip.	*Droppelen*, to drip constantly.
Huppen, to hop.	*Huppelen*, to continue hopping, to skip.
Wenden, to turn, to move.	*Wandelen*, to take a walk, to be constantly moving.
Stooten, to dash, to push.	*Stotteren* to stammer.
Kikken, to utter a sound.	{ *Kakelen* / *Kekkelen* } to cackle.

OBS.—Mark that Verbs in *elen* and *eren* belong to the class of Frequentatives *only when they indicate a repetition* of the action. Many other verbs have the same endings, being derived from nouns which end in *el* and *er*:

Grendelen, to bolt (from *grendel*, a bolt); *hameren*, to hammer (from *hamer*, a hammer).

XXV. COMPOUND VERBS (*Samengestelde Werkwoorden*) are of two kinds—first, those in which the first part is **inseparably connected** with the verb-stem; second, those whose first part is **occasionally separated** from the stem. The following rules assist the student in overcoming the apparent difficulty which arises from this fact.

Rule 1.—All Verbs compounded with a Noun are separable: *houthakken,* to chop wood; *leerlooien,* to tan leather; *huishouden,* to manage a household.

Rule 2.—All Verbs compounded with an Adjective are separable, except those with "*vol,*" and "*mis,*" when unaccented: *grootspreken,* to boast; *vrijlaten,* to set free; inseparable: *volhárden,* to endure; *voldóen,* to satisfy; *mishágen,* to displease; *misdóen,* to do wrong.

- Note.—*Vólhouden,* to continue, is separable, as are also those verbs in which *vol* has the meaning of "full," and has the accent.

Rule 3.—When verbs are compounded with an Adverb or preposition, the pronunciation must decide the case. When the accent lies on their first part, they are separably compounded; when the accent is on their second part, they are inseparably compounded.

Examples:—

Separable are, *áanlachen,* to smile at; *áchterhouden,* to keep back; *ómloopen,* to take a round-about way; *nádenken,* to reflect upon.

Inseparable are: *overdénken,* to consider; *aanbídden,* to adore; *weerkáatsen,* to reflect; *ontgaán,* to escape.

Rule 4.—Verbs derived from existing ones by means of the verbal prefixes, *be, ge, er, her, ont,* and *ver,* are inseparable, as: *beginnen,* to begin; *geleiden,* to lead; *erkennen,* to acknowledge; *herroepen,* to recall; *ontvangen,* to receive; *vergeten,* to forget.

Obs.—The difference in conjugation between the inseparably compounded verbs and those separably compounded is so marked that attention should be given to it here.

Separably Compounded Verbs, when conjugated, separate

themselves from their prefix throughout the entire conjugation, and in their Past Participles insert the prefix "*ge*" between their two parts.

INSEPARABLY COMPOUNDED VERBS, on the other hand, remain intact, and their Past Participles reject the prefix "*ge*."

Examples:

1. **Verbs separably compounded**: *náloopen*, to follow; Inf. *náloopen*; Pres. Part. *náloopende*; Past Part. *nágeloopen*, Pres. *ik loop na*; Imp. *ik liep na*; Perf. *ik heb nageloopen*; Plup. *ik had nageloopen*; Fut. *ik zal naloopen*; Fut. Perf. *ik zal nageloopen hebben*; Imperative, *loop na*; Inf. with Prep. *na te loopen*.

2. **Verbs inseparably compounded**: *volhárden*, to endure; Inf. *volhárden*; Pres. Part. *volhárdende* Past Part. *volhard*; Pres. *ik volhard*; Imp. *ik volhardde*; Perf. *ik heb volhard*; Plup. *ik had volhard*; Fut. *ik zal volharden*; Fut. Perf. *ik zal volhard hebben*; Imperative, *volhard*; Inf. with Prep. *te volharden*.

NOTE 1.—Derived verbs (referred to under Rule 4) having one of the verbal prefixes (*be, ge, er, her, ont,* or *ver*) likewise reject the participial prefix *ge*:

Infinitives: *beginnen, geleiden, erkennen, herroepen, ontvangen, vergeten.*

Past Participle: *begonnen, geleid, erkend, herroepen, ontvangen, vergeten.*

NOTE 2.—The verbs *antwoorden*, to answer; *argwanen*, to suspect; *dagvaarden*, to summon; *glimlachen*, to smile; *handhaven*, to maintain; *waarborgen*, to guarantee; *zegepralen*, to triumph; *beeldhouwen*, to sculpture; *zegevieren*, to triumph; *evenaren*, to equal; *wanhopen*, to despair, which are derived from compound nouns, are inseparable, but take the prefix *ge* in their past participle: *geantwoord, gezegepraald.*

NOTE 3.—The following verbs change their meaning according to the way their accent is placed:

Dóordringen,   *De vijand is in het bosch dóorgedrongen,* the enemy has penetrated into the wood.
Doordrìngen,   *Ik ben van de waarheid uwer woorden doordròngen,* I am impressed with the truth of your words.
Dóorloopen,   *Het kind is de kamer dóorgeloopen,* the child has gone through the room.
Doorlòopen,   *De boden hebben de stad in alle richtingen doorlòopen,* the messengers have traversed the town in every direction.

Dóorreizen,	Deze man is door Perzië naar Palestina gereisd, this man has travelled through Persia on his way to Palestine.
Doorrèizen,	Mijn vader heeft de geheele Kaap-Kolonie doorreisd, my father has travelled all about in Cape Colony.
Dóorsteken,	Ik heb de naald hier dóorgestoken, here I have put the needle through.
Doorstèken,	De soldaat werd doorstòken met eene lans, the soldier was stabbed with a lance.
O'ndergaan,	De maan is zooeven óndergegaan, the moon has just set.
Ondergàan,	Hij ondergàat zijn lot met kalmte, he submits to his fate with calmness.
O'nderhouden,	Hij heeft zijne woede lang óndergehouden, he has long suppressed his rage.
Onderhòuden,	De ouders worden door hunnen zoon onderhòuden, the parents are provided for by their son.
O'verdrijven,	Het onweder is óvergedreven in de richting van de zee, the thunderstorm passed over us in the direction of the sea.
Overdrìjven,	Mijn broeder heeft de zaak gewis overdrèven, my brother has no doubt exaggerated the matter.
O'verwegen,	Hij heeft de pakjes óvergewogen, he has weighed the parcels again.
Overwègen,	Men heeft het voorstel overwògen, the motion has been considered.
O'verwerken,	Ik heb het geheele opstel óvergewerkt, I have done the composition all over again.
Overwèrken,	Zijne zuster heeft zich verleden maand overwèrkt, his sister overworked herself last month.
O'verzien,	De onderwijzer heeft het huiswerk óvergezien, the teacher has looked over the homework.
Overzièn,	Van hier overziet men de geheele stad, from here one has a view of the whole town.
Vóorkomen,	Er komen veel ongelukken vóor, many accidents happen.
Voorkòmen,	Men had dien ramp kunnen voorkòmen, that calamity might have been prevented.
Vóorzeggen,	Het kind heeft zijn zusje de les vóorgezegd, the child has prompted his sister in saying the lesson.
Voorzèggen,	De val van Jeruzalem was voorzègd (geworden), Jerusalem's fall had been predicted.

THE VERB.

XXVI. LIST OF STRONG VERBS:—

Class I.

		Infinitive (ij).	Past Tense (ĕ).	Past Part. (ĕ).
1.	To confess,	belijden,	beleed,	beleden.
2.	,, succumb,	— bezwijken,	bezweek,	bezweken.
3.	,, bite,	bijten,	beet,	gebeten.
4.	,, appear (to be),	blijken,	bleek,	gebleken.
5.	,, remain,	blijven,	bleef,	gebleven.
6.	,, drive,	drijven,	dreef,	gedreven.
7.	,, resemble,	gelijken,	geleek,	geleken.
8.	,, glide,	glijden,	gleed,	gegleden.
9.	,, seize,	grijpen,	greep,	gegrepen.
10.	,, hoist,	hijschen,	heesch,	geheschen.
11.	,, look,	kijken,	keek,	gekeken.
12.	,, pinch,	knijpen,	kneep,	geknepen.
13.	,, get,	krijgen,(1)	kreeg,	gekregen.
14.	,, croak,	krijschen,	kreesch,	gekreschen.
15.	,, acquit oneself,	kwijten,(2)	kweet,	gekweten.
16.	,, suffer,	lijden,	leed,	geleden.
17.	,, seem (to be),	lijken,	leek,	geleken.
18.	,, avoid,	mijden,	meed,	gemeden.
19.	,, incline (bow),	nijgen,	neeg,	genegen.
20.	,, pass away (die),	overlijden,	overleed,	overleden.
21.	,, praise,	prijzen,(3)	prees,	geprezen.
22.	,, ride,	rijden,	reed,	gereden.
23.	,, lace,	rijgen,	reeg,	geregen.
24.	,, tear,	rijten,	reet,	gereten.
25.	,, rise up,	rijzen,	rees,	gerezen.
26.	,, seem, to shine,	schijnen,	scheen,	geschenen.
27.	,, saunter,	schrijden,	schreed,	geschreden.
28.	,, write,	schrijven,	schreef,	geschreven.
29.	,, sharpen,	slijpen,	sleep,	geslepen.
30.	,, wear out,	slijten,	sleet,	gesleten.
31.	,, fling,	smijten,	smeet,	gesmeten.
32.	,, cut,	snijden,	sneed,	gesneden.
33.	,, be sorry,	spijten,(4)	speet,	gespeten.
34.	,, split,	splijten,	spleet,	gespleten.
35.	,, ascend,	stijgen,	steeg,	gestegen.
36.	,, starch,	stijven,(5)	steef,	gesteven.
37.	,, strive (fight),	strijden,	streed,	gestreden.
38.	,, iron, to skim over,	strijken,	streek,	gestreken.
39.	,, disappear,	verdwijnen,	verdween,	verdwenen.
40.	,, give way, to yield,	wijken,	week,	geweken.
41.	,, impute,	wijten,	weet,	geweten.
42.	,, show,	wijzen,	wees,	gewezen.
43.	,, rub,	wrijven,	wreef,	gewreven.
44.	,, sink, to filter,	zijgen,	zeeg,	gezegen.
45.	,, be silent,	zwijgen,	zweeg,	gezwegen.

THE COMMERCIAL DUTCH GRAMMAR.

Notes.—1. *Krijgen*, to wage war, is weak.
2. *Kwijten* is reflexive: *ik heb mij van mijnen plicht gekweten*, I have fulfilled my duty.
3. *Prijzen*, to price, is weak: *hij heeft het linnen geprijsd*, he has marked the price on the linen.
4. *Spijten* is impersonal: *het spijt mij*, I am sorry.
5. *Stijven*, to encourage (harden), is weak: *hij stijfde mij in het kwade*.

Class II.	Infinitive (a) ĭ, (b) ĕ.	Past Tense (ŏ).	Past Part. (ŏ).
(a) 1. To begin,	beginnen,	begon,	begonnen.
2. ,, bind,	binden,	bond,	gebonden.
3. ,, shine,	blinken,	blonk,	geblonken.
4. ,, strive for,	dingen,	dong,	gedongen.
5. ,, urge,	dringen,	drong,	gedrongen.
6. ,, drink,	drinken,	dronk,	gedronken.
7. ,, force (coerce),	dwingen,	dwong,	gedwongen.
8. ,, gleam,	glimmen,	glom,	geglommen.
9. ,, climb,	klimmen,	klom,	geklommen.
10. ,, sound,	klinken,	klonk,	geklonken.
11. ,, shrink,	krimpen,	kromp,	gekrompen.
12. ,, fallow (to open),	ontginnen,	ontgon,	ontgonnen.
13. ,, get startled,	schrikken,(1)	schrok,	geschrokken.
14. ,, diminish in size,	slinken,	slonk,	geslonken.
15. ,, spin,	spinnen,	spon,	gesponnen.
16. ,, jump,	springen,	sprong,	gesprongen.
17. ,, stink,	stinken,	stonk,	gestonken.
18. ,, devour,	verslinden,	verslond,	verslonden.
19. ,, vanish,	verzwinden,	verzwond,	verzwonden.
20. ,, find,	vinden,	vond,	gevonden.
21. ,, wind,	winden,	wond,	gewonden.
22. ,, win, to gain,	winnen,	won,	gewonnen.
23. ,, wring,	wringen,	wrong,	gewrongen.
24. ,, sing,	zingen,	zong,	gezongen.
25. ,, sink,	zinken,	zonk,	gezonken.
26. ,, meditate,	zinnen,	zon,	gezonnen.
(b) 1. ,, put by,	bergen,	borg,	geborgen.
2. ,, delve (dig),	delven,	dolf,	gedolven.
3. ,, be worth,	gelden,	gold,	gegolden.
4. ,, carve,	kerven,	korf,	gekorven.
5. ,, milk,	melken,(2)	molk,	gemolken.
6. ,, call names,	schelden,	schold,	gescholden.
7. ,, violate,	schenden,	schond,	geschonden.
8. ,, make a present, to pour,	schenken,	schonk,	geschonken.
9. ,, melt,	smelten,	smolt,	gesmolten.
10. ,, hit,	treffen,	trof,	getroffen.

THE VERB.

Class II.	Infinitive (a) ĭ, (b) ĕ.	Past Tense (ŏ).	Past Part. (ö).
11. To pull, to journey,	trekken,	trok,	getrokken.
12. „ fight,	vechten,	vocht,	gevochten.
13. „ plait,	vlechten,	vlocht,	gevlochten.
14. „ send,	zenden,	zond,	gezonden.
15. „ swallow,	zwelgen,	zwolg,	gezwolgen.
16. „ swell,	zwellen,	zwol,	gezwollen.
17. „ swim,	zwemmen,	zwom,	gezwommen.

NOTES.—1. *Schrikken*, to startle (trans.), is weak. It is usually replaced by *verschrikken*: *De tijding heeft ons allen verschrikt.*

2. *Melken* is also used weak.

Class III.	Infinitive (a) ie, (b) ē, (c) u, (d) ui, (e) ij.	Past Tense (ō).	Past Part. (ö).
(a) 1. To deceive,	bedriegen,	bedroog,	bedrogen.
2. „ offer,	bieden,	bood,	geboden.
3. „ enjoy,	genieten,	genoot,	genoten.
4. „ pour, to water,	gieten,	goot,	gegoten.
5. „ choose,	kiezen,	koos,	gekozen.
6. „ tell lies.	liegen,	loog,	gelogen.
7. „ shoot,	schieten,	schoot,	geschoten.
8. „ grieve,	verdrieten, (1)	verdroot,	verdroten.
9. „ loose,	verliezen,	verloor,	verloren.
10. „ flee,	vlieden,	vlood,	gevloden.
11. „ fly,	vliegen,	vloog,	gevlogen.
12. „ flow,	vlieten,	vloot,	gevloten.
13. „ freeze,	vriezen, (2)	vroor,	gevroren.
14. „ boil (seethe),	zieden, (3)	zood,	gezoden.
(b) 1. „ shave (shear),	scheren,	schoor,	geschoren.
2. „ weigh,	wegen,	woog,	gewogen.
3. „ ulcerate,	zweren,	zwoor,	gezworen.
(c) 1. „ spit,	spugen, (4)	spoog,	gespogen.
(d) 1. „ bend,	buigen,	boog,	gebogen.
2. „ drip,	druipen,	droop,	gedropen.
3. „ dive,	duiken,	dook,	gedoken.
4. „ whistle,	fluiten,	floot,	gefloten.
5. „ gnaw (a bone),	kluiven,	kloof,	gekloven.
6. „ wheel (on a barrow),	kruien, (5)	krooi,	gekrooien.
7. „ creep,	kruipen,	kroop,	gekropen.
8. „ close,	luiken, (6)	look,	geloken.

H

Class III.

Infinitive: (a) ie, (b) ē, (c) u, (d) ui, (e) ij.
Past Tense: (ŏ).
Past Part.: (ō).

		Infinitive	Past Tense	Past Part.
9.	To ravel out,	pluizen, (7)	ploos,	geplozen.
10.	,, smell,	ruiken,	rook,	geroken.
11.	,, take shelter,	schuilen, (8)	school.	gescholen.
12.	,, move (shove)	schuiven,	schoof,	geschoven.
13.	,, smuggle,	sluiken,	slook,	gesloken.
14.	,, sneak,	sluipen,	sloop,	geslopen.
15.	,, lock,	sluiten,	sloot,	gesloten.
16.	,, blow (the nose),	snuiten,	snoot,	gesnoten.
17.	,, sniff (take snuff).	snuiven,	snoof,	gesnoven.
18.	,, sprout,	spruiten,	sproot,	gesproten.
19.	,, spout,	spuiten,	spoot,	gespoten.
20.	,, raise dust,	stuiven,	stoof,	gestoven.
21.	,, suck,	zuigen,	zoog,	gezogen,
22.	,, tipple,	zuipen,	zoop,	gezopen.
(e) 1.	,, go (journey),	tijgen, (9)	toog,	getogen.

NOTES.—1. *Verdrieten* is impersonal: *het verdriet mij,* it grieves me.
2. *Vriezen* is likewise conjugated : *vroos, gevrozen.*
3. *Zieden* is rarely used.
4. *Spugen* is also used weak.
5. *Kruien* is also used weak.
6. *Luiken* is only used of flowers and the human eye.
7. *Pluizen* is used for picking out (as wool), and examining (any matter) closely; it is used both strong and weak.
8. *Schuilen* is also used weak.
9. *Tijgen* has a complete conjugation, but the present tense is rarely used.

Class IV.

Infinitive: (a) ē, (b) ĭ, (c) ē.
Past Tense: (a).
Past Part.: (a) ē, (b) ē, (c) ō.

		Infinitive	Past Tense	Past Part.
(a) 1.	To eat,	eten,	at,	gegeten.
2.	,, cure,	genezen,	genas,	genezen.
3.	,, give,	geven,	gaf,	gegeven.
4.	,, read,	lezen,	las,	gelezen.
5.	,, measure,	meten,	mat,	gemeten.
6.	,, tread (step),	treden,	trad,	getreden.
7.	,, forget,	vergeten,	vergat,	vergeten.
8.	,, gorge,	vreten,	vrat,	gevreten.
(b) 1.	,, pray,	bidden,	bad,	gebeden.
2.	,, lie down,	liggen,	lag,	gelegen.

THE VERB.

Class IV.	Infinitive (a) ē, (b) ĭ, (c) ē.	Past Tense (a).	Past Part. (a) ē, (b) ē, (c) ō.
3. To be sitting,	zitten,	zat,	gezeten.
(c) 1. ,, command,	bevelen,	beval,	bevolen.
2. ,, break,	breken,	brak,	gebroken.
3. ,, take,	nemen,	nam,	genomen.
4. ,, speak,	spreken,	sprak,	gesproken.
5. ,, stab (put through),	steken,	stak,	gestoken.
6. ,, steal,	stelen,	stal,	gestolen.

Class V.	Infinitive (a) ā, (b) ă, (c) ō, (d) oe, (e) ou, (f) ē, (g) ě, (h) ĕ.	Past Tense (ie).	Past Part. (a) ā, (b) ă, (c) ō, (d) oe, (e) ou, (f) ē, (g) ŏ, (h) ū.
(a) 1. To blow,	blazen,	blies,	geblazen.
2. ,, let,	laten,	liet,	gelaten.
3. ,, sleep,	slapen,	sliep,	geslapen.
(b) 1. ,, fall,	vallen,	viel,	gevallen.
2. ,, grow (wax),	wassen, (1)	wies,	gewassen.
(c) 1. ,, run (walk),	loopen,	liep,	geloopen.
(d) 1. ,, call,	roepen,	riep,	geroepen.
(e) 1. ,, hew,	houwen,	hieuw,	gehouwen.
(f) 1. ,, lift,	heffen,	hief,	geheven.
(g) 1. ,, corrupt (spoil),	bederven,	bedierf,	bedorven.
2. ,, help,	helpen,	hielp,	geholpen.
3. ,, die,	sterven,	stierf,	gestorven.
4. ,, throw,	werpen,	wierp,	geworpen.
5. ,, recruit,	werven,	wierf,	geworven.
6. ,, wander,	zwerven,	zwierf,	gezworven.
(h) 1. ,, create,	scheppen, (2)	schiep,	geschapen.

Notes.—1. *Wassen*, to cover with wax, is weak.
2. *Scheppen*, to scoop or dip out, is weak.

Class VI.	Infinitive (a) ā, (b) ē.	Past Tense (oe).	Past Part. (a) ā, (b) ō.
(a) 1. To carry (bear),	dragen,	droeg,	gedragen.
2. ,, dig,	graven,	groef,	gegraven.
3. ,, navigate (sail),	varen,	voer,	gevaren.
(b) 1. ,, swear (take oath),	zweren,	zwoer,	gezworen.

H 2

	Infinitive	Past Tense	Past Part.
Class VII.	(ă).	(ĭ).	(ă).
1. To hang,	hangen,	hing,	gehangen.
2. „ catch.	vangen,	ving,	gevangen.

	Infinitive	Past Tense	Past Part.
Class VIII.	(ŏ).	(ĕ).	(ŏ).
1. To become,	worden,	werd,	geworden.

GRAMMAR EXERCISES.—*Taaloefeningen.*

EXERCISE LIX.*

1. Determine the stems of the following verbs.

Denken; doen; vragen; blijven; zoeken; leven; zien; hangen; zagen (to saw); *liggen; brengen; drogen; voelen; gaan; onderwijzen* (to teach); *proeven* (to taste); *lesschen* (to quench); *visschen; suizen* (to rustle); *ruischen* (to rustle); *hakken; schoppen* (to kick); *dwalen* (to wander); *pochen* (to brag); *bogen* (to boast); *zuchten; lachen; wezen; bedelen* (to beg); *verblinden* (to blind); *ontdoen* (to strip); *rekken* (to stretch); *tornen* (to unpick); *naaien; mazen* (to darn); *breien* (to knit); *haken* (to crochet); *zoomen* (to hem); *stikken* (to stitch); *bedragen* (to amount to); *gebeuren; voorvallen* (to take place); *lezen; vreezen; kussen* (to kiss); *kuchen* (to cough); *stoven* (to stew); *koeren* (to coo); *kweelen* (to warble); *tjilpen* (to chirp); *slaan; piepen; gichelen* (to giggle); *oorlogen* (to wage war); *vuren* (to fire); *schieten; vellen* (to fell); *villen* (to skin); *vallen; bespotten* (to mock); *verbreken* (to break); *verhuren* (to hire out).

2. Write out the singular and the plural form of the Imperative Mood of all the above verbs; and the first person, singular and plural, of the Indicative Present.

Exercise LX.

1. Write out the first person, singular, of the Indicative and Subjunctive Present of the following verbs.

Besteden (to spend); *vertellen;* *ergeren* (to vex); *spitten* (to dig); *raden* (to guess); *overreden* (to prevail upon); *duwen* (to push); *duren* (to last); *zetten;* *plaatsen;* *missen;* *fronsen* (to frown); *heelen* (to heal); *verhelen* (to hide); *gedijen* (to thrive); *ontleden* (to analyse); *verschepen* (to ship); *temmen* (to tame); *laven* (to refresh); *zalven* (to anoint); *inenten* (to vaccinate); *mesten* (to manure); *landen;* *rusten;* *planten;* *dulden* (to endure); *troosten* (to comfort); *branden;* *roosten* (to roast); *braveeren* (to brave); *ontberen* (to do without); *geschieden* (to happen); *kwaken* (to croak); *schroeven* (to screw); *gooien* (to throw); *schrobben* (to scrub); *schuren* (to scour); *beletten* (to prevent); *draven* (to trot); *verlaten* (to leave); *ontzetten* (to set free); *kruisen* (to cross).

2. Of the above verbs write out the stem, the Past Tense (first person, singular) and the Past Participle.

Exercise LXI.

In the following exercise write the words in italics in the plural.

Hoe laat *is uw broeder* aangekomen? Het paard kan *den wagen* niet trekken; *de jongen zal het* moeten uitspannen: zulk een dier is veel te zwak voor *die vracht.* Waarom *heeft de man het gat* zoo diep gegraven? *Ik vertelde hem* dat *het boek* niet gedrukt *kon* worden; maar *hij wilde mij* niet gelooven. Kind, kind, wat zal er toch van *je* groeien? Hoe dikwijls *heb ik je* niet gewaarschuwd! *Ik had mij* gewasschen vóór ik in de kamer *kwam.* Wie *is* vandaag hier geweest? Wanneer *wordt uw vriend* verwacht? Mijn vader zeide *mij,* dat *ik mij* in dien persoon vergist *moest* hebben. *Denk* aan wat ik *u* zoo dikwijls gezegd heb: het *is de slechtste perzik* niet waaraan *de wesp knaagt. De timmerman zaagt* het hout. *Het jonge meisje bood mij eenen kleinen ruiker* aan. Hoe dikwijls *baadt hij zich* gewoonlijk? *De ooievaar kuiert* langs *de sloot*, om te zien of *hij* er geen *kikker* uit *kan halen, dien hij* dan lekker *opsmult. De telegraafpaal staat* eenzaam in het veld. *De adelaar bouwt zijn* nest op den *top* van *eenen hoogen berg.*

Exercise LXII.

Of the following verbs write out the third person, singular and plural, of the Indicative Present.

Binden; delven (to dig); *spelen; straffen; beloven* (to promise); *wasschen; bepalen* (to decide); *vragen, snijden; onthalen* (to treat); *lezen; gaan; scheiden* (to separate); *weven* (to weave); *schrijven; vreezen; streven* (to strive); *beseffen* (to realise); *oorlogen* (to wage war); *staren* (to stare); *zaaien; voeden; heeten* (to be called); *zich herinneren* (to remember); *bewijzen* (to prove); *bidden* (to pray); *antwoorden, slaan.*

Exercise LXIII.

Of the following sets of verbs write out the Stem, Past Tense (first person, singular), and Past Participle.

1.

Strong verbs (§§ III and XXVI):

Bieden (to offer); *blijken* (to appear); *bergen* (to put aside); *drinken; eten; genezen* (to cure); *breken; fluiten* (to whistle); *kiezen* (to choose); *vriezen; hangen; glimmen* (to gleam); *lezen; loopen; nemen; schelden* (to call names); *meten* (to measure); *schrijven; sluiten; slijten* (to wear out); *schenken* (to give or pour); *stelen; spreken; smelten; vangen; vechten.*

2.

Strong, Mixed, and Anomalous verbs (§§ XX, XXI, XXVI):

Houden; sluipen (to steal); *raden; zoeken; zeggen; vergeten; plegen; verliezen; lachen; wassen; dunken; wezen; werven* (to levy an army); *zitten; jagen; bakken; zullen; zweren* (to swear); *moeten; wasschen; laden; zwijgen; wrijven; koopen; brouwen; weven; zweren* (to ulcerate) *sterven; wreken; begraven; denken; zien; komen.*

3.

Compound and Derivative verbs (§ XXV):

Leerlooien; losmaken; beeldhouwen (to sculpture); *liefhebben; volhouden; volharden; volgieten; volbrengen* (to accomplish); *ontvangen; antwoorden; dagvaarden; òverwerken; ondergàan; herroepen; grootspreken; vrijlaten; náloopen; doorrèizen; zegevieren; wanhopen: mishàgen; misschieten* (to miss aim in shooting); *vólloopen* (to run full); *veroveren* (to conquer); *onderwèrpen* (to subdue); *doorblàderen* (to peruse); *evenaren; vóorkomen; úitloopen* (to sprout); *ontluiken* (to open, of flowers); *overdrìjven; voorzèggen.*

Exercise LXIV.

Write out the following exercise, first in the third person, singular; then in the second person, singular; and lastly in the third person, plural, using throughout the tenses as they are given.

Ik sprak met mijnen vader en wees hem den brief, dien ik geschreven had. Ik vertelde mijnen oom wat mij op den weg overkomen was, en hoe ik bijna een ongeluk had gekregen. Op school hoorde ik van mijnen onderwijzer, dat ik de eerste op de lijst stond en dat ik dus eenen prijs zou krijgen. Ik schreef het blad vol, en vouwde toen den brief op, en deed hem in een envelop. Ik riep den postbode toe, dat ik hem zou verklagen, indien ik weer zoo iets merkte. Ik zal het aannemen, als ik mag, maar ik weet niet, of mijn vader het mij zal toelaten Ik geloof niet, dat ik mijzelf zooveel kwaad doe, als hij mij wijs wil maken. Ik kan het niet helpen, dat ik niet eerder gekomen ben: mijn vader heeft mij om eene boodschap gezonden, en daardoor moest ik wel later komen. Ik ben van morgen vroeg op geweest, maar nu ga ik ook vroeg naar bed. Ik wil het hem niet zeggen, want ik houd er niet van, geheimen te verraden. Het zal mij wezenlijk veel genoegen doen, als ik morgen door dit werk heen kom. Ik behoef mij daarover niet te schamen, dat ik met mijne eigene handen mijn brood verdien. Ik kan ervan zeggen, wat ik wil; gehoorzaamd word ik toch niet. Ik zou wel graag naar de kerk gaan, maar ik ben bang dat ik erg verkouden worden zal. Heb ik mij niet altijd fatsoenlijk gedragen? Heb ik mij ooit aan die familie opgedrongen? Had ik mij niet kunnen verrijken ten koste van mijne vrienden, en heb ik ooit iemand te kort gedaan? Wil ik eens gaan rijden, dan zadel ik zelf mijn paard, want ik houd er niet van den knecht altijd lastig te vallen voor mijn plezier.

Exercise LXV.

In the following exercise change the Infinitive form of the verb into the required form of (1st) the Present Tense, (2nd) the Past, and (3rd) the Future of the Indicative Mood.

Mijne tante (geven) les aan vier kinderen; zij (doen) hun best en (maken) goede vorderingen. Er (zijn) eene zware wolk op den berg; het (duren) niet meer lang of het (regenen). De trein (razen) en (rommelen), terwijl hij ons (voorbijvliegen). De mannen (werken) vandaag aan den weg; zij (rusten) en (gebruiken) hun middagmaal. Met welke boot (vertrekken) uw vriend naar Australië? Een jager (loopen) over het veld en (dragen) zijn geweer onder den arm. De kinderen (baden) zich eerst in den dam en (kleeden) zich daarna aan. De zwaluw (zitten) op eenen tak en (fluiten) een vroolijk deuntje

terwijl zijn wijfje de eieren (broeden). Waarom (laden) de
soldaat zijn geweer? Een hevig onweer (losbreken) over de
stad. De zon om zeven uur (ondergaan). De man (graven)
diep in den grond. De wind (suizen) door de boomen en (doen)
de dorre bladeren ritselen. De generaal (handhaven) de eer
der republiek. Het gedrag van mijnen neef (mishagen) onzen
rector. Onze tuinman (leiden) water in den tuin. Het
koper (verscheept worden) te Port Nolloth. De luie kinderen
(gestraft worden) door den onderwijzer. Na een uur de pijn
óvergaan.

Exercise LXVI.

Fill in the endings and complete the verbal forms in
the following exercises.

De boer ploeg-, zaai- en eg- het land, en hoop- dan op
regen om het zaad te laat- groei-. De man en zijn zoon zat-
in de kar en reed- ons voorbij zonder ons te merken in. Toen
wij ons van morgen in de rivier wild- baad-, zaag- wij er
een- groot- slang in rondzwem-. Houd- u van warm- melk?
De metselaar- heb- de muur- gepleister-. Wanneer word-
dit meel gemaal-? Had- uw neef zich niet zoo ver gewaag-,
hij zou zijn been niet gebrook- heb-. Hoor- u die twee vogels,
welk- daar boven in den boom zit- te zing-? Hij ga- morgen
verneem-, of hij kans heef- de betrekking te krijg-. Wij kon-
uw- broeder niet overreed- met ons mede te kom-. Deze
boeken zou- al uitgegeef- zijn, als de kist vroeg- bezorgd was.
Uw- ouders waar- zeer ongerus-, toen zij niets van u hoor-.
De boom- word- dit jaar niet gesnoei-. Door wien zul- de
proef- van dit werk gelees- wor-? Heef- hij niet beloof- u
te help- als gij in nood waar-? Waarom kom- hij nu zijn
belofte niet na? Hoelang waar- vader en zoon gescheid-
gewees-? Al de pad- in ons- tuin zijn gegruis-. Het kind
heef- maar drie uur- geleef-, nadat het geval- was.

Exercise LXVII.

In the following exercises change the Infinitive form of the Verb into (1st) the Present Perfect, and (2nd) the Future Perfect.
(Mind the use of the Auxiliaries *hebben* and *zijn*, § IV.)

Mijn vader — mij niet (straffen), maar — mij (zeggen) dat het niet weer gebeuren moet. De vogels — een rustig plekje (uitzoeken) en — daar een nestje (bouwen) waarin zij hunne eieren — (leggen). De kinderen — zich vlug (wasschen) en (aankleeden) en — nu den tuin (ingaan). De vleermuis — den geheelen nacht in de kamer (rondvliegen), hij — door het open raam (inkomen). Al de leerlingen — een halven dag vrij (hebben) en — dien tijd (gebruiken) om de brieven te beantwoorden, die zij van huis (ontvangen) —. Dit kind — lang ziek (wezen), en al dien tijd — hare onderwijzeres haar geregeld (opzoeken). — er zooveel ongelukken op dit pad (gebeuren)? Neen, de municipaliteit — het in orde laten brengen (see § XI, Obs.). De kleine varkens — onder de heg (doorkruipen), en — veel schade in den tuin (doen). Hoe lang — het Romeinsche Rijk (bestaan)? Mijn broer — ziek (worden), nadat hij — (vallen). Om hoe laat — de les (beginnen)? Onze beste koeien — dezen winter (sterven). Men — dat ongeluk niet (kunnen voorkomen). Wanneer — de begrafenis (plaats hebben). Ik — er niet bij tegenwoordig (zijn). Door wien — deze peren (geplukt worden)? Deze vaas — (breken), omdat de kat erop (springen) —. Het ijs in de sloot — (ontdooien), zoodra de zon warm — (worden).

Exercise LXVIII.

Express the following in the Passive Voice (§ X, c. 5).

De slager slacht de koe. De os trekt den ploeg. De ezel heeft de kar getrokken. De man had den hond geslagen. Ik schreef eenen brief. Waarom heeft mijne moeder mij geroepen.

Had het onweer veel schade gedaan? In twee uren leer ik al mijne lessen. De hond zal zijnen meester gevonden hebben. Het menschelijk lichaam kan veel ziekte verdragen. Men vindt in sommige deelen van dit land nog olifanten. De wet beschermt den secretarisvogel. Verscheidene malen heb ik aan uwe deur geklopt, maar niemand heeft mij gehoord. Waarom had men hem niet gezegd, dat men hem zijn verzoek niet kon toestaan? Wij zullen onze reis voortzetten, zoodra de zware regens ophouden. Waarin vangt men het regenwater op? — heeft u dat al ooit onderzocht? Napoleon de Groote won den slag bij Austerlitz. Men speelde in dat hotel veel biljart. Mijn oom zou dien man vertrouwd hebben, als ik hem niet gewaarschuwd had. De goudmijnen hebben Zuid-Afrika in menig opzicht voordeel aangebracht. Wie heeft de boekdrukkunst uitgevonden? De Duitschers zeggen, dat Gutenberg haar uitgevonden heeft. Men heeft de luiheid des duivels oorkussen genoemd. Men kan dien man niet overreden zijn testament te maken. Zouden de kinderen hunnen vader niet hebben kunnen weerhouden van zulk een dwazen stap? Men zegt, dat de vijand den bergpas bezet heeft.

Exercise LXIX.

Express the following in the Active Voice (§ X, c. 5).

Het huis zou door dien metselaar gebouwd (geworden) zijn, indien ik eerder van dien man gehoord had. De haas is door den jager neergeschoten (geworden), nadat hij door den hond opgejaagd was (geworden). Werden de paarden in vroegere eeuwen ook beslagen, of werd hun hoef toen niet beveiligd tegen de ruwe steenen, die toch altijd op de wegen gevonden worden? De muizen zouden in de val gevangen kunnen worden, indien er een stukje spek ingelegd werd. Er wordt gezegd, dat de mijn gesloten zal worden. Er werd gisteren avond laat aan de deur geklopt. Er is mij vandaag eenen brief gezonden (geworden) door iemand, die mij geheel onbekend is. Door zulke hulp zal deze vrouw niet veel gebaat worden. Den *geheelen dag werd daar piano gespeeld. Alle boomen waren door den tuinman verplant (geworden) zonder dat hem daarvan door mijnen vader iets gezegd was (geworden). Het geld, dat door u verkwist wordt, zou gebruikt kunnen worden tot leniging van den nood der armen, die in den omtrek gevonden worden. Dit onrecht zou u niet aangedaan (geworden) zijn, als ik hier geweest was. Er zijn hier in den laatsten tijd veel paarden van edel ras ingevoerd (geworden). Door wie zijn deze woorden in mijn boek geschreven (geworden)? Door wie wordt nog aan zulke dwaasheden geloofd?*

Exercise LXX.

In the following exercises put the verbs in the tenses indicated.

De dief — niet — — (inbreken, Subj., Fut., Perf.*), als mijn vader t'huis — — (wezen,* Pluperf.*). Het huis, dat ik — — — (laten bouwen,* Perf.*), is nu — (verhuren,* Past Part.*). — (hebben,* Subj., Past*) ik maar eenen vriend tot wien ik mij — — (wenden kunnen,* Past*)! Gisteren — ik eenen brief — (schrijven,* Perf.*), en morgen — ik er twee — (schrijven,* Fut.*). Al de melk — — — (overkoken,* Subj., Fut., Perf.*) als ik niet in de keuken — — (komen,* Pluperf.*). — (weten,* Subj., Pluperf.*) ik —, dat mijn vader zoo ziek — (wezen,* Past*), ik — dadelijk — (terugkeeren,* Subj., Pluperf.*). In minder dan eene maand tijds — (verliezen,* Past*) deze man het geheele fortuin, dat hij met speculeeren — — (maken,* Pluperf.*) — (leven,* Subj., Past*) mijn goede vader nu nog maar! Deze dame — al hare kinderen — (verliezen,* Perf.*); zij — allen jong — (sterven,* Perf.*); nu — ook haar echtgenoot — (overlijden,* Perf.*), en — (achterblijven,* Pres.*) zij geheel alleen —. Als alles goed — (gaan,* Pres.*), — (weerzien,* Pres.*) u mij vandaag over veertien dagen —. Het — vannacht zoo zwaar — (regenen,* Perf.*), dat de geheele tuin — — onderloopen,* Perf.*) Waarom — u niet aan den heer B. — (schrijven,* Perf.*)? Ik — hem — (schrijven,* Fut.*), zoodra ik tijd — (krijgen,* Pres.*). Deze jonge dames — (besteden,*

Past) *al haren tijd aan muziek en teekennen, toen zij op school* — (zijn, Past). *Het schip* — (komen, Past) *gisteren avond in de baai, en* — (landen, Past) *van morgen. Juist toen wij* — — (verhuizen, Pluperf.) — (worden, Past) *mijne moeder zoo zwaar ziek, dat de dokter het ergste (vreezen,* Past); — (zijn, Subj., Pluperf.) *Maria toen niet bij mij* —, *ik* — *niet* — — (weten, Subj., Fut. Perf.) *wat* — — (doen, Inf.). *Het hof* — *gisteren* — (zitten, Perf.), *en de zaak van den heer A.* — *voor* — (wezen, Perf.); *de rechter* — *echter nog geene uitspraak* (doen, Perf.). *Hoe lang* — *de vergadering* — (duren, Fut.).

Exercise LXXI.

Use all verbs reflexive and in the tenses indicated (§ XIX).

Mijn paard — — (bezeeren, Perf.) *door* — *tegen den post van de staldeur* — — (stooten, Inf.). — (vergissen, Pres.) *gij* — *niet, als gij zegt, dat al die menschen* — — — (verkleeden, Pluperf.) — (verbeelden, Imperative) —, *dat men mij vertelt, dat hij* — *in dien man* — — (bedriegen, Perf.). *Mijn vriend* — (storen, Pres.) — *niet aan wat men van hem zegt, hierdoor* — (benadeelen, Pres.) *hij* — *dikwijls. Toen de zon opging* — (wasschen, Past) *de vogels* — *in het beekje, en* — (strijken, Past) — *toen de veertjes glad. De kinderen*— (aanmatigen, Past) — *te veel vrijheid* —. — (bedenken, Imperative) — *wel, eer gij* — *tot zoo iets* — (verbinden, Pres.). *Deze vrouw* — — *niet* — (ontzien, Perf.) — *op mijne vroegere vriendschap* — — (beroepen, Inf.). *Vroeger geloofde men, dat de zon* — *om de aarde* — (bewegen, Past). *Ik* — (schamen, Pres.) — *niet alleen over uw gedrag, maar* — (bedroeven, Pres.) *er* — *over. Wij* — — *gisteren avond zeer aangenaam met dat jonge meisje* — (onderhòuden, Perf.). *Wij* — (zullen, Past) — *op die partij* — — (amuseeren, Perf.), *als wij de gasten wat beter gekend hadden. Ik* — (kunnen, Pres.) — *niet* — (begrijpen, Inf.), *dat gij* — *over deze handelwijze* — (beklagen, Pres.); *gij* — (kunnen, Pres.)—

toch niet — — *(verbeelden,* Inf., Perf.*), dat ik* — *niet de geheele zorg* — — *(belasten,* Subj., Fut.*), zoodat er niets voor u te doen overbleef.* — *(herinneren,* Pres.*) zij* — *den naam niet meer? Als gij* — *niet* — — *(haasten,* Pluperf.*), waart gij den trein misgeloopen. Heb ik u niet gezegd, dat gij* — *voor dien man* — — *(hoeden moeten,* Past*)? Voor hem* — *(kunnen,* Past*) ik* — *al die moeite niet* — *(getroosten,* Inf.*). Als wij* — *niet over dat arme mensch* — — *(ontfermen,* Pluperf.*), was zij zeker van gebrek omgekomen.*

Exercise LXXII.

Substitute for the Infinitive forms whatever tense fits in with the context.

De bijbel (zeggen), dat die (Sing.) *niet werken (willen) ook niet eten (moeten). Al (zijn) de leugen nog zoo snel, de waarheid (achterhalen) haar wel. Het oog des meesters (maken) het paard vet. De ware wijsheid (wegen) hare woorden; de zot (flappen) ze gedachteloos uit. Gisteren (lezen) ik een mooi boek. Van morgen (zeggen,* § XV, Obs. 3*) mijn vader mij, dat hij een nieuw paard (koopen). Rome (verwoesten) Karthago. Julius Cæsar (zijn) een Romeinsch veldheer. Als het morgen nog zoo (regenen), ik t'huis (moeten blijven). Waarom (zeggen) u hem niet, dat u het niet (doen)? Verleden jaar (dragen) onze vruchtboomen zoo veel dat wij meer vruchten (hebben) dan wij gebruiken (kunnen). Waaraan (sterven) uwe koe? Komen de dokter toch maar. Door wien (teekenen) deze kaart? Mijne moeder hoopt, dat zij u nog (zien). Als hij het doet, ik hem (straffen). Als zij het deed, ik haar (straffen). De dienst in de kerk gisteren lang (duren). Wat hij ook (zeggen), (gelooven) hem niet. Zij vroeg of ik haar nu betalen (kunnen). Als gij uwen plicht (doen), gij niet in moeielijkheid (raken). Als mijn vader mij roept, (komen) ik. Als hij mij riep, (komen) ik. Als hij mij roepen zal, ik (komen). Als hij mij geroepen had, ik (komen). Toen de Hollanders zich aan de Kaap*

(*vestigen*), (*worden*) *het land door wilde stammen bewoond.
Nadat hij het telegram* (*lezen*), (*overhandigen*) *hij het aan
mij.* (*Mogen*) *deze vreeselijke gebeurtenis u tot waarschuwing
strekken.* (*Luisteren*) *mijn zoon maar naar mijne vermaningen!
Toen de vogel* (*zien*), *dat het deurtje van de kooi open* (*zijn*),
(*vliegen*) *hij er uit. Als het paard* (*voelen*), *dat het los* (*zijn*),
het (*wegloopen*).

Exercise LXXIII.

Fill up the blanks and complete the verbal forms in the following exercises.

*Beide de aarde en de maan word– door d– zon verlich–,
en laat– dus schaduw val– in d– ruimte achter zich. Kom–
de maan nu bij haa– omloop juist achter d– aarde dan word–
zij verduister–. Goed– kinderen heb– het altijd druk. Een
verstandig kind zorg– voor tijd tot slaap–, eet–, speel– en
leer–. Gij verbeuzel– de oogenblik–, en uur– en dag– zijn
uit oogenblik– samengestel–. Het waar– te wensch– dat hij
eindelijk naar mijn– raad luister–. Gij en uw broer kun–
beid– gaan. Hij of zijn vader moet d– boom omhak–.
Vroeger werd– door d– vorsten een– overgroot– macht uit–
geoefen–, toen d– gemeen– man geloof–, dat de edellieden van
ander– bloed gemaak– waar– dan zijzelv–. Wij baad– ons
gisteren tweemaal in d– dam. Zijwormen leef– van moerbei–
blad–. Louw Wepeners mannen had– d– berg bestorm–, maar
waar– teruggeslaag–: hij zou hem neem–. Toen d– verrader–
lijk — kogel hem vel–, ent– zij hun– bloed met het zijn– en
bewees– op heidensch– wijze hem de grootst– eer. Zuid-
Afrika, hij behoor– tot uw– dapperst– zoon–! Kostbaar
blijf– zijn– voorbeeld aan allen. Neen, gij stierf– niet ver–
geef–: uw– volk volg– uw– voorbeeld, en strijd– als gij, tot–
dat all– hinderpaal– uit d– weg geruim– zijn. De arm–
boer geloof– d– schelmerij en reed– verheug– naar huis, om
er zijn– vrouw van te vertel–. D– oneerlijk– telegrafist had–
d– nieuw– schoenen gestool– en zijn– eigen– oud– aan d–
draad gehang–.*

TRANSLATION EXERCISES.—*Vertaaloefeningen.*

Exercise LXXIV.
(On § XIII, the translation of the Infinitive.)

Tell the waiter to bring me a glass of water. Can you lend me some money? I have not got enough with (*bij*) me to pay this bill. The distance is too long to walk, we will have to (*moeten*) drive there (*er heen*). To have told (if one had told) the girl of her friend's death in her present weak state, might (it) have caused a serious relapse. But one man escaped alive to tell the fearful tale. Go and tell Mr. B. that I (*bij hem*) will call at (*op*) his office at three o'clock this afternoon. To read good books (see Rule II, p. 67) improves the mind. It would have been pleasant to take a ride before sunrise this morning. Why don't you come to see me oftener? You know it is too cold now for me to go out. To (*voor*) that poor woman to live would have been to suffer. Since my friends have gone to live in (the) town, I feel very lonely. Why did (are) you not come and tell me that you had no money to pay your tram fare? Can't you teach that boy to speak properly? To try is to succeed.

Exercise LXXV.
(On § XV, the use of Tenses, and § IV, the use of the auxiliaries *hebben* and *zijn*.)

While I was sweeping the room this morning, I found the lost ring. Did you tell the man not to go to the front door? I wonder (*zou wel eens willen weten*) what (*er*) has become of my cousin, who left for America two years ago. When shall I see you again (Present tense). To-day (*over*) fortnight. The French have gradually extended their power in Madagascar. My brother has just arrived in time for the concert. I have been walking about the whole morning, and feel very tired. Did you walk or drive to the station? I walked, because I found I had plenty of time. To-day week (*over eene week*) we intend leaving for Natal. How did the fire originate? By the carelessness of a man who lit his pipe in the workshop, and dropped the burning match among the shavings. I have crossed the brook without the least trouble. There have been poor people at all times. How long has this company been in existence (existed)? It was (is) founded in 1886. These girls have grown very much since last I saw them. The accident would not have happened, if the guard had remained at his post. Since the boy's father died he has had to (*moeten*) provide for himself.

Exercise LXXVI.
(On §§ IX, X, A, B, C, the use of the Passive.)

The flowers are being planted by the gardener this morning. Has he been told where to plant them? Yes, I told him (that) they should be planted along the grass border. All these exercises were (have been) corrected by the teacher this morning. This child is (being) punished for the second time to-day. If I had been warned in time, I would not have got into trouble. My room will be papered to-morrow. Did you think the child would be punished for not knowing (because he did not know) his lesson? He certainly ought to (*behoorde*) have been punished. I was present when the names of the applicants were (being) read out. If the new town-hall had been built of hewn stone, it would look more imposing. If the murderer were found out, he would be hanged. The camel is found in the desert regions of Africa and Asia. Heavy firing was going on when I left the camp. Flowers should (*behooren*) not be picked while the sun is hot. Is enough wheat raised in this country to meet the demands of consumption? Was the boy told (had — been told) to attend to the horse?

Exercise LXXVII.

(On § X, A, B, and C, the use of *zijn* and *worden*.)

Translate into English :—

Zou u tevreden geweest zijn, als men u de helft van uw loon (earnings) *onthouden* (kept back) *had?* Waarom werd de kerkklok van middag geluid (to ring). Omdat een der oudste bewoners van het dorp, die gestorven is, begraven werd. De boot zou gisteren avond al aangekomen zijn, als de wind niet zoo tegen (contrary) geweest was. De boomen zijn van hunne laatste bladeren *beroofd* (deprived) door den wind en regen der laatste dagen. De lichten in de kerk waren om zes uur al *aangestoken* (lit). De kracht van den stoom is op zeer eenvoudige wijze door Sir Isaac Newton ontdekt. Is uw broeder reeds vertrokken? Is uw oom tot magistraat *benoemd* (appointed)? Is uw vriend *bevoegd* (qualified) tot het vervullen van zulk eene gewichtige (important) *betrekking* (post)? Geschiedenis wordt in die school niet uit boeken geleerd, maar alles wordt den kinderen verteld. Zijn al uwe paarden *beslagen* (shod)? De boomen waren niet omgehakt, toen ik den grond kocht. Ik zou niet zoo angstig geweest zijn, als mij niet verteld was, dat de spoorlijn door de zware regens op verscheidene plaatsen *weggespoeld* (washed away) was. De haas is door den jager neergeschoten, nadat hij door den hond *opgejaagd was* (had startled him). Was de man niet ziek geworden, dan zou dit werk al lang klaar zijn.

Exercise LXXVIII.

(On § X, A, B, and C, the different renderings of "to be" as a Copulative and an Auxiliary of Voice.)

Do not take the bread out of the oven, it is not sufficiently baked yet. All the cake has been eaten by the children. If there had been time, these boxes would have been labelled. The peculiar properties of the loadstone were known to the Chinese long before the compass was introduced into Europe by the Venetian traveller Marco Polo. If I had been called in time, I would not have been late for breakfast. The dictionary has been carefully revised, so that the new edition will be much improved. The child would have been delighted if she had been asked to take part in the entertainment. During that severe winter all our rivers were frozen over, and there was a good deal of (*er werd veel*) skating and sledging (*schaatsen gereden en gesleed*). The poor child was so frightfully burned that his life was despaired of from the first (*van het begin af*). The poor man would have been satisfied if he had only been told that his child was out of danger. There have been several fires on the mountains round about lately, and it is to be feared (to fear) that the wood about some of the fountains has been destroyed. Would you have believed this man to be (that ... was) capable of such a vile act?

Exercise LXXIX.
(On § XIV, the translation of the Present and Past Part.)

My father is very fond of walking. I saw the man picking up the letter. It is only by working from early morning till late at night, that the poor widow has been able to provide for her children thus far (*tot nu toe*). Early rising is conducive to (the) health. Thinking the child had gone with his father, the mother was not anxious at not finding him (when she did not find him) on (*bij*) her return home (*thuiskomst*). Crossing this bridge at night is very dangerous. Having lost the letter, the boy ran home in great distress. The young people spent the evening (*met*) dancing and playing games. Travelling in foreign countries is not only pleasant but instructive. Walking up St. John's Street this morning, I met an old college friend of mine (see Chapter VIII, p. 134). Columbus supposed that (he), by sailing due west [he] would reach India. The boy not noticing that he kept making (continually (*steeds*) made) the same mistake, spent an hour trying to get his sum right. On hearing his father's hard accusation the young man left the house in despair. The boys, not being aware of the depth of the river, were on the point of jumping in, when I called to them. What have you been doing this morning? I have been reading in my room. Have you ever heard Miss B. recite? My mother asks me to tell you that she will come to see you before you leave. As a last resource the poor man has gone to work in the mines.

Exercise LXXX.

(On § XII, (*b*), and Notes, the use of the Subjunctive Mood.)

Translate into Dutch, employing the Subjunctive Mood.

Had you done your duty, you would have been rewarded. However that be, I know that I cannot trust him. Were he in better circumstances, he would not be so sad. If he had done right, he would have no fear. If I were your teacher, I should not allow it. Whatever may happen, I shall remain true to you. Be that as it may, I consider myself free to think as I choose. If he had only had a loving mother he would not have been so reckless. If the doctor had a larger practice, he would be happier. That would never have occurred, had he had you to advise him. If every man were prudent and conscientious there would be very little poverty. (The) Heaven grant that I may see my native country once more! God forbid that you should ever steal. May the king grant our urgent request! May South Africa once be one large united country.

Exercise LXXXI.

(On § XIX, and Chap. VIII, p. 132, Obs. 6, Reflexive Verbs and the use of *zelf*.)

My brother has hurt himself on the knee, while chopping down the old apple-tree at the back of (*achter in*) the garden. I find I have not been mistaken in the good opinion I had of that young girl. Fancy, when I came home this morning, I heard that my dog had died. Why do you want me to do (that I should do) a thing which you would not do yourself? When we were at the farm, we bathed in the large pond every morning before sunrise. Instead of repenting of his misdeeds, this young fellow boasts of (it) having (that he has) deceived his employer so cleverly. Are you going out this morning? No, I have changed my mind; I shall rather stay at home and prepare for the reading class this evening. You ought to be ashamed of yourself; this is the second time (that) you have failed in the examination. The pioneers who settled in Mashonaland, have had to put up with many hardships. Before going out to a new country, these young people ought to have made sure of what opportunities they would have there of getting on. Don't you remember (that) I told you at the time (that) you should hesitate to accept so much kindness from a mere stranger? I cannot understand why your brother did not complain of the unjust treatment he was undergoing at school (*die hem aangedaan werd*). He did not do so, because he would rather suffer himself, than bring disgrace to his schoolmates.

Exercise LXXXII.

(On § XXV, Note 3, Compound Verbs changing their meaning according to the way the accent falls.)

Just (*toch eens*) weigh this letter over again, I am afraid it is overweight. My brother has been travelling all over

Europe (*doorreizen*); and has brought a fine collection of views and curios from the different countries he has visited. Our gardener predicts (*voorspellen*) fine weather for to-morrow, and as the old man very rarely makes a mistake, I think we can safely arrange for the picnic. All these years this young girl has provided for her mother. The man seemed so convinced of the truth of my statement that he walked away without uttering a (*enkel*) word in reply. When I returned to the study, I found that the ink-pot had been upset over my work, and that the ink had penetrated (*door . . . heengedrongen*) (the) most of my papers, so that I had to write the greater (greatest) part of my work over again. It was quite touching to see the clerk, when my father told him that he would overlook his misdeed, and give him a chance to undo the past; the tears rushed to his eyes (him in the eyes), and he had the greatest difficulty to keep down his emotion. I have carefully considered the contents of this letter, but the (*hoe*) more I think of it (*erover*) the more (*des te*) convinced I feel (myself) that the report is much exaggerated. Many of the railway accidents that have happened in the course of this year might have been prevented, if the responsible persons had simply done their duty. The sun was (*aan het*) setting as we reached home. The heavy rain-clouds were dispersing; the moon rose stately behind the pine-wood, and threw her soft light over the peaceful earth.

EXERCISE LXXXIII.

(On § XXII, Impersonal Verbs.)

You must have been surprised not to see me at the station, since I made an appointment to meet you there; but as it was very windy and I had a bad cold, I could not venture out. I was very sorry indeed, to miss my last opportunity of seeing you before your departure. It had been raining and blowing all (the whole) night, but in the morning the clouds parted, and the rising sun brought rest to nature and joy to man and beast. I have been instructed (to me is instructed) to inform you that the council have (has) been pleased to accede to your request. It did strike me (insert '*wel*'), that your friend did not look well, but I had no idea he was really ill. Of course you are free to do as you please, but it is so misty this evening, that I think it would be very risky for you to go out. I am grieved to hear you speak so disrespectfully of your teachers; even if they should be to blame (*schuld hebben*) in this matter, you have got no right to speak like that (so). I was overtaken by such a severe thunderstorm on my way to the village, that I had to take shelter in a deserted hut that happened to be near (*die zich gelukkig in de nabijheid bevond*). I do not recollect ever to have witnessed such thunder and lightning. It struck me that the reading was particularly good at that school; it certainly reflects great credit on the teacher who has got (the) charge of that particular branch of instruction. I do not know what is the matter with this tree, that it will not grow. My watch differs so much from the station-clock, that I very nearly missed the train. It would have made a great difference to me, if I had had some one to show me how to do the work. He does not care if he has got to work hard, as long as he earns enough to support his family.

Exercise LXXXIV.

The English verb "to mean" has various equivalents in Dutch.

1. *Meenen:*

   Hij meent het goed, he means well.
   Ik wist niet, wat zij meende, I did not know what she meant.
   Meent u wat u zegt? do you mean what you say?

2. *Bedoelen*, with the strength of "bringing out the meaning of some one's words":

Hij bedoelde dat hij zelf wilde gaan, he meant (with what he said) that he wanted to go himself.
U bedoelde het beter dan u het zei, you meant it better than you said it.

3. *Beteekenen*, with the force of Eng. "to signify":

Het opsteken eener witte vlag beteekent vrede, the flying of a white flag means peace.
Het woord "erkentelijkheid" beteekent "dankbaarheid," the word "gratitude" means "thankfulness."

4. *Van plan zijn*, with the special meaning of "to intend":

Ik was van plan de courant te gaan lezen, I meant to go and read the paper.
Zij is van plan mij dit present te geven, she means to make me a present of this.

5. A special sense in which the Dutch "*meenen*" is used, is that of "being of opinion," on account of which it is commonly translated by "to think":

Meent gij, dat het te duur is? do you think it is too expensive?

The verb "*meenen*," so used, is always followed by a noun sentence (object).

If he meant all (that) he said, he would not be so kind to me. Do you mean, that you would rather be in the Free State than in Natal? The girls meant that they had not been in your garden, and had therefore not picked your flowers. The woman always meant (it) well with that ungrateful son of hers (of her). Did he really think it was too far for him to walk to Wellington? No, but he meant, I think, that his feet might (would perhaps) get (become) sore. I am sure (*er zeker van*) (that) he did not mean (that) his brother to (should) read his letters! It was a shame for him to do so (that he did it)! What did you think the word meant? Oh, I thought it meant something wrong, but my brother was of opinion that it had quite a different meaning. You knew, that he meant it, did you not (*niet waar*)? What he means is that it is not right for you to (that you) go to such a place. I always meant to ask my father for the book, but whenever (*wanneer . . . ook*) I saw him, I forgot it. It has meant a good deal (*heel wat*) to him, that his brother would not share the profit with him. You mean, the potatoes are too expensive? You had better ask your mother (*vraag het maar eens aan*); she knows more about (*van*) these (*die*) things than you do.

Exercise LXXXV.

A.

Commit to memory the following idiomatic expressions.

I can give it,	*Ik kan het geven.*
I could give it,	*Ik kon het geven.*
	Ik zou het kunnen geven.
I can have given it,	*Ik heb het kunnen geven.*
I could have given it,	*Ik had het kunnen geven.*
	Ik zou het hebben kunnen geven.
I shall be able to give it,	*Ik zal het kunnen geven.*
I shall have been able to give it.	*Ik zal het hebben kunnen geven.*

I could not get the book, even if I wanted (*zelfs niet al wou ik*). You can get some (*wat*) apples for me, I hope! You could have got them yesterday, but now they are al gone (*weg*). I shall not be able to ask my brother to-day because he is not at home. He could send me some money, if he wanted, but I believe (that) he does not want to (*het niet wil*). They cannot finish that work in a day! they could not finish it in a week! We could have come, if we had known that you were in (the) town.

B.

Likewise the following idiomatic expressions.

Will he give it to me?	*Zal hij het mij geven?*
	Zal hij het mij willen geven?
Would he give it to me?	*Zou hij het mij geven?*
	Zou hij het mij willen geven?
Will he have given it?	*Zal hij het gegeven hebben?*
	Zal hij het hebben willen geven?
Would he have given it?	*Zou hij het gegeven hebben?*
	Zou hij het hebben willen geven?

Can he give it to me ?	*Kan hij het mij geven ?*
	Zal hij het mij kunnen geven ?
Could he give it to me ?	*Kon hij het mij geven ?*
	Zou hij het mij kunnen geven ?
Can he have given it ?	*Kan hij het gegeven hebben ?*
	Heeft hij het kunnen geven ?
	Zal hij het hebben kunnen geven ?
Could he have given it ?	*Kon hij het gegeven hebben ?*
	Had hij het kunnen geven ?
	Zou hij het hebben kunnen geven ?

I could not have shown you the picture, if you had not been in the room. Do you think (that) he would give me a shilling, if I asked for it (*erom*)? Can he help me with my exercise? Yes, he could help you if he would. Would you not bring me a glass of water? Could they not do something for the poor woman. They could no doubt sing that song if they only wanted to (*wilden*). How can that boy ever have given such a disrespectful answer? How could your sisters have gone to (the) church without you? Would you take this letter to the post for me, my child? Yes, I would, if I only knew where the post-office was. Would your father give you permission, do you think? How could he? I was (have been) out yesterday, and I may never go more than once a week. But, Jane, could you not sew on those buttons? I could even do it myself, I think! Could you? well then try (*het eens*). I am sure you cannot sew!

Exercise LXXXVI.

A.

"Should," "ought to," as translated by the verb "*behooren*," (see Ex. LIV, p. 149).

Learn the following:

He should say so,	(Present)	*Hij behoorde het te zeggen.*
He should have said so,	(Past)	*Hij behoorde het gezegd te hebben.*
		Hij had het behooren te zeggen.

We ought to do as you say. You should not speak in (*op*) this way. My brother should have gone this morning. The butcher should have called to-day, but he has not done so (*het*). Should he not state why he has been absent this morning? Should we not have said that we were very sorry that this had occurred? Why do you answer me like this?—you ought to be ashamed of yourself. A teacher ought to be careful about (*met*) praising his pupils. You should read that book, my friend; that would be better than to idle away your time in this way. Should our neighbours share the expense of building this wall, or have we to bear it all alone? He ought to apply to the government for a situation. You should have laid out your garden as I have laid out mine. She should not have been out on (such) a cold night [like that].

B.

"To have to," "to be to," "to be bound to," synonymous with "must," are both translated by the verb "*moeten.*"

Learn the following:

The boy has to (is to) work,	De jongen moet werken.
The boy had to (was to) work,	De jongen moest werken.
The boy has had to work (is to have worked),	De jongen heeft moeten werken.
The boy had had to work (was to have worked),	De jongen had moeten werken.
The boy will have to work,	De jongen zal moeten werken.
The boy will have had to work,	De jongen zal hebben moeten werken.

If I am to do all this work before 12 o'clock, you must leave me at peace. The gardener will have to clear up all the rubbish before he goes. Will the boy have to say his lesson this afternoon, or to-morrow morning? It is hard to have to go [all] this (whole) way alone. Were you to take the letter to the post, or to the man's private house? I should have taken it to his house, but I put a stamp on it and posted it. You will be bound to acknowledge that I have done you no wrong. Would it do (go) to make him stay three nights a (*per*) week? It would hardly do, for he would have to go home all alone in the dark. You are not to go beyond the church—mind (*hoor*) what I say. If people were always to be punished for what they do wrong, there would be little pleasure in (*the*) life. You are to accompany your father to Europe, you said. Yes, but I do not like leaving mother alone. To have to work for one's daily bread is a pleasure to some people and a great hardship (*verdriet, o.*) to others. It would have done him good to have had to practise strict obedience at the boarding school. Now (*that*) he is gone, I shall be bound to go as well.

Exercise LXXXVII.

A.

Commit to memory the following idiomatic expressions:

We make him say it,	*Wij laten het hem zeggen.*
We made him say it,	*Wij lieten het hem zeggen.*
We have made him say it,	*Wij hebben het hem laten zeggen.*
We had made him say it,	*Wij hadden het hem laten zeggen.*
We shall make him say it,	*Wij zullen het hem laten zeggen.*
We shall have made him say it,	*Wij zullen het hem hebben laten zeggen.*

We made the poor bird sing by whistling to it. Will you make the child write his exercise over again? He makes me laugh when he looks at (*naar*) me. If you do not lend me your pencil, so that I can put down the name, you will make me forget the message. The sun makes the moon shine by night, and the moon again makes the stars glitter less brightly than they do on (*in*) clear but dark nights. The wind was so violent that he made the forest trees (trees in the forest) [to] tremble. We shall undoubtedly have made him confess before you come back. To make him go against his will, would be both unpleasant for him and awkward for us. If you do not learn your lessons for to-morrow, my child, I shall make you write them out.

B.

Learn likewise the following idioms:

I have the floor washed,	Ik laat den vloer wasschen.
I had the floor washed,	Ik liet den vloer wasschen.
I have had the floor washed,	Ik heb den vloer laten wasschen.
I had had the floor washed,	Ik had den vloer laten wasschen.
I shall have the floor washed,	Ik zal den vloer laten wasschen.
I shall have had the floor washed,	Ik zal den vloer hebben laten wasschen.

We have had this wall built, because the neighbours annoyed us. I shall have the books taken down and cleaned. You will have the watch seen to, will you not (*niet waar*)? Yes, I shall have it put right for you. He would have had his hair cut very short, if he had not been afraid of (*voor*) the cold weather. You had the garden dug up, you said. Yes, and we had the gardener search it well, but no trace of a box was found in the soil anywhere. Several countries, but especially France, used to (*plachten*) have their political criminals work on galleys in former times. I hear you have found diamonds on your farm? Will you have the ground worked? I shall have a hole drilled, and the ground tested. But would you have a drill decide this matter? If I were you, I should certainly have a large hole dug and the soil washed. To-morrow about this time we shall have the horses brought in, and start on our trip. I have had the boy saddle the horses; so if you care for a ride, we shall go—if not, I shall have them taken back to the stable.

C.

Learn once more the following idioms:

He likes (doing) it,	Hij heeft er lust in (heeft lust), het te doen.
He does not like doing it,	Hij heeft geen lust, het te doen.
He did not like doing it,	Hij had geen lust, het te doen.
	Hij heeft geen lust gehad, het te doen.
	Hij had geen lust gehad, het te doen.
He won't like doing it,	Hij zal geen lust hebben, het te doen.
He won't have liked doing it,	Hij zal geen lust gehad hebben, het te doen.

Charles does that work because he has to, but he does not like doing it. You did not like writing out the exercise, but you did it nevertheless. I like going on (with) reading; may I, mother? Yes, if you like (it), you may go on. Oh, I should like so much (*zoo'n lust hebben*) telling that man that he should stop writing me such letters! You would not like studying on, if you had spent so many years at school as I have! Wait till you have heard what I have to say, and then consider whether you would not like going. (*Of*) Would I like it, (*er ... in*) you ask. Of course, I would. She likes it, and that is sufficient reason for me to like it too. We did not like letting you (know) that we were going. Many a one does not like the work (which) (the) circumstances compel him to do. I should have liked better (*meer*) to be your secretary than to be a clerk in the civil service.

CONVERSATIE.	CONVERSATION.
Reizen op Zee.	**Travelling by Sea.**

1. *Ik wensch u goede reis.*
2. *Dank u, maar ik ben een slechte op zee.*
3. *Ik hoop recht te genieten van de reis.*
4. *Zijn er veel passagiers?*
5. *Ik hoor dat iedere kajuit bezet is.*
6. *Wanneer vertrekt de boot?*
7. *Van middag om drie uur.*
8. *Ik kom om u te zien vertrekken.*
9. *Vriendelijk dank; houd u aan uw woord.*
10. *'t Is een prachtige boot.*
11. *Gewis, en de kajuiten zijn groot en luchtig.*
12. *Is u al in de salon geweest?*

1. I wish you a pleasant voyage.
2. Thanks, but I am a very bad sailor.
3. I hope to enjoy the voyage immensely.
4. Are there many passengers?
5. I hear that every berth is taken.
6. When does the steamer leave?
7. This afternoon at three o'clock.
8. I shall come and see you off.
9. Thanks, be sure to keep your promise.
10. This is a splendid steamer.
11. Yes, and the cabins are large and airy.
12. Have you been in the saloon?

13. *De tafel is gedekt voor tachtig passagiers eerste klasse.*
14. *Ik breng het grootste gedeelte van mijn tijd op dek of in de rookkamer door.*
15. *Is er eene bibliotheek aan boord?*
16. *Ja, en de hofmeester heeft er den sleutel van.*
17. *Wie is de kapitein?*
18. *De kapitein heet Harris, en de eerste officier Crutchley.*
19. *Is dat de betaalmeester?*
20. *Neen, dat is de scheepsdokter.*
21. *Die matrozen zijn flinke menschen.*
22. *Laat ons eens kijken, hoe ze de zware bagage in het ruim neerlaten.*
23. *Hoe effen is de zee!*
24. *'t Zal ruw zijn, als we de Sond oversteken.*
25. *Als we maar geen water scheppen, kan het mij niet schelen.*
26. *Kom mee naar voren; ik zou graag de accomodatie zien voor de passagiers 2de en 3de klasse.*
27. *Het dek is te vol daar: kom liever mee naar den achtersteven.*
28. *Men mag niet spreken tegen den man aan het roer.*
29. *Dit is het kompas van het schip.*
30. *Hoe schommelt en slingert het schip!*
31. *Het behoorde meer ballast te hebben.*
32. *Zie dien man eens in den top van den mast.*
33. *Vraag den machinist, ons de machinekamer te wijzen.*

13. The table is laid for eighty first-class passengers.
14. I spend most of my time either on deck or in the smoking-room.
15. Have they got a library on board?
16. Yes, and the head-steward keeps the key.
17. Who is the captain?
18. The captain's name is Harris, and the chief officer is Mr. Crutchley.
19. Is that the purser?
20. No, that is the ship's doctor.
21. Those sailors are fine fellows.
22. Let us watch them lower the heavy luggage into the hold.
23. How very smooth the sea is!
24. We shall have it rough crossing the Sound.
25. As long as we do not ship seas I shall not mind.
26. Come forward; I want to see the accommodation for the 2nd and 3rd class passengers.
27. The deck is crowded there: come rather to the stern.
28. You must not speak to the man at the wheel.
29. This is the ship's compass.
30. How the ship rolls and pitches!
31. It wants more ballast.
32. Look at the man at the mast-head.
33. Ask the engineer to show us the engine-room.

34. *Heeft u ooit met een zeilschip gereisd?*
35. *Ik ben er eens mee het Kanaal overgestoken, maar ik kan niet zeggen dat het mij bevallen is.*

34. Have you ever gone by a sailing ship?
35. I once crossed the Channel in one, but I cannot say that I liked it.

CHAPTER X.
THE ADVERB.
(*Het Bijwoord.*)

I. WHAT the Adjective is to the Noun, that the Adverb is to the Verb. As Adjectives express attributes and qualities of persons and things, so Adverbs express peculiarities which mark an action. Adverbs are accordingly principally meant for modifying (*a*) Verbs, yet they may likewise modify (*b*) Adjectives, (*c*) Adverbs, and (*d*) even Nouns in some particular cases.

EXAMPLES:

(*a*) *Het kind leest goed*, the child reads well.
Het paard loopt snel, the horse runs swiftly.
De vogel zit ginds, the bird sits yonder.
Mijne dochter belooft veel, my daughter promises much.

(*b*) *Dat is bijzonder goed schrift*, that is particularly good writing.
Dit pakje schijnt ongemeen zwaar, this parcel seems uncommonly heavy.
Uwe begeerte wordt te sterk, your desire is becoming too strong.

(*c*) *Ik had het lang te voren gedaan*, I had done it long before.
Mijne zuster leest bijzonder mooi, my sister reads particularly well.
De zonnestralen vallen bijna loodrecht, the sunbeams fall almost perpendicularly.

(d) *De menschen* **hierachter** *zijn zindelijk*, the people at the back are cleanly.
Die steilte **daar** *is gevaarlijk*, that steep place there is dangerous.

NOTE.—The Cape Dutch, which has only one demonstrative pronoun, *die*, avails itself of the adverbs *hier* and *daar* to indicate that an object is close by or at a distance: *Hier die boek en die eene daar;* Dutch: *Dit boek en dat*, this book and that one.

OBS. 1.—The copulative verbs, *i.e.*, those which take a nominative case before and after them (*zijn, blijven, worden, heeten, schijnen, gelijken, blijken*), are followed by adjectives, and not adverbs: *Hij schijnt* **rijk**, he seems to be rich; *Hij blijft* **trouw**, he remains faithful. Here the words *rich* and *faithful* evidently do not qualify an action, but the doer of the action, and so are adjectives.

OBS. 2.—Other verbs besides the copulative may be followed by an adjective instead of an adverb: *De schilder verft het raam* **groen**, the painter paints the window green; *Het is die vriend, die hem zoo* **slecht** *gemaakt heeft*, it is that friend, who has made him so wicked. Here the colour *green*, and the quality *wicked*, evidently have nothing to do with the actions *painting* or *making*. It is the *door* which is *green*, and not the *painting*; likewise it is *he* that is wicked, and not the *making*; so that *green* and *wicked* are adjectives, and not adverbs.

II. The following are the Adverbs in use:

1. *Bijwoorden van wijze*, Adverbs of manner.
2. *Bijwoorden van graad*, Adverbs of degree.
3. *Bijwoorden van getal*, Adverbs of number.
4. *Bijwoorden van plaats*, Adverbs of place.
5. *Bijwoorden van tijd*, Adverbs of time.
6. *Bijwoorden van oorzaak*, Adverbs of cause.
7. *Voegwoordelijke Bijwoorden*, Adverbial Conjunctions.

8. *Modale Bijwoorden*, Adverbs of mood, divided into:
   (a) Adverbs of affirmation (*Bevestiging*).
   (b) Adverbs of negation (*Ontkenning*).
   (c) Adverbs of doubt (*Twijfel*).
   (d) Optative (*Wenschende*) Adverbs.

EXAMPLES:

(1) ADVERBS OF MANNER: *slecht*, badly, *schoon*, beautifully, *langzaam*, slowly. "*Hoe*" is an interrog. adv. of manner. Every adjective denoting a quality may be used as an adverb of manner without any change of form. Those, however, which end in *lijksch, lingsch* and *waartsch* drop their *ch* when used as adverbs: *dagelijks*, daily (adv.), *voorwaarts*, onward (adv.).

(2) ADVERBS OF DEGREE: *genoeg*, enough; *uitermate*, exceedingly; *overtollig*, excessively; *nauwelijks*, scarcely; *bijna*, nearly; *bijzonder*, especially; *zoo*, so; *te*, too, *volkomen*, quite; *zeer*, very; *vreeselijk*, terribly; *heelemaal*, altogether; *erg*, very.

(3) ADVERBS OF NUMBER: all the *Herhalingsgetallen* (see p. 122), and further—*ten eerste, ten tweede, ten derde, ten vierde, enz.*, first, second, third, fourth, etc.; *ten laatste*, lastly; *ten slotte*, finally.

(4) ADVERBS OF PLACE: *af*, down; *rond*, about; *om*, round; *henen*, away; *voort*, on; *heen*, towards; *daarheen*, thither; *herwaarts*, hither; *huiswaarts*, home; *berg op*, uphill; *berg af*, downhill; *noordwaarts*, northward; *naar boven*, upstairs; *naar beneden*, downstairs; *hier*, here; *in*, into; *nabij*, near; *nergens*, nowhere; *ergens*, somewhere; *overal*, everywhere, *ergens anders*, elsewhere; *boven*, above; *beneden*, beneath; *achter*, behind; *terzijde*, aside; *aan boord*, aboard; *aan wal*, ashore; *vooruit*, ahead; *ginds*, yonder; *hier en daar*, here and there; *heinde en ver*, far and wide. Also the interrog. adv. *waar*, where; *waarheen*, whither; *vanwaar*, whence, etc.

NOTE.—A good many of these words may be used as prepositions, but then they invariably take a noun after them: *Hij liep den tuin* uit *en de kamer* in (*uit* and *in* adverbs), he walked out of the garden and into the room; *De vogel zit* in *den boom* (in prep.), the bird is in the tree.

(5) ADVERBS OF TIME:

(a) Time, definite or indefinite: *nu*, now; *dan*, then; *heden*, to-day; *morgen*, to-morrow; *'s daags*, per diem; *'s nachts*, by night; *'s jaars*, per annum; *maandelijks*, every month; *van avond*, this evening; *thans*, now; *gisteren*, yesterday; *reeds*, already; *eens*, once upon a time; *ooit*, ever; *nooit* or *nimmer*, never; *voorheen*, formerly; *weleer*, before; *nauwelijks* (*nauw*), scarcely; *straks*, just now; *intusschen*, meanwhile.

(b) Duration of time: *altijd*, always; *steeds*, constantly; *immer*, always; *voortaan*, henceforward; *onderwijl*, in the meantime; *van lieverlede*, in course of time; *sedert*, since.

(c) Repetition of time: *dikwijls*, often; *vaak*, often; *zelden*, seldom; *telkens*, every now and then; *opnieuw*, once more; *somtijds*, sometimes; *nu en dan*, now and then; *gewoonlijk*, usually; *doorgaans*, commonly; *weder*, again. *Wanneer*, when, is an interr. adv. of time.

(6) ADVERBS OF CAUSE: *daarom*, therefore; *derhalve*, therefore; *dienvolgens*, on that account; *vandaar*, for that reason; *daartoe*, for that purpose, etc.

Interrogative: *waarom*, why; *waartoe*, for what purpose; *weshalve*, on what account, etc.

(7.) ADVERBIAL CONJUNCTIONS: *evenwel*, however; *toch*, yet; *niettemin*, yet; *nochtans*, yet, nevertheless; *desniettegenstaande*, notwithstanding; *integendeel*, on the contrary; *bijgevolg*, consequently; and the words *daarvan, ervan, daarmee, ermee, daarop, erop, daaruit, eruit*, etc., called SAMENGETROKKEN BIJWOORDEN (see their formation, p. 136).

(8) ADVERBS OF MOOD:

(a) Affirmation : *ja*, yes; *wel*, indeed; *voorwaar*, verily; *immers* (see the example); *volstrekt* (see the example); *inderdaad*, indeed; *zeker*, certainly; *voorzeker*, to be sure; *gewis*, undoubtedly; *stellig*, positively. The way in which "*wel*," "*immers*," and "*volstrekt*" are used can be best gathered from the following sentences:

1. *Hij heeft het* **wel** *gedaan, maar niet zooals ik het wilde*, he did it indeed, but not as I wanted it.
2. *Ik heb u* **immers** *trouw gediend*, I served you faithfully, did I not?
3. *Hij wilde het* **volstrekt** *zóó hebben*, he was determined to have it so.

(b) Negation : *neen*, no; *niet*, not; *geenszins*, in no wise, not at all; *volstrekt niet*, not at all.

(c) Probability or doubt: *misschien*, perhaps; *mogelijk*, probably; *wellicht*, perhaps; *vermoedelijk*, presumably; *waarschijnlijk*, probably; **wel** (see example).

Ex. *Ik denk* **wel**, *dat hij thuis zal zijn*, I rather think he will be at home.

(d) Wish : *dan* and *toch*.

Ex. *Kom* **dan**, *waarom zouden wij wachten*, do come, why should we wait? *Zeg hem* **toch**, *dat hij haast make*, please tell him to make haste.

OBS. I.—Adverbs of manner (see par. II, 1) are for the greater part adjectives used as adverbs, without any change of form. The student is requested to note this fact. The adverbial ending *lijk* (Eng. ly) exists in Dutch, but is now very little used. There are adverbs which take it, not because it makes them adverbs, but because it has been used in the formation of the adjective from a noun or a verb; *e.g.*, *moeielijk* is an adverb, signifying "with difficulty," but the adjective "difficult" is translated likewise by *moeielijk*: *De oude man loopt moeielijk*, the old man walks with difficulty; *Het is een moeielijk geval*, it is a difficult case. The student should therefore beware of placing the ending "*lijk*" after adjectives of manner, in order to make adverbs of them. Formerly it was customary to do so; now it is not admitted in colloquial language, though in high-flown style and in Bible language it is still done, as: *Wij hebben goddelooslijk gehandeld*, we have done wickedly.

OBS. 2.—Adverbs never change their form. The Adverbs of manner, however, take degrees of comparison, like adjectives. (See on Comparison, p. 105). The Superlative degree is always preceded by the def. article *het*.

> Ex. *Mijn zoon werkt het vlijtigst*, my son works most diligently (of all).
> *Uwe dochter leert het best*, your daughter learns best (of all).
> *Mijne borst plaagt mij 's winters het meest*, my chest troubles me most in winter.

OBS. 3.—The following are irregular in their forms:

Positive.	Comparative.	Superlative.
Goed, well,	*beter*,	*het best*.
Slecht, badly,	*erger*,	*het ergst*.
Veel, many a time,	*meer*,	*het meest*.
Weinig, a few times,	*minder*,	*het minst*.
Vroeg, early,	*eerder*,	*het eerst*.
Dikwijls, often,	*meermalen*,	*het meest*.
Gaarne, willingly,	*liever*,	*het liefst*.

NOTE.—*Het eerst*, or *eerst*, *het laatst*, or *laatst*, *het best*, or *best*, *het liefst*, or *liefst*, are used with different meanings, as follows:

Compare: *Ik was het eerst op school*, I was the first at school.

Adv. of time: *Ik was eerst op school en daarna in het museum*, I was first at school, and then at the museum.

Compare: *Mijn broeder kwam het laatst boven*, my brother was the last to come upstairs.

Adv. of time: *Mijn broeder bezocht laatst de mijnen*, my brother visited the mines some time ago.

Compare: *Dit meisje leert het best*, this little girl learns best of all.

Adv. of mood: *Deze jongen kan best naar het dorp gaan*, this boy can very well go the village.

Compare: *De man heeft zijn kind het liefst bij zich*, the man prefers having his child with him.

Adv. of degree: *Ik zou van avond liefst niet uitgaan*, I would rather not go out this evening.

NOTE.—Some Adverbs of manner have been formed from adjectives by the diminutive ending *je* followed by an adverbial final *s: zoet*, sweet; *zoetjes*, nicely, softly; *stil*, quiet; *stilletjes*, quietly, etc. Such adverbs *do not* take any degrees of comparison. The Cape expression: *Sla den bal zoetjester*, beat the ball more softly,—is absurd.

III. The meaning and use of the following Adverbs require special notice:

1 *a. Zelden*, rarely (seldom), is only an adverb, and never an adjective: *Wij zien onzen broeder zelden*, we seldom see our brother.

1 *b. Zeldzaam*, rare, wrongly used in the place of *zelden*, is an adjective, and not an adverb: *Volkomen zwarte katten zijn zeldzaam*, perfectly black cats are rare.

2 *a. Heen* is an Adverb of place, indicating direction towards an object: *Waar gaat gij morgen heen?* whither do you go to-morrow? *Mijn plan is van middag nergens heen te gaan*, my intention is, not to go anywhere this afternoon.

2 *b. Henen* is an adverb, indicating motion away from a place: *Ga niet henen, vóór het donker is*, do not go away before dark.

NOTE.—The difference between the words *heen* and *henen* is not observed in colloquial Dutch. For either meaning *heen* is used.

3 a. *Immer*, ever, and *nimmer*, never, point to a future time: *Zal ik u immer wederzien?* Shall I ever see you back? *Hij zal ons nimmer beschamen!* he will never put us to shame!

3 b. *Ooit*, ever, refers only to the past: *Heb ik ooit in mijn leven zoo iets gezien?* did I ever see such a thing in my life?

3 c. *Nooit*, never, may indicate a past or a future time: *Ik heb mij nooit met zoo iets beziggehouden, en ik zal er mij nooit mede bezighouden*, I have never occupied myself with such a thing, nor shall I ever occupy myself with it.

4. *Wijlen*, late, is an Adverb of time taking its place before the name of a person: *Wijlen de Graaf van Chambord*, the late Count Chambord.

5. *Met*, a preposition (the adverbial form of which is *mede*), may be used as an Adverb of time: *Met dat hij binnenkwam, hield het geraas op*, the moment he came in, the noise stopped.

6. *Kwansuis* (Cape pronunciation: *konsuis*), sometimes written *kwanswijs*, a word found in several of the Saxon languages, means "as it were," or, "pretending." It is commonly used in telling about a trick which has been played on anyone: *Omdat de jongen lust had in een der lekkere appelen, liet hij kwansuis het geld vallen, om de aandacht zijner tante af te leiden*, because the boy longed for one of the nice apples, he (as it were by mistake) dropped the money, in order to divert his aunt's attention.

7. *Averechts* (a compound of *af*, from, and *recht*, right, with an adverbial *s*) means in the wrong direction. *Zij breit den éénen toer recht, en de anderen averechts*, she knits one round plain and the next pearl.

8. *Na*, after, is an Adverb of time; *naar*, towards, is a preposition. *Hij kwam daar na mij*, he came there after me; *Ik vertrek naar Engeland*, I am leaving for England.

9. *Af*, down, is an adverb; *van*, from, is a preposition: *Wij klommen den berg af*, we came down the mountain; *Hij nam het boek van mij weg*, he took the book away from me.

10. *Toe* is an adverb expressing direction; *tot* is a preposition: *Waar gaan wij naar toe*, where are we going? *Wij zullen maar tot daar gaan*, we shall only go till there.

11. The use of the adverbs "*af*" and "*neer*," both meaning "down," which are found in composition with many everyday verbs, requires special attention.

> 1. Use "*af*" when the "motion **from** an object" is the prominent idea.
> 2. Use "*neer*," when "motion **towards** an object" is the prominent idea.

EXAMPLES OF 1:
> *Hij kwam van zijn paard af*, he came down from his horse.
> *Hij viel van het dak af*, he fell from the roof.
> *De vogel vliegt van den boom af*, the bird flies down from the tree.
> *De jongen trekt de vlieg een poot af*, the boy pulls out one of the legs of the fly.

EXAMPLES OF 2:
> *Hij kwam op den vloer neer*, he came down on the floor.
> *Hij valt bij den stoel neer*, he falls down at the chair.
> *De jager schoot den bok neer*, the hunter shot down the buck.
> *Ik trek het gordijn neer*, I pull the curtain down.

Consequently, when separation is to be indicated, *af* should be taken: *Hij sloeg hem het hoofd af*, he cut his head off.

When a directly downward motion must be expressed, "*neer*" is used: *De regen valt uit de wolken neer*, the rain falls from the clouds.

Downward motion, along a slope, is expressed by "*af*": *Hij loopt de trap af*, he goes down the stairs.

Motion resulting in rest upon an object, is expressed by "*neer*" only: *Ik legde hem op het bed neer*, I laid him down on the bed.

GRAMMAR EXERCISES.—*Taaloefeningen.*

EXERCISE LXXXVIII.

Fill up the blanks with appropriate Adverbs.

Mijn paard trekt—*dan het uwe.* — *schreit dat kind?* *Deze oefening is* — (degree) — *geschreven, gij moet ze overschrijven. Die man gaat* — (time) — (place) *voorbij. Wij zijn* — *den berg opgeloopen. Het kind is gestraft,* — (cause) *wil het niet binnenkomen.* — (interrog. of time) *vertrekt u naar Natal? Zeg hem* — (of mood), *dat ik* — (time) *op reis ga. Ik sta* — (repetition of time) *om zes uur op. Kunt gij* — (compound adv.) *iets verstaan? Deze klerk schijnt* — (degree) *geschikt voor zijn werk. Ik kan* — (place) *mijn boek vinden. Mijne moeder is nu* — (degree) *gezond. Wij laten* — (repetition of time) *ons goed uit Parijs komen.* — (probability) *regent het morgen, en* — (time) *kunnen wij* — (neg.) *gaan.* — (interrog. of cause) *worden de lichten* — (degree) — *opgestoken? Zij zouden* — (affirmation) *bij ons geweest zijn, als zij tijd gehad hadden. De man is* — (time) *ziek geweest,* — (cause) *dat hij er* — (degree) *slecht uitziet.*

EXERCISE LXXXIX.

Give the Dutch Adverb of the English form.

Als deze man niet so terribly *lui was, zouden wij hem* certainly *werk gegeven hebben. Toen het Amerikaansche schip here in de baai lag, ben ik* aboard *geweest. By night *zijn alle katten grauw. Ik ben* yesterday *ziek geweest,* for that reason *dat ik mijne lessen* not *geleerd heb. Het kind zal in* course of time *aan zijne nieuwe omgeving gewoon worden. Het bericht der overwinning was in weinige uren* far and wide *verbreid. De inspecteur zal* one of these days *de school bezoeken. Ofschoon zijn vader hem* strictly *verboden had* tonight *uit te gaan, deed hij het yet. Ik heb* everywhere *naar mijne pen gezocht, ik heb ze* this morning somewhere *neergelegd, maar ik kan mij* not at all *herinneren* where. *Ik* *lees* usually *mijne courant* in the evening. *Heeft u* indeed never *geweten*, why *uw vader* thither *gegaan is? Dit boek is* exceedingly *vervelend.* For what purpose *geeft gij u zooveel moeite? De kinderen vermaakten zich* especially well; *en* merrily *keerden allen* home. Henceforward *zullen de booten* every week *varen.*

TRANSLATION EXERCISES.—*Vertaaloefeningen.*

EXERCISE XC.

Translate the following (minding especially § II, (1), and OBS. 1, 2, 3, also § III).

All these roses blossom a long time, but that one yonder blossoms longest of all. Notwithstanding the heavy rains, the troops marched courageously onward. I would rather not tell you why he prefers going to-morrow. The seasons are caused by the annual rotation of the earth round the sun. My father visits his old friend daily. They will have to act very cautiously in that matter. Of all the young ladies that sang last night, I liked (*beviel mij*) your niece's voice best. Whoever comes in last should close the door. When I was in (the) town some time ago, I called on Mrs. B. This girl can very well learn this piece of poetry, but won't recite it best of all. Please, let the curtain down a little, the sun is shining right in my face (me right in the face). The price of wheat has considerably fallen lately. The unfortunate man must have dropped asleep near the edge of the precipice, and must have fallen down in his sleep. Don't jump down from that height; you will hurt yourself. The children amused themselves by (*met*) running up and down the sand-hills. The bride is a near relative to the late President Brand. I told you, didn't I? that the stamp was a very rare one, and that you should not give it away; you will never get such a one again. I got up half an hour after you, and yet I was downstairs earlier than you. The children ran up to their teacher, and wished him many happy returns of the day (*geluk met zijnen verjaardag*).

Exercise XCI.

Note.—"*Na*," "after," is a preposition expressing time, and rank or order.

Zijn broeder is na hem gestorven, his brother died after him.

Na het zingen kwam de preek, on the singing followed the sermon.

"*Nadat*," "after," is an adverbial conjunction, binding two sentences:

Hij kwam nadat zijn broeder vertrokken was, he came after his brother had gone.

Nadat hij dit gezegd had, ging hij zitten, after he had said so, he sat down.

"*Daarna*" is the Dutch equivalent for "after that (afterwards)":

Ik vroeg het hem eerst, en antwoordde u daarna, I asked him first, and answered you afterwards.

It may be replaced by "*dan*," with the present and future tenses, and "*toen*" with the past tense:

Ik vraag het hem, en vertel het u dan, I ask him, and then tell you.

Ik zal het hem vragen, en u dan vertellen, I shall ask him, and then tell you.

Ik vroeg het hem eerst, en vertelde het u toen, I asked him first, and then told you.

After I had finished my drawing, I packed my box and went (*naar*) home. The ship arrived after you had left. His brother died just after his arrival. After this rain we shall have fine weather. I invited my parents first, and afterwards my uncle as well (too). Let me eat first, and then I shall speak to (*met*) you. He sat down (*ging zitten*) on that chair there, and shortly after he fainted. I promise to take him in after he is discharged from (*uit*) (the) prison. Who would first sow, and then plough? Is it not natural, first to plough, and then to sow? You saw him after he had written his letter. After the rain had stopped, we went out for a walk (*wandelen*). You should not say no, after you have once said yes. He told me of all the pain he had suffered, and then he fell into a quiet sleep. I shall have the boy wash the floor after he comes back from the butcher's (butcher). After my father had started for Europe, my mother got very ill. He came to East London shortly after the third Kafir war. After you, please, madam! After a day's (day of) hard work it is pleasant to have (some) music. Who shall say that (*er*) after this cruel war there won't be a long spell (*tijdperk, o*) of peace in these parts (*streek, v*).

Exercise XCII.

NOTE.—"To put" is translated by "*leggen*," "*zetten*," "*steken*," "*doen*," "*plaatsen*."

Use "*leggen*" whenever an object is to be placed on its broad side:

Ik heb dat boek op de tafel gelegd, I have put that book on the table.

Use "*zetten*" whenever an object is to be placed on end:

Ik heb het boek op de plank gezet, I have put the book on the shelf.

Use "*steken*" whenever an object is passed through a close-fitting opening:

Steek uwen zakdoek in uwen zak, put your handkerchief into your pocket.
Steek den draad door de naald, thread the needle.

Use "*doen*" for "putting into," "passing through":

Hij deed de brieven in een zak, he put the letters into a bag.

Compare: *Ik steek het geld in mijnen zak*, I put the money into my pocket;

to: *Ik doe het geld in mijne beurs*, I put the money into my purse.

"To put on," and "to take off," of clothing, should be translated by "*aandoen*," and "*afdoen*," when there is no passing of limbs into or out of such garments:

Hij doet zijn boord, zijne das, zijnen mantel aan, he puts on his collar, his neck-tie, his cloak.

Hij deed zijne manchetten, zijne kappen af, he took off his cuffs, his leggings.

But when there is such passing, "*aantrekken*" and "*uittrekken*" are used:

Trek uwe jas, uwe schoenen aan, put on your coat, your boots.

Hij trekt zijne handschoenen, zijne kousen uit, he takes off his gloves, his stockings.

Of hats, "*opzetten*" and "*afzetten*" are used.

"*Plaatsen*," English "to place," is used for Dutch "*zetten*" in more formal expressions.

For the many other and varied meanings of "to put," a translation of the synonym which applies best to the action, is advisable.

He put (wrote) it down in the book, *hij schreef het in het boek op*.

I put (said) it straight to him, *ik zei het hem rechtuit*.

I shall put (lay) that money by (away) for you, *ik zal dat geld voor u wegbergen*.

Will you put the inkpot on the table for me? I have put the inkpot there, and I have also put the paper on your desk. They put a bucket under the spout to catch up the rain-water. Let us put our clothes into our boxes. Put a chair ready for your uncle: he will be here just now. The man put the horse into the stable, and put the cart into the waggon-house. Have you put sugar in my tea? Yes, and I have also put in (it) milk. The boy had a number of marbles which he quickly put into his pocket. Put on (*om*) a shawl, it is cold. Must I put on a veil too? No, you need not put on a veil, as long as (*als* . . . *maar*) you put on gloves. Don't put sheep and oxen into one fold. Take off your hat and your boots too. Shall I put on my slippers? Yes, and take off that heavy coat; I shall (*er*) bring you a light one. Put away your books, the teacher is coming. Jane had a bird which she had put in a cage. I have put the cups on the table in the kitchen. And where have you put the meat? I have put the meat into the sideboard.

Exercise XCIII.

What is your salary? I get three hundred pounds sterling per annum, which makes exactly twenty-five pounds per month. Is the salary paid out monthly? We can get it by the month, or at the end of every three months, just as we like it best. Every other day (*om den anderen dag*) we drive down to yonder farm; it is so very pleasant to be there. At 7 p.m. (*n.m.* = *in den namiddag*) the train starts for (*naar*) Edinburgh, where it is due (*hij aankomt*) at 5 a.m. (*v.m.* = *in den voormiddag*). We do not intend being (trans., to be) out all (the) morning; before noon (trans., at 12 o'clock) we shall be back. He came just in time to see the balloon rise. What a grand sight it was! I think I should like to go up some time (*eens*); it must be glorious to be drifting about in the air, and to see the beautiful earth at such a distance. Last night somebody called (trans., has called) on me; I am so sorry that I was not at home. Next week we have to part, and next month, just about this time, we shall be in different parts of the globe. Will you be back in a fortnight? I can not tell (it) you at present. About a week ago I met my uncle and three of my cousins (fem.) at a railway station near Dartmouth.

Conversatie.	Conversation.
Over verschillende Ambachtslieden.	**About various Artisans.**

1. *Er moet eene ruit in dit venster gezet worden; haal een glazenmaker om het te doen.*
2. *Vraag hem, dit stuk hout voor mij te zagen, en leen mij eene boor om een gat te maken.*
3. *Heeft u nog andere werktuigen noodig?*
4. *Ja, breng mij als 't u blieft een schroefdraaier, een hamer, eene schaaf, en wat groote spijkers met koperen koppen; ook wat tinnen nageltjes.*
5. *Dat uithangbord is slecht geschilderd; de schilder was maar een leerjongen.*
6. *Laat mij eens wat zinken platen zien voor dekking.*
7. *Leien of dakpannen worden hier zelden voor dat doel gebruikt.*
8. *Rieten daken zijn boven alle andere te verkiezen.*
9. *De metselaar, die dien muur gebouwd heeft, moet slechte kalk gehad hebben.*
10. *Vraag den straatmaker wat hij rekenen zou voor het bestraten der plaats.*
11. *Deze laden moeten naar een schrijnwerker gaan om nagezien te worden.*
12. *De kuiper zal het vat repareeren, er hoepels om slaan en het oversturen.*

1. This window needs a pane of glass; call a glazier to put one in.
2. Ask him to saw this piece of wood for me, and lend me a gimblet to bore a hole.
3. Do you require any other tools?
4. Yes, bring me please a screw-driver, a hammer, a plane, and some large brass-headed nails; also a few tin tacks.
5. That sign-board is badly painted; the painter was only an apprentice.
6. Show me some corrugated iron for roofing.
7. One seldom uses slates or tiles for that purpose here.
8. Thatched roofs are to be preferred to either.
9. The bricklayer who built that wall, must have had bad mortar.
10. Ask the paviour what he would charge for paving the yard.
11. These drawers must be taken to a cabinet-maker to be mended.
12. The cooper will repair the cask, hoop it, and send it across.

THE ADVERB.

13. Heeft u hem gesproken over de duigen en den boom (bodem)?
14. De smid legde het ijzer op het aanbeeld, en smeedde het terwijl het heet was.
15. Deze waterkan lekt; breng haar naar den blikslager en laat hem haar soldeeren.
16. De smid kan de kolenschop en pook repareeren.
17. De schelledraad is gebroken; waar kan ik een belleider vinden?
18. Ik heb deze voorsnijmessen bij den messenmaker in de D-straat gekocht.
19. Hoe mooi zijn de pooten van die tafel gedraaid! Heeft u al eene draaibank gezien?
20. Laat ons naar den schrijnwerker gaan, en wat lijm en een paar krullen vragen.
21. Die schilder is beroemd; prins Alexander heeft zijne laatste schilderij gekocht.
22. Dat houtsneewerk is uitmuntend gedaan. Wie is de beeldhouwer?
23. Mijnheer N; hij heeft het opschrift op dien grafsteen gemaakt.
24. Deze messen en scharen zijn niet scherp; breng ze naar een scharenslijper, als 't u blieft.

13. Did you tell him about the staves and the bottom?
14. The blacksmith laid the iron on the anvil, and struck it while it was hot.
15. This water-can leaks; take it to the tinsmith and ask him to solder it.
16. The blacksmith can repair the coal-scuttle and fire-irons.
17. The bell-wire is broken; where can one find a bell-hanger?
18. I bought these carving-knives at the cutler's in D-street.
19. How beautifully the legs of that table are turned. Have you seen a turner's lathe?
20. Let us go to the joiner's, and ask for some glue and a few shavings.
21. That artist is celebrated; Prince Alexander bought his last painting.
22. That carving is exquisitely done. Who is the sculptor?
23. Mr. N.; he did the engraving on that tombstone.
24. These knives and scissors are not sharp; please take them to a grinder.

CHAPTER XI.
THE PREPOSITION.
(*Het Voorzetsel.*)

I. PREPOSITIONS, *Voorzetsels*, are real particles, *i.e.* indeclinable words. They may have different meanings according to the various relations between actions, persons, and objects which they are made use of to express. One of the two nouns between which a preposition takes its place in a sentence, is the name of the person or thing to which attention is chiefly drawn, whereas the other noun merely serves to indicate in what relation or position that principal person or thing is placed. In the sentence for instance: *de hond is in zijn hok*, the dog is in its kennel, the *dog* is the principal thing spoken about, whereas *kennel* is used to define the place the dog occupies. Any such defining noun is under the direct influence of the preposition that precedes it, by which preposition it is said to be governed.

II. The usual place of prepositions is *before* the nouns they govern: *Wij speelden* op *de plaats*, we played in the yard; *De vogels zaten* in *de kooi*, the birds sat in the cage.

NOTE.—"*Halve*" and "*wegen*" are placed after the noun or pronoun with which they stand, forming one word with them: *mijnentwege*, for my sake; *uwentwege*, for your sake; *zijnentwege*, for his sake; *veiligheidshalve*, for the sake of safety.

III. Formerly Prepositions and words used as such,

governed different cases, *i.e.*, required either the Genitive, Dative, or Accusative case of the noun after them.

Now, however, one common rule applies to every Preposition, viz., that it governs the Accusative case—and the obsolete use of the Genitive and Dative cases is only discernible in some expressions, few in number, yet sufficient to remind us of what once has been.

EXAMPLES.—Feminine Dative: *uitermate* (*uit der mate*), exceedingly; *bij der hand*, close at hand; *mettertijd*, in time; *uitter ooge, uitter herte*, out of sight, out of mind; *ter oore komen*, to come to one's notice; *ter feest gaan*, to go to a feast.

Neuter Dative: *in den beginne*, in the beginning; *van goeden huize*, *ten top stijgen*, to reach the highest point; *met dien verstande*, with this understanding; *bij levenden lijve*, alive.

Neuter Genitive: *binnenshuis*, inside (the house); *buitenslands*, outside of the country; *tusschendeks*, between deck.

Masculine Genitive: *buitenstijds*, out of season; *binnensmonds*, mutteringly.

IV. The relations pointed out by Prepositions may be:

1. A relation of place { *a.* Rest in a place.
        { *b.* Motion to or from a place.
2. A relation of time.
3. An abstract relation expressing a cause, an object in view, etc.
4. A positive or negative connection.

1. Rest in a place is indicated by: *boven*, above; *onder*, under; *buiten*, outside; *binnen*, inside; *nabij*, near; *naast*, next to; *aan*, at; *te*, at; *in*, in; *op*, on; *tusschen*, between; *tegen*, against, etc.

Motion to or from a place is indicated by: *over*, over; *van*, from; *naar*, towards; *tot aan*, as far as; *langs*, along *rond*, round; *rondom*, round about; *voorbij*, past, etc.

OBS.—Notice the following sentences:

Hij loopt in de school, he walks about in the school (*in* = Prep.).
Hij loopt de school in, he walks into the school (*in* = Adverb).
De koeien grazen op de weide, the cows are grazing in the meadow (*op* = Prep.).
Zij klimmen den berg op, they climb the mountain (*op* = Adverb).
Ik lees uit Homerus, I read from Homer (*uit* = Prep.).
Ik las het geheele boek dien avond uit, I read through the whole of the book that night (*uit* = Adverb).

2. A relation of time is indicated by: *in*, in; *binnen*, within; *omstreeks*, about; *bij*, near by; *om*, at; *over*, past, in; *aan*, on; *tegen*, towards; *voor*, for; *tusschen*, between; *tot*, to; *sedert*, since; *gedurende*, during.

3. An abstract relation of cause, etc., is expressed by: *door*, by; *voor*, for; *uit kracht van*, by virtue of; *ten spijt van*, in spite of; *naar gelang van*, according to; *in weerwil van*, in spite of; *aangaande*, touching; *wegens*, on account of; *betreffende*, touching; *aangezien*, for as much; *ter oorzake van*, on account of; *ten gevolge van*, in consequence of; *in tegenstelling van*, in opposition to; *in vergelijking van*, in comparison to; *ter wille van*, for the sake of; *instede van*, instead of; *ten behoeve van*, on behalf of; *overeenkomstig met*, conformably to.

4. A positive connection is expressed by: *met*, with; *benevens*, together with; a negative connection by: *zonder*, without; *uitgenomen*, except; *behalve*, except.

NOTE.—Seeing that the same word may occur as an adverb and a preposition, or as a preposition and a conjunction, the student should notice that every preposition must necessarily be followed by a noun or pronoun in the accusative (objective) case.

VI. Prepositions used for indicating different relations.

AAN.

1. Rest in a place: *De stad ligt aan zee*, the town lies on the sea-coast.

2. Indicating a beginning: *De vogel gaat aan 't vliegen,* the bird begins to fly.
3. Used instead of the Dative case: *Geef het boek aan uwen broeder,* give the book to your brother.

VAN.

1. Instead of the Possessive case: *Dit is de lei van mijnen broeder,* this is my brother's slate.
2. Meaning "*from*": *Ik ontving eenen brief van hem,* I got a letter from him.

DOOR.

1. Meaning "*through*": *De kogel ging door het huis,* the bullet went through the house.
2. Meaning "*by*": *Door uw vermogen zijt gij in staat, veel goed te doen,* by your fortune you are able to do a great deal of good.
3. Meaning "*with*": *Door uwe vriendelijke hulp is het mij gelukt,* with your kind assistance I have succeeded.
4. Meaning "*throughout*": *Door alle landen zal het gehoord worden,* it will be heard throughout every country.

BIJ.

1. Meaning "*by*": *Bij geval,* by chance; *bij beurten,* by turns; *bij nacht,* by night; *dicht bij,* close by; *bij lamplicht,* by lamplight.
2. Meaning "*near*," "*nearly*": *Het is bij tweeën,* it is close upon two o'clock; *Zijn huis is bij het kerkhof,* his house is near the churchyard; *Mijne grootmoeder is bij de tachtig,* my grandmother is nearly eighty years of age.
3. Meaning "*with*": *Zij logeert eene week bij ons,* she is staying with us for a week; *Heeft hij geld bij zich?* has he any money about him?
4. Meaning "*to*": *Kom bij mij, lief kind!* come to me, my dear child!
5. Meaning "*about*": *Hij kwam eerst bij twaalven,* he only came about twelve o'clock.

ONDER.

1. Meaning "*among*": *Dat is zoo de gewoonte onder soldaten*, that is the custom among soldiers.
2. Meaning "*during*": *Onder het ontbijt wordt ons altijd iets voorgelezen*, during breakfast we have always something read to us.
3. Meaning "*under*": *Die boot kan geheel onder water gebracht worden*, that boat can be completely brought under water.
4. Meaning "*amongst*": *De roovers verdeelden de buit onder elkander*, the robbers divided the spoil amongst them.
5. Indicating a time: *Onder de lange regeering van Keizer Wilhelm I.*, during the long reign of the emperor Wilhelm I.

OP

May be translated by "*upon*," "*on*," "*in*," "*after*," "*at*," "*with*," "*but*," "*into*," "*to*."

1. *Upon*: *Hij legt het eene boek op het andere*, he places one book upon another; *Op mijn woord ik weet het niet*, upon my word I don't know.
2. *On*: *Ik ontmoette hem eerst op eenen Maandag, en daarna op eenen Woensdag*, I met him first on a Monday and then on a Wednesday.
3. *In*: *Doe het eens op eene andere manier*, just try it in a different way.
4. *After*: *Hij kleedt zich op zijn Duitsch*, he dresses after the German style.
5. *At*: *Op uw verzoek zal ik gaan*, I shall go at your request.
6. *With*: *Mijn vader is waarlijk boos op mij*, my father is indeed angry with me.
7. *But*: *Alle kinderen op één na zijn dood*, all the children but one are dead.
8. *Into*: *Dien fraaien hoed zal ik u op den koop toegeven*, I shall throw that pretty hat into the bargain.

9. *To*: *Weet ge, dat we op souper (pron. sou-pé) gevraagd zijn?* do you know that we have been invited to supper?

NAAR.

1. Meaning "*to*," "*towards*": *Mijn plan is, morgen naar mijn stil dorp terug te gaan*, my intention is to return to my quiet village to-morrow; *De vogels vliegen naar de kust*, the birds are flying towards the shore.
2. Meaning "*from*": *Dat is naar de natuur geteekend*, that is drawn from nature.
3. Meaning "*according to*": *Ik heb gehandeld naar mijne overtuiging*, I acted according to my conviction.
4. Meaning "*about*": *Hij doet er onderzoek naar*, he is making enquiries about it.
5. Meaning "*for*": *Hij zoekt naar zijn boek*, he is looking for his book.
6. Meaning "*after*": *Hij kleedt zich naar de Duitsche mode*, he dresses after the German fashion.

OM.

1. Indicating a place: *Er is eene heining om den tuin*, there is a fence round the garden.
2. Indicating a time: *Hij gaat om de veertien dagen naar huis*, he goes home every fortnight; *de vergadering begint om zeven uur*, the meeting begins at 7 o'clock.
3. Preceding the Infinitive of a verb: *Hij doet het alleen om te plagen*, he just does it to tease; *Ik ben gekomen om onze rekening te vereffenen*, I have come to square our account.
4. Meaning "*for*": *Om welke reden is hij vertrokken?* for what reason did he leave? *Denk eraan om mijnentwil*, remember it for my sake.
5. Meaning "*up*": *Uw bepaalde tijd is om*, your fixed time is up.

UIT.

1. Meaning "*out*": *Zal hij ooit uit de moeite komen?* will he ever be out of trouble?
2. Meaning "*from*": *Hij komt uit de kerk*, he is coming from church.
3. Meaning "*out of*": *Uit oprechte liefde*, out of real love.

VII. Preposition-Verbs requiring for the greater part different prepositions in Dutch from those which they are followed by in English, a list is here appended from which those which occur most frequently may be learned.

VIII. List of Preposition-Verbs with unlike Prepositions in English and Dutch.

Aanbevelen aan,	To recommend to.	Ik heb dien klerk aan den raad aanbevolen,	I have recommended that clerk to the board.
Aandringen op,	,, insist on.	Hij dringt er op aan, dat ik komen zal,	He insists upon my coming.
Aankomen te,	,, arrive at.	Wij kwamen laat in den avond te Napels aan,	We arrived at Naples late at night.
Aanvraag doen om,	,, apply for.	Zult gij aanvraag doen om die betrekking,	Will you apply for that situation?
Aanzien,	,, look at.	Kind, zie mij aan,	Child, look at me.
Aanzoek doen om,	,, make application for.	Wij hebben aanzoek gedaan om opname in het hospitaal,	We have made application for a place in the hospital.
Acht geven op,	,, pay attention to.	Gij behoort meer acht te geven op uw schrift,	You should pay more attention to your handwriting.
Adresseeren aan,	,, address to.	Wij hebben den brief aan uzelf geadresseerd,	We have addressed the letter to yourself.
Adresseeren naar,	,, label for.	Hebt gij het koffer naar Wellington geädresseerd,	Have you labelled the trunk for Wellington?
Afgaan op,	,, go by.	Ik moet afgaan op wat hij schrijft,	I must go by what he writes.
Afhangen van,	,, depend on.	Uw slagen zal er van afhangen,	Your success will depend on it.
Afwijken van,	,, depart from.	De regel is daar, en wij kunnen er niet van afwijken,	The rule is there, and we cannot depart from it.
Antwoorden op,	,, reply to.	Ik heb nog niet op uwen brief geäntwoord,	I have not replied to your letter yet.
Beamen,	,, assent to.	Hij beaamt al wat zijn vader zegt,	He assents to all his father says.
Beboeten met,	,, fine.	De rechter heeft hem met honderd pond beboet,	The judge has fined him a hundred pounds.

LIST OF PREPOSITIONS—continued.

(Zich) bedienen van,	To make use of.	Wij bedienen ons van messen en vorken bij het eten,	We make use of knives and forks when we eat.
(Zich) bedroeven over.	" be grieved at.	Ik bedroef mij over uwe woorden, mijn vriend,	I am grieved at your words, my friend.
Begaan zijn met,	" be grieved at.	Waarlijk, ik ben met u begaan,	Really, I do pity you.
(Zich) begeven naar,	" repair to.	De troepen begaven zich naar hunne tenten,	The troops repaired to their tents.
Behoeden voor,	" keep from.	God behoede u voor kwaad!	May God keep you from harm!
Behooren aan,	" belong to.	Behoort die pen aan u, of aan hem?	Does that pen belong to you, or to him?
(Zich) beklagen over,	" complain of.	Ik heb mij bij mijnen buurman over zijnen zoon beklaagd,	I have complained to my neighbour about his son.
(Zich) bekommeren over,	" trouble (oneself) about.	Waarom bekommert gij u over die zaak?	Why do you trouble yourself about that matter?
Belang hebben bij,	" have an interest in.	Deze man heeft belang bij die onderneming,	This man has an interest in that enterprise.
(Zich) belasten met,	" take upon oneself.	Ik zal mij met genoegen met die zaak belasten,	I shall gladly take that matter upon myself.
Belenden aan,	" be adjoining to.	Zijn eigendom belendt aan het mijne,	His property is adjoining to mine.
Beloopen,	" amount to.	De som beloopt over de duizend pond,	The sum amounts to more than a thousand pounds.
Benoemen tot,	" appoint.	Hij is gisteren tot magistraat benoemd,	He was appointed magistrate yesterday.
(Zich) beroemen op,	" boast of.	Die menschen beroemen zich op hunne afkomst,	Those people boast of their lineage.

THE PREPOSITION.

Dutch	English	Dutch example	English example
(Zich) beroepen op,	To appeal to.	Paulus beriep zich op den keizer,	Paul appealed to Cæsar.
Berouw hebben van,	" regret.	Ik heb er berouw van, dat ik er in toegestemd heb,	I regret having consented to it.
Bersten van,	" burst with.	De jongen berstte bijna van het lachen,	The boy almost burst with laughter.
Berucht zijn wegens,	" be notorious for.	Die mannen zijn berucht wegens hunne bedriegerijen,	Those men are notorious for their cheating.
Beschaamd zijn over,	" be ashamed of.	Ik ben beschaamd over u, Karel,	I am ashamed of you, Charles.
Beschermen tegen,	" protect from.	Eene paraplu beschermt ons tegen den regen,	An umbrella protects us from the rain.
Beschikken over,	" dispose of.	Gij kunt te allen tijd over mij beschikken,	You can dispose of me (I shall be at your service) at any time.
Bestaan uit,	" consist of.	Mijn pennenhouder bestaat uit drie deelen,	My penholder consists of three parts.
Bestand zijn tegen,	" be proof against.	Het dak is bestand tegen alle weer en wind,	The roof is proof against all wind and weather.
Besteden aan,	" bestow upon.	Ik heb er veel tijd en arbeid aan besteed,	I have bestowed much time and labour on it.
Beven van,	" tremble with.	De man beefde van woede,	The man trembled with rage.
Bevoegd zijn tot,	" be qualified for.	Hij is niet bevoegd tot het vervullen van die betrekking,	He is not qualified to fill that post.
Bevreesd zijn voor,	" be afraid of.	Mijn zoon is niet voor heel veel bang,	My son is not afraid of very much.
Bewaken,	" watch over.	De arend bewaakt zijne jongen,	The eagle watches over his young.
Bewilligen in,	" consent to.	Zoudt gij er in bewilligen, het te geven,	Would you consent to give it?

List of Prepositions—continued.

Bezorgd zijn over,	To be anxious about.	Ik ben bezorgd over mijnen broeder,	I am anxious about my brother.
Bezwijken van,	,, be overcome with.	Wij bezweken van dorst,	We were overcome with thirst.
Bibberen van,	,, shiver with.	De kinderen bibberen van de kou,	The children shiver with cold.
Blaffen tegen,	,, bark at.	Blaffen die honden altijd tegen u?	Do these dogs always bark at you?
Blijven bij,	,, stick to.	Zult gij bij uw voornemen blijven?	Will you stick to your intention?
Boos zijn op/over	,, be angry with/at	Ik ben boos op u, Willem,	I am angry with you, William.
		Ik ben niet boos om wat u deed, maar om wat u zei,	I am not angry at what you did, but at what you said.
Branden van,	,, burn with.	De soldaten branden van verlangen om den vijand te ontmoeten,	The soldiers burn with desire to meet the enemy.
Brengen naar,	,, take to.	Breng dezen heer naar het station,	Take this gentleman to the station.
Deelnemen aan,	,, share in.	Hebben alle troepen deelgenomen aan het gevecht?	Have all the troops shared in the fight?
Denken aan,	,, think of.	Denk er toch niet meer aan,	Do not think of it any more.
Dienen tot,	,, serve as.	Mijn jongen diende mij tot gids,	My boy served me as a guide.
Dingen naar,	,, aim at.	Gij behoort allen naar den prijs te dingen,	You should all aim at getting the prize.
Doelen op,	,, refer to.	Deze brief doelt op wat ik u gisteren gezegd heb,	This letter refers to what I told you yesterday.
Droomen over,	,, dream about.	Ik heb den geheelen nacht van brand gedroomd,	I have been dreaming about fire all night.
(Zich) erbarmen over,	,, take pity on.	Mijn vader heeft zich erbarmd over dezen jongen man,	My father has taken pity on this young man.

THE PREPOSITION.

(Zich) ergeren over,	To be vexed at.	Dat onzinnig lachen ergert mij,	That silly laughing vexes me.
Gebrek hebben aan,	,, be in want of.	De metselaar heeft gebrek aan steenen,	The mason is in want of bricks.
Gedachtig zijn aan,	,, be mindful of.	Ik ben gedachtig aan uwe woorden,	I am mindful of your words.
Gelooven aan,	,, believe in.	Ik geloof niet aan wat gij zegt,	I do not believe in what you say.
Gelijken op,	,, resemble.	Het kind gelijkt op zijnen vader,	The child resembles his father.
Genieten van,	,, enjoy.	De zieke geniet van den zonneschijn,	The invalid enjoys the sunlight.
Geschikt zijn tot,	,, be fit for.	De man is geschikt tot dit werk,	The man is fit for this work.
Gesteld zijn op,	,, be fond of.	Deze boer is zeer gesteld op zijne paarden,	This farmer is very fond of his horses.
Getroffen zijn door,	,, be struck with.	Ik was getroffen door de tevredenheid van dien armen man,	I was struck by the contentment of that poor man.
Geven om,	,, mind (care for).	Mijn neef geeft niets om bloemen,	My cousin does not care for flowers.
Gewennen aan,	,, accustom to.	Hij heeft zich aan vroeg opstaan gewend,	He has accustomed himself to early rising.
Goedkeuren,	,, approve of.	Mijn vader keurde mijn besluit goed,	My father approved of my resolution.
Gooien naar,	,, throw at.	De man gooide met eenen steen naar het paard,	The man was throwing a stone at the horse.
Grabbelen naar,	,, scramble for.	De jongens grabbelden naar de knikkers,	The boys were scrambling for the marbles.
Graven naar,	,, dig for.	Er wordt op die plaats naar water gegraven,	They are digging for water at that farm.
Grenzen aan,	,, border on.	Onze tuin grenst aan den hoofdweg,	Our garden borders on the main road.

List of Prepositions—continued.

Gruwen van,	To shudder at.	Wie zou niet gruwen van zulk eene misdaad,	Who would not shudder at such a crime.
Haken naar,	,, long for.	Ik haak naar het oogenblik, waarop ik u ontmoeten zal,	I long for the moment when I shall meet you.
(Zich) hechten aan,	,, get attached to.	De hond hecht zich sterk aan zijnen meester,	The dog gets very much attached to his master.
Helpen aan,	,, help to.	Mijn broeder heeft mij aan eenen post geholpen,	My brother has helped me to a post.
Herinneren aan,	,, remind of.	Ik herinnerde hem aan zijne belofte,	I reminded him of his promise.
Hinderen in,	,, keep from.	Dat kind hindert mij in mijne studie,	That child keeps me from my studies.
(Zich) hoeden voor,	,, beware of.	Hoed u voor kwaad gezelschap,	Beware of bad company.
Hopen op,	,, hope for.	Wij hopen op een mooien dag morgen,	We hope for a fine day to-morrow.
Houden van,	,, like.	Het kind houdt van lezen,	The child likes to read.
(Zich) houden voor,	,, consider (oneself).	Die jongen houdt zich voor heel knap,	That boy considers himself very clever.
Hunkeren naar,	,, long for.	De kinderen hunkeren naar de vacantie,	The children long for the holidays.
(Zich) interesseeren voor,	,, take an interest in.	Die man interesseert zich voor photographie,	That man takes an interest in photography.
Introduceeren aan,	,, introduce to.	Hij heeft mij aan uwen vader geïntroduceerd,	He has introduced me to your father.

THE PREPOSITION.

Jagen naar,	To hunt after.	De menschen jagen naar rijkdom en eer,	People strive after riches and honour.
Jammeren over,	,, lament.	De slaven jammerden over hun harde lot,	The slaves lamented their hard fate.
Keeren naar,	,, turn to.	De bloem keert zich naar de zon,	The flower turns to the sun.
Kenbaar zijn aan,	,, be known by.	Een haan is kenbaar aan zijne sporen,	A cock can be known by its spurs.
Kermen van,	,, groan with.	De hond kermde van pijn,	The dog groaned with pain.
Klagen over,	,, complain of.	De menschen klagen over den regen,	People complain of the rain.
Kleven aan,	,, stick to.	Het papier kleeft aan mijnen vinger,	The paper sticks to my finger.
Klimmen in,	,, climb up.	Alle katten kunnen in boomen klimmen,	All cats can climb up trees.
Knabbelen aan,	,, nibble at.	De konijnen knabbelden aan de kool,	The rabbits were nibbling at the cabbage.
Knagen aan,	,, gnaw (at).	De hond knaagt aan een been,	The dog gnaws at a bone.
Knielen voor,	,, kneel to.	Heidenen knielen voor afgoden,	Heathen kneel to idols.
Kniezen over,	,, fret about.	Hij kniest over zijn verloren geld,	He frets about his lost money.
Koken van,	,, boil with.	Zij scheen te koken van verontwaardiging,	She seemed to boil with indignation.
Kwaad zijn over,	,, be angry about.	Ik ben kwaad over de manier waarop hij u toespak,	I am angry about the way he spoke to you.
(Zich) kwellen over,	,, worry about.	Hij kwelt er zich over dat de tijding zoo lang uitblijft,	He worries about the news being delayed so long.
(Zich) kwijten van,	,, acquit (oneself of).	Hij heeft zich altijd trouw gekweten van zijnen plicht,	He has always acquitted himself faithfully of his duty.
Kijken naar,	,, look at.	Kijk eens naar den hond, die daar ligt,	Just look at the dog lying there.

List of Prepositions—continued.

Lachen om,	To laugh at.	Zij lacht om alles wat ik zeg,	She laughs at all I say.
Leenen aan,	,, lend to.	Hebt gij die boeken aan uwen neef geleend?	Have you lent those books to your cousin?
Leenen van,	,, borrow of.	Wij hebben wat melk van onze buren geleend,	We have borrowed some milk from our neighbours.
Leiden naar,	,, lead to.	Leidt deze weg naar het dorp?	Does this road lead to the village?
Letten op,	,, pay attention to.	Let op wat ik u ga zeggen,	Pay attention to what I shall tell you.
Leven van,	,, live on.	Zij leven van de opbrengst van hun land,	They live on the produce of their land.
Leveren aan,	,, supply with.	Wij hebben dikwijls steenkolen aan die firma geleverd,	We have often supplied that firm with coal.
Liggen aan,	,, lie with (depend on).	Het zal geheel aan u liggen,	It will entirely lie with (depend on) you.
Logeeren bij,	,, stay with.	Zij logeert een paar dagen bij ons,	She is staying with us for a few days.
Loeren op,	,, be watching for.	De tijger ligt op eenen bok te loeren,	The tiger is watching for a buck.
Luisteren naar	,, listen to.	Wij luisteren naar de vogels in den boom,	We are listening to the birds in the tree.
Lijden aan,	,, suffer from.	Zij lijdt aan de jicht,	She suffers from gout.
Lijden van,	,, suffer by.	Heeft u van de bankbreuk geleden?	Have you suffered by the failure of the bank.
Lijken op,	,, resemble.	Het kind lijkt op hare moeder,	The child resembles her mother.
Mikken op,	,, aim at.	De soldaat mikte op de schijf,	The soldier aimed at the target.

THE PREPOSITION.   257

Mijmeren over,	To cogitate on.	Waar zit gij nu weer over te mijmeren?	What are you cogitating on again?
Morren over,	,, grumble about.	De matrozen morren over het schrale eten,	The sailors grumble about the poor food.
Nadenken over,	,, consider.	Ik heb rijpelijk over de zaak nagedacht,	I have carefully considered this matter.
Navraag doen naar,	,, enquire into.	Er wordt navraag gedaan naar den diefstal,	The theft is being enquired into.
Nopen tot,	,, bring to.	Uwe zachtheid zal hem tot gehoorzamen nopen,	Your gentleness will bring him to obey.
Oefenen in,	,, practise.	Wij oefenen ons in de muziek,	We are practising music.
Omzien naar,	,, look after.	Deze vrouw ziet niet eens naar hare kinderen om,	This woman does not even look after her children.
Onbekwaam zijn tot,	,, be incapable of.	Ik gevoel er mij gansch onbekwaam toe,	I feel quite incapable of it.
Onderdoen voor,	,, be inferior to.	De meeste dieren doen in kracht voor den leeuw onder,	Most animals are inferior to the lion in strength.
Onderwerpen aan,	,, subject to.	Wij moeten ons aan deze regelen onderwerpen,	We must subject ourselves to these regulations.
(Zich) onfermen over,	,, have mercy on.	Ontferm u over dien armen ouden man,	Have mercy on that poor old man.
Onthalen op,	,, treat to.	Wij wilden u op koek en chocolade onthalen,	We wanted to treat you to cake and chocolate.
Ontsnappen aan,	,, escape from.	De gevangenen zijn aan hunnen bewaker ontsnapt,	The prisoners have escaped from their guard.

K

LIST OF PREPOSITIONS—continued.

Oordeelen over,	To judge about.	Hoe zou ik over die zaak kunnen oordeelen,	How should I be able to judge of this matter?
Opofferen aan,	,, sacrifice to.	De ziekenverpleegster heeft alles aan hare plichten opgeofferd,	The hospital nurse has sacrificed all to her duties.
Overeenstemmen met,	,, correspond to.	Deze tijding stemt overeen met de laatste,	These tidings correspond to the former.
Passen bij,	,, go with.	De voering past uitstekend bij het goed,	The lining goes very well with the material.
Passen op,	,, take care of.	Pas op uwe tanden, kleine!	Take care of your teeth, little one!
Passen voor,	,, be fit for.	Deze man past juist voor zulke soort van werk,	This man is just fit for that kind of work.
Peinzen over,	,, meditate upon.	Hij peinsde over den inhoud van het boek,	He meditated upon the contents of the book.
Plagen met,	,, tease about.	Hij wordt erg geplaagd met zijne lange haren,	He gets dreadfully teased about his long hair.
Pochen op,	,, boast of.	Mijn neef pocht op zijnen rijkdom,	My cousin boasts of his riches.
Praten over,	,, talk about.	Zij zaten te praten over den brand,	They were talking about the fire.
Raadplegen over,	,, consult about.	Wij zullen over die zaak eerst moeten raadplegen,	We shall first have to consider that matter.
		Ik heb mijnen vader over de zaak geraadpleegd,	I have consulted my father about this matter.
Raken aan,	,, touch.	Als men maar aan dat blad raakt, krult het ineen,	If one only touches that leaf it curls up.

THE PREPOSITION.

Redeneeren over,	To talk about.	Gij zijt veel te jong om over zulke zaken te redeneeren,	You are much too young to talk about such matters.
(Zich) regelen naar,	,, be ruled by.	Hij regelt zich naar de wenschen zijner ouders,	He is ruled by his parents' wishes.
Reikhalzen naar,	,, long for.	De reizigers reikhalsden naar het eind van den tocht,	The travellers were longing for the end of the journey.
Reizen naar,	,, travel to.	Er reizen jaarlijks veel Mahomedanen naar Mecca,	Every year many Mohammedans travel to Mecca.
Rekenen op,	,, rely on.	Mag ik op uwe ondersteuning rekenen?	Can I rely on your support?
Rekenen met,	,, take into account.	Gij zult met uwe zwakke gezondheid moeten rekenen,	You will have to take your weak health into account.
Roemen op,	,, glory in.	Deze man roemt op zijn groot vermogen,	This man glories in his great wealth.
(Zich) schamen over	,, be ashamed of.	De jongen schaamde zich over zijne armoedige kleeren,	The boy is ashamed of his poor clothing.
Schatten op,	,, value at.	Zijn vermogen wordt op tien duizend pond geschat,	His riches are valued at ten thousand pounds.
Schieten op,	,, shoot at.	De jagers schieten op wilde eenden,	The hunters are shooting at wild ducks.
(Zich) schikken naar,	,, accommodate oneself to.	Ik heb mij naar mijne nieuwe omgeving moeten schikken,	I have had to accommodate myself to my new surroundings.
(Zich) schikken in,	,, resign oneself to.	De arme vrouw schikt zich in haar ongeluk,	The poor woman resigns herself to her misfortune.
Schreien over,	,, weep for.	Het kleine meisje schreide over den dood van haar vogeltje,	The little girl wept for the death of her bird.

LIST OF PREPOSITIONS—continued.

Schrikken voor,	To startle at.	Mijn paard schrikt voor het minste geraas,	My horse startles at the least noise.
Schrijven om,	,, write for.	Ik zal met deze post om de boeken schrijven,	I will write for the books with this post.
Schuilen voor,	,, take shelter from.	Onder dien boom kunnen wij voor den regen schuilen,	Under that tree we can take shelter from the rain.
Sidderen bij,	,, shudder at.	Ik sidder bij de gedachte aan wat er had kunnen gebeuren,	I shudder at the thought of what might have happened.
Smachten naar,	,, long for.	De geheele natuur smacht naar regen,	All nature is longing for rain.
Smaken naar,	,, taste of.	Dit water smaakt naar ijzer,	This water tastes of iron.
Smalen op,	,, run down.	Deze vreemdeling smaalt op alles wat hij hier ziet,	This stranger runs down (rails at) anything he sees here.
	,, rail at.		
Smeeken om,	,, beg for.	De misdadiger smeekte om genade,	The criminal begged for mercy.
Snakken naar,	,, crave for.	Het zieke kind snakte naar frissche lucht,	The sick child was craving for fresh air.
Snoeven op,	,, boast of.	De jonge man snoeft op zijne goede afkomst,	The young man boasts of his good connections.
Spelen om,	,, play for.	Er mag hier niet om geld gespeeld worden,	Playing for money is not allowed here.
Spijt hebben van,	,, be sorry for.	Ik heb spijt van het geld dat ik voor dit kind uitgegeven heb,	I am sorry for the money I spent on that child.
Spotten met,	,, mock at.	Het is slecht om met de gebreken van den ouderdom te spotten,	It is wrong to mock at the defects of old age.
Spreken over,	,, talk about.	Heeft u hem over de zaak gesproken,	Have you talked about the matter to him?

Staan op,	To insist on.	Ik sta er op, dat het kind zijne lessen leert,	I insist on the child learning his lessons.
Sterven aan,	„ die of.	Er zijn hier heel wat menschen aan de koorts gestorven,	A good many people have died of fever here.
Steunen op,	„ rely upon.	De vader steunt op de hulp van zijn oudsten zoon,	The father relies on the help of his eldest son.
Stikken van	„ choke with.	Het kleine kind stikte bijna van den rook,	The little child was almost choking with the smoke.
(Zich) storen aan,	„ mind.	Deze hond stoort zich weinig aan zijn baas,	This dog does not mind his master much.
Straffen om	„ punish for.	Deze kinderen zijn om hunne luiheid gestraft,	These children have been punished for their laziness.
Stralen van,	„ beam with.	Mijn vriend straalde van genoegen, toen hij den brief las,	My friend was beaming with joy when he read the letter.
Strekken tot,	„ serve.	Laat deze gebeurtenis u tot waarschuwing strekken!	May this incident serve as a warning to you!
Streven naar,	„ strive for.	Hoeveel die man ook gewonnen heeft, hij streeft altijd nog naar meer,	However much that man may have won, he is always striving for more.
Strooken met,	„ agree with.	Dit verhaal strookt niet met wat hij mij gezegd heeft,	This story does not agree with what he told me.
Strijden over	„ quarrel about.	Deze menschen strijden over de minste kleinigheid,	These people are quarrelling about the least little thing.
Talen naar,	„ have a desire for.	Van het begin harer ziekte aan heeft het kind niet naar voedsel getaald,	From the commencement of her illness the child has not felt the least desire for any food.
Teren op,	„ live on.	De zoon teert op het vermogen van zijnen vader.	The son lives on his father's fortune.

List of Prepositions—continued.

Tintelen van,	To tingle with.	*Ik tintel van verlangen om het haar te zeggen,*	I tingle with desire to tell her of it.
(Zich) toeleggen op,	,, apply (oneself) to.	*Hij heeft zich met ijver op het aanleeren der taal toegelegd,*	He has zealously applied himself to the study of the language.
Trakteeren op,	,, treat to.	*De kinderen werden op koffie en koek getrakteerd,*	The children were treated to coffee and cake.
Trekken naar,	,, go to.	*Veel jonge menschen zijn naar Mashonaland getrokken,*	Many young people have gone to Mashonaland.
Treuren over,	,, sorrow for.	*Het kind treurt over den dood harer moeder,*	The child is sorrowing (pining) for her mother's death.
Turen naar,	,, gaze at.	*Waarom staat u zoo naar de lucht te turen?*	Why do you stand gazing at the sky like this?
Twijfelen aan,	,, doubt.	*Ik heb altijd aan zijne oprechtheid getwijfeld,*	I have always doubted his sincerity.
Twisten over,	,, quarrel about.	*Mijn oom heeft jaren lang met mijnen vader over deze zaak getwist,*	My uncle has quarrelled for years with my father about this matter.
Uitgeven aan,	,, spend on.	*Al het geld, dat ik verdiend heb, heb ik aan medicijnen moeten uitgeven,*	All the money I have earned I have had to spend on medicines.
Uitscheiden met,	,, cease (stop).	*Het is tijd om met uwe lessen uit te scheiden,*	It is time now to stop your lessons.
Uitschelden voor,	,, call.	*Van dien tijd aan werd de jongen altijd voor dief uitgescholden,*	From that time the boy was always called a thief.
Uitzicht hebben op,	,, have in view.	*Mijn broer heeft uitzicht op eene goede betrekking,*	My brother has got a good position in view.

Varen naar,	To sail for.	De boot is naar het eiland gevaren,	The boat has sailed for the island.
Vasthouden aan,	" cling to.	De vader houdt vast aan zijne overtuiging, dat zijn zoon onschuldig is,	The father clings to his conviction, that his son is innocent.
Vat hebben op,	" have a hold on.	Heeft u eenig vat op dat kind?	Have you got any hold on that child?
Veranderen van,	" change.	In dien korten tijd is deze man driemaal van woonplaats veranderd,	In that short time this man has changed his domicile three times.
Verbergen voor,	" hide from.	Hij heeft de waarheid voor zijnen vader verborgen,	He has hidden the truth from his father.
(Zich) verblijden over,	" rejoice at.	Wij verblijden ons over de goede tijding, die wij omtrent u gehoord hebben,	We rejoice at the good news we have heard about you.
(Zich) vergasten aan,	" feast on.	De kinderen vergastten zich aan de heerlijke vruchten,	The children feasted on the delicious fruit.
Vergelijken bij,	" compare to.	Dit linnen is niet te vergelijken bij hetgeen ik van Ierland gekregen heb,	This linen cannot be compared to what I got from Ireland.
Vergen van,	" demand from.	Hij vergt te veel van zulk een jong kind.	He demands too much from such a young child.
(Zich) vergenoegen met,	" content (oneself) with.	De man zal zich moeten vergenoegen met de helft van wat hij eischt,	The man will have to content himself with half of what he claims.
(Zich) vergrijpen aan,	" outrage.	Hij heeft zich aan al de regels der betamelijkheid vergrepen,	He has outraged all rules of decency.
(Zich) verheugen over,	" rejoice at.	Ik verheug mij over uw welslagen,	I rejoice at your success.

List of Prepositions—continued.

Verkiezen boven,	To prefer to.	Verkiest u dit boek boven het andere?	Do you prefer this book to the other?
Verlangen naar,	,, wish for.	De kinderen verlangen naar de thuiskomst van hunnen vader,	The children are wishing for their father to come home.
(Zich) verlaten op,	,, rely on.	De arme vrouw verlaat zich op de woorden van den dokter,	The poor woman relies on the words of the doctor.
Vernemen naar,	,, enquire for.	Velen zijn naar den welstand van den ouden heer komen vernemen,	Many have come to enquire for the old gentleman's health.
Vertalen uit,	,, translate from.	Dit boek is uit het Duitsch vertaald,	This book has been translated from the German.
Vertrekken naar,	,, set out for.	De geheele familie is naar Engeland vertrokken,	The whole family has set out for England.
Vertrouwen op,	,, to trust in.	Hij is een man op wien gij vertrouwen kunt,	He is a man in whom you can trust.
Verwerken tot	,, work into.	De vezels van de hennep worden tot touw verwerkt,	The fibres of the hemp are worked into rope.
(Zich) verwonderen over,	,, wonder at.	Ik heb mij zeer over zijn gedrag verwonderd,	I have very much wondered at his behaviour.
Verzenden naar,	,, send to.	Deze boer verzendt al zijn wol naar East-London,	This farmer sends all his wool to East-London.
Verzot zijn op,	,, be mad after.	Dit vogeltje is verzot op suiker,	This little bird is mad after sugar.
Visschen naar,	,, fish for.	Deze mannen hebben den geheelen dag naar kabeljouw gevischt,	These men have been fishing for cod-fish all day.
Vitten op,	,, cavil at.	Dit kind vit op al wat haar gezegd wordt te doen,	This child cavils at all that she is told to do.

(Zich) vleien met,	To flatter (oneself) with.	De moeder vleit zich met de hoop d't haar kind nog beter zal worden,	The mother is flattering herself with the hope that her child may yet recover.
(Zich) voeden met,	" feed on.	Roofvogels voeden zich met aas,	Birds of prey feed on carrion.
Voldoen aan,	" fulfil.	Deze machine voldoet aan onze verwachting,	This machine fulfils our expectations.
(Zich) voorbereiden op,	" prepare (oneself) for.	Ik heb mij op het ergste voorbereid,	I have prepared myself for the worst.
Voorgaan in,	" set an example of.	De ouders zijn hunne kinderen in eerlijkheid voorgegaan,	The parents have set their children an example of honesty.
Voorstellen aan,	" introduce to.	Wees zoo goed mij aan die dame voor te stellen,	Be so good as to introduce me to that lady.
Voorzien van,	" provide with.	De soldaten waren voorzien van al wat zij op den tocht zouden noodig kunnen hebben,	The soldiers were provided with all they might need on the journey.
Voorzien in,	" provide for.	Mijn vader heeft in de behoeften der weduwe voorzien,	My father has provided for the widow.
Vorschen naar,	" search for.	Wij vorschen te vergeefs naar de oorzaak,	We are searching for the cause in vain.
Vragen om,	" ask for.	Waar vraagt het kind om?	What is the child asking for?
Vreezen voor,	" be afraid of.	Waarvoor zou ik vreezen, als gij bij mij zijt?	What would I be afraid of, if you are with me?
Vrijstellen van,	" exempt from.	Vreemdelingen zijn van den militairen dienst vrijgesteld,	Foreigners are exempt from military service.
Vuren op,	" fire at.	Onze troepen hebben op den vijand gevuurd,	Our troops have fired at the enemy.

List of Prepositions—continued.

Waarschuwen voor,	To warn of.	Ik heb u voor het gevaar gewaarschuwd,	I warned you of the danger.
Wachten op,	,, wait for.	Wil u op mij wachten?	Will you wait for me?
(Zich) wachten voor,	,, beware of.	Wacht u voor dit paard; het is niet te vertrouwen,	Beware of this horse; it cannot be trusted.
(Zich) wagen aan,	,, venture on.	Zult gij u aan dat werk wagen?	Will you venture on that work?
Waken voor,	,, watch over.	De wet waakt over onze vrijheid,	The law watches over our liberty.
Wanhopen aan,	,, despair of.	De dokters wanhopen aan zijn leven,	The doctors despair of his life.
Wedden om,	,, bet for.	Wedden die menschen om geld?	Do these people bet for money?
(Zich) weerhouden van,	,, refrain from.	Ik weerhoud mij van aanmerkingen te maken,	I refrain from passing remarks.
Wegkwijnen van,	,, pine with.	Het meisje is weggekwijnd van verdriet,	The girl has pined away with sorrow.
Weldoen aan,	,, do good to.	Hij heeft veel goed gedaan aan die familie,	He has done much good to that family.
(Zich) wenden tot,	,, apply to.	Wij hebben ons tot de regeering gewend,	We have applied to the government.
(Zich) wennen aan,	,, got used to.	Ik heb mij aan die soort van leven gewend,	I have got used to that kind of life.
Wenschen naar,	,, wish for.	Hoe wensch ik er naar, dat hij terugkomt,	How I wish for him to get back.
Werken aan,	,, work at.	Wij hebben den ganschen dag aan deze papieren gewerkt,	We have worked all day at these papers.
Werpen naar,	,, fling at.	Zij wierpen de stokken naar zijn hoofd,	They flung the sticks at his head.

Wonen te,	To reside at.	Mijne neven wonen te Dieprivier,	My cousins reside at Dieprivier.
Worden uit,	„ become of.	Wat zal er van u worden, arme vogel!	What will become of you, poor bird!
Wijden tot,	„ ordain.	Hij is onlangs tot priester gewijd (geworden),	He has recently been ordained priest.
(Zich) wijden aan,	„ devote oneself to.	Mijne nicht heeft zich geheel aan de muziek gewijd,	My niece has quite devoted herself to music.
Wijten aan,	„ impute to.	Ik wijt mijne verliezen alleen aan hem,	I impute my losses to him only.
Zaniken over,	„ bother about.	Het kind zanikt den heelen morgen over zijne knikkers,	The child is bothering me all the morning about his marbles.
Zenden naar,	„ send to.	Laat hem naar den winkel zenden (sturen) om meer te krijgen,	Let him send to the shop to get more.
Zenden om,	„ send for.	Het is tijd dat gij om den dokter zendt (stuurt),	It is time that you should send for the doctor.
Zien naar,	„ look at.	Zie eens naar dat vogeltje, dat hier zit,	Look at that little bird sitting here.
Zoeken naar,	„ look for.	Waar zoekt u naar, Karel?	What are you looking for, Charles?
Zorgen voor,	„ take care of.	Zorg voor mijn kind, terwijl ik weg ben,	Take care of my child, while I am gone.
Zuchten om,	„ sigh for.	De meisjes zuchten om de vacantie,	The girls are sighing for the holidays.
Zweven boven,	„ hover over.	De aasvogels zweven boven het aas,	The vultures are hovering over the carrion.
Zwichten voor,	„ succumb to.	Alles moest zwichten voor den huilenden storm,	Everything succumbed to the roaring storm.

TRANSLATION EXERCISES.—*Vertaaloefeningen.*

EXERCISE XCIV.

We wish to take a little preserve instead of cheese. Before the day dawned we were all up and ready. At what time (*Hoe laat*) do you wish to be called? My ink is done, I shall have to buy a new bottle. Among yonder trees there is one which looks particularly pretty. During (the) dinner people were continually knocking at our door to [the] annoyance of our guests as well as of ourselves. We met the travellers on their way to Berlin, and spent a couple of hours with them. Not every heart requires a large number of friends to be happy. I have known persons who had very few true friends, and yet were happy and contented. Three of the pupils have failed in the examination, on account of many mistakes (that) they made in the translation from German into (the) English. Forasmuch as the news has reached you, you will be obliged to go at once. All the people ran to the market-house for (to) shelter, on account of the unexpected shower. The bird flew into the church, and went right through it. He came to me about a quarter of an hour after my brother had left me, and stayed for some (a) twenty-five minutes.

EXERCISE XCV.

Once upon a time a fox saw a pretty wood-pigeon sitting on one of the lowest branches of an oak-tree in a large wood. "Pretty dove," said the fox, "I have been running (I have run) about all (the) morning (for) to find somebody to have a chat with; do come down and sit in the brushwood, and we shall have a pleasant talk." The silly pigeon actually came down and sat in the brushwood, close to the ground. Then the fox said: "Why do you think (that) it is, that birds are so much prettier than four-footed animals?" "Oh," said the pigeon, "I do not consider (that) they are (that), but this I know, that our feathery coat is of much more use to (*voor*) us than your hairy skin is to you." The fox seemed to get interested, and replied: "Little creature, where do you get such wisdom (*vandaan*)? Did I ever hear (have I heard) a wood-pigeon speak (such) intelligent words [like those]? Surely, if foxes are called cunning, pigeons might (*zouden kunnen*) be called wise. But now explain your statement." The poor dove, which perhaps had never been flattered before, was almost beside (*buiten*) herself with (of) joy and pride when she gave the following explanation: "$_2$You $_1$see, the first and most important duty of every living creature, whether in the wood or elsewhere, is to protect his head against every injury from outside. Now that is just (of) what (*waartoe*) you, hairy animals, are not capable [of]. With us it is different. From whatever side the wind blows, we are always able to shield our head and keep it warm."

Exercise XCVI.

"Suppose for instance (that) the wind should come (came) from the south, and I should be sitting (sat) just like at present. I would simply lift my right wing and (*er*) cover my head with (*mede*) it. If the wind blew from the north, I should only require to lift my left wing and do the same." "That's well explained," said the fox, "but now just (*eens*) show (it) me." The pigeon then (*toen*) lifted first her right wing, and then her left [one], and with either (both) covered her head entirely, so that the fox seemed quite satisfied. "But now," he added (to it), "that's all right (*dat is goed en wel*) for southerly and northerly winds, but what would you do if the breeze should come (came) from the west, while you were sitting (sat) like that (*zoo*)? You see, now I have caught you, that's a thing that you do not know, my little dove!" "What!" said the pigeon, "do not know? Pigeons know everything about (of) that matter. Shall I show you how we do?" "I should be so glad if you would (did it)" replied the fox, "I do like to (*zoo graag*) learn things from wiser people than myself (I am)." This answer again stung the poor dove's pride. She ventured (it) to come down from her twig in the brushwood, and sat (went to sit) down on the ground right in front of (*recht vóór*) the fox. "Now mind," (*let nu op*) she went on (*voort*), "this is what we do" (so do we). Saying this, she buried her pretty head in the soft down of her neck. That was (it) what (*waar*) the fox had been looking for (*op gewacht had*) with all the desire of his cruel heart. The very (same) minute (that) the head turned round, he seized the poor pigeon with his strong claws, ate it (*op*) and went away.

Exercise XCVII.

I dare not go out, for fear (that) I might (*zou kunnen*) catch cold. Let him do it, if he likes (*wil*). How delightful! I shall have you all (*geheel*) to (*voor*) myself; we shall have a happy fortnight. Evil communications corrupt good manners. You won't go out, will you? I would not be able to act against your desire. May I leave the work [undone]? What is it that puts you up to (*dat er u toe brengt*) neglecting (neglect) your duties? He is so anxious (desirous) to become acquainted with you. What will (*er*) have become of my poor boy? The last news (plur.) from him was disheartening. All the people (whom) you see assembled in that spacious hall are descendants of the late Duke of A., a man of great physical strength, great activity and zeal, and true nobility of heart. What a pity (*hoe jammer*) (that) you have not been able to (*kunnen*) travel more! To spend a couple of years in (*met*) (the) visiting (of) countries, (the) seeing (of) strange nations, (the) observing (of) their manners and customs, and (the) inquiring into (of) their religion, affords more real development than double the time spent in study or in an office.

THE PREPOSITION. 271

CONVERSATIE.	CONVERSATION.

Ambachten en Beroepen. — **Trades and Occupations.**

1. Hij is smid van beroep.
2. Hij is van alle markten thuis.
3. Deze man heeft een lakenwinkel in de Langstraat.
4. Waar kan men een exemplaar van dit boek bekomen?
5. Men kan het, meen ik, krijgen bij Mason, boekhandelaar, in de Georgestraat.
6. Als u bij den drogist voorbijkomt, koop dan wat citroenzuur voor mij.
7. Neem dit recept, en wacht bij den apotheker tot de medicijnen klaar zijn.
8. Laat dit bij den blikslager repareeren.
9. Laat den timmerman die tafels en banken repareeren.
10. Een metselaar moet dien muur nazien.
11. De stoffeerder heeft de voorkamer behangen en gemeubileerd.
12. Wees zoo goed, dit naar den slotenmaker te sturen.
13. Waar kan ik een glazenmaker vinden?
14. De man, die voor mij werkt, woont dicht bij Johnston, den schoenmaker.
15. Mijne paarden moeten beslagen worden; breng ze naar den hoefsmid.
16. Die wagenmaker maakt uitmuntende wagens voor den transporthandel.
17. Ga met mij mee naar den goudsmid om een gouden ketting te koopen.

1. He is a blacksmith by trade.
2. He is a jack of all trades.
3. This man has a draper's shop in Long St.
4. Where can one get a copy of this book?
5. I believe it can be had at Mason's, booksellers, in George Street.
6. If you pass the chemist's, buy some citric acid for me.
7. Take this prescription, and wait at the apothecary's till the medicine is ready.
8. Have this mended at the tinsmith's.
9. Get the carpenter to mend these tables and benches.
10. A mason must repair that wall.
11. The upholsterer has papered and furnished the drawing-room.
12. Please have this taken to the locksmith's.
13. Where can one find a glazier?
14. The man whom I emp'oy lives near Johnston, the shoemaker's.
15. My horses must be shod; take them to the farrier.
16. That waggon-builder makes excellent waggons for transport-trade.
17. Go with me to the jeweller's to buy a gold chain.

18. De horlogemaker heeft juist een nieuwen voorraad ontvangen.
19. Zullen wij bij den vischhandelaar aangaan en wat visch voor het diner bestellen?
20. De slager heeft in den laatsten tijd geen heel goed schapevleesch gestuurd.
21. Waar koopt u groenten?
22. Wij koopen er zelden: onze tuinier voorziet ons.
23. De boeren zeggen, dat de oogst van 't jaar slecht zal zijn.
24. Deze man is boekbinder, en die heeft een boekenstalletje.
25. Vraag den drukker, die fout te verbeteren.
26. Stuur naar den kruidenier om eene kist beste thee.
27. Heeft u sigaren?
28. Neen, maar de tabakshandelaar heeft er zeer goede op het oogenblik.
29. Heeft de kleermaker mijne jas gestuurd?
30. Neen, mijnheer, maar de hoedenmaker heeft den hoed gestuurd, dien u besteld had.

18. The watch-maker has had a fresh supply just lately.
19. Shall we call at the fishmonger's, and order some fish for dinner.
20. The butcher has not been sending very good mutton lately.
21. Where do you buy your vegetables?
22. We seldom buy any; our gardener keeps us supplied.
23. The farmers say the harvest will be bad this year.
24. This man is a bookbinder, and that one has a bookstall.
25. Ask the printer to correct that mistake.
26. Send to the' grocer's for a box of his best tea.
27. Have you any cigars?'
28. No, but the tobacconist has excellent ones at present.
29. Has the tailor sent my coat?
30. No, sir, but the hatter has sent the hat you ordered.

CHAPTER XII.

THE CONJUNCTION.

(*Het Voegwoord.*)

I. As Prepositions express relations between objects, or between an object and an action, so CONJUNCTIONS establish relations between thoughts. CONJUNCTIONS are indeclinable words (particles), and have no meaning in themselves. They are used for expressing the connection between sentences, or different parts of the same sentence. Consequently they are connective words. To distinguish them from Adverbs, which may be connectives as well, it must be observed that Adverbs do not derive their meaning from the place they take in the sentence, and though used as connectives, must always qualify some other word. Adverbs, moreover, when used as connectives, are not necessarily placed *between* two sentences; they may be included in one of the sentences, which is not the case with Conjunctions.

> NOTE.—The difficulty of distinguishing between adverbs and conjunctions is most apparent where the same word is used in both qualities: *Reken er op*, nu *zal het geschieden*, be sure of it, now it will happen (*nu* is adv.); *Al mijne vreugde is weg* nu *mijne ouders dood zijn*, all my joy is gone now that my parents are dead (*nu* is conj.)

II. Conjunctions may be divided into two principal classes, viz. A., those which connect two independent sentences, CO-ORDINATIVE CONJUNCTIONS, *Nevenschikkende Voegwoorden*, and B., those which connect sentences of which the one is dependent upon the other, SUBORDINATIVE CONJUNCTIONS, *Ondergeschikte Voegwoorden*.

> *Note.*—Subordinate Conjunctions remove the verb to the end of a clause. Of the Co-ordinate Conjunctions, those that are adverbial place the subject after the verb.

A. Co-ordinative Conjunctions are subdivided into:

1. those which unite or couple together, *Verbindende* or *Aaneenschakelende Voegwoorden*.
2. those which oppose, *Tegenstellende Voegwoorden*.
3. those which limit or separate, *Scheidende Voegwoorden*.
4. those which express a reason, *Redengevende Voegwoorden*.

EXAMPLES OF 1.—*en*, and, *ook*, also, *niet alleen* or *niet slechts* or *niet enkel* . . . . *maar ook*, not only . . . . but also, *benevens*, and also, *alsmede*, and also, *zoowel* . . . . *als ook*, as well . . . . as, *noch* . . . . *noch*, neither . . . . nor, and the adverbial conjunctions *daarenboven*, besides, *daarna*, after that, *bovendien*, besides, *ja zelfs*, even.

Laat mij u zeggen, hoe wij den dag hebben doorgebracht: niet alleen hebben we eene lange wandeling gemaakt, maar we zijn ook wat gaan lezen, en hebben toen gedineerd, vervolgens zijn we te paard uit geweest, eindelijk hebben we ons huiswerk voor morgen gemaakt. Let me tell you how we spent the day: not only did we take a long walk, but we also read a little, and then had dinner, then again we went out on horseback, and finally we did our homework for to-morrow.

EXAMPLES OF 2.—*maar*, but, *doch*, but, *nu*, now that, *dan*, then, and the adverbial conjunctions *integendeel*, on the contrary, *echter*, however, *desniettegenstaande*, notwithstanding, *evenwel*, however, *intusschen*, in the meantime.

Ik zou het u gaarne geven, doch het is onmogelijk, I should like to give it to you, but it is impossible: *op die wijze zult gij mij niet van u vervreemden, integendeel gij zult mij u meer doen achten en liefhebben*, in that way you will not estrange me from you, on the contrary you will cause me to esteem and love you more; *Ik heb hem dikwijls gewaarschuwd, echter heeft hij er geene acht op geslagen,* I have often warned him, but he has not heeded it.

EXAMPLES OF 3.—*of,* or, *of* .... *of,* either .... or, *hetzij* .... *hetzij,* either .... or, *hetzij* .... *of,* whether .... or.

Hetzij wij werken of spelen, ons hoofd moet er bij zijn, whether we work or play, our mind must be in it; *Of de brief is reeds verzonden, of hij zal van morgen op de post gaan,* either the letter has been sent already, or it will be posted this morning.

EXAMPLES OF 4.—*want,* for, *bijgevolg,* consequently, *dus,* so, *alzoo,* so, *daarom,* so, therefore, *hierom,* on this account, *derhalve,* for that reason, *dan,* then, so, *toch* (see sentence), *immers* (see sentence), all of which may be called adverbial conjunctions.

Wij zullen moeten ophouden, want het begint te regenen, we shall have to stop, for it begins to rain; *Verklaar u nader, mij toch komt toe, alles te weten,* or *immers komt mij toe, enz.,* explain yourself further, it is meet for me to know all, *or,* is it not meet for me, etc.?

B. Subordinative Conjunctions are subdivided into:

1. those that express a comparison, *Vergelijkende Voegwoorden.*
2. those that express a proportion, *Verhoudingaanwijzende Voegwoorden.*
3. those that define a time, *Tijdbepalende Voegwoorden.*
4. those that define a place, *Plaatsbepalende Voegwoorden.*
5. those that express a condition, *Voorwaardelijke Voegwoorden.*
6. those that indicate a concession, *Toegevende Voegwoorden*

7. those that express a purpose, *Doelaanwijzende Voegwoorden.*
8. those that express the reason of an action, *Redengevende Voegwoorden.*
9. those that join noun-sentences to principal sentences, *Verklarende Voegworden.*

EXAMPLES OF 1.—*gelijk*, as; *evenals*, just as; *als*, as; *dan*, than; *zooals*, as; *dat*, so that; *alsof*, as if.

Hij is grooter geworden, dan ik verwacht had, he has grown taller than I had expected; *Doe alsof gij thuis waart,* make yourself at home.

EXAMPLES OF 2.—*hoe . . . . hoe . . . ,* the . . . . the; *hoe . . . . des te,* the . . . . so much the; *naarmate* or *naar gelang,* according as; *naar, naardat,* according as, in proportion to.

Hoe minder hoe liever, als ge maar gezond zijt, the less the better as long as you are healthy; *Hoe meer ik hem aanzette tot zijn werk, des te meer vertraagde hij,* the more I put him up to his work, the more he became lazy; *Naardat gij werkt, zullen uwe vorderingen zijn,* your progress will be according to your work.

EXAMPLES OF 3.—*als,* if; *toen,* when; *wanneer,* when; *zoodra als,* as soon as; *zoo dikwijls als,* as often as; *vóórdat,* before; *nu,* now that; *terwijl,* whereas. These conjunctions are for the greater part adverbs and prepositions changed into conjunctions by the addition of "*als*" or "*dat.*"

De haan begon te kraaien, zoodra als wij buiten kwamen, the cock began to crow as soon as we came outside; *Het vuur ging dadelijk uit, toen de blaasbalg ophield met blazen,* the fire went out immediately, when the bellows ceased blowing.

EXAMPLES OF 4.—*waar,* where; *alwaar,* where; *waarheen,* whither; *werwaarts,* whither; *van waar,* from where.

Wijs mij de plaats, waar ik gezaaid heb, show me the

place where I have sown ; *Ik reis naar hetzelfde onbekende land, werwaarts mijn vader twee jaren geleden vertrokken is,* I am travelling to the same unknown country, whither my father went two years ago ; *Ik herinner mij nog duidelijk de hoogte, vanwaar wij u het laatst vaarwel toewuifden,* I distinctly remember the height from where we beckoned a last farewell to you.

EXAMPLES OF 5.—*indien,* if ; *in geval dat,* in case that ; *zoo,* if ; *tenzij,* unless ; *mits,* provided ; *wanneer,* if.

Ik wil het niet doen, tenzij gij uwe volle toestemming geeft, I don't want to do it, unless you give your full consent ; *Gij kunt op mijne hulp rekenen, mits gij zelf al uwe krachten inspant,* you may be sure of my assistance, provided you yourself do everything in your power.

EXAMPLES OF 6.—*schoon, hoewel, alhoewel, ofschoon, al,* though ; *niettegenstaande,* although.

Ofschoon dit woord verouderd mag heeten, wordt het toch door verschillende schrijvers nog gebruikt, though this word may be called obsolete, it is still being used by several authors ; *Hij waagt zich gedurig nog 's avonds in de lucht, niettegenstaande hij gewaarschuwd is,* although he has been warned, he still often goes out at night; *al is de leugen nog zoo snel, de waarheid achterhaalt haar wel,* though falsehood be ever so swift, truth is sure to overtake it.

EXAMPLES OF 7.—*opdat,* in order that ; *dat,* that ; *teneinde,* for the purpose of.

De vader werkte wat hij kan, opdat de zoon de vruchten van zijnen arbeid zou plukken, the father worked with all his might, in order that the son should gather the fruits of his labour ; *Eert uwen vader en uwe moeder, opdat uwe dagen verlengd worden,* honour thy father and thy mother, that thy days may be long ; *Hij spoort zijn paard aan, ten einde nog vóór zonsondergang thuis te zijn,* he spurs on his horse, for the purpose of being home before sunset.

NOTE.—Mark that adverbial sentences of purpose are not *usually* formed with the words *opdat* and *ten einde.* In fact, in colloquial language, those two conjunctions are rarely used. The common expression for the thoughts contained in the first and last of the sentences under 7 would be: *De vader werkt wat hij kan, om den zoon de vruchten van zijnen arbeid te laten plukken*, the father works with all his might, to let the son gather, etc.; *Hij spoort zijn paard aan om nog vóór zonsondergang thuis te zijn*, he spurs on his horse to be home before sunset. Foreigners should try to accustom themselves to the constant use of the preposition *om* for the sake of fluency.

EXAMPLES OF 8.—*omdat, dewijl, naardien, doordien, aangezien, wijl*, because; *daar, vermits*, since; *om reden (dat)*, for the reason (that); *op grond (dat)*, on the ground (that); *nademaal*, for as much.

De verkooping kon niet doorgaan, omdat het regende, the sale could not come off, because it was raining. *Ik zal u in rechten moeten vervolgen, aangezien gij mijnen naam hebt trachten te benadeelen*, I shall have to take legal steps against you, for as much as you have tried to injure my reputation.

EXAMPLES OF 9.—*dat*, that; *of*, whether, if. These conjunctions occur after verbs which express an assertion, an assurance, a question, etc.

Hij verzekert mij, dat hij er geene schuld aan heeft, he assures me that it is not his fault; *Gij verlangdet te weten, of ik u helpen zou?* you wished to know whether I would help you? *Zeg mij of alles in orde is*, tell me if all is right.

OBSERVATIONS.

1. *Dat*, that, may mean *omdat*, because, *opdat*, in order that, and *zoodat*, so that: *a*) *ik ben heel dankbaar, dat ge gekomen zijt*, I am very thankful that (because) you have come; *b*) *Ik span alle krachten in, dat ik slagen moge*, I do my very best that (in order that) I may succeed; *c*) *het regent, dat het giet*, (literal trans.) it rains so that it pours.
2. *Wijl* ought to be taken for *dewijl*, because, and not for *terwijl*, while.

3. *Zonder, in plaats van, behalve,* when they are conjunctions, can never be used without the conjunction "*dat:*" *a) Hij zegt zulke dingen, zonder dat hij er bij denkt,* he says such things without thinking what he says; *b) In plaats van dat hij onmiddellijk naar hem toeging, kwam hij eerst bij mij,* instead of going to him straight, he first came to me; *c) Alles bevalt mij, behalve dat ge hem zijn verzoek geweigerd hebt,* I am pleased with everything but that you have refused his request.
4. After real conjunctions the connective "*dat*" may not be used.
5. "*Now that*" may be translated "*nu dat,*" but "*nu*" only is more common.
6. "*Maar*" and "*doch*" both mean "but." "*Maar,*" however, opposes the thoughts, expressed in the sentences it connects, in a stronger way than "*doch.*" *Hij is rijk, maar blind; wat baat hem zijn rijkdom?* he is rich but blind; of what good are his riches to him? *Hij zegt nooit veel, doch als hij spreekt, verraadt ieder woord de helderheid zijner gedachte,* he never says much, but if he does speak, each word betrays the clearness of his thoughts. In common speaking, however, "*doch*" is uncommon.
7. "Good-hearted though he was, many people shunned him" may be translated, *Goedhartig als hij was, werd hij toch door velen gemijd*—yet a better translation is, *Hoewel hij goedhartig was, werd hij, enz.*

TRANSLATION EXERCISES.—*Vertaaloefeningen.*

EXERCISE XCVIII.

A thrush, a linnet, and a thistle-finch were once caught by a fowler in one day and under the same (*een en hetzelfde*) net. Since they were all equally pretty, he did not like (*wilde hij niet graag*) to kill [any] one of the three; so he put them together into one large cage. At first they were all on very good terms (*op zeer goeden voet*), most (*heel*) likely because none of them liked the fate (to none of them was the fate agreeable) (to which) they were condemned [to]; but when₂ after a while₁ they had got accustomed to the small room, (to which) they were confined [to], the thistle-finch began to be very disagreeable. He scolded his two companions either for singing (because they sang) too high or too low, or for not keeping time (*maat, v*), when they were trying to sing together. At last his temper grew (became) so bad, that the other two birds could not bear his company any longer. In fact, the little linnet got so nervous from being (to be) scolded all day long (the whole day), that it (*hun*) soon became impossible for him (*om*) to sing. So (on) one morning, when the fowler—who on the whole was very good to (*voor*) them—took them out (brought them outside) into the sun, the linnet spoke to him on this wise (*hem aldus aan*): Good man, I am perfectly aware (of it) that I am doing a hazardous thing by openly complaining about the thistle-finch here present; but yet I must speak out. His temper has grown bad beyond measure (*uitermate*), so much so (*zoozeer*), that I have given up (the) singing for fear of being scolded incessantly, and I am even beginning to hate (the) life. I frankly ask you, for my own sake and that (*ter wille van mijzelven en van*) of my good companion, the thrush, to relieve us of the company of this miserable thistle-finch, and to do it soon, lest (*opdat . . . niet*) he kill me.

Exercise XCIX.

A certain man had three sons. When he had grown (become) old, and was about to die (soon would die) he called his sons to (*bij*) him (*zich*), telling them (and told them) that he wanted to divide his goods. After the necessary arrangements had been made, he thus spoke to (*aanspreken*) them: "My sons, besides what I have now assigned to you, there is in my possession a large diamond of great value, which I received from my father on the day of his death. This jewel I cannot divide, and may (I) not sell. I have therefore made up my mind (resolved), that I shall give it to that one of my three sons who within three months will give me proof that he possesses a better character than his brothers." Upon this (*Hierop*) the sons took leave of their father, and separated (*uit elkaar gaan*) on the promise of reassembling at the old man's sick-bed after a lapse of (*na verloop van*) three months. When the time had arrived (*komen*), they all met (*samenkomen*) once again in their old home. And this is what they had to report. "Father," said the eldest, "in the course of these three months a friend of mine (see p. 134) wished to undertake a journey into a far-off land. He brought me a large amount (sum) of gold, which I undertook (*op zich nemen*) to keep for him, but for which he refused to (would not) take a written acknowledgment. When he came back, I returned all the money to him without (*er*) keeping any of (something) [it] back, though there was nothing to show how large the sum had b en (which) he had entrusted to me. What does my father think of such a character?"—"My son," replied the old man, "this was only ordinary honesty; I should not have expected anything (nothing) less of my son!"

Exercise C.

Thereupon the second son stepped (came) forward, and spoke: "My father, in the course of these three months I came to the shore(s) of a lake, just at (*op*) the moment when (*dat*) a little child, playing on the bank (*kant, m*), happened to (accidentally) fall into the water. The poor mother, who stood by (*erbij*), screamed for (*om*) help, and wildly threw up (*in de hoogte gooien*) her arms in despair. I hurried to the spot, sprang (*er*) in, dived after (*naar*) the sinking child, caught it, brought it up (*naar boven*), swam with it (*ermede*) to the shore, and handed it to the distressed mother. Far gone (*heen*) though (*hoe...ook*) it was, (*the*) life was not extinct (*er ... uit*) and our combined efforts brought the poor child back to (*tot het*) life. The mother found (could find) no words with which (*om*) to thank me; but drawing a purse filled with gold from her pocket, she spoke [to] me thus (*aan*): 'Stranger, take this. Though the reward be little in comparison to the noble deed, do not despise what I offer you from (*uit*) a heart overflowing with (*van*) gratitude. Take it, and if you will make no personal use of it, let it (*then*) be the price for buying something which will remind you of this happy day, and this glorious deed!'—But I refused the money, saying that to see the boy breathe was sufficient reward for me. What does my father think of such a character?"—The old man replied, "My son, this is nothing but ordinary love of man (*menschenliefde*), and just what I should have expected of my son."

Exercise CI.

Then the youngest son came to tell his tale, and this is what he said: "Father, in the course of these three months I was travelling in the mountains. On a certain day, when darkness had set in (*de avond gevallen was*) and the road was but faintly lit up by the glimmer of the stars, my attention was attracted by (*doordat*) my dog sniffing (sniffed) at something lying off the roadside (*aan den kant van den weg*). The spot being [a] dangerous [one], I dismounted, and went to see what my dog had found. It was a man who was lying fast asleep on the very (*uiterst*) edge of a fearful chasm. I scanned his face, and knew it to be (that it was) that of my worst enemy. Now I know that (if) should I leave (I left) him there, he would undoubtedly move about (*zich bewegen*) in his sleep, and (*er*) no more of him would be heard; yea, and (that) even if I should try to rouse him, he might (*zou kunnen*) move and drop down, so near he lay to (*bij*) the outermost edge. I therefore seized his arm (him by the arm), dragged him away a few yards, and then woke him up. He startled when he recognised my voice, but I spoke reassuringly [to] him (*toe*), and asked him to tell me what had made (*bewogen*) him lie down in such a horrible place. He then told me that he had lost his way (*verdwalen*), and that (he), being overwhelmed with (*uitgeput van*) fatigue at the approach of (the) night, [he] had dropped down, not knowing where. I then showed him his way (*naar*) home, and let him go. What does my father think of such a character?"—The eyes of the dying man brightened up as the question was put (*gedaan*), and he exclaimed, "Oh my son, that was indeed more than common honesty, more also than common love of man—that was magnanimity! You have shown to possess the best character, and gladly (*volgaarne*) do I bequeath the jewel to you!"

Conversatie.
Onderwijs en School.

1. *Onze school zal op den 23sten April weer beginnen, en gesloten worden op den 21sten Juni.*
2. *Op welke school is uw zoon?*
3. *Hij is op de Normaalschool, op het openbare Gymnasium.*
4. *Mijn zoon is op het Athenaeum.*
5. *Hij zal 't volgende jaar naar het Theologisch Seminarie gaan.*
6. *Wat onderwijsstaf heeft u?*

Conversation.
Teaching and Schools.

1. Our school re-opens on the 23rd of April and closes on the 21st of June.
2. What school does your son attend?
3. He goes to the Normal school, to the Public Gymnasium.
4. My son is at the College.
5. He enters the Theological Seminary next year.
6. What staff of teachers have you?

7. Een hoofdonderwijzer en vier assistenten.
8. Hij is taalonderwijzer, teekenonderwijzer, enz.
9. Bij wien neemt u les?
10. Professor Schmidt geeft mij muziekles.
11. Woont u de taalklassen bij?
12. Neen, ik neem privaatles in Fransch en Duitsch.
13. Mijn onderwijzer komt Maandags en Donderdags.
14. Hij rekent vijf shillings per les.
15. Mijne zuster gaat naar eene kostschool.
16. Zij is eene leerlinge van eene collegiale school.
17. Hij heeft bij het laatste examen eene beurs gekregen.
18. Hij was een schoolkameraad van mij.
19. In welke klasse is u?
20. In de eerste, tweede, vierde, laagste, enz.
21. Dat kind kent alleen het a, b, c.
22. Hij heeft een certificaat gekregen.
23. De zomervacantie begint in December.
24. Elementair schoolexamen.
25. Elementair onderwijzersexamen.
26. Toelatingsexamen tot de universiteit.
27. Examen in de Rechten.
28. Landmetersexamen.
29. De bijzondere vakken, in dat examen vereischt, zijn: Algemeene Geschiedenis, Engelsche Geschiedenis, de Engelsche Taal, Gricksch en Latijn.

7. A head-master, and four assistants.
8. He is a teacher of languages, a drawing-master, etc.
9. With whom do you take lessons?
10. Professor Schmidt gives me music lessons.
11. Have you joined the language classes?
12. No, I take private lessons in French and German.
13. My master comes on Mondays and Thursdays.
14. The fee is five shillings a lesson.
15. My sister is going to a boarding-school.
16. She is a pupil of a collegiate school.
17. He gained a bursary at the last examination.
18. He was a school-fellow of mine.
19. In what class are you?
20. The first, second, fourth, lowest, etc.
21. That child only knows the alphabet.
22. He has obtained a certificate.
23. The summer holidays begin in December.
24. School Elementary examination.
25. Elementary Teachers' Examination.
26. Matriculation Examination.
27. Law Examination.
28. Survey Examination.
29. The special Subjects required for that examination are: General History, English History, English language, Greek and Latin.

30. *Noem mij de studieboeken eens op voor den graad van doctor in de letteren.*
31. *Ik heb mijne klasse kwart voor twaalf laten uitgaan.*
32. *Iederen morgen wordt de presentielijst afgelezen.*
33. *Alle drie maanden worden er rapporten gepubliceerd, waaruit ouders en voogden kunnen opmaken, hoe het met de leerlingen onzer school staat.*

30. Tell me the text-books for the M.A. degree in literature, please.
31. I dismissed my class at a quarter to twelve.
32. Every morning the roll is called.
33. Every three months reports are published from which parents and guardians may know how the pupils of our school are doing.

CHAPTER XIII.

THE INTERJECTION.

(*Het Tusschenwerpsel.*)

1. INTERJECTIONS, *Tusschenwerpsels*, are sounds without a definite meaning, which serve to give utterance to some momentary emotion of the mind. They are indeclinable, and may be placed in a sentence anywhere without ever effecting any change in its construction. Some grammarians object to their being called words, on the ground of their having no definite meaning. A good many Interjections are imitations of sounds. A few nouns, verbs in the imperative mood, and adverbs, are used as Interjections. The name 'interjection,' as will be easily seen from the Dutch equivalent, means "cast in between."

The following are the most common Interjections:

1. For the expression of grief: *ach!*=ah! *helaas!*= alas! *wee!*=woe! *wee mij!*=woe to me! *o Hemel!* =good Heavens!
2. For the expression of pain: *ai! au!*=oh!
3. For the expression of wonder: *hé!*=oh! *aha!*=I say!
4. For the expression of excitement and joy: *heisa! hoezee! hoera!*=hurrah!
5. For the expression of a wish: *och!*=oh!
6. For the expression of dislike: *ba! aba!*=bah! *foci!* =fy!
7. For the expression of encouragement: *bravo!*=well done! *welaan!*=go on! *komaan!*=come on.

8. For the expression of any emotion whatever: *o!* = oh!
9. For the imitation of sounds: *bom, bam* (of a tolling bell), *bim, bam* (of a striking clock), *tik, tak* (of any timepiece in motion), *pief, paf* (of a gun), *krik, krak* (of breaking wood), *kukeleku* (of a crowing cock), *tok, tok, tok* (of a cackling hen), *miauw* (of a mewing cat), *boe, boe* (of a lowing cow), *klingelingeling* (of a common door-bell), *flap* (of any unexpected clap), *bons* (of a heavy object falling).

CHAPTER XIV.

ETYMOLOGY.

(*Woordvorming.*)

I. ETYMOLOGY treats of the formation of words. Words are of three kinds—PRIMITIVE, COMPOUND, and DERIVATIVE.

PRIMITIVE words (*stamwoorden*) are not derived from other words.

COMPOUND (*samengestelde*) words are made up of two other words.

DERIVATIVE (*afgeleide*) words are derived from primitive words, or roots.

> OBS.—Derivation is brought about partly by changes in the radical vowels of words, with or without modifications of their consonants; and partly by means of prefixes and suffixes. In determining the different changes by which words have received their present form, we are led through the successive stages of the history of the language, a field of study and research beyond the limits of a concise grammar. As an example, however, of the way in which a great number of words have come into existence, the following may be given:

Words derived from the same roots.

To revenge,	*wreken,*	*wraak,*	*wrok.*
To smell,	*ruiken,*	*reuk,*	*ruiker—rieken.*
To split,	*splijten,*	*spleet,*	*split.*
To grip,	*grijpen,*	*greep,*	*begrip.*
To break,	*breken,*	*breuk,*	*brok—bres—bros.*
To dig,	*graven,*	*graaf,*	*graf—groef—gracht— greppel.*
To drink,	*drinken,*	*drank,*	*dronk—drenken.*
To give,	*geven,*	*gave,*	*gift.*

To wade,	waden,	wed,	wadde.
To spring,	springen,	sprong,	sprank.
To ride,	rijden,	rit,	ridder.
To fly,	vliegen,	vlucht,	vleugel—vlok.
To lock,	sluiten,	sloot,	slot—sleutel.
To bend,	buigen,	boog,	bocht—beugel.
To swell,	dijgen (dijen),	duig,	deeg—dik.
To lie,	liegen,	leugen,	logen—loochenen.
To draw,	tiegen,	teugel,	tocht—teug.
To bind,	linden,	band,	bundel—bond.
To bite,	bijten,	bit,	bete—bijt.

II. FORMATION OF NOUNS.

(a) By means of prefixes (*Voorvoegsels*):

Aarts (meaning *eerste*, first): *aartsvader*, patriarch; *aartsengel*, archangel.

On (meaning *geen*, no): *onmensch*, brute; *onkunde*, ignorance; *ongeloof*, unbelief.

Mis (meaning *verkeerd*, wrong): *misdaad*, crime; *misdruk*, paper wasted in printing.

Wan (meaning *slecht*, bad): *wanorde*, disorder; *wantrouwen*, distrust.

Oor (meaning *uit*, out of): *oorsprong*, origin; *oorlog*, war.

Et (meaning *opnieuw*, again): *etmaal*, period of 24 hours; *etgroen*, second crop of grass after it has been mown.

Ant (meaning *tegen*, against): *antwoord*, answer.

Ge (before nouns " belonging to "): *gebroeders*, brethren; *gemaal*, consort.

(In connection with suffix *te*—a collection): *geboomte*, collection of trees; *gebladerte*, foliage.

(Before stems of Verbs—the product of the action): *gebak*, confectionery; *geschenk*, present.

(b) By means of suffixes (*Achtervoegsels*):

Masculine names of persons are formed by the help of the suffixes *aar* (*er, ier, enaar, enier*), *aard* (*erd*), *ik* and *and*.

Aar, er, ier form substantives from verbs, and names of persons from the proper names of countries and towns.

Er stands for *aar*, when the preceding syllable has the accent; *ier* is rarely used; *enaar* and *enier* form names of persons from other substantives.

EXAMPLES: *leeraar*, professor; *dienaar*, servant; *schrijver*, author; *gever*, donor; *tuinier*, gardener; *kunstenaar*, artist; *kruidenier*, grocer; *hovenier*, gardener; *Hollander*, Hollander; *Haarlemmer*, inhabitant of Haarlem.

Aard, erd, ik, and *erik*, indicate a fulness of the (mostly bad) quality expressed by the original verb or adjective: *grijnzaard*, one who grins; *veinzaard*, dissembler; *blufferd*, boaster; *luiaard*, idler; *gauwerd*, one who has a quick hand; *slimmerd*, cunning person; *vuilik*, filthy person; *stommerik*, dunce.

And is the old form for *end*, the ending of every present participle, and consequently indicates that the individual whose appellation it helps to form, is the doer of the action expressed by the verb which forms the first part of the word: *heiland* (*de heilende, de heelende, de geneesmeester*), Saviour; *vijand* (*de vijende, de hatende*), enemy (foe); *vriend* (*vrijand, de vrijende, de beminnende*), friend.

III. Feminine names of persons and animals are formed by the suffixes *ster, in, es*. *Ster* is placed after the stems of verbs: *bakster*, female baker; *schoonmaakster*, charwoman, etc.

If the stem is dissyllabic and has no accent on the last syllable, the feminine substantive is derived from the masculine by adding *ster* to the latter: *bedelaarster*, female beggar; *toovenaarster*, witch.

Es and *in* form feminine substantives from masculine ones: *dienares*, female servant; *voogdes*, female guardian; *dichteres*, poetess; *zangeres*, professional lady singer; *godin*, goddess; *koningin*, queen; *boerin*, farmer's wife.

NOTE.—*Zangster* means muse, songstress.

With '*in*' names of female animals are likewise derived from masculine forms: *berin*, she-bear; *leeuwin*, lioness; *tijgerin*, tigress; *wolvin*, she-wolf.

IV. *Er (aar), el (eel, sel)* are used for the formation of names of instruments or tools with modifications of the root-vowel before *el: stoffer*, broom; *klopper*, knocker; *tuimelaar*, tumbler (kind of pigeon); *hevel*, siphon; *troffel*, trowel; *beugel* (fr. *buigen*, to bend), iron hoop; *teugel* (fr. *tiegen, trekken*, to pull), bridle; *sleutel* (fr. *sluiten*, to close), key; *vleugel* (fr. *vliegen*, to fly), wing; *tooneel* (fr. *toonen*, to show), stage; *houweel* (fr. *houwen*, to hew), pick-axe; *stijfsel*, starch; *schoeisel*, shoes; *voedsel*, food.

> NOTE.—The ending *sel* is, however, principally used for indicating the product of an action: *baksel*, anything produced by baking; *kooksel* (product of *koken*, to boil); *zaagsel* (product of *zagen*, to saw).

V. *Je (tje, etje), ke (kijn), elijn, ing*, and *el* form diminutives. *Je* is the most common diminutive ending, of which *tje, etje, pje*, and *kje* are only modified forms required in special instances.

Je occurs whenever a word ends in one of the sharp consonants (*'t kofschip*) or in *d* or *g: kopje*, small head; *vischje*, small fish; *lesje*, small lesson; *kuifje*, small tuft; *haakje*, small hook; *matje*, small mat. Exc. *meid* (contracted form of *maagd*) has *meisje*, girl.

> NOTE.—The Cape Dutch *meidje* means a little servant-girl.

Tje occurs after words ending in a vowel or diphthong: *knietje*, little knee; *zeetje*, small sea.

Tje also occurs when the word ends in *l, n, r*, or *w*, preceded either by a full vowel or diphthong, or sometimes by a mute vowel: *kooltje*, small cabbage; *nageltje*, small nail; *deuntje*, ditty; *dekentje*, coverlet; *boortje*, small gimlet; *kamertje*, little room; *pauwtje*, young peacock; *zwaluwtje*, young swallow.

Words ending in *m* preceded by a long or by a mute vowel, or by either of the consonants *l* and *r*, take *je* for their diminutive ending, inserting *p* between it and the word: *boompje*, small tree; *bezempje*, small broom; *halmpje*, tiny stalk; *wormpje*, little worm.

Etje occurs when a final *b, ng, l, m, n,* or *r* is preceded by a modified vowel: *tobbetje,* small tub; *dingetje,* small thing; *rolletje,* small roll; *kommetje,* small cup; *zonnetje,* little sun; *karretje,* small cart. Nouns in *g* preceded by a modified vowel may take either *je* or *etje* · *mugje,* little gnat; *ruggetje,* little back.

Some nouns in *ng* take *je* while sharpening *g* into *k,* in consequence of their last syllable being unaccented, which would render the addition of mute *etje* impossible: *rottinkje,* small cane; *koninkje,* little king.

Ke and *ken* were much more frequently used in former times than they are now. They render the language sweet and tender, as may be felt on reading Jan van Beers' poem: "*Het broerken.*"

Kijn and *lijn* belong almost exclusively to poetry. For examples read Jan van Beers': "*De bloem op het graf.*"

Words with final *e* generally drop that letter before a diminutive ending: *einde,* end, makes *eindje; koelte,* breeze, makes *koeltje.* Sometimes, however, the *e* is retained: *dieptetje,* little hollow; *diktetje,* small swelling.

Ing serves less to derive real diminutives from existing words than rather to indicate small objects: *krakeling,* cracknell; *hokkeling,* calf less than a year old; *nesteling,* nestling.

El is an obsolete diminutive ending, only to be found in a small number of words, in which it has so entirely lost its original meaning, that a new ending is now added, whenever an actual diminutive is required: *kruimel* (from *kruim,* crumb), *kruimeltje; eikel,* acorn (fr. *eik,* oak-tree), *eikeltje; bundel,* bundle, *bundeltje.*

> OBS.—It may here be observed both that the Dutch are fond of using diminutives, and that these forms have lost much of their original signification, in consequence of which, if a thing is actually small, the use of the adjective *klein* together with the diminutive ending, is not infrequent; e.g. *Daar zit een klein muisje,* a tiny little mouse sits there.

VI. Collective nouns are formed by means of the suffixes: *age, dom, heid, schap, te* and *ij;* e.g. *plantage,* plantation; *pakkage*, collection of packages; *menschdom*, mankind; *christenheid*, christianity; *gereedschap*, tools; *gevogelte*, all the birds; *ruigte*, shrubbery; *ruiterij*, cavalry.

VII. ABSTRACT NOUNS are derived:

1. From concrete nouns by means of the suffixes *schap*, *dom*, *ij*. Ex.: *koningschap*, kingship; *priesterdom*, priesthood; *slavernij*, slavery.

2. From adjectives by the suffixes *schap*, *dom*, *nis*, *e*, and *te*, representing qualities as substantives: *blijdschap*, gladness; *adeldom*, nobility; *droefenis*, sadness; *koude*, cold; *diepte*, depth.

3. From verbs by the suffixes: *schap*, *dom*, *nis*, *ij*, *age*, *st*. Ex.: *rekenschap*, account; *wasdom*, growth; *ergernis*, annoyance; *razernij*, madness; *lekkage*, leakage; *kunst*, art.

VIII. FORMATION OF ADJECTIVES.

(a) By means of prefixes (*Voorvoegsels*):

Aarts (in a high degree, with words having an unfavourable meaning): *aartsdom*, very stupid; *aartslui*, very lazy.

On (not): *onnut*, useless; *onwetend*, ignorant.

Wan (bad): *wanschapen*, misshapen; *wanstaltig*, deformed.

Be and *ge* form adjectives from nouns and stems of verbs; *behendig*, dexterous (from *hand*); *bekommerd*, anxious (from *kommer*); *bewust*, conscious (from *weten*); *gewoon*, accustomed (from *wennen*).

(b) By means of suffixes (*Achtervoegsels*):

Achtig: one suffix "*achtig*" is accented, another with a different meaning is unaccented. The first, which we also meet with under the German form *haftig* (*haft*), expresses full possession of what the word to which it is affixed indicates: *waarachtig*, true; *twijfelachtig*, doubtful; *krijgshaftig*, soldier-like; *manhaftig*, manly.

Achtig, not accented, has the meaning of the English *y*, *ish*, and indicates a similarity with the meaning of the principal word: *zwartachtig*, blackish; *houtachtig*, woodlike; *winterachtig*, wintry.

Baar (derived from *beren*, to bear), means a bringing

forth, a producing, or a possibility of the action: *wonderbaạr*, wonderful; *vruchtbaar*, fertile; *leesbaar*, legible.

En and *sch* form adjectives which indicate a material: *zilveren, koperen, houten* (unaltered by any inflexion of gender, number, or case), *duffelsch, lakensch*.

Ig (Engl. *y*) indicates possession, or, with stems of verbs, a repetition of the action: *krachtig, kundig, begeerig, levendig*.

NOTE.—*Eenig* is formed of a num. adj.; *innig, overig*, and *nietig* are formed of particles.

Zaam signifies "fitness" or "desire": *buigzaam, leerzaam, werkzaam*.

Lijk means similitude, belonging to, being of the nature of: *koninklijk, vorstelijk, zedelijk, armelijk, liefelijk, vroolijk*; —after verbs, a possibility of the action: *sterfelijk, schadelijk*.

Loos means "destitute of": *eerloos, naamloos, broodeloos*; —after verbs, impossibility of the action: *reddeloos, stoorloos*.

Isch and *sch* are used to derive adjectives from proper nouns: *Aziatisch, Perzisch, Egyptisch, Zweedsch, Deensch, Poolsch*. It is also found in a good many adjectives of foreign origin, and then stands for the English *ic: grammatisch, alfabetisch*.

In *afgodisch* and *wettisch* it has the meaning of *lijk*.

Sch likewise forms adjectives from nouns and adverbs: *wereldsch, buitenlandsch, dagelijksch, achterwaartsch*.

IX. FORMATION OF VERBS.

(a) By direct derivation:

1. CAUSATIVES (*Causatieven*), through changes in the radical vowel: *vellen* (from *vallen*), to fell; *zetten* (from *zitten*), to put down; *leiden* (from *lijden*), to lead.

2. INTENSIVES (*Intensieven*), through changes in the radical vowel and final consonant: *bukken* (from *buigen*), to stoop; *vluchten* (from *vliegen*), to flee; *slachten* (from *slagen, slaan*), to kill; *knippen* (from *knijpen*), to nip.

3. DENOMINATIVES (*Denominatieven*), through suffixing the verbal infinitive ending '*en*' to

Nouns: *ademen*, to breathe; *lijmen*, to glue; *regenen*, to rain; *schaven*, to plane.

Adjectives, *witten*, to whitewash; *drogen*, to dry; *dooden*, to kill; *stijven*, to starch.

Num. adjectives: *vereenen*, to unite; *verdubbelen*, to double.

Particles: *innen*, to collect; *uiten*, to utter.

(*b*) By means of Prefixes (*Voorvoegsels*):

Be (by) has the meaning of "all round;" it signifies that the action is extended to every part of the object in *bezien, bedekken, bespreken, beschieten, behandelen, bevoelen*; —its meaning is that of the Dutch preposition "*bij*" in *bereiken, behooren, bespringen, besparen, bekomen*.

> NOTE.—On account of this meaning *be* has the power of changing any intransitive verb into a transitive one, and of forming verbs of substantives which otherwise could not (as in English) be used as such: *sterven—het vleesch besterft een nacht; bemannen*, to man; *beschijnen*, to shine upon; *bevruchten*, to fertilize.

Er originally has the meaning of "obtaining by means of the action": *erlangen, erkennen, ervaren, erbarmen*. The prefix is little used. Its meaning is expressed by *be*, and *ver*.

Ge does not materially change the meaning of a verb: *winnen* or *gewinnen, lukken* or *gelukken*, etc., are alike in signification.

In some cases *ge* takes the place of a preposition following the verb: *gelijken* for *lijken op, genaken* for *naken tot*.

Of some verbs the original form is no longer in use: *genezen, geschieden, genieten*.

Of a few verbs this prefix changes the meaning: *beuren*, to lift, and *gebeuren*, to happen; *raken*, to touch, and *geraken*, to get to.

Wan expresses a negation of the meaning of the stem-word: *wantrouwen*, to distrust; *wanhopen*, to despair.

Her means again, anew: *herdenken, herkauwen, hereenigen*.

Ont originally meant *ant*, i.e., back, against, away from: *ontraden, ontmoeten, onthouden, ontloopen, ontzien*. But it may also mean a change either from an old condition, or into a new one: *ontsluiten, ontdekken, onttronen, ontaarden, ontbinden, ontslapen, ontdooien, ontspringen, ontspruiten*.

Ver, an important prefix, has several distinct meanings:

1. When prefixed to a verb it expresses the contrary of the original meaning of that verb: *verachten, verleeren, veroordeelen, verleiden*.

2. It expresses a continuation of the action, until a complete change is brought about: *verdrogen*, to die by drought; *verteren*, to consume; *vreten=vereten*, to devour; *verspelen*, to game away; *verdrinken*, to be drowned; *verouderen*, to pine away through age; *verpletten*, to crush.

3. It signifies "away from": *verplaatsen, verjagen, verwerpen*.

4. It expresses transition or change: *verbedden, verharen, vertalen, vervellen*.

5. It has the meaning of covering or closing: *vermommen, vergulden, verzilveren, verglazen, vernagelen, verhelen*.

6. It forms verbs from nouns and adjectives, once more indicating a change: *verbroederen, vergoden, verzwageren, vernieuwen, verouderen, verfijnen*.

7. In a few cases it merely stands for the preposition "over": *vernachten* and *overnachten; vermannen* and *overmannen*.

(*c*) By means of Suffixes (*achtervoegsels*):

Elen and *eren* (with or without change in radical vowel) form frequentative verbs (*Frequentatieven*), those that express a repetition of the action, from existing ones:

kakelen (from *kekken*), to cackle; *sprenkelen* (from *springen*), to sprinkle; *bedelen* (from *bidden*), to beg; *bibberen* (from *beven*), to shiver; *stotteren* (from *stooten*), to stammer.

X. Adverbs may have the following suffixes: *e, s, lijk* (*lijks*), *ling* (*lings*), *waart* (*waarts*), *wijs* (*wijze, gewijs, gewijze*), *jes* (*pjes, tjes, etjes*).

E changes adjectives into adverbs. It is little used: *dicht(e)-bij, verre, noode, alreede.*

S changes nouns, adjectives, and present participles into adverbs, apocopating final *d* in the latter: *daags, dikwijls, ondanks, rechts, slechts, willens, wetens.*

Lijk (*lijks*) are suffixes to nouns and adjectives: *maandelijks, schriftelijk, herhaaldelijk, gewisselijk.*

Ling (*lings*) converts nouns into adverbs of manner: *zijdelings, mondelings, blindelings.*

Waart (*waarts*), with the meaning "in the direction of," occurs after nouns, pronouns and prepositions: *hemelwaarts, landwaarts, te mijnwaart, te uwaart, voorwaarts, herwaarts.*

Wijs (*wijze gewijs, gewijze*), meaning "on this wise," occurs after nouns in the genitive case, or after verbs with inserted *s*: *trapsgewijze, steelsgewijze, kwanswijs.*

Jes (*pjes, tjes, etjes*) makes of adjectives adverbial diminutives: *zoetjes, liefjes, zachtjes, kalmpjes, eventjes.* These are all used as adverbs of manner.

XI. FORMATION OF COMPOUND WORDS.

(*a*) Compound Nouns are formed:

1. By writing the two parts together, so as to make them appear one word: *huisdeur, vuurhaard, reisgenoot, uitgaaf.* In this way by far the greater part of the compound nouns are formed in Dutch.

2. By inserting an *s* between the two parts of the compound, as a mark of the genitive case, a plural form, or for the sake of euphony: *jagerstasch, handelsbank; meisjesschool, jongensboek; leidsman, scheidsrechter.*

3. By inserting *e* or *en* between the two parts (see the rules, p. 21).

4. In uncommon compositions, geographical names or compounds derived from foreign languages, the hyphen is used: *vergeet-mij-niet*, forget-me-not (the flower); *kruidje-roer-mij-niet*, touch-me-not (the sensitive plant); *Zuid-Afrika, Oost-London, Mokka-koffie, Procureur-Generaal, Luitenant-Admiraal*.

(*b*) Compound Adjectives are formed—

1. By writing the two parts together so as to make them appear one word: *lichtgroen, blauwgrijs, driedubbel, doodarm*.

2. When the first part is a verb, by the insertion of *s* between the parts: *noemenswaard, werkensmoe*.

(*c*) Compound Verbs are formed—

1. By the composition of infinitives with nouns, adjectives, adverbs, and prepositions, when the two parts are written as one word without undergoing any change; *schijfschieten, huishouden, doodslaan, wegnemen, ophouden, loslaten*.

2. By the composition of two infinitives, the first of which loses its final *n*, or sometimes the entire infinitive-ending *en*: *ginnegappen, harrewarren, trekkebekken;—staroogen, reikhalzen, vrijwaren*.

(*d*) Compound Adverbs are formed—

1. Without changing either part of the composition *bergop, tweemaal, driewerf, achteruit*.

2. By the insertion of a genitive-ending between the parts; *blootshoofds, goedsmoeds, geenszins;—langzamerhand, middelerwijl*.

3. By the insertion of a dative-ending between the parts, strengthened by a *t: zijnentwege, om uwentwille, harenthalve*.

ETYMOLOGY.

XII. LIST OF WORDS which require some explanation on account of the altered or obsolete meaning of one of their component parts, or on account of the difference between their original and present meanings, and alterations in their spelling.

Adelaar, adel aar, noble bird, (now) eagle.
Adelborst, noble breast, noble youth, (now) navy-cadet.
Achterbaks, achter den rug, behind one's back, on the sly.
Bakboord, rugboord, larboard, left hand of a ship.
Baker (contraction of *bakermoeder*), baby-nurse.
Barnsteen, (by common metathesis of *r*) *brandsteen*, burnt stone, (now) amber.
Bongerd (boogaard), boomgaard, tree-garden, orchard.
Bordpapier, plankpapier, board-paper, cardboard.
Crediet, credit (commercial term); *krediet*, trust, faith.
Deemoed,* *dienaarsmoed*, servant's mind, humility.
Dertien, drietien, thirteen.
Dokter, physician; *doctor*, university degree in literature, theology, etc.
Drempel, dorpel, deurpaal, door-post, threshold.
Elf, eenlif, overblijvende een, one over, eleven.
Ellende, ander land, other country, *ballingschap*, banishment, (now) misery.
Etmaal, edmaal, nog eens maal(tijd), again (the same) time, a period of 24 hours.
Godsvrucht, godsvurcht (metathesis of *r*), *vreeze Gods*, fear of God, piety.
Handhaven, (bij de) hand hebben, to maintain, manu tenere; *verdedigen*, to defend, hold.
Heimwee, woning-smart, home-pain, home-sickness.
Hertog, (met het) heir tiegende, (met het) leger trekkende, leider, leader (dux), (now) duke.
Honingraat, honingratel, honigweefsel, honeycomb (pron. distinctly *honing-raat*).

* The word *moed*, found in many compounds, may always be translated by "mind."

Hoovaardig, hoogvaardig, trachtende naar hoogheid, desirous of being great, proud.
Huisraad, huisgeraad, huisgereedschap, utensils for housekeeping, (now) furniture.
Juffrouw, jufvrouw, jungvrouw, jonge vrouw, young lady, miss (as a form of address).
Kermis, kerkmis, church-mass, (now) fair.
Kerspel, kerkspel, kerkspaal, kerkelijke grens, parish.
Kerstfeest, krestfeest (metathesis of *r*), *kristfeest, Christus-feest,* Christmas.
Kinds, childish; *kindsheid,* childhood; *kindsch,* doting; *kindschheid,* dotage, childishness of old age.
Komédie, theatre; *comédie,* comedy.
Kwik, kwikzilver, quicksilver, mercury.
Kwikstaart, levende staart, wagtail (a bird).
Landouw, land aue, goed land, fertile tract of land.
Landpaal, landgrens, land-mark.
Lichaam, likhaam, lijkbedekking (from *hemen,* to cover), flesh-covering, body.
Likdoren, lijkdoren, doren (in het) vleesch, thorn (in the) flesh, corn.
Litteeken, lijkteeken, teeken (in het) vleesch, mark (in the) flesh, scar.
Madeliefje, weideliefje, weidebloem, meadow-flower, daisy.
Maarschalk, (mare knecht), paardeknecht, groom, (now) *hoogste generaal,* chief officer, marshal.
Meineed, valsche eed, false oath, perjury.
Mevrouw, mijne vrouw, my wife, (now) madam.
Misdruk, misdruksel, paper wasted in printing.
Moer, moerschroef, screw-nut.
Muizenesten, muizenissen, musings, *diepe gedachten,* deep thoughts.
Nachtvorst, nachtvrost (metathesis of *r*), night-frost.
Nameloos, innumerable; *naamloos,* without a name.
Nooddruft, nooddurft (metathesis of *r*), *groote behoefte,* great want, need, from *durven (derven), behoeven.*

Ooievaar, ode baar (from *beren*, to bear), *schatdrager*, treasure-bearer, (now) stork.
Ooglid, oogdeksel, eyelid (the Dutch *lid* for *deksel* is sometimes heard).
Orde, order (arrangement), rank; *order, bestelling*, order (commercial term).
Overlijden, overgaan, to pass over, (now) to die.
Paarlemoer, parelmoeder, mother-of-pearl.
Practijk, practice, application of rules; *praktijk*, practice of a physician.
Ruiken, to smell; *rieken*, to scent.
Schauw (in poetry) *schaduw*, shadow; *schouw*, chimney, or hut.
Spin, spinnekobbe, spinnekop, spider.
Tachtig, (t)achtig, (t)achttig, eighty.
Twaalf, tweelif, overblijvende twee, two over, twelve.
Veertien, viertien, fourteen.
Veertig, viertig, forty.
Vierschaar, vier scharen, vier banken, four seats (in an ancient court), (now) tribunal.
Vorst, voorste, eerste, gebieder, prince (monarch).
Wieroo, kwijrook, gewijde or *heilige rook*, consecrated smoke, incense.
Wissel, wisselbrief, bill of exchange.
Wijwater, gewijd water, holy water.
Zinloos, meaningless; *zinneloos*, senseless, foolish.
Zinnelijk, sensual; *zindelijk*, clean, neat.

XIII. WHERE TO PLACE THE ACCENT:—Generally speaking the accent lies on the first syllable of a word.

The following detailed rules may prove useful to students:

(a) Of the prefixes of Ch. XIV, § II, (a), *aarts, on, mis, wan, oor, et*, and *ant* have the accent: *aártsvader, óngeloof, misbaksel, wántrouwen, oórsprong, étmaal, ántwoord*.

(b) Of the suffixes of § II, (b), only *ier* is accented: *tuiniér* (whereas *kúnstenaar, schríjver*, etc.).

(c) Of the suffixes of § III, *es* and *in* have the accent: *zangerés, tijgerín.*

(d) Of the suffixes of § IV, *eel* takes the accent: *houweél, tooneél.*

(e) Of the suffixes of § VI, *áge* and *ij* have the accent: *lekkáge, plantáge, bakkeríj, dieveríj.*

(f) Except a few enumerated under (b) to (e) no one suffix—whether in nouns, adjectives, adverbs, or verbs, has the accent, except "*achtig*," as explained under § VIII, (b).

(g) Of the prefixes of § VIII, (a), *aarts, on,* and *wan* are accented.

(h) Of the prefixes of § IX, (b), *wan* is the only one which has the accent. The other verbal prefixes, *be, ge, er, her, ont,* and *ver,* by means of which a great many verbs, and nouns derived from them, are made, have no accent, but the accent lies on the first syllable after them.

(i) In verbs, and words derived from verbs, the accent lies on the stem-part.

(j) Separably compounded verbs, however (see p. 188), have the accent on the noun, adjective, adverb, or preposition with which they are compounded.

(k) Compound nouns have the accent on their first part.

(l) Non-Dutch words, as a rule, have the accent on their last syllable: accént, presónt, absént, muzíek, physíek, concórt, talént, corsét, kanáal, harpóen, kantóor, muskét, seizóen, schavót—or if they are of more than two syllables, on the second last one: kanárie, monopólie, kalénder, operátie, tradítie, piáno.

(m) When such foreign words of three or more syllables end in *aaf, gram, fie, ment, uut, ist, ant, aan, iek, ier,* or *aat,* they take the accent on their final syllable: telegráaf, monográm, photografíé, firmamént, instítúut, telegrafíst, foliánt, oceáan, republíek, formulíer, potentáat.

TRANSLATION EXERCISES.—*Vertaaloefeningen.*

Exercise CII.

Very long ago, about the year 550 B.C. (*V.C.*), Asia had two mighty kings, viz., Cyrus, King of Persia, a man renowned for his courage and military skill, and Crœsus, whose riches surpassed all comprehension. The latter once happened to meet (met by chance) the Greek philosopher Solon, whom he treated with the greatest distinction and to whom he showed all his riches and treasures. Then he said : "Solon, I know (that) you have seen much of the world—tell me whom you consider (as) the happiest of men." Of course the proud king could himself have given the answer (that) he expected; he merely used the philosopher as an instrument for flattering (to flatter) his vanity. How disappointed he must have been, when he heard the following reply from the mouth of the sage:—"He whom I consider (the) happiest among mortals is Tellus, a burgher of Athens, a man upright and good, esteemed by all his fellow-citizens, a man who spent his life in promoting the good of the city of his fathers ; a man who had a happy home, healthy, beautiful, strong children, whom he saw grow up as dutiful youths, esteemed by (the) society as the father *was* himself; a man who, when his beard had become grey and the hair of his head snow-white, when his eyes were getting dim and his knees feeble, went to war for the rescue of his country, and died on the battle-field, to seal with his blood the glorious victory of the day." "Him," Solon repeated, "I certainly consider (as) the happiest of all men."

Exercise CIII.

"And after *him*," hastily replied the king, who had grown (become) indignant at the philosopher's boldness of preferring (to prefer) a common citizen of Athens to the richest of kings—"after that, tell us, who do you think is happiest?" "Two Greek youths," was the disappointing answer, "Cleobis and Biton, both of whom were handsome and strong, and they even once gained laurels in the Olympian games. Their mother was a priestess, and when one day the hour of service in the temple was drawing near (approached), and the mother sat ready in her cart, waiting in vain for the oxen, which were to pull the vehicle, the two sons, lest she should be (too) late, harnessed themselves to the chariot, and conveyed their mother to the place of worship. The people looked on (it) in amazement, and began to praise the happy priestess on account of her worthy sons. The mother, moved at heart, straightway entered the temple, knelt down before the images of her gods, and entreated them to reward her sons and (to) do to them what they might think best (*wat hun het best mocht dunken*). Then she called her sons into the temple and made them lie down for a while, because she saw (that) they were tired. Both fell asleep and neither of them ever woke again. The gods had granted the mother's request, and translated the youths to the world of undisturbed happiness."

Exercise CIV.

After having listened impatiently to Solon's second reply, Crœsus exclaimed: "Stranger from Athens, tell me why I, whom everyone acknowledges to be the richest of men, should be inferior in happiness to common citizens of your native country!" "O Crœsus," was the answer, "do not be offended at my words. I know you are happy at present; but I, who have seen much of life, can only call him happy, who continues to be so (*het*) until the day of his death. You are young and may have fifty more (*nog*) years to live (may perhaps live, etc.); who knows what may happen in the course of your days!"— Crœsus failed to see (*inzien*) (could not see) the sound wisdom of the philosopher's reply, and declined speaking to him (any) more. But let us see what happened: Crœsus, stung by pride, sent messengers to the celebrated oracle of Delphi, in Greece, for the sake of ascertaining what would be the result if he should make war with Cyrus of Persia. The messengers came back in (on the) due time with the following message from the gods—for which they had paid a sum as only a man like Crœsus could offer:—"If Crœsus passes the Halys—the eastern border of his dominion—a great empire will be destroyed."

Exercise CV.

A man (somebody) of common sense would have noticed the apparent ambiguity of this answer—every answer from the priests at Delphi was ambiguous—but Crœsus felt sure that the empire whose doom had been announced, must be the Persian one. He therefore raised a mighty army, crossed the border into Persia, and attacked his great opponent. From the very (first) beginning the tide of war seemed to turn against him, and very soon after (*daarna*), we find (the) poor Crœsus fettered to a stake in the market-place of his own capital, just on the point of being burned. Suddenly, however, he exclaims: "Solon, Solon, Solon!"—and goes on repeating that foreign name until the attention of King Cyrus is drawn to it, and he sends an interpreter to his enemy to inquire what he wants. Crœsus tells about Solon's visit to Sardes, and what remarkable words he had spoken to him. Cyrus, to whom every syllable of the conversation is translated, is deeply moved. He feels himself a human being, weak in himself, great only through circumstances. He fancies how an equal fate might befall him some day (*de eene of andere*), and commands the Lydian king to be loosed (commands that . . . . . be loosed) from his bonds on the spot. Not only (the) life was granted unto Crœsus, but he became Cyrus's friend and counsellor.

CHAPTER XV.
CONSTRUCTION.
(*Woordschikking.*)
The Principal Sentence.
(*De Hoofdzin.*)

I. THE common order of the Assertive sentence, whose verb is in a simple tense, is the same in Dutch as in English:

Subject—Predicate—Object—Extension.

He saw a house in the wood, *hij zag een huis in het bosch.*

II. A. When the Predicate consists of more than one word, *i.e.,* when it is made up of a verb and its auxiliary, or a verb in conjunction with an adverb, noun, or any other part of speech, the verb (whichever comes first) takes the place of the English verb, whereas the other parts of the predicate must be removed to the end of the sentence:

He has seen a house in the wood, *hij heeft een huis in het bosch gezien.*
He seems to have called the child, *hij schijnt het kind geroepen te hebben.*
My brother wants a book, *mijn broeder heeft een boek noodig.*
You must have used the knife, *gij moet het mes gebruikt hebben,* or *hebben gebruikt.*
He has been obliged to give it, *hij heeft het moeten geven,* not *geven moeten.*

OBS.—Notice that in the last two sentences the Aux. of time, *hebben*, can either precede or follow the principal verb, whereas the Aux. of mood, *moeten*, cannot follow it. Whenever an Aux. of mood, used as a Past Part., takes the form of the Infinitive, *i.e.*, when it is used with another infinitive verb—it *must precede* the principal verb:

He has not been allowed to say it, *hij heeft het niet mogen zeggen.*

OBS. 2.—The only case in which the rule of § II may be broken, is when various extensions, or a sub-ordinate sentence intervening, the distance between the two parts of the verb is rendered greater than is consistent with clearness:

He did it this morning, as soon as he was up, *hij heeft het van morgen, zoodra hij op was, gedaan,* or *hij heeft het van morgen gedaan, zoodra hij op was.*

B. Separably compounded verbs in their simple tenses follow this rule:

He travels through the Free State to go to Pretoria, *hij reist den Vrijstaat door, om . . . .*
The anxiety about his sister keeps him down, *de zorg over zijne zuster houdt hem onder.*

III. When there are two Objects, one in the Dative case (indirect), and the other in the Objective case (direct), the indirect object representing a person, and the direct object a thing, the person must precede the thing:

He gave the scholar a book, *hij gaf den scholier een boek.*

IV. When two objects (as under III) are represented by personal pronouns, the direct object goes first:

He has given it to him, *hij heeft het hem gegeven.*

V. Generally speaking, the place of the adverbial extension is in Dutch where it is in English, viz., after the object at the end of the sentence. This position is taken to emphasize the idea expressed by the adverb:

> He has told him distinctly, yesterday, often, for the last time, here, etc., *hij heeft het hem duidelijk, gisteren dikwijls, voor het laatst, hier, enz. gezegd.*

VI. When the object itself requires more emphasis than the adverb, the latter (in Dutch) is placed before the object, whereas its place in English is between Subject and Verb:

> I plainly see the house, but not the window, *ik zie duidelijk het huis, maar niet het raam.*

VII. When the object is a noun in the singular, preceded by the article *een* (a, an) or a plural noun without any distinguishing word, all adverbs except those of manner must precede such an object:

Compare
{ I wrote a letter yesterday, *ik heb gisteren eenen brief geschreven.*
I wrote that letter yesterday, *ik heb dien brief gisteren geschreven.* }

Compare again
{ I wrote some letters yesterday, *ik heb gisteren brieven geschreven.*
He treats children well, *hij behandelt kinderen goed.* }

VIII. When the object is a personal pronoun, the adverbs cannot precede it;

> I shall see him often, *ik zal hem dikwijls zien.*
> I have heard her very well, *ik heb haar heel goed gehoord.*

IX. Adverbs must precede the preposition-object:

> He always relies on his memory, *hij vertrouwt altijd op zijn geheugen.*

Compare
{ He relied on his memory foolishly, *hij vertrouwde op eene dwaze manier op zijn geheugen.*
He foolishly relied on his memory, *hij was dwaas genoeg op zijn geheugen te vertrouwen.* }

X. True adverbs must precede adverbial phrases:

> He saw my brother here in the wood, *hij heeft mijnen broeder hier in het bosch gezien.*
>
> He will see him for the last time to-morrow, *hij zal hem morgen voor het laatst zien.*
>
> He will start at seven to-morrow, *hij zal morgen om zeven uur vertrekken.*

XI. Adverbs of time usually precede the other adverbs:

> The man has been looking for the child everywhere to-day, *de man heeft het kind vandaag overal gezocht.*

XII. The adverb of negation (*niet*, not) stands:

1. After the verb in a single tense:
The child does not eat, *het kind eet niet.*

2. Before the principal verb in compound tenses:
> The child has taken no food to-day, *het kind heeft vandaag niet gegeten.*

3. After the object (direct or indirect, or both) of a verb:
> I did not pick those flowers, *ik heb die bloemen niet geplukt.*
>
> Did he not tell it to you? *heeft hij het u niet verteld?*

4. If intended to negative the meaning of any other word but the verb, its place is immediately before such word:
> The child would not eat at once, *het kind heeft niet dadelijk willen eten.*
>
> My brother, not I, has read the book, *niet ik, maar mijn broeder, heeft het boek gelezen.*

The Sub-ordinate Sentence.
(*De Ondergeschikte Zin.*)

XIII. The great characteristic of the Dutch sub-ordinate sentence is, that the whole of the Predicate is placed at the end of the sentence:

> He said, he would have called me at once, *hij zei, dat hij mij dadelijk zou laten roepen.*
> The woman who lives opposite my uncle's house is very ill, *de vrouw, die tegenover het huis van mijnen oom woont, is erg ziek.*

> OBS.—When a sub-ordinate sentence has a lengthy extension, the verb *may* be made to precede it, but may never be in front of the Direct Object:
>> I knew you would never be able to do it, *ik wist, dat gij het nooit zoudt kunnen doen.*
>> Do you think I shall see your brother before six o'clock this evening? *denkt gij, dat ik uwen broeder zal zien vóór van avond zes uur?*

> NOTE.—An infinitive phrase forming part of a sub-ordinate sentence, is not counted an extension, but is (see p. 323) analysed as a separate sentence; hence the verb of the sub-ordinate sentence precedes such phrase:
>> He said he did it to tease you, *hij zei, dat hij het deed om u te plagen.*
>> He called to me to stop calling his brother names, *hij riep, dat ik het laten moest, zijnen broeder uit te schelden.*

XIV, A. When the verb of the sub-ordinate sentence is used in a compound tense, or in conjunction with an auxiliary of mood, the principal verb and the auxiliaries may change places at the end of the sentence:

The book I must have read,
{ *Het boek, dat ik gelezen moet hebben.**
Het boek, dat ik gelezen hebben moet.
Het boek, dat ik moet hebben gelezen.
Het boek, dat ik moet gelezen hebben.

B. But when the auxiliaries of mood, *kunnen, mogen, moeten, willen* and *durven,* are joined to the principal verb

---
* The second of these four ways is least used.

in their infinitive form (see p. 171, obs.), they must always precede the principal verb:

> He wanted me to let him do it, *hij wilde, dat ik het hem zou laten doen,* not *doen laten.*

XV. There are a few cases in which it is preferable to keep to one form of construction:

1. When the subject of a sub-ordinate sentence is a RELATIVE PRONOUN, the auxiliary should come after the principal verb:

> The lecturer who is expected, *de spreker die verwacht wordt,* rather than *wordt verwacht.*

2. The verbs, *doen, gaan, helpen, hooren, komen, leeren, voelen, zien,* take their places in front of their principal verb:

> If the boy hears me coming, he will run away, *als de jongen mij hoort komen, zal hij wegloopen.*
> I felt it as soon as I sat down, *ik voelde het, zoodra ik ging zitten.*

Inversion in the Principal Sentence.

XVI. The inversion of Subject and Predicate occurs in Dutch as also sometimes in English:

> In Interrogative and Exclamatory sentences:
> Do you see that child playing? *ziet u dat kind spelen?*
> Have you heard that man? *heeft u dien man gehoord?*
> If I could only see him! *kon ik hem toch maar zien!*
> Would that my brother were here! *ware mijn broeder maar hier!*

XVII. If, for the sake of emphasis, any other part of the sentence but the subject is placed at the beginning of the sentence, the subject in Dutch is always placed after the verb, if such verb be in a simple tense, and after the first auxiliary, if the verb be in a compound tense:

> There you see him, *daar ziet gij hem.*
> Yesterday I saw him, *gisteren heb ik hem gezien.*
> I do not like the book at all, *mij bevalt het boek in het geheel niet.*
> His letter I have not read, *zijnen brief heb ik niet gelezen.*
> Hate him I do not, *haten doe ik hem niet.*

XVIII. In sentences in which "it"—*het*, is the Subject, and a personal pronoun forms part of the Predicate, such personal pronoun takes the place of the subject:

> It is he, *hij is het.* It is we, *wij zijn het.*

XIX. When the first word of a principal sentence is one of the adverbial conjunctions, *toch*, yet, *niettemin*, nevertheless, *desniettegenstaande*, notwithstanding, *evenwel*, yet, *intusschen*, meanwhile, *integendeel*, on the contrary, *daarentegen*, on the other hand, *ook*, likewise, *daarenboven*, besides, *dus, derhalve*, consequently, *vandaar*, that is why, *daarom*, for this reason, *bijgevolg*, consequently, *daardoor*, that is why, *voorts*, further, etc., the Subject and Predicate change places:

> It should not be forgotten in the meantime, *intusschen moet men niet vergeten.*
> Further I have to say, *voorts moet ik zeggen.*
>
> Obs.—The above sentence also appears in the following form: *Intusschen, moet men niet vergeten*, etc. It should be noticed that the inserted comma does away with the need of inversion. This comma, however, is not used after *ook*, *vandaar, daardoor, voorts.*

XX. The adverbial conjunctions *nu*, now, and *echter*, however, are usually placed in the body of the sentence, in which case they do not influence the construction:

> My parents, however, have decided for me, *mijne ouders hebben echter voor mij besloten.*
> Now the judge was of opinion, *de rechter nu meende.*
> Now to-morrow there would be a holiday, *morgen nu zou er vacantie zijn.*

Toch, yet, is sometimes used in the same way:

> Yet he is not ashamed of his ignorance, *zijner onwetendheid toch schaamt hij zich niet.*

XXI. When a sub-ordinate sentence precedes a principal one, the order of the latter is inverted:

> I have told him all, answered the man, *ik heb hem alles gezegd, antwoordde de man.*
> After having spoken to him a long time, I left him alone, *nadat ik lang met hem gesproken had, liet ik hem alleen.*
>
> OBS.—After sub-ordinate sentences with *wie ook*, whoever, *wat ook*, whatever, *hoe ook*, however, and *hoe het zij*, however it be, the order of the principal verb is *not* inverted.
>
> Whoever may tell you, I shall not believe it, *wie het u ook zegt, ik zal het niet gelooven.*
> However that may be, I shall rest satisfied, *hoe dat ook zij, ik zal tevreden zijn.*

XXII. When verbs like *zeggen*, to say, *antwoorden*, to answer, *hernemen*, to go on (speaking), *voortgaan*, to continue (speaking), *denken*, to think, etc., occur with their subject between the two parts of a quotation, such subject must be placed after its verb:—

> "Those books," said he, "I shall give you anyway."
> "*Die boeken*," *zei hij*, "*zal ik u in elk geval geven.*"

Inversion in the Sub-ordinate Sentence.

XXIII. In conditional sentences, when the conjunction *als* = if, is omitted, the sub-ordinate sentence takes the form of the inverted principal sentence, instead of having the whole of its predicate at the end (see XIII).

> Could I but see him, I should ask him, *kon ik hem maar zien, ik zou het hem vragen.*
> Were I but ten years younger, I should go, *was ik maar tien jaar jonger, ik zou gaan.*
>
> OBS.—The conditional sentence without the conjunction *als* =

if, has no influence on the construction of the principal sentence (see XXI); whereas when *als* = if, is expressed, it has:

Compare { Could I but see him, I should ask him, *kon ik hem maar zien, ik zou het hem vragen.*
If I could but see him, I should ask him, *als ik hem maar zien kon, zou ik het hem vragen.*

XXIV. Sub-ordinate sentences, introduced by *als* = as if, and *al* = although, take the inverted construction of the principal sentence:—

He speaks as if he knew all about it, *hij spreekt, als wist hij er alles van* (for: *alsof hij er alles van wist*).

I shall not understand it, though I read it ten times, *ik zal het toch niet verstaan, al lees ik het tienmaal over* (for: *ofschoon ik het tienmaal overlees*).

Obs.—In the sentence, *Al hoorde hij u, hij zou toch niet komen,* even if he heard you, he would not come, the sub-ordinate sentence, not having its regular construction form, cannot influence the construction of the principal sentence (see XXIII, Obs.).

XXV. In statements and indirect questions beginning with *who, which, what,* or with *how* and an adjective, in English a Noun-subject *may follow* the verb *to be,* whereas in Dutch these sentences follow the regular construction of the sub-ordinate sentence (see XIII):—

He asked what was my opinion of the matter, *hij vroeg, wat mijn oordeel over de zaak was.*

I know how delicate are her feelings, *ik weet, hoe teer hare gevoelens zijn.*

TRANSLATION EXERCISES.—*Vertaaloefeningen.*

Exercise CVI.

One of the greatest men of (the) old Hellas was the son of a sculptor, Socrates by name. When (he was) yet a boy, his lofty spirit made him (already) a wonder to (for) his parents and friends. (The) Tradition says that his father had received a message from (the) heaven, instructing him to let the boy have (transl., go) his own way in everything, and never to oblige him to do anything against his own will and conviction, because the gods had granted to the young man a sure guide that would unfailingly lead him in (*op*) the right path. (The) young Socrates at first seemed to show some inclination to become [a] sculptor like his father; yet he soon found out that this occupation did not suit him. No lifeless material would he work; he would try his hand at himself and his fellow-men. From that time Socrates, who had now grown to manhood, became a philosopher, a teacher of profound wisdom, a blessing to his native country, and a model to the world at large. After [the] lapse of many ages we still find Socrates (transl., Socrates is still) beloved, admired; though generations on generations have appeared, lived, and acted, yet the people of the present day think it an honour to imitate the great sculptor's son on account of his purity, his modesty, his love of truth, his impartial distribution of justice, his unshaken calmness at the approach of (the) death.

Exercise CVII.

There can be no doubt (*Er valt niet aan te twijfelen*), that the study of Socrates' character must be profitable to every right-minded youth. The beginning of all virtue to (for) him was soberness. His doctrine was not, to make food and drink as pleasant [as] possible, and take them in the greatest quantity possible—he took food to sustain (the) life, and never for any other purpose. Even the most exquisite dainties could not induce him to take any more than he considered necessary. He likewise never drank but (*behalve*) when he was thirsty, and never more than was necessary to quench his thirst. The gods, he used to say, know no wants, so (*met*) the (*hoe*) less we are contented [with] the (*des te*) more we resemble them. Naturally quick-tempered, he managed to bring his temper under full subjection to his will, and thereby acquired an amount of equanimity, as is seldom seen (*gelijk men . . . aantreft*) in (a) man. The inward peace and calm which he enjoyed, became manifest in every deed he performed, in every word he said; his inward joy, sprung from an (the) uninterrupted practice of (the) virtue, seasoned his speech and shone from his eyes.

Exercise CVIII.

(*Even*) Calm and self-possessed as he was in his life, [so] Socrates was in his death. At the age of seventy (years) he was accused as one (somebody), whose existence was dangerous to the state, seeing that he did not believe in the gods of his country and corrupted the manners of the rising generation by perverted doctrines. He begged the judges to take into consideration his public life, and how he had devoted himself to the general happiness of his fellow-citizens both young and old. The frankness with which he defended himself, embittered the judges, and he was condemned to drink the poisoned cup. When (he was) in (the) prison, one of his followers brought him an elaborate defence, fit to be read in (the) public. Socrates took the document from (*uit*) his hands, perused it, and handed it back with the reply: "Lysias, if you brought me a pair of soft sandals, you would know that I could not accept them, because I should think it unmanly. Take back your speech and pardon me for refusing (transl., that I refuse) to make use of it." (On) Another day, one of Socrates' dearest friends entered his cell and tried to induce him to flee, saying that he had bribed the jailer, and that no ill would befall him in (*op*) the flight. This time (*ditmaal*), however, his answer was decisive and firm. "What," he said, "would a true friend induce me to disobey the laws of my city? Many years have I enjoyed the just laws of the city of my fathers, and do you think that now [that] I am become a martyr by (the) misapplication of those laws, I would rebel against them?"

Exercise CIX.

On the morning of the day of the execution some officials entered the prison [and] telling (transl., told) Socrates that his last day had come, (and) loosed him from his shackles. Shortly after (*daarna*) his dearest friends, to the number of fifteen (*vijftien in getal*), came in to spend the last hours with him. One of these said to him: "Master, what will do you leave us, and what can we do for you when you are gone?" "I charge you all," was the grave reply, "to live as you have seen me live—more you cannot do for me. Moreover, do not speak at my grave, here we lay Socrates to rest; for surely Socrates will then have long since departed to the land of eternal bliss." Hereupon he began to speak some parting words, first to his friends and then to his wife and children. This (being) done, he received the fatal draught (transl., drink) from an official (who was) present, drank it [off] with a smile, and, after having paced the room for some time, laid himself down to die. When about (*toen hij op het punt was*) to breathe his last, he suddenly opened his eyes, looked at his friends with a last smile and whispered: "I am cured; sacrifice (bring) a thank-offering to Esculapius on my behalf."

CHAPTER XVI.
PARSING AND ANALYSIS.

Parsing.—(*Woordontleding.*)

DUTCH parsing differs in form materially from English parsing. The student should endeavour to make himself familiar with the points of dissimilarity.

Dutch names for the different parts of speech :—

Zelfstandignaamwoord, Noun; *Lidwoord*, Article; *Bijvoegelijknaamwoord*, Adjective; *Telwoord*, Numeral Adjective; *Voornaamwoord*, Pronoun; *Werkwoord*, Verb; *Bijwoord*, Adverb; *Voegwoord*, Conjunction; *Voorzetsel*, Preposition; *Tusschenwerpsel*, Interjection.

Abbreviations used in Dutch Parsing:

Zelfstnw.	*Zelfstandignaamwoord.*	Noun.
Lidw.	*Lidwoord.*	Article.
Bijvnw.	*Bijvoegelijknaamwoord.*	Adjective.
Telw.	*Telwoord.*	Num. Adjct.
Vnw.	*Voornaamwoord.*	Pronoun.
Ww.	*Werkwoord.*	Verb.
Bijw.	*Bijwoord.*	Adverb.
Voegw.	*Voegwoord.*	Conjunction.
Voorz.	*Voorzetsel.*	Preposition.
Tusschenw.	*Tusschenwerpsel.*	Interjection.
Overg.	*Overgankelijk.*	Transitive.
Onoverg.	*Onovergankelijk.*	Intransitive.
Onregm.	*Onregelmatig.*	Anomalous.
Gem.	*Gemeen.*	Common.
Eig.	*Eigen.*	Proper.
Afgetr.	*Afgetrokken.*	Abstract.
Sameng.	*Samengesteld.*	Compound.
Pers.	*Persoon.*	Person.
Mann.	*Mannelijk.*	Masculine.
Vr.	*Vrouwelijk.*	Feminine.
Onz.	*Onzijdig.*	Neuter.

PARSING AND ANALYSIS. 319

Abbreviations—*continued.*

Nv.	Naamval.	Case.
Bep.	Bepaald.	Definite.
Niet-bep.	Niet-bepalend.	Indefinite.
Meerv.	Meervoud.	Plural.
Enk.	Enkelvoud.	Singular.
Aant. w.	Aantoonende wijs.	Indic. Mood.
Aanv. w.	Aanvoegende wijs.	Subj. Mood.
Geb. w.	Gebiedende wijs.	Imper. Mood.
Onb. w.	Onbepaalde wijs.	Infin. Mood.
Teg. deelw.	Tegenwoordig deelwoord.	Present Part.
Verl. deelw.	Verleden deelwoord.	Past Part.
Onv. teg. t.	Onvolmaakt tegenwoordige tijd.	Present Tense.
Volm. verl. t.	Volmaakt verleden tijd.	Pluperfect Tense.
Onv. toek. t.	Onvolmaakt toekomende tijd.	Future Tense.

OBS. 1.—In Dutch, such terms as *Nominative to, Objective after, Qualifying, Modifying, Limiting*, etc., are not in use. The relations between verbs and their Subjects and Objects, and between Nouns and their Articles and Adjectives are differently expressed, as will be seen from the examples.

OBS. 2.—In Dutch parsing each Verb is treated as a separate one, except the Auxiliaries of Tense, *hebben, zijn*, and *zullen*, and the Auxiliary of Voice, *worden*, which form an inseparable part of the Verbs which they help to conjugate.

EXAMPLES OF PARSING.

I.

SENTENCE :—" *Zij werden getroost door de zekerheid, dat zij het goede gedaan hadden, en zich niet bemoeid hadden met den laster, dien men van hunnen buurman verspreid had.*"

Zij	Pers. Vnw. 3ᵉ Pers. Gem. gesl. Meerv. 1ᵉ nv.
werden getroost	Zwak Onoverg. Ww. Lijdende Vorm. Aant. W. Onv. Verl. T. 3ᵉ Pers. Meerv.
door	Voorz.—wijst de betrekking aan tusschen " werden getroost " en " zekerheid."
de	Bep. Lidw. Vrouw. Enk. 4ᵉ nv.
zekerheid	Afg. Zelfstnw. Vrouw. Enk. 4ᵉ nv.
dat	Voegw.—verbindt twee zinnen.

zij	Pers. Vnw. 3° Pers. Gem. gesl. Meerv. 1° nv.
het	Bep. Lidw. Onz. Enk. 4° nv.
goede	Afg. Zelfstnw. Onz. Enk. 4° nv.
gedaan hadden	Onreg. Overg. Ww. Aant. W. Volm. Verl. T. 3° Pers. Meerv.
en	Voegw.—verbindt twee zinnen.
zich	Terugw. Pers. Vnw. 3° Pers. Gem. gesl. Meerv. 4° nv.
niet	Bijw.—van ontkenning.
bemoeid hadden	Zwak Onoverg. Ww. Aant. W. Volm. Verl. T. 3° Pers. Meerv.
met	Voorz. — wijst de betrekking aan tusschen "bemoeid hadden" en "laster."
den	Bep. Lidw. Mann. Enk. 4° nv.
laster	Afg. Zelfstnw. Mann. Enk. 4° nv.
dien	Betrokk. Vnw. 3° Pers. Mann Enk. 4° nv.
men	Onbep. Pers. Vnw. 3° Pers. Gem. gesl Enk. 1° nv.
van	Voorz.—duidt de betrekking aan tusschen "verspreid had" en "buurman."
hunnen	Bez. Vnw. 3° Pers. Mann. Enk. 4° nv.
buurman	Gem. Zelfstnw. Mann. Enk. 4° nv.
verspreid had.	Zwak Onverg. Ww. Aant. W. Volm. Verl. T. 3° Pers. Enk.

II.

SENTENCE :—

"*Of het zonnevuur al blaker',
Of natuur te middag zucht,—
Bij der mane minnetint'ling
Schept zij nieuwe levenslucht.*"

Of (al)	Toegevend. Voegw.
het	Bep. Lidw. Onz. Enk. 1° nv.
zonnevuur	Sameng. Zelfstw. Onz. Enk. 1° nv.
al	(behoort bij "*of*")
blaker'	Zwak Onoverg. Ww. Aanv. Wijs. Onv. Teg. T. 3° Pers. Enk.

Of	Toegevend Voegw.
natuur	Gem. Zelfstnw. Vrouw Enk. 1ᵉ nv.
te	Voorz. ⎱ Bijwoordelijke
middag	Gem. Zelfstnw. Mann. ⎰ uitdrukking
	Enk. 4ᵉ nv. van Tijd.
zucht'	Zwak Onoverg. Ww. Aanv. Wijs. Onv. Teg. t. 3ᵉ Pers. Enk.
Bij	Voorz.—drukt betrekking uit tusschen "*schept*" en "*minnetint'ling.*"
der	Bep. Lidw. Vrouw. Enk. 2ᵉ nv.
mane	Gem. Zelfstnw. Vrouw Enk. 2ᵉ nv.
minnetint'ling	Afgetr. Zelfstnw. Vrouw. Enk. 4ᵉ nv.
Schept	Zwak Overg. Ww. Aant. Wijs. Onv. Teg. t. 3ᵉ Pers. Enk.
zij	Pers. Vnw. 3ᵉ Pers. Vrouw Enk. 1ᵉ nv.
nieuwe	Bijvnw. Vrouw. Enk. 4ᵉ nv.
levenslucht.	Sameng. Zelfstnw. Vrouw. Enk. 4ᵉ nv.

III.

SENTENCE:

"*Wien Neerlands bloed in d' aad'ren vloeit,
Van vreemde smetten vrij,
Wiens hart voor land en koning gloeit
Verheff' den zang als wij.*"

Wien	Betrekk. Vnw. 3ᵉ Pers. Mann. Enk. 3ᵉ nv.
Neerlands	Eig. Zelfstnw. Onz. Enk. 2ᵉ nv.
bloed	Gem. Zelfstnw. Onz. Enk. 1ᵉ nv.
in	Voorz.—duidt de betrekking aan tusschen "*aderen*" en "*vloeit.*"
de	Bep. Lidw. Vrouw. Meerv. 4ᵉ nv.
aderen	Gem. Zelfstnw. Vrouw. Meerv. 4ᵉ nv.
vloeit	Zwak Onoverg. Ww. Aant. w. Onv. Teg. t. 3ᵉ Pers. Enk.
Van	Voorz.—duidt de betrekking aan tusschen "*vrij*" en "*smetten.*"
vreemde	Bijvnw. Vrouw. Meer. 4ᵉ nv.
smetten	Gem. Zelfstnw. Vrouw. Meerv. 4ᵉ nv.
vrij	Bijvnw. Onz. Enk. 1ᵉ nv. (behoort bij "*bloed*").

Wiens	Betrekk. Vnw. 3ᵉ Pers. Mann. Enk. 2ᵉ nv.
hart	Gem. Zelfstnw. Onz. Enk. 1ᵉ nv.
voor	Voorz.—drukt de betrekking uit tusschen "*gloeit*" en "*land*."
land	Gem. Zelfstnw. Onz. Enk. 4ᵉ nv.
en	Verbindend Voegw.
koning	Gem. Zelfstnw. Mann. Enk. 4ᵉ nv.
gloeit	Zwak Onoverg. Ww. Aant. w. Onv. Teg. t. 3ᵉ P. Enk.
Verheff'	Sterk Overg. Ww. Aanv. w. Onv. Teg. t. 3ᵉ P. Enk.
den	Bep. Lidw. Mann. Enk. 4ᵉ nv.
zang	Gem. Zelfstnw. Mann. Enk. 4ᵉ nv.
als	Vergelijkend Voegw.
wij.	Pers. Vnw. 1ᵉ Pers. Gem. Gesl. Meerv. 1ᵉ nv.

ANALYSIS.—(*Zinsontleding*).

The Dutch way of Analysing Sentences is a perfect parallel of English analysis, and, as far as principal features are concerned, differs from it only in its terms. The translation of those terms is as follows:

Sentence	*Zin.*
Simple Sentence	*Enkelvoudige Zin.*
Complex Sentence	} *Samengestelde Zin.*
Compound Sentence . . .	
Simple Sentence with composite parts	*Enkelvoudige Zin met veelvoudige deelen.*
Principal Sentence	*Hoofdzin.*
Co-ordinate Sentence . . .	*Nevengeschikte Zin.*
Sub-ordinate Sentence . . .	*Afhankelijke Zin.*
Complete Sentence	*Volledige Zin.*
Incomplete Sentence . . .	*Onvolledige Zin.*
Elliptic Sentence	*Elliptische Zin.*
Noun Sentence	*Zelfstandig Afhankelijke Zin.*
Adjective Sentence	*Bijvoegelijk Afhankelijke Zin.*
Adverbial Sentence	*Bijwoordelijk Afhankelijke Zin.*
Of Time	*Van Tijd.*
Of Place	*Van Plaats.*

Of Manner	Van Wijze.
Of Cause	Redengevende.
Of Purpose	Doelaanwijzende.
Of Comparison	Van Vergelijking.
Concessive	Toegevende.
Copulative	Aaneenschakelende.
Disjunctive	Scheidende.
Adversative	Tegenstellende.
Illative	Besluitende.
Subject	Onderwerp.
Enlargement of the Subject .	Uitbreiding van het Onderwerp.
Understood Subject. . . .	Verzwegen Onderwerp.
Connective	Verbinding.
Predicate	Gezegde.
Object	Voorwerp.
Direct Object	Lijdend (Direct) Voorwerp.
Indirect Object	Oneigenlijk (Indirect) Voorwerp.
Preposition Object	Voorwerp met een Voorzetsel.
Extension	Bepaling.
Extension of Time	Bepaling van Tijd.
Extension of Place	Bepaling van Plaats.
Extension of Manner . . .	Bepaling van Wijze.
Extension of Cause	Bepaling van Oorzaak.

The following peculiarities should be noted:

1. Dutch analysis favours the embodiment in separate sentences of phrases, which in English are treated as belonging to the main sentence. For example: "*Seeing his brother, he began to cry,*" would in Dutch be analysed as, "*As (he) saw his brother, he began to cry.*"

This custom allows of no exception when an infinitive verb is concerned. For example, "*I told you to go*" should be analysed, "*I told you (that you should) go.*" Likewise: "*I shot the cat (in order that I should) get rid of it.*"

2. No distinction in name is made between the Complex and the Compound Sentences, both going by the name of "*Samengestelde Zin.*"

The Compound Sentence, however, is sometimes called "*Veelvoudige Zin.*"

The following example will illustrate the similarity of Dutch and English analysis:

Example of Analysis.

"*Zoo is het genoeg,*" *zeide hij, en keerde zich om, om te zien, wie het was, die achter hem dat vreemde geluid maakte. Nooit had hij kunnen denken, dat zijn eigen zoon, wien hij jaren geleden wegens schandelijk wangedrag de deur gewezen had, op 't onverwachtst was teruggekeerd, om wraak te oefenen, en in volle wapenrusting nu achter hem stond, gereed, hem het leven te benemen.*

Sentence (zin).	Kind of Sentence (Soort van zin).	Connective (Verbindingswoord).	Subject (Onderwerp).	Predicate (Gezegde).	Object (Voorwerp).	Extension (bepaling).
"Zoo is het genoeg"	Zelfstand. Aflankel. Voorwerpszin		het	is genoeg		zoo (van wijze
zeide hij	Hoofdzin		hij	zeide		
en hij keerde zich om	Nevengeschikte Hoofdzin	en	hij	keerde om	zich (direct)	
(dat) hij zien (zou)	Do-laanwijzende Bijwoord. Afhank. zin	(dat) (verzwegen)	(hij) (verzwegen)	zien (zou)		
wie het was	Zelfstand. Afhankel Voorwerpszin		het	was wie		
die achter hem dat vreemde geluid maakte	Bijvoeg. Afhank. zin		die	maakte	dat vreemde geluid (direct)	achter hem (van plaats)
Nooit had hij kunnen denken	Hoofdzin		hij	had kunnen denken		nooit (van tijd)
dat zijn eigen zoon op 't onverwachtst was teruggekeerd	Zelfstand. Afhankel.Voorwerpszin	dat	zijn eigen zoon	was teruggekeerd		op 't onverwachtst (van tijd)
wien hij jaren geleden wegens schandelijk wangedrag de deur gewezen had	Bijvoeg. Afhank. zin		hij	had gewezen	de deur (direct) wien (indirect)	jaren geleden (van tijd) wegens enz. (van oorzaak)
(opdat) hij wraak oefende	Bijwoord Afhank. Doelaanwijzende zin	(opdat) (verzwegen)	(hij) (verzwegen)	oefende	wraak (direct)	
en (dat hij) in volle wapenrusting nu achter hem stond, gereed	Zelfstand. Afhankel. zin, nevengeschikt aan II. b	en (verzwegen) gereel—uitbreiding van 't onderwerp	(hij) (verzwegen)	stond		in volle wapenrusting (van wijze) achter hem (van plaats)
(dat hij) hem het leven benamm	Zelfstand. Afhankelijk Doelaanwijzende zin	(dat) (verzwegen)	(hij) (verzwegen)	benamm	het leven (direct) hem	

CHAPTER XVII.

CORRESPONDENCE.—*Correspondentie.*

THE difficulties of corresponding in the Dutch language lie in the forms of address, which in Dutch are more elaborate than in English; in the phrases preceding the correspondent's signature, which are less varied in Dutch than in English; and in the use of certain set terms, of which every language has its own stock, and which cannot always be literal translations of those used in another language.

The necessary indications for the removal of these difficulties will here be given.

I. WAYS of BEGINNING and CLOSING LETTERS.

1.	1.
To the Governor:	Aan den Goeverneur:
His Excellency Sir Andrew Cosnett, K.C.M.G., etc., etc. Governor of the Colony of the Cape of Good Hope.	*Zijne Excellentie, Sir Andrew Cosnett, K.C.M.G., etc., etc. Goeverneur der Kolonie der Kaap de Goede Hoop.*
May it please your Excellency,	Excellentie,
I have the honour to remain, Sir, Your obedient Servant, C. D.	Ik heb de eer te zijn, Excellentie, Uw onderdanige Dienaar, C. D.
2.	2.
To a President:	Aan een President:
His Honour President Reitz, Bloemfontein.	*Den HoogEdelen Heer President Reitz, Bloemfontein.*
Sir,	HoogEdele Heer,
I have the honour to remain, Sir, Your obedient Servant, C. D.	Ik heb de eer, mij te noemen, HoogEdele Heer, Uw onderdanige Dienaar, C. D.

3.

To a Member of Parliament, or Cabinet Minister:

The Honourable A. B.
Sir,
I have the honour to be, Sir,
 Your obedient Servant,
  C. D.

4.

To a Chief Justice:

His Honour the Chief Justice, Cape-Town.

Sir,
I have the honour to be,
 Sir,
 Your obedient Servant,
  C. D.

5.

To a Judge,
The Hon. Mr. Justice A. B.

Sir,
I have the honour to be,
 Sir,
  C. D.

6.

To a Barrister:
A. B., Esq.

Dear Sir,
Believe me, Sir,
 Yours faithfully,
  C. D.

7.

To a Consul:

A. B., Esq.,
 Consul General of Belgium.
Sir,
I have the honour to remain,
 Sir,
 Yours obediently,
  C. D.

3.

Aan een Lid van het Parlement of Minister:

Den Edelen Heer A. B.
Edele Heer,
Ik heb de eer te zijn, Edele Heer,
 U Eds. Dienstw. Dienaar,
  C. D.

4.

Aan een Hoofdrechter:

Den HoogEdel Gestrengen Heer A. B., Hoofdrechter, Kaapstad.
HoogEdel Gestrenge Heer,
Ik heb de eer te zijn, HoogEdel Gestrenge Heer,
 Uw onderdanige Dienaar,
  C. D.

5.

Aan een Rechter:
Den HoogEdel Gestrengen Heer A. B.
HoogEdel Gestrenge Heer,
Ik heb de eer te zijn, HoogEdel Gestr. Heer,
  C. D.

6.

Aan een Advokaat:
Den Weledel Gestrengen Heer A. B.
Weledel Gestrenge Heer,
Geloof mij, Weled. Gestr. Heer,
 Uw Dienstw. Dienaar,
  C. D.

7.

Aan een Consul:
Den Weledel Gestrengen Heer, A. B.,
 Consul Genraal voor België.
Weledel Gestrenge Heer,
Ik heb de eer mij te noemen,
 Weled. Gestr. Heer,
 Uw Dienstw. Dien,
  C. D.

8.

To a General:
General Sir Michael Jonstone, K.C.M.G., etc., etc.

Sir,
I have the honour to be,
Sir,
Your obedient Servant,
C. D.

8.

Aan een Generaal:
Den HoogEdel Gestrengen Heer Generaal Sir Michael Jonstone, K.C.M.G., etc. etc.

HoogEdel Gestrenge Heer,
Ik heb te eer te zijn, HoogEdel Gestr. Heer,
Uw onderdanige Dienaar,
C. D.

9.

To a Colonel:
Colonel A. B.

Sir,
I remain, Sir,

Yours obediently,
C. D.

9.

Aan een Kolonel:
Den Weledel Gestrengen Heer A. B.

Weledel Gestrenge Heer,
Ik verblijve, Weledel Gestr. Heer,
UEds. Dienstw. Dien.,
C. D.

10.

To a Baronet:
Sir James Cosby, Bart.

Sir,
I have the honour to be,
Sir,
Your obedient Servant,
C. D.

10.

Aan een Jonkheer:
Den Hoogedel Geboren Heer James Cosby.

Weledel Geboren Heer,
Ik heb de eer te zijn, Weled. Geb. Heer,
Uw Dienstw. Dien.,
C. D.

11.

To a Bishop:
The Right Reverend W. Clarke, D.D.

Right Reverend Sir (My lord),

I have the honour to be,
Right Reverend Sir,
Yours obediently,
B. F.

11.

Aan een Bisschop:
Den Doorluchtigen Hoogwaardigen Heer Dr. W. Clarke.

Doorluchtige Hoogwaardige Heer,

Ik heb de eer te verblijven,
Doorl. Hoogw. Heer,
Uw Dienstw. Dienaar,
B. F.

12.

To a Doctor of Divinity:

The Rev. W. Williams, D.D.

Reverend Sir,
I have the honour to be, Reverend Sir,
Yours faithfully,
R. F.

13.

To a Clergyman:
The Rev. A. B.,
Reverend Sir,
I have the pleasure to remain, Sir,
Yours faithfully,
E. F.

14.

To a Consistory:
The Rev. A. Bevell, and the Gentlemen the Members of the Consistory of Trinity Church.

Gentlemen,
I have the honour to be, Gentlemen,
Yours obediently,
C. D.

15.

To a Superintendent of Education:
The Superintendent General of Education, Cape Town.

Sir,
I have the honour to be, Sir,

Yours obediently,
C. D.

12.

Aan een Doctor in de Godgeleerdheid:

Den Weleerw. Zeergeleerden Heer, Dr. W. Williams.

Weleerw. Zeergeleerde Heer,
Ik heb de eer te zijn, Weleerw. Zeergel. Heer,
Uw Dienstw. Dienaar,
R. F.

13.

Aan een Predikant:
Den Weleerwaarden Heer A. B.
Weleerw. Heer,
Ik heb het genoegen te blijven, Weleerw. Heer,
Uw Dienstw. Dienaar,
E. F.

14.

Aan een Kerkeraad:
Den Weleerw. Heer, A. Bevell, en de Heeren Leden van den Kerkeraad der Trinity Kerk.

Heeren,
I heb de eer te zijn, Heeren,

Uw Dienstwillige Dienaar,
C. D.

15.

Aan een Superintendent van Onderwijs:
Den Superintendent Generaal van Onderwijs, Kaapstad.

Weledele Heer,
Ik heb de eer te zijn, Weledele Heer,
Uw Dienstw. Dienaar,
C. D.

16.
To a Doctor of Literature or Laws:
J. Brink, Esq., M.A., LL.D.

Sir,
    I remain, dear Sir,

        Yours faithfully,
                F. M.

16.
Aan een Doctor in de Letteren of de Rechtsgeleerdheid:
Den Weledel Zeergeleerden Heer, J. Brink.

Weledel Zeergeleerde Heer,
    Verblijve hoogachtend, Weled. Zeergel. Heer,
        Uw Dienstw. Dien.,
            F. M.

17.
To a Professor at a University or College:
Professor A. Bennett.

Professor,
    I remain, Professor,

        Yours faithfully,
                C. D.

17.
Aan een Professor van eene Universiteit of Athenæum:
Den Hooggeleerden Heer Professor A. Bennett.

Hooggeleerde Heer,
    Verblijve met hoogachting, Hooggel. Heer,
        Uw Dienstw. Dien.,
            C. D.

18.
To a Physician:
J. B. Clarke, Esq., M.D. (Dr. J. B. Clarke).

Sir,
    I remain, dear Sir,

        Yours faithfully,
                F. K.

18.
Aan een Geneesheer:
Den Weledel Zeergeleerden Heer Dr. J. B. Clarke.

Weledel Zeergeleerde Heer,
    Verblijve hoogachtend, Weledel Zeergel. Heer,
        Uw Dienstw. Dien.,
            F. K.

19.
To a Town Council:
The Mayor and Members of the Town Council of A.

Gentlemen,
    I have the honour to be, Gentlemen,
        Your obedient Servant,
            B. C.

19.
Aan een Stadsraad:
Den Edelachtbaren Heeren, den Burgemeester en Leden van den Raad der stad A.

Edelachtbare Heeren,
    Ik heb de eer te zijn, Edelachtbare Heeren,
        Uw Dienstw. Dien,
            B. C.

20.
To a School Board:

The President and Members of the Wellington School Board.

Gentlemen,
    I remain, Gentlemen,
        Your obedient Servant,
            A. B.

21.
A Firm to another Firm:

Messrs. A. B. & E. F.

Gentlemen,
    We remain, Gentlemen,
        Yours obediently,
            C. D. & G. H.

22.
An Individual to a Firm:

Messrs. A. B. & E. F.

Gentlemen,
    I remain,
        Gentlemen,
        Yours obediently,
           C. D.

23.
To a Man of Station, or of means, (anyone addressed as Esq.):

A. B., Esq.

Dear Sir,
    I remain,
        dear Sir,
           Yours truly,
              C. D.

20.
Aan eene Schoolcommissie:

Den Voorzitter en Leden van de Wellingtonsche School Commissie.

Weledele Heeren,
    Verblijve met hoogachting,
        UEdeler Dienstw. Dien.,
            A. B.

21.
Eene Firma aan eene andere firma:

Den Heeren A. B. & E. F.

Heeren,
    Wij verblijven hoogachtend,
        Uwe Dienstw. Dienaren,
           C. D. & G. H.

22.
Een Privaat Persoon aan eene Firma:

Den Heeren A. B. & E. F.

Mijne Heeren,
    Ik heb de eer te zijn, Mijne Heeren,
        Uw Dienstw. Dien.,
           C. D.

23.
Aan Iemand uit Hoogeren Stand:

Den Weledelen Heer A. B.

Weledele Heer,
    Hoogachtend noem ik mij,
        Weledele Heer,
        Uw Dienstw. Dien,
           C. D.

24.

To a Tradesman or other in similar social position, (any one addressed as Mr.).

Mr. A. B.
Dear Sir,
    I remain, dear Sir,
        Yours truly,
            C. D.

24.

Aan een Handwerksman of iemand van gelijke positie in de maatschappij:

Den Heer A. B.
Mijnheer,
        Verblijve,
         De Uwe,
           C. D.

Notes.—1. In writing to a gentleman of like social standing with the correspondent, and in respect of whom he is allowed to make use of terms of intimacy, "*Waarde Heer*" may be substituted for either "*Mijnheer*," or "*Weledele Heer*."

2. The wife of a man addressed as "*Mijnheer*" (see No. 24) is addressed as "*Mejuffrouw*."

3. The wife of a gentleman is addressed as "*Mevrouw*."

4. An unmarried lady is addressed as "*Mejuffrouw*." N.B. "*Jongejuffrouw*," used extensively in the Cape Dutch, only applies to girls under the age of sixteen.

5. A widow is addressed either as "*Mejuffrouw de Weduwe*," or, "*Mevrouw de Weduwe*."

6. Ladies do not have the title of their husbands added to any form of address: "Mrs. Professor Dummy," is simply "*Mevrouw Dummy*."

7. Surnames are not excluded in terms of address: "Dear Mr. Hancock," should be rendered "*Mijnheer*," or, "*Waarde Heer*," but not "*Waarde Mijnheer Hancock*."

8. The English "My" before the name of a person in terms of address, is not translated: "My dear sister," therefore, becomes "*Lieve Zuster*."

9. The adjective "dear" is, in correspondence, only translated by "*lieve*" when friendship or familiarity are intended to be indicated. This should be noticed well, since a word-for-word translation of, for example, "My dear Mr. Goodson," would be an absurdity, when that gentleman is not a special friend of the correspondent.

The term "dear," therefore, commonly remains untranslated, or is (and at the Cape frequently so) rendered by "*waarde*," the use of which term, however, should neither be encouraged, seeing it finds no place in strict correspondence style.

II. List of terms and phrases common in ordinary correspondence.

Account,	*Rekening.*
Acknowledge (to),	*Erkennen.*
Acknowledgment,	*Bewijs.*
Address,	*Adres.*
Address (to),	*Adresseeren.*
Advice,	*Advies.*
Advise (to),	*Aanraden, raden.*
Anticipate (to),	*Verwachten.*
Anxious,	*Erop gesteld.*
Approach (to),	*Zich wenden tot.*
Arrangement,	*Schikking.*
Assure (to),	*Verzekeren.*
Assured (feel),	*Overtuigd (zich . . . gevoelen).*
Attached,	*Bijgevoegd, nevensgaand.*
Attention,	*Aandacht.*
August 10th,	10 *Augustus.*
Await (to),	*Afwachten.*
Awaiting,	*In afwachting van.*
Aware (to be),	*Ingelicht zijn (over).*
Beg (I beg to),	*Ik heb de eer te.*
Beg to say,	*Heb de eer te doen dienen.*
Bill,	*Wissel.*
Book (to. . . . orders),	*Bestellingen aannemen.*
Brand,	*Merk.*
Cash,	*Kontant.*
Co. (company)	*Co., Cie., (Compagnie).*
Competition,	*Competitie.*
Concerns (as),	*Wat aangaat.*
Condition,	*Voorwaarde.*
Consequently,	*Dus, bijgevolg.*
Considerably,	*Aanzienlijk, veel.*
Consume (to),	*Verbruiken.*
Consumption,	*Verbruik.*
Contained in it,	*Daarin vervat.*
Copy,	*Copie.*
Copy (to),	*Copiëeren.*

Correct,	Correct, in orde, accoord.
Cwt.	Centenaar.
Date,	Datum.
Dealer,	Handelaar.
Dealings (to have),	Handelen.
Decision,	Beslissing.
De dato (d.d.),	Gedateerd.
Delay,	Uitstel.
Demand (to be in),	Veel gevraagd worden.
Despatch,	Spoed.
Despatch (to),	Verzenden.
Discount,	Korting, disconto.
Discount (to),	Inwisselen, verdisconteeren.
Docks,	Dok.
Due,	Betaalbaar.
Duly to hand,	In orde ontvangen.
Enclosed,	Ingesloten.
Endorse (to),	Endorseeren.
Enquiry,	Navraag.
Enquire (to),	Navraag doen.
Error,	Abuis, fout.
Event (in the),	In geval.
Execute (to),	Uitvoeren.
Expenditure,	Uitgaven.
Expense,	Kosten.
Expense (at your own),	Op uwe eigene kosten.
Export trade,	Buitenlandsche handel.
Fashion,	Mode.
Favour (your),	De Uwe, Uw brief, Uwe letteren.
Figure (the lowest),	Prijs (de laagste).
Firm,	Firma.
Further,	Verder.
Future,	In de toekomst.
Glad,	Blij.
Goodbye,	Vaarwel.
Goods,	Goederen.
Grace,	Gratie.
Guarantee (to),	Garandeeren.
Hope (to),	Hopen.
Intimate (to),	Melden.
I. O. U.,	Schuldbewijs.
Instant,	Dezer.
Institution,	Inrichting.

Land (to),	Landen, lossen.
Last (your),	Uw laatste schrijven.
Learn (to),	Hooren, vernemen
Liabilities,	Schulden.
Limited,	Beperkt.
Mail (next —),	Per volgende post (mail).
March 3rd,	3 Maart.
Market,	Markt.
Matter,	Zaak.
Meet (to),	Voldoen.
Merchant,	Koopman.
Mistake,	Fout, vergissing.
Money,	Geld.
Money-matters,	Geldzaken.
Oblige (to),	Verplichten.
Offer,	Aanbod.
Offer (to),	Aanbieden.
Opportunity,	Gelegenheid.
Order,	Bestelling.
Order (to),	Bestellen.
Original,	Origineel.
Overdue,	Achterstallig.
Pack (to),	Pakken, inpakken.
Parcel,	Pakket, pakje.
Pay (to),	Betalen.
Payment,	Betaling.
Payment will be made,	Betaling zal geschieden.
Percentage,	Percent.
Please find,	Zult Gij vinden.
Pound Stg.	Pond Stg.
Prepared (to be),	Gewillig zijn, bereid zijn.
Practicable,	Bruikbaar, doenlijk.
Price,	Prijs.
Price list,	Prijscourant.
Profit,	Voordeel, Profijt.
Profit by (to),	Voordeel trekken uit.
Promissory note,	Promesse.
Prompt (ly),	Prompt.
Proximo,	Eerstkomende (e.k.).
Public,	Publiek.
Quality,	Hoedanigheid, kwaliteit.
Quantity,	Hoeveelheid, kwantiteit.
Receipt,	Kwitantie.
Receipt (to),	Voldaan teekenen, kwiteeren.

Reference (with .... to)	Met referte naar, met verwijzing naar.
Remember me to,	Doe mijne groeten aan.
Repairs,	Reparatie.
Reply (in .... to),	In antwoord op.
Request (to),	Verzoeken.
Require (to),	Behoeven, noodig hebben.
Return (by .... of mail),	Per keerende post.
Sample,	Staal, monster.
Said,	Gezegde.
Season,	Seizoen.
Secure (to),	(Zich) verzekeren (van).
Send (to),	Zenden, sturen.
Send back (to),	Terugzenden.
Servant,	Dienaar.
Share,	Aandeel.
Sharp (time),	Precies.
Ship (to),	Verschepen.
Shipment,	Scheepslading.
Solicit (to),	Verzoeken.
Special,	Bijzonder, speciaal.
Stock (in),	In voorraad.
Style,	Stijl.
Supply,	Voorraad.
Supply (to),	Leveren.
Ton,	Ton.
Trade,	Handel, bedrijf, ambacht.
Tradesman,	Ambachtsman.
Trial,	Proefneming.
Trifle (a),	Een weinig.
Trip,	Reisje.
Trust (to),	Vertrouwen.
Ultimo,	Laatstleden, (l.l.).
Understand (to),	Verstaan, vernemen, opmaken.
Understanding,	Verstandhouding.
Undertake (to),	Op zich nemen.
Want (for .... of),	Uit gebrek aan.
Want (to),	Noodig hebben.
Warrant (to),	Toelaten, gedoogen.
Way,	Manier, wijze.
Whereas,	Terwijl, daar.
Whole (the),	Het geheel.
Yesterday's date	Van gisteren.

CHAPTER XVIII.

OFFICIAL AND DOCUMENTARY LANGUAGE.

LIST of Words and Phrases used in official correspondence and documents, with their Dutch equivalents:

Accident,	Ongeluk.
Accordance (in—with), } According to, }	Overkomstig met, naar luid van, volgens.
Accordingly,	Dienvolgens, dienovereenkomstig.
Account,	Rekening.
Accountant,	Boekhouder, kashouder.
Account (on—of),	Op rekening van, wegens.
Accounting Department,	Departement van rekeningen.
Act,	Wet, akte, handeling.
Acting,	Ageerend.
Action,	Actie.
Addition,	Toevoegsel, bijvoegsel.
Addition (in—to),	Behalve.
Adjacent thereto,	Daaraan grenzend.
Adjourn (to),	Verdagen.
Adjournment,	Verdaging.
Adjoining,	Belendend, naast aanliggend, aangrenzend.
Administer (to),	Besturen, beheeren, waarnemen.
Administer an oath (to),	Een eed opleggen.
Administrate (to),	Besturen, beheeren, administreeren.
Administration,	Administratie, beheer, bestuur.
Administration of justice,	Bediening van het recht.
Administrator,	Administrateur.
Admit (to),	Toelaten, inlaten, toegeven, erkennen.
Admitted (to be),	Toegelaten worden.
Advance (in),	Vooruit.
Affidavit,	Affidavit.
Aforesaid,	Voorzegd.
Aforewritten,	Voorschreven, voormeld.
Agree to (to),	Overeenstemmen, instemmen.
Agree upon (to),	Overeenkomen.

Agreement,	Overeenkomst, schikking.
Agriculture,	Landbouw.
Agricultural Department,	Landbouw departement.
Aid and assist (to),	Helpen en bijstaan.
Alien,	Uitlander.
Alteration,	Verandering.
Allow (to),	Toestaan, toelaten, erkennen.
Allowed in law,	Wettiglijk gangbaar, toegestaan bij de wet.
Allowable,	Geoorloofd.
Alluvial,	Alluviaal.
Amend (to),	Verbeteren, amendeeren.
Amendment,	Amendement, wijziging.
Annex (to),	Aanhechten, annexeeren, insluiten.
Annexure,	Het aangehechte, ingeslotene.
Annual(ly),	Jaarlijks(ch).
Annul (to),	Vernietigen, te niet doen.
Annulment,	Vernietiging.
Annum (per),	Jaarlijks, per jaar.
Ante-nuptial contract,	Huwelijkskontrakt.
Appeal,	Apèl.
Appeal (to),	Apelleeren, beroep doen op.
Appear (to),	Verschijnen, compareeren.
Appearer,	Comparant.
Applicant,	Eischer.
Application,	Aanvraag, applicatie, toepassing.
Apply (to),	Aanvragen, aanwenden, bezigen, gebruiken.
Apply to (to),	Van toepassing zijn.
Appoint (to),	Aanstellen.
Appointment,	Aanstelling.
Appraise (to),	Schatten, taxeeren.
Appraiser,	Taxateur, schatter.
Apprehend (to),	Aanhouden, in hechtenis nemen.
Apprehension,	Aanhouding, in hechtenis neming.
Approval,	Goedkeuring.
Approve (to),	Goedkeuren.
Arbitration,	Arbitratie.
Arbitrator,	Scheidsrechter, arbiter.
Area,	Deel, district, streek, cirkel, oppervlakte.
Arrest (to),	Arresteeren, aanhouden.
Article,	Artikel.
Assembly,	Vergadering.
Assembly (House of—),	Parlement.
Assent (to—to),	Goedkeuren.
Assess (to—rates),	Belasting opleggen.
Assets and liabilities,	Baten en schulden.

Assign (to),	Toewijzen, overdragen, assigneeren.
Assignee,	Rechtverkrijgende.
Assistant,	Assistent, hulp.
Association,	Genootschap, associatie.
As such,	Als zoodanig.
Assume (to),	Aanvaarden, in bezit nemen.
Assumption,	Assumptie, op-zich-neming.
Attend (to—a meeting),	Bijwonen.
Attorney,	Procureur, zaakgelastigde.
Attorney-General,	Procureur-Generaal.
Auction,	Veiling, auctie, verkooping.
Auction duty,	Opgelden.
Auctioneer,	Afslager, vendumeester.
Audience,	Gehoor, audientie.
Audit Office,	Auditeurs kantoor.
Authorise (to),	Authoriseeren, machtigen.
Authority,	Authoriteit, macht, gezag, last.
Available,	Beschikbaar.
Bail,	Borgtocht.
Bail (out on),	Op borgtocht ontslagen.
Bailiff,	Baljuw.
Balance,	Balans, saldo.
Ballot (by),	Bij ballotage, met stembriefjes.
Ballot box,	Stembus.
Ballot paper,	Stembriefje.
Banns,	Huwelijksgeboden.
Bar,	Balie.
Barrister,	Rechtsgeleerde, pleitbezorger, advokaat.
Beacon,	Baken.
Be it herewith made known.	Zij het mits dezen kennelijk.
Behalf (on my),	Te mijnen behoeve, om mijnentwil.
Behalf (on—of),	Ten behoeve van.
Below (the Court—),	Het lagere hof.
Bequeath (to),	Vermaken.
Best (to the) of his knowledge,	Zoo ver hem bekend is.
Bidder (highest),	Meestbiedende.
Bill,	Wetsontwerp, concept.
Board,	Raad, bestuur.
Bond,	Verband, schepenkennis.
Bond (goods in—),	Goederen in entrepôt.
Borough-council,	Stadsraad.
Bound,	Verplicht, gehouden.
Boundary,	Grens.
Branch,	Tak.

Breach,	Verbreking.
Bring (to—to justice),	Voor het gerecht brengen.
British and Foreign,	Britsch en buitenlandsch.
Business,	Zaken, handel, bezigheid.
Bye-law,	Reglement, toevoegsel.
Cabinet,	Kabinet, ministerraad.
Calendar (within 3 months),	Binnen 3 maanden.
Cancel (to),	Vernietigen.
Candidate,	Kandidaat.
Capacity,	Capaciteit, bevoegheid.
Cargo,	Lading.
Case (in the—of),	In het geval van.
Case in point,	Voorbeeld, soortgelijk geval.
Case in point (to state—),	Voorbeeld geven, geval opnoemen.
Cash,	Kontant.
Cash (to pay—),	Kontant betalen.
Central,	Centraal.
Certain,	Zeker.
Certificate,	Certificaat, bewijs, getuigschrift.
Certificate of Birth,	Geboortebewijs.
Certificate of Death,	Sterftebewijs, certificaat van overlijden.
Chairman,	Voorzitter.
Charges,	Prijs, rekening.
Charge and command (to),	Gelasten en bevelen.
Chief (adj.),	Voornaamste, opper-, hoofd-.
Chief of Police,	Hoofd der politie.
Circuit Court,	Rondgaand hof.
Civil,	Civiel, burgerlijk.
Civil Commissioner,	Civiele Commissaris.
Civil imprisonment,	Gijzeling.
Civilisation,	Beschaving.
Claim,	Eisch, delfplek.
Claim (to),	Eischen.
Claimant,	Eischer.
Claim inspector,	Inspecteur van delfplekken.
Clause,	Clausule.
Clear (three—days),	Drie volle dagen.
Codicil,	Codicil, aanhangsel.
Cognisance (with),	Met medeweten.
Colonial,	Koloniaal.
Colonial Secretary,	Koloniale Secretaris.
Colony,	Kolonie.
Commence (to),	Beginnen, aanvangen.
Commissary-General,	Commissaris-Generaal.

Commission,	Commissie, opdracht.
Commit (to),	Bedrijven, zich blootstellen, in staat van beschuldiging stellen.
Committed for trial,	Naar de strafzitting verwezen.
Committee,	Comité.
Commonage,	Gemeenteweide.
Comply with (to),	Nakomen.
Compromise,	Compromise, schikking, vergelijk.
Compulsory sequestration,	Gedwongen sequestratie.
Concerning,	Omtrent, aangaande, betreffende.
Concession,	Concessie.
Condition,	Konditie, toestand, voorwaarde.
Conditions of sale,	Koopkonditiën.
Conduct (to),	Leiden, voeren, besturen.
Confirm (to),	Bevestigen, confirmeeren.
Confirmation,	Bevestiging, confirmatie.
Conformity (in—with),	In overeenstemming met.
Conjunction (in—with),	Samengaande met, in verbintenis met, vereenigd met.
Connection (in — therewith),	Daarmede in verband staande.
Connection (in—with),	In verband met.
Consent,	Verlof, toestemming, consent.
Consent (to),	Toestaan, inwilligen, verlof geven.
Consent to (to),	Bewilligen, toestemmen in.
Consider (to),	Beschouwen, overwegen.
Consignee,	Geadresseerde, ontvanger.
Consignor,	Afzender.
Consist (to—with law),	Bestaanbaar zijn met de wet.
Consistent with,	Overeenkomstig.
Consolidate (to),	Consolidceren, vereenigen, samensmelten.
Constitute (to),	Vaststellen, samenstellen, benoemen.
Constitute and appoint (to),	Kiezen en aanstellen.
Construct (to),	Bouwen, oprichten.
Construction (for the—of),	Tot het bouwen (aanleggen) van.
Consul,	Consul.
Consulate,	Consulaat.
Consul-General,	Consul-Generaal.
Consumption,	Verbruik.
Contract,	Kontrakt, overeenkomst.
Contract (to),	Kontrakteeren, overeenkomen.
Contracting parties,	Kontrakteerende partijen.
Contract of lease,	Huurkontrakt, pachtkontrakt.
Contrary to,	Strijdig met, in strijd met.
Contravene (to),	Overtreden, inbreuk maken op.
Conveniently,	Behoorlijk, betamelijk.
Convention,	Conventie, verdrag.

Conveyance,	Voertuig, rijtuig, expeditie.
Conveyance (law),	Transport, overdracht.
Conveyancer,	Transportbezorger.
Convict,	Bandiet, boef.
Convict (to),	Schuldig verklaren.
Convict Department,	Bandieten-departement.
Convict guard,	Bandietenoppasser, gevangenbewaarder.
Conviction (on),	Schuldigverklaring (bij).
Corporal punishment,	Lijfstraf.
Council,	Raad.
Council (Divisional),	Afdeelingsraad.
Council (Legislative),	Wetgevende raad.
Council (in);	In rade.
Councillor,	Raadslid.
Counterfoil,	Tegenblad.
Court,	Hof, Gerechtshof.
Cover (to),	Dekken.
Credit,	Krediet.
Creditor,	Crediteur, schuldeischer.
Crime,	Misdaad.
Criminal,	Crimineel.
Criminal Session,	Strafzitting.
Crown land,	Kroonland.
Crown Prosecutor,	Publieke aanklager.
Current,	Dezer.
Current (account),	Rekening courant.
Customs,	Tol, in- en uitgaande rechten,
Customs duty,	Invoerende Rechten.
Custom house,	Tolkantoor, kantoor van in- en uitgaande rechten.
Custom officer,	Tolbeambte.
Customs Union,	Tolverbond.
Damage,	Schade.
Damages,	Schadevergoeding.
Dative,	Datief.
Debentures,	Schuldbrieven.
Debt,	Schuld.
Debtor,	Schuldenaar, debiteur.
Decease,	Dood, overlijden.
Deceased,	Overledene.
Decide (to),	Besluiten, beslissen.
Declaration,	Verklaring, declaratie.
Declaration of Insolvency	Insolvent verklaring.
Declare, proclaim and make known (I),	Verklaar, proclameer en maak bekend (ik).

Decree (to),	Bepalen, verordenen.
Decreed (to be—entitled),	(Aan iemand) toegekend worden.
Deed,	Akte, document.
Deed of transfer,	Akte van transport.
Deeds' Office,	Registratie kantoor.
Default (in—of),	Bij gebreke van.
Default (judgment by—),	Vonnis bij verstek.
Defence Department,	Departement van landsverdediging.
Defend (to),	Verdedigen.
Defendant,	Verweerder.
Delay,	Uitstel, oponthoud.
Deliver (to) up,	Afgeven, opgeven, overgeven.
Delivery,	Levering.
Demand,	Eisch.
Demand (to),	Eischen.
Dependency,	Aanhoorigheid.
Deputy sheriff,	Ondersherif.
Derelict land,	Verlaten grond.
Derive (to),	Trekken van.
Design,	Plan, teekening.
Despatch (to),	Verzenden, afzenden.
Deviate (to),	Verleggen; afslaan; uiteenloopen.
Diagram,	Schets, figuur.
Diggings,	Delfplek.
Direct (to),	Last geven, verordenen.
Directed (I am—),	Mij is gelast (opgedragen).
Directions,	Aanwijzingen.
Disallowance,	Afkeuring, weigering.
Discipline,	Tucht.
Discount,	Disconto, korting.
Disposal,	Verkooping.
Dispose (to) of,	Van de hand zetten, verkoopen.
Disposing mind,	Wel bij—verstand.
Disqualified,	Onbevoegd.
Distribution,	Distributie, uitdeeling.
District,	District, afdeeling.
Divert (to),	Van richting veranderen, afslaan.
Division,	Afdeeling, divisie.
Divisional Council,	Afdeelingsraad.
Docks,	Dok.
Due (to be—and payable),	Vervallen en betaalbaar zijn.
Due to (to be),	Schuldig zijn aan, te danken zijn aan, vervallen.
Duly,	Behoorlijk, in orde.
Duly sworn,	Behoorlijk beëedigd.
Duty,	Belasting, inkomende rechten.
Dwelling-house,	Woonhuis.

Edict,	*Edict, bevelschrift, plakkaat.*
Edictal citation,	*Edictale citatie.*
Education,	*Opvoeding, onderwijs.*
Education Office,	*Onderwijs kantoor.*
Effect,	*Gevolg, uitwerking.*
Effect (to have),	*Uitwerking hebben.*
Effects,	*Goederen, bezitting, have.*
Effectual,	*Doeltreffend.*
Ejectment (from a house),	*Het uitzetten (uit een huis).*
Elaborately,	*Uitvoerig.*
Election,	*Verkiezing, electie.*
Elector,	*Kiezer.*
Electoral division,	*Kiesafdeeling.*
Eligible,	*Verkiesbaar.*
Employ,	*Dienst.*
Employ (to),	*Gebruiken, huren, in dienst hebben.*
Empower (to),	*Machtigen.*
Enable (to),	*In staat stellen.*
Enact (to),	*Bepalen, vaststellen.*
Endorse (to),	*Endorseeren.*
Enter appeal (to),	*Appèl aanteekenen.*
Enter into (to—a contract),	*Een kontrakt aangaan.*
Entitle (to),	*Machtigen.*
Entitled to,	*Bevoegd om (tot).*
Entitled (to be—to),	*Aanspraak (recht) hebben op.*
Entituled,	*Getiteld.*
Equip (to),	*Inrichten.*
Equitable,	*Billijk.*
Estate,	*Boedel.*
Estimate,	*Raming, schatting.*
Estimate (to),	*Beramen, schatten.*
Event (in the—of),	*In geval.*
Evidence,	*Getuigenis.*
Evident,	*Blijkbaar.*
Exceed (to),	*Te boven gaan.*
Exceeding (not),	*Niet te boven gaande.*
Excellency (His),	*Excellentie (Zijne).*
Except,	*Behalve.*
Except (to),	*Uitzonderen.*
Excepting,	*Uitgezonderd.*
Exception,	*Uitzondering.*
Exception (with the—of),	*Met uitzondering van.*
Exclusive (of),	*Met uitsluiting van.*
Execute (to),	*Oefenen, uitoefenen, bekrachtigen.*
Executive Council,	*Uitvoerende Raad.*
Executor,	*Executeur.*
Exercise,	*Uitoefening.*

Exercise (in—of),	Uitoefenende.
Expectancy,	Erfenis.
Expedient,	Raadzaam, dienstig.
Expenditure,	Uitgaven.
Expense,	Kosten, onkosten.
Expiration,	Afloop, einde, verschijning (van een
Explicit,	Duidelijk. [termijn).
Export (to),	Uitvoeren, exporteeren.
Export trade,	Buitenlandsche handel.
Extend (to),	Verlengen, uitbreiden.
Extension,	Verlenging, uitbreiding.
Facility (greater),	Vergemakkelijking.
Failing which,	In gebreke waarvan.
Favour (in—of),	Ten gunste van, ten behoeve van, ten faveure van.
Fee,	Loon, honorarium, leen, fooi.
Field cornet,	Veldkornet.
Fill (to—a vacancy),	Eene vacature opvullen.
File (to),	Inzenden, overleggen.
Fine,	Boete.
Fine (to),	Beloeten.
Firm,	Firma.
First (the—dying),	Eerststervende.
Fix (to),	Vaststellen.
Fix (to—up),	Aanplakken.
Force (to be in—),	Van kracht zijn.
Forest Department,	Departement van houtvesterijen.
Forfeit (to),	Verbeuren, verliezen.
Frame (to),	Opstellen, optrekken.
Furnish (to—names),	Namen opgeven.
Further,	Verder, voorts.
Fulfil (to),	Vervullen.
Fulfilment,	Vervulling.
Funds,	Fondsen.
Further examination,	Verder onderzoek.
Further proof,	Verder bewijs.
General (noun),	Generaal, veldheer.
General (in),	In het algemeen.
General information (for),	Tot algemeen naricht.
Generally,	Over het algemeen.
General Manager,	Algemeen bestuurder.
Given under my hand,	Gegeven onder mijne hand.
God save the Queen,	God behoede de Koningin.
Goods,	Goederen, bezitting.
Government,	Gouvernement, regeering, bestuur.
Government measure,	Maatregel der regeering.

Government railways,	Gouvernements spoorwegen.
Governor,	Gouverneur.
Grant,	Toelage.
Grant to,	Toestaan, toewijzen, geven.
Grazing rights,	Weiderechten.
Greeting,	Saluut.
Guarantee,	Waarborg.
Guarantor,	Borg, waarborg.
Guardian,	Voogd, voogdes.
Harbour,	Haven.
Harbour Board,	Havenbestuur.
Harbour works,	Havenwerken.
Health Department,	Gezondheids departement.
Hereby,	Hierbij, hiermede, hierdoor.
Hereinafter,	Hierna.
Hereto annexed,	Hier bijgevoegd.
Heretofore,	Vóór dezen.
High Commissioner,	Hooge commissaris.
Hindrance,	Verhindering, beletsel, hinder.
Hire (to),	Huren.
Hire out (to),	Verhuren.
House of Assembly,	Volksvertegenwoordiging, parlement.
House of Correction,	Verbeteringshuis.
House duty,	Huisbelasting.
Immovable property,	Onroerende goederen, vastgoed.
Imperial Consulate,	Keizerlijk consulaat.
Imperial Government,	Rijksregeering.
Import,	Belang.
Import (to),	Importeeren, invoeren.
Imprison (to),	Gevangen zetten.
Imprisonment,	Gevangenisstraf.
Improve (to),	Verbeteren.
Include (to),	Insluiten.
Inclusive of,	Insluitend, ingesloten, met inbegrip van.
Incorporate (to),	Inlijven, incorporeeren.
Indemnify (to),	Schadeloos stellen.
Indemnification,	Schadeloosstelling.
Ineligible,	Niet-verkiesbaar.
Inevitable,	Onvermijdelijk.
Infected (to be),	Besmet zijn.
Infectious,	Besmettelijk.
Information (for general—),	Tot algemeen naricht.
Inheritance,	Erfenis.
In lieu of,	In plaats van.
Insert (to),	Invoegen, inscreeren.

Insolvency,	Bankroetschap, insolventie.
Insolvent (noun),	Bankroetier, insolvent.
Insolvent (adj.),	Bankroet, insolvent.
Insolvent estate,	Insolvente (bankroete) boedel.
Inspector,	Inspecteur.
Inspection,	Inspectie, onderzoek.
Instalment,	Paaiement, termijn.
Instant (inst.),	Dezer.
Institute (to),	Instellen.
Instructions,	Instructies, aanwijzingen.
Insubordination,	Insubordinatie, verzet.
Interested,	Belanghebbende, betreffende.
Interested (to be—in),	Belang hebben bij.
Interfere (to),	Zich bemoeien, tusschen beide komen.
Interference,	Tusschenkomst, bemoeiing.
Interpreter,	Tolk.
Intituled,	Getiteld, genoemd.
Invention,	Uitvinding.
Inventor,	Uitvinder.
Inventory,	Inventaris.
Issue,	Uitgifte.
Issue (to),	Uitgeven, in het licht geven, openbaar maken.
Jail,	Gevangenis, tronk.
Jailer,	Gevangenbewaarder, cipier.
Joint,	Gezamenlijk.
Joint lives,	Beider leven, gemeenschappelijk leven.
Joint stock company,	Naamlooze vennootschap.
Journal,	Journaal, dagblad.
Judge,	Rechter.
Judgment,	Vonnis, uitspraak.
Judicial,	Gerechtelijk.
Jurisdiction,	Jurisdictie, rechtsgebied.
Juror,	Jurielid.
Jury,	Jurie.
Justice,	Recht, gerecht, rechter.
Justice (Court of—)	Gerechtshof.
Justice (to bring to—)	Voor het gerecht brengen.
Justice of the peace,	Vrederechter.
Know all men whom it may concern,	Zij het mits dezen kennelijk, aan allen wien het moge aangaan.
Knowledge (to the—of),	Zoover het bekend is.
Lands and Mines Department,	Departement van landen en mijnen.
Landlord,	Huisbaas.

Landowner,	Landeigenaar.
Late,	Gewezen, vorige, overleden, wijlen.
Law,	Wet.
Law agent,	Wetsagent.
Law Department,	Rechtsdepartement.
Lawful,	Wettig, wettelijk.
Lawful (it shall not be—),	Het is verboden.
Lawful authority,	Wettig gezag.
Lease,	Huurkontrakt, pacht.
Leasehold estate,	Pachthoeve, pachtgoed.
Ledger,	Grootboek.
Legislature,	Wetgevende macht.
Leper,	Melaatsche.
Leprosy,	Melaatschheid.
Lessee,	Huurder.
Lessor,	Verhuurder.
Let (to),	Verhuren.
Letter of demand,	Aanmaning.
Letters patent,	Octrooibrief.
Levy (to—taxes),	Belasting innen.
Liable (person—to pay),	Aansprakelijke persoon.
Liable (shall be—to a fine),	Zal beboet kunnen worden.
Liberation,	Vrijlating, vrijstelling, ontslag.
License,	Licentie, patent, vergunning.
Licensed to,	Gepatenteerd, gelicentieerd, gemachtigd tot.
Licensing Court,	Licentie-hof.
Lieu (in—of),	In plaats van.
Limit,	Limite, grens.
Limit (of weight),	Hoogste gewicht.
Limited,	Beperkt.
Liquidation,	Liquidatie, vereffening.
Liquidator,	Liquidateur, redderaar.
Local,	Plaatselijk, locaal.
Local military forces,	Plaatselijke krijgsmacht.
Location (native),	Naturellen locatie.
Lock-up,	Bewaarplaats.
Lodge (to),	Ingeven, inzenden.
Lot,	Perceel.
Lunacy Act,	Krankzinnigenwet.
Lunatic Asylum,	Krankzinnigengesticht.
Lung sickness,	Longziekte.
Magistrate,	Magistraat, landdrost.
Magistrate's clerk,	Magistraatsklerk.
Magistrate's court,	Magistraatshof.
Maintenance (the—of),	Het handhaven van.

Majesty,	Majesteit.
Majority,	Meerderheid, meerderjarigheid.
Make request (to),	Verzoek (aanvraag) doen om.
Management,	Bestuur.
Marriage,	Huwelijk.
Marriage laws,	Huwelijkswetten.
Marriage officer,	Huwelijksambtenaar.
Master of the Supreme Court,	Meester van het hoog gerechtshof.
Material (noun),	Materiaal, bouwstof.
Material (adj.),	Belangrijk, gewichtig.
Materially,	In groote mate.
Matter,	Zaak.
May concern,	Moge aangaan.
Mayor,	Burgemeester.
Meaning (within the—of),	Naar luid van.
Medical Board,	Geneeskundige raad.
Medical examination,	Geneeskundig onderzoek.
Meet (to—an amount),	Betalen, vinden.
Meeting,	Bijeenkomst, vergadering.
Member,	Lid.
Minor,	Minderjarig, minder, gering, onmondig.
Minority,	Minderheid, minderjarigheid.
Minor heir,	Minderjarige erfgenaam.
Minutes,	Notulen.
Monthly,	Maandelijks (ch).
Mortgaged,	Verbonden, onder verband, bezwaard.
Mortgage bond,	Hypotheek, verband, schepenkennis.
Mortgagee,	Verbandhouder.
Motion,	Voorstel, motie.
Mover,	Voorsteller.
Municipal Act,	Municipale wet.
Municipality,	Municipaliteit.
Mutually,	Onderling.
Natives,	Inboorlingen, naturellen.
Native location,	Inboorlingen locatie.
Next,	Eerstkomende (e.k.).
Next of kin,	Nabestaande.
Nett,	Netto.
Nominate (to),	Benoemen, nomineeren.
Nominate and appoint (to),	Benoemen en aanstellen.
Nomination,	Nominatie.
Nominee,	Benoemde, candidaat.
Non-fulfilment,	(Het) niet-vervullen.
Notary public,	Notaris publiek.
Notice,	Kennisgeving.

Notice (to give—),	Kennisgeven, opzeggen.
Notice is hereby given,	Hiermede geschiedt kennisgeving.
Notify for general information (to),	Ter algemeene kennis brengen.
Notify (to),	Melden, aanzeggen, ter kennis brengen.
Oath,	Eed.
Oath (to put on—),	Onder eede stellen, beëedigen.
Oath (on),	Onder eede.
Obey (to),	Gehoorzamen.
Observance,	Naleving, opvolging, gebruik.
Observe (to),	Waarnemen, acht slaan op, opmerken, in acht nemen.
Observation,	Naleving, opvolging, gebruik.
Occupation,	In bezit neming, bezetting, beroep.
Occupier,	Bewoner, inwoner.
Occupy (to),	Hebben, vervullen, bezetten.
Offence,	Overtreding.
Offender,	Schuldige, overtreder.
Officer,	Beambte.
Officer (in the army),	Officier.
Official (noun),	Beambte, ambtenaar.
Official (adj.),	Officiëel, ambtelijk.
Option,	Keus.
Order,	Bevel, bestelling; orde, rangschikking.
Order (to),	Bevelen, bestellen; ordenen, schikken.
Order of court,	Bevelschrift.
Order (by),	Op last.
Order, direct, and appoint (I),	Beveel, gelast en verorden (ik).
Ordinance,	Ordinantie.
Orphan chamber,	Weeskamer.
Overdrawn,	Overtrokken.
Parliament,	Parlement.
Parliament (Act of),	Wet van het parlement.
Parliamentary,	Parlementair.
Particularly,	In het bijzonder.
Party,	Persoon.
Pass (to—a document),	Passeeren (een document).
Payable in advance,	Vooruit betaalbaar.
Payment,	Betaling.
Penalty,	Verbeuring.
Penal servitude,	Dwangarbeid.
Per centum,	Percent, ten honderd.
Period (for a—),	Gedurende een tijdperk.

Periodically,	Periodiek.
Permission,	Vergunning, verlof.
Perpetual quitrent,	Eeuwigdurende erfpacht.
Petitioner,	Petitionaris.
Place (of this—),	Alhier.
Plaintiff,	Klager.
Poll,	Stembus, verkiezing.
Polling officer,	Kiesbeambte.
Polling station,	Stemplek.
Policy,	Polis.
Possess (to),	Bezitten.
Possession,	Bezit.
Post Office,	Postkantoor.
Pound,	Schut.
Pound master,	Schutmeester.
Power of attorney,	Volmacht, procuratie.
Power and authority vested in me,	Macht en gazag mij verleend.
Preceding,	Voorgaande, vorige, tevoren.
Precisely,	Precies.
Precision,	Nauwkeurigheid, juistheid.
Premises,	Erf.
Premium,	Premie.
Prescriptive right,	Verjaringsrecht.
Presence (in the—of),	In tegenwoordigheid van.
Presents (by these—),	Bij deze, hiermede, hieruit.
Prevent (to),	Voorkomen, verhinderen.
Prevention,	Voorkoming.
Prime Minister,	Eerste minister.
Prison,	Gevangenis, tronk.
Prisoner,	Gevangene.
Private (adj.),	Privaat.
Private secretary,	Privaat secretaris, geheimschrijver.
Procedure,	Procedure, rechtsvervolging.
Proceed (to),	Overgaan.
Proceedings,	Verrichtingen, proces.
Proceeds,	Opbrengst.
Proclaim (to),	Proclameeren, uitvaardigen.
Proclaim, declare and make known,	Proclameer, verklaar en maak bekend.
Proclamation,	Proclamatie, kennisgeving.
Produce (to),	Opbrengen, voortbrengen, produceeren.
Produce,	Opbrengst, produkten.
Profits,	Profijt, winst, voordeel.
Promise (noun),	Belofte.
Promise (to),	Beloven.
Property,	Eigendom.

Propose (to),	Voorstellen.
Propriety,	Gepastheid.
Prorogue (to),	Verdagen.
Prosecute (to),	Vervolgen, doorzetten.
Provide (to),	Voorzien, verschaffen.
Provided with,	Voorzien van.
Provided,	Mits, onder voorwaarde.
Provision (to make—),	Voorziening maken.
Provisionally,	Voorloopig. provisoir, provisioneel.
Provisions,	Levensmiddelen.
Proxy,	Volmacht; gemachtigde, plaatsvervanger.
Public,	Publiek, openbaar.
Public auction,	Publieke veiling (verkooping).
Public seal,	Publick zegel.
Public works,	Publieke werken.
Publish (to),	Publiceeren.
Published by authority,	Op last gepubliceerd.
Publisher,	Uitgever.
Purchase (to),	Koopen, aanschaffen.
Purchase amount,	Koopschat.
Purchase money,	Kooppenningen.
Purchase price,	Koopprijs.
Purchaser,	Kooper.
Purpose (for the—of),	Met het doel om, ten doel hebbende.
Qualified,	Bevoegd.
Question (in),	In kwestie.
Railway,	Spoorweg.
Raise (to),	Opnemen.
Raise (to—a loan),	Eene leening sluiten.
Raise (to—objections),	Objecteeren, tegenwerpingen maken.
Rank (to),	Rangschikken.
Rate,	Rato, bedrag, schaal, koers.
Rato (at the—of),	Tegen.
Rates,	Belasting, aanslag.
Ratepayer,	Belastingschuldige.
Reason (by—of),	Wegens, om, om reden van.
Reasonable,	Redelijk.
Reasonable reward,	Billijke belooning.
Reasonable wear and tear,	Billijke slijtage.
Rebate,	Rabat, korting.
Receipt,	Kwitantie.
Reciprocally,	Wederzijds, over en weer.
Recognise (to),	Erkennen.
Recommendation,	Aanbeveling.
Record,	Oorkonde, kroniek, verhaal.

Record (to),	Aanteekenen, registreeren, notuleeren.
Recover (to—money),	Invorderen (van geld).
Recruiting Depôt,	Werfdepôt.
Reduce (to),	Verminderen, afbrengen, verlagen.
Reduction,	Vermindering, verlaging.
Reference (with—to),	Met referte naar, met verwijzing naar.
Referring to,	Refereerende naar.
Register,	Register, lijst.
Registered,	Geregistreerd.
Registrar,	Griffier, registrateur.
Registration,	Registratie.
Registrar of Deeds,	Registrateur van akten.
Regulation,	Regulatie, regel, reglement.
Relating to,	Betreffende.
Relation (with—to),	Met betrekking tot.
Relation,	Betrekking; verwante (fam.).
Relet,	Weder verhuren.
Relict,	Weduwe.
Relative to,	In verband met.
Remand (prisoner was remanded),	Het verhoor werd uitgesteld.
Removal,	Verplaatsing, verwijdering.
Remove (to),	Vervoeren, verplaatsen.
Rent,	Huur, pacht.
Repeal,	Herroeping.
Report,	Rapport, verslag.
Report (to),	Rapporteeren, verslag doen.
Repression,	Onderdrukking.
Republic,	Republiek.
Republican,	Republikeinsch.
Request,	Verzoek, aanvraag, verzoekschrift.
Request (to),	Verzoeken, aanvraag doen.
Required,	Noodig, benoodigd.
Required (to be),	Moeten zijn, benoodigd zijn, verzoeken.
Requisition,	Requisitie.
Reserve to oneself (to),	Zich voorbehouden.
Reside (to),	Wonen.
Residence,	Woning, woonplaats.
Resident,	Woonachtig.
Resident Magistrate,	Plaatselijke magistraat.
Resign (to),	Opgeven, bedanken voor, resigneeren.
Respect (in—of),	Wat betreft, ten aanzien van.
Respect (with—to),	Ten aanzien van.
Respectfully,	Met verschuldigden eerbied.
Respective,	Respectieve.
Respectively,	Respectievelijk.

N

Responsible,	Verantwoordelijk.
Returning officer,	Verslaggevend beambte, stemopnemer.
Returns,	Staten, opgaven.
Revenue,	Inkomsten.
Revert (to),	Terugkeeren, terugvallen aan.
Rights,	Rechten.
Same (the),	Dezelve, hetzelve.
Sanction (to),	Goedkeuren, toestemmen.
Sanitary (commission),	Gezondheids (commissie).
Sanitary officer,	Sanitair beambte.
Savings bank,	Spaarbank.
Scab Act,	Brandziektewet.
Schedule,	Schedule, bijlage.
Seal,	Zegel.
Second (to),	Secondeeren, ondersteunen.
Seconder,	Fecondant.
Secretary,	Secretaris, schrijver.
Secretary for Agriculture,	Landbouwsecretaris.
Secretary for Native Affairs,	Secretaris voor Naturellenzaken.
Section,	Sectie, deel, afdeeling, artikel.
Security,	Securiteit.
See fit (to),	Goeddunken.
Select (to),	Kiezen.
Set forth (to),	Omschrijven, Nitleggen, uiteenzetten.
Several,	Verschillende, onderscheidene.
Share,	Deel, aandeel.
Share (to),	Deelen, aandeel hebben (nemen).
Sheriff,	Sherif, kantonrechter.
Shortcomings,	Tekortkomingen.
Sign (to),	Teekenen, onderteekenen.
Signatory,	Onderteekenaar.
Signature,	Onderteekening, handteekening.
Signed,	Geteekend.
Signify (to),	Te kennen geven.
Sinking fund,	Amortisatie.
Situated,	Gelegen.
Sole,	Eenig.
Solely,	Geheel en al.
Sole and universal heir,	Eenige en algemeene erfgenaam.
Solemn,	Plechtig, solemneel.
Solemn declaration,	Plechtige verklaring.
Solemnise (to—marriages),	Huwelijken sluiten.
Solemnly declare (to),	Plechtig verklaren.
Solitary confinement,	Eenzame opsluiting.
Sound and disposing mind (of),	In het genot van alle geestvermogens.

OFFICIAL AND DOCUMENTARY LANGUAGE. 355

Spare diet,	Water en brood, rijst en water.
Special,	Bijzonder, speciaal.
Specifications and drawings,	Specificatiën en teekeningen.
Spouse,	Echtgenoot.
Stamp,	Zegel.
State (to),	Opgeven, aangeven, zeggen, te kennen geven.
Statement,	Opgave, verklaring.
Stationery Department,	Departement van schrijfbenoodigdheden.
Statistics,	Statistiek, opgaven.
Stipulation,	Bedinging, bepaling.
Stipulate (to),	Vaststellen, bepalen, bedingen.
Strictly (I—charge),	Ik gelast u uitdrukkelijk.
Styled (to be—),	Genoemd te worden.
Subdivision,	Onderverdeeling, onderafdeeling, subdivisie.
Sub-guarantor,	Achterwaarborg.
Subject,	Onderwerp, onderdaan.
Subject (to),	Onderwerpen.
Subjoined,	Hier bijgevoegd, hierna volgend.
Sublet (to),	Onderverhuren.
Submit (to),	Onderwerpen.
Subscription,	Inschrijving, subscriptie, abonnementsprijs.
Subsequent,	Daarna volgende.
Substitute (to),	Substitueeren, in de plaats stellen.
Substitution,	Substitutie, plaatsvervanging.
Successive,	Achtereenvolgend.
Such,	Zoodanig, zulk een.
Sue (to),	Vervolgen.
Suit (law—),	Rechtsgeding.
Summary,	Uittreksel, korte inhoud.
Summon (to),	Dagvaarden.
Summons,	Dagvaarding, oproeping.
Superintendent General,	Superintendent Generaal.
Supervision,	Opzicht, overzicht, supervisie.
Supreme Court,	Hoog gerechtshof.
Surety,	Borg.
Surrender (to),	Zich overgeven, boedel overgeven.
Surrender (voluntary),	Vrijwillige overgave.
Surrogation,	Surrogatie, subrogatie.
Survey,	Opmeting.
Survey (to),	Opmeten.
Surveyor,	Landmeter.
Survivor,	Langstlevende, overblijvende.
Swear (to),	Zweren, bezweren.

Sworn (duly),	Behoorlijk gezworen (bezworen, beëedigd).
Sworn declaration,	Beëedigde verklaring.
Sworn translator,	Beëedigd vertaler.
Tariff,	Tarief.
Tariff Act,	Tariefwet.
Taxes,	Belasting.
Telegraph,	Telegraaf.
Telegraph (to),	Telegrafeeren.
Telegraphist,	Telegrafist.
Telegram,	Telegram.
Tenancy,	Huurbezit, pachting.
Tenant,	Huurder, pachter.
Tender,	Inschrijving, tender.
Tender (to give out by—),	Aanbesteden.
Term,	Termijn, tijd, tijdperk.
Terms (in—of),	Krachtens, naar luid van.
Terminate (to),	Ten einde brengen, voleindigen, afloopen.
Territory,	Gebied, grondgebied.
Testament,	Testament, wilsbeschikking.
Testator,	Testateur.
Thus done and passed,	Aldus gedaan en gepasseerd.
Time table,	Tijdtafel, rooster.
Times (at all—),	Te allen tijde.
Title,	Recht, aanspraak.
Title deed,	Grondbrief.
Town,	Stad, dorp, gemeente.
Town-council,	Stadsraad.
Trade-mark,	Handelsmerk.
Tradesman,	Handwerksman.
Transfer,	Transport, overdracht.
Transfer (to),	Transporteeren, overdragen.
Transit (in),	In transito.
Transit duty,	Doorvoerbelasting.
Transmit (to),	Overzenden, toezenden.
Transport,	Transport.
Transport (to),	Transporteeren.
Treasurer,	Thesaurier.
Treasury,	Thesaurie.
Trial,	Onderzoek.
Trial (the—is postponed),	De zaak is uitgesteld.
Trial (to be put up for—),	Voorbrengen.
Trial (to take one's—)	Terechtstaan.
Try (to),	Onderzoeken, gerechtelijk onderzoeken.
Trustee,	Curator.

Ultimately,	Ten laatste.
Ultimo (ult.),	Laatstleden (l. l.).
Umpire,	Scheidsrechter.
Unauthorised,	Niet-geauthoriseerd, ongemachtigd.
Under and by virtue of,	Onder en uit kracht van.
Under provision of,	Onder voorziening van.
Undersigned,	Ondergeteekende.
Undue,	Onbehoorlijk, ongepast.
Unemployed,	Buiten werk.
Upset price,	Inzet.
Usher,	Ceremoniemeester, concierge.
Usufruct,	Vruchtgebruik.
Vacancy,	Vacature.
Vacant,	Vacant.
Valid and effectual,	Geldig en van kracht.
Verdict,	Uitspraak.
Vest in (to),	Verleenen.
Vested in me,	Mij verleend.
View (in—of),	Met het oog op.
View (with a—to),	Met het oog op.
Village board of management,	Dorpsbestuur.
Virtue of the powers (by),	Krachtens de macht.
Void (null and—),	Van nul en geener waarde.
Vote,	Stem.
Voter,	Stemmer.
Voucher,	Bewijs.
Warehouse (to),	Op entrepôt leggen.
War Office,	Oorlogskantoor.
Ward,	Wijk, afdeeling; pupil.
Warder,	Bewaarder.
Warrant,	Machtiging, bevelschrift.
Whereas,	Nademaal, aangezien.
Will (last),	Uiterste wil.
Witness,	Getuige.
Witness (to),	Als getuige teekenen.
Writ,	Lastbrief.

(358)

CHAPTER XIX.

LIST OF CAPE IDIOMS, WITH THEIR DUTCH AND ENGLISH EQUIVALENTS.

Words in Alphabetic Order.	Cape Idioms.	Dutch for the Idioms.	English for the Idioms.
Aanstellen.	1. Jij stel baign ver jou aan; 2. aanstellerig; 3. vol aanstelling.	1. Ge verbeeldt u heel wat; 2. gemaakt; 3. vol verbeelding.	1. You are very conceited; 2. affected; 3. full of affectation.
Aap.	Apie.	Je zijt beetgenomen.	You are taken in.
Aardappelkop.	Hij is een aardappelkop.	Hij is een weetniet, domoor.	He is a know-nothing (booby).
Aarig.	1. Ik voel zoo aarig; 2. Sies, da's een aarige ding!	Aardig, wonderlijk, minder mooi; 1. ik voel mij zoo wonderlijk; 2. Bah, wat een akelig ding is dat!	1. I feel so queer; 2. Bah, that's a nasty thing!
Aas.	Hij zoek aas.	Hij zit ledig rond te gapen.	He stares vacantly.
Achterlaaier.	Achterlaaier.	Pandjas.	Frock-coat.
Afdra'and.	Afdra'and en opdra'and (afdragend en opragend).	Afhellend en hellend (ook gemakkelijk en moeielijk).	Down-hill and up-hill (also easy and difficult).
Afdra'anshoogte.	Afdra'anshoogte.	Scheldnaam voor iemand, die zich niet wil laten gezeggen.	Nickname for a self-willed person.
Afkloppen.	Hij klop af.	Hij neemt af en is aan 't sterven (van paarden gesproken).	It is falling off and about to die (said of horses).
Aja.	Aja.	Kindermeid.	Nursemaid.

LIST OF CAPE IDIOMS.

Akerdissie.	Akerdissie.	Lizard.
Albaster.	1 Albaster; 2. Albaster speul.	1. Marble — 2. To play at marbles.
Anklammen.	Hij is bietjie angeklam.	He is tipsy.
Apevlooi.	Apevlooi.	Nickname for a little boy who fancies himself a man.
As.	1. As (asch); 2. de hand in de asch slaan.	1. Ashes; 2. to get the slip.
Assemblief.	Assemblief.	If you please.
Baaitje.	Baaitje.	Jacket.
Baign.	Baign (ook bajang).	Much, very.
Baken.	Hij het baken gesteek.	He has fallen from a horse.
Bakooren.	Bakooren.	Big ears.
Bandiet.	1. Bandiet; 2. die bandieten breek deur.	1. Prisoner; 2. You are out at toes.
Bakklei.	Bakklei.	To fight (said of men and animals).
Baroe.	Baroe.	Edible turnip of white colour, milky.
Bawer.	Bawer.	Barbel.
Beest.	1. Beest; 2. beestovleesch.	1. Ox, cow or bull; 2. beef.
Begaai.	Jij begaai.	You dig badly.
Beenen.	1. Spaansch-riet-beenen; 2. hij het zijn beenen te lang weggesteek.	1. Long legs; 2. his trousers are too short.

LIST OF IDIOMS—continued.

Words in Alphabetic Order.	Cape Idioms.	Dutch for the Idioms.	English for the Idioms.
Bits.	1. Bits; 2. Hij het bits geeet.	1. Giftplant; 2. Hij is dronken.	1. Poisonous plant; He is drunk.
Biljethuis.	Biljethuis.	Lommerd, pandjeshuis.	Lombard-house, pawn-broker's shop.
Blatjang.	Blatjang.	Mengsel van jonge perziken en Spaansche peper (als specerij gebruikt).	Green peaches pickled with Cayenne-pepper.
Blazen.	Hij blaas.	Hij liegt.	He lies (tells a story).
Blikooren.	Blikooren.	Vrijstaters.	People of the Orange Free State.
Blij.	1. Blij (blijven); 2. Waar blij hij?	1. Wonen; 2. Waar woont hij?	1. To dwell (live); 2. Where does he live?
Blus.	1. Zijn blus hang; 2. zijn blus is uit.	1. Hij is bijna dood (meest van dieren); 2. Hij is te moe om nog iets te doen.	1. It is half dead (said of animals); 2. He is too tired for anything.
Boedel.	Boedel o'ergé (overgeven).	Bankroet gaan; onpasselijk worden.	To become bankrupt; to turn sick.
Bockpens.	Bockpens.	Benaming voor een corpulenten man.	Nick-name for a corpulent man.
Boch.	Boch (bocht).	Ruigte om veekralen mede te voorzien (ook "onzin").	Shrubs strewn on the floors of kraals (also used for "nonsense").

LIST OF CAPE IDIOMS.

Bok.	1. Bok; 2. Hij het die bok bij die stert gehad; 3. Bokmelk.	1. Goat; 2. He has returned from the brink of the grave; 3. Goat's milk.
Bokkie.	Bokkie.	Buggy.
Bokman.	Bokman.	A man who smoothes the ground that has just been dug up.
Bokveld.	Hij is bokveld toe.	He is dead.
Boord.	Bo'ord.	Orchard.
Botter.	1. Botter; 2. Botterkop.	1. Butter; 2. Stupid fellow, (some one whose hair has been closely cropped).
Botterkopezel.	Botterkopezel.	A kind of mule with a very small head.
Broek.	Hij het te vinnig deur die broek gespring. Zijn broek is te kort.	His trousers are too short.
Brommer.	1. Brommer; 2. Zijn brommer is af.	1. Big fly; 2. He has lost his tongue.
Bulperd.	Bulperd.	Particularly fine horse.
Daarom.	1. Daarom; 2. Die jas is wel wat groot vcr hom, maar hij lijk daarom mooi.	1. Toch; 2. De jas is hem wel recht groot, maar hij ziet er toch mooi mee uit. 1. Yet, nevertheless; 2. The coat is rather large for him, yet he looks well in it.
Dalkies.	Dalkies.	Just now; presently.
Dam.	Dam.	1. Pool, pond; 2. Reservoir.
Diamant.	Hij graaf diamant.	Exclamation on seeing any one fall from his horse.

LIST OF IDIOMS—continued.

Words in Alphabetic Order.	Cape Idioms.	Dutch for the Idioms.	English for the Idioms.
Doen.	Die perd is gedaan.	Het is gedaan met dat paard.	That horse is done for.
Don.	't Is don met hom (English "done").	Het is met hem gedaan.	He is done for.
Dons.	Hij het ver hom opgedons.	Hij heeft zich opgeschikt.	He has tricked himself out.
Dop.	1. Dop; 2. Dophouden; 3. Hij houdt daar dop; 4. Laat dop.	1. Nap; 2. Den melkemmer vasthouden bij 't melken; 3. Hij maakt het hof aan dat meisje; 4. Weggaan.	1. Bowl; 2. To hold the pail while some one else is milking; 3. He courts that girl; 4. To go away.
Dopsteker.	Dopsteker (Hij steck' een goeie dop).	Dronkaard.	Drunkard.
Draf.	Mijn kind, loop op een hondedraffie.	Mijn kind, loop op een 'sukkeldrafje.	My child, trot on gently.
Drift.	Drift.	Doorwaadbare plaats in ene rivier.	Ford.
Droster.	Droster.	Deserteur.	Deserter.
Effen.	Ver effen.	Even; daarzoeven.	Just now.
Engelsch.	Hij het met hom Engelsch gepraat.	Hij heeft hem hard aangesproken.	He has spoken sharply to him.
Ezel.	1. Ezel; 2. Donkey.	1. Muilezel; 2. ezel.	1. Mule; 2. Donkey.
Fiemish.	Fiemish.	Stilzeneurig	Peevish.

LIST OF CAPE IDIOMS.

Finkel.	Finkel.	Spierwit fijn blad, onder roisen groeiend, eetbaar, verkoelend, buitengewoon zoet.	A perfectly white, feathery plant, growing under rocks, edible, cooling and with a very sweet taste.
Frisch.	1. Frisch; 2. Hoe vaar je nog? Frisch, dankie; 3. Een frissche mensch.	1. Gezond; 2. Hoe vaart u? Wel, dank u; 3. Een gezet mensch.	1. Healthy; 2. How do you do? Well, thank you; 3. A rather stout person.
Gannabos.	Gannabos (ook Aschbos).	Lage struik met sappige loten zonder bladeren (wordt verbrand en de -asch dient als toog).	A low shrub having juicy twigs without leaves (when burned, its ashes serve for making lye).
Gantang. Geef.	Gantang. 1. Ik geef nie om nie; 2. Al wat om ge' is hond zijn kind.	Vrijer. 1. Ik stoor er mij niet aan; 't is mij onverschillig; 2. Al wie er om maalt, is een gek.	Sweet-heart. 1. I don't care; I don't mind; 2. We should be fools to care about it.
Geil.	1. Geil; 2. Een geile smaak aan vleesch of melk.	1. Wedig opgegroeid (van mensch, dier en plant); 2. Smaak, veroorzaakt door 't eten van een zekere soort kruiden door de koe.	1. Lusty (said of men and animals); 2. A strong taste in meat and milk, caused by certain herbs that the cow has eaten.
Getips. Goeverneur.	Getips (van 't Eng. tipsy). Goeverneur zijn hond is zijn oom.	Aangeschoten. Keizers kat is zijne nicht.	Tipsy. He is a cousin of the Emperor's cat (said of upstarts who pretend to genteel connections).
Gons.	1. Gons; 2. laat gons.	1. Gonzen; 2. Loop hard.	1. To hum; 2. Run.

LIST OF IDIOMS—continued.

Words in Alphabetic Order.	Cape Idioms.	Dutch for the Idioms.	English for the Idioms.
Grap.	1. Grap; 2. da's amper een grap en een half.	1. Grap; 2. Dat's wezenlijk een goede ui.	1. Joke; 2. That's a capital joke.
Grau.	Grau (ook: graaf).	Graaf, spade.	Spade.
Grieksch.	Hij praat Grieksch.	Hij spreekt onzin.	He talks nonsense.
Haak af.	Haak af (druk af).	Schiet af; gooi op; sta toe.	Fire away.
Hulfnaatje.	Halfnaatje.	Kind van een blanken vader en bruine moeder (of omgekeerd).	Half-cast.
Hamerkop.	Hamerkop.	Bruine vogel ter grootte van eene kraai; draagt een vederbos, gelijkende op eenen hamer, achter op den kop.	Brown bird of the size of a crow, with a feather-bush on the back of its head, giving it a shape like a hammer.
Hang.	Hij kan lekker hang.	Hij kan mooi een slag ontduiken, (goed pareeren).	He can parry well.
Hanglip.	Hanglip.	Overhangende rots.	An overhanging cliff.
Hart.	Hartsvergå'ring hou.	Eene zaak ernstig overdenken.	To cogitate about a matter.
Haartebees.	1. Hartebees(t); 2. Hartbeeshuis, (eigenlijk hard-bieshuis).	1. Hert; 2. Huisje gedekt met stroo of riet.	1. Deer; 2. Hut thatched with straw or rushes.
Hartzeer.	Hartzeer; 2. Wees hartzeer, maar moe' nie huil nie.	1. Bedroefd; 2. Wees verdrietig (zoo ye wilt) maar schrei niet.	1. Down-hearted; 2. If you must be down-hearted, don't cry.

LIST OF CAPE IDIOMS.

Hempie.	Hempie; Hij 's hempie.	Shirt; He is done for; He has lost all (in a game).
Hoed.	1. Hoed; 2. Druk vas(t) die hoed.	1. Hat: 2. Run fast.
Hoender.	1. Hoender; 2. Hij is hoenderkop; 3. Loop na die hoenders; 4. Die hoenders het zijn kos(t) afgeneem.	1. Fowl; 2. He is half drunk; 3. Go about your business; 4. (Said of one who sits moping in company).
Hondblij.	Hondblij.	As pleased as Punch.
Horak.	Wat zeg' Horak?	You exaggerate.
Hottentotsgod.	Hottentotsgod.	A mantis.
Jag'.	1. Jag'; 2. Hij gaat jag.	1. To hunt; 2. He has got his first frock-coat on.
Jantje.	Jantje-trap-zuutjes.	Cameleon.
Jas.	Jas.	Lady's jacket.
Jongens.	Jongens (jongetjes).	Young (of animals).
Jonkas.	Jonkas.	Boon companion.
Juffer.	1. Juffer; 2. Ou' juffer tijds genoeg.	1. Lady; 2. A slow-coach.
Kaalvoet.	Kaalvoet.	Bare-footed.
Kakoenetje.	Kakoenetje.	Flat round bulb, growing at the surface, turnip-shaped, sweet.
Kalkoencier.	Kalkoencier.	A person with freckles in the face.

List of Idioms—continued.

Words in Alphabetic Order.	Cape Idioms.	Dutch for the Idioms.	English for the Idioms.
Kalvers.	1. Kalvers; 2. Hij span jonge kalvers in.	1. Kalveren; 2. Hij voneert.	1. Calves; 2. He vomits.
Kambroe.	Kambroe.	Knolgewas in zandigen grond groeiend, hard als radijs, zeer goed van smaak.	Tuber growing in sandy soil, hard like a radish, well-flavoured.
Kamma-Kamma Kampta.	Kamma - Kamma (zie Kampta). 1. Kampta; 2. Hij is kampta mooi; 3. Hij zegt kampta zoo.	2. Hij houdt zich voor mooi; 3. Hij zegt het om te vleien.	2. He fancies himself handsome; 3. He says it in order to flatter.
Kapok. Kapokhaantje. Karkoer. Karmasten.	1. Kapok; 2. Kapokken. Hij is een kapokhaantje. Karkoer. Karmasten. (Duitsch "Gamaschen")	1. Sneeuw; 2. Sneeuwen. Hij is een dwerg. Bitterappel (eene vrucht als een [melon]). Rijkappen.	1. Snow; 2. To snow. He is a dwarf. Bitter melon. Gaiters.
Kanis.	(Scheldwoord) Jou snerige kanis.	Jou vuilik.	You dirty pig. (Latin Canis = a dog.)
Karretje.	1. Karretje; 2. Hij het uitgerij met Jan thuisblij' zijn karretje	1. Karretje; 2. Hij is van zins geweest uit te gaan, maar verhinderd.	1. Cart; 2. He had a mind to go out, but was prevented.
Karoo.	Karoo.	1. Woestijn; 2. Steenachtige bodem, bedekt met laag, dun struikgewas.	1. Waste; 2. Stony ground, thinly-covered with low shrubs.

LIST OF CAPE IDIOMS.

Kasta.	1. Kasta; 2. Hij gaat kasta na die pos.	1. Apparently; 2. He pretends to go to the post-office.
Kenta. Keil.	Hij is kenta. Keil (van het Duitsch).	He won't play any more. 1. Wedge; 2. Tile (high-crowned hat).
Kits. Kirie. Klaaswaarzegger.	1. Kits; 2. Zij is kits. 1. Kirie; 2. Knopkirie. Klaaswaarzegger.	1. Mad; 2. She is cracked. 1. Walking-stick; 2. Club. Story-teller.
Klam.	1. Klam; 2. Anklam; 3. Ik het die spons gevat om die tabbertje an to klam.	1. Damp; 2. To damp; 3. I took the sponge to damp the dress.
Klavier. Klau'.	Klavier (van het Duitsch). 1. Klau; Gooi klau in die grond!	Piano. 1. Paw, foot; 2. Run along!
Kleinneef. Kleinnicht. Klip.	Achterneef. Achternicht. 1. Klip; 2. een klip in die pad gooi.	Second cousin. Second cousin. 1. Rock, boulder, and stone; 2. To do anyone a good turn.
Klok.	1. Klok; 2. pas op, anders gaat 't na die klok.	1. Bell; 2. Take care, or you will become bankrupt.
Klonk.	Klonk (klein jonk) ook: klonkie.	Little chap (coloured).
Kluitjes.	1. Kluitjes; 2. Hij bak' kluitjes.	1. Fibs; 2. He tells fibs.

List of Idioms—continued.

Words in Alphabetic Order.	Cape Idioms.	Dutch for the Idioms.	English for the Idioms.
Knie. Kniehalter'.	Een kniediep vóór dag. Kniehalteren.	Zeer vroeg in den morgen. De knie van het paard door een riem met den kop verbinden.	Some time before daybreak. To connect the knee and head of a horse by means of a strap.
Knipmes.	1. Knipmes 2. hij rij' knipmes.	1. Knipmes; 2. Hij laat zijn paard den nek mooi krommen.	1. Pocket-knife; 2. He makes his horse arch its neck.
Koekemakran- ka.	Kockemakranka.	Een bol, die eene vrucht onder den grond draagt, welke als medicijn gebruikt wordt.	A bulb producing a fruit underground, used as medicine.
Kool.	1. Kool; 2. Kool zonder spek.	1. Kool; 2. Gezelschap dames zonder heeren.	1. Cabbage; 2. A ladies' party without gentlemen.
Kop.	1. Kop; 2. Hij wil nio kop gé nie; 3. Hij het kop uitgotrek'.	1. Hoofd; 2. Hij wil niet ingeven; 3. (Gezegd van een deelhebber in eene firma, die bankroet gegaan is).	1. Head; 2. He won't give in; 3. He has failed and withdrawn from the business.
Koppie.	Koppie.	Uitstekende, kale rots op den top eens heuvels.	Bare rock on the top of a hill.
Kort.	Hij is kort gespan (geno- men van het spannen der achterpooten eener koe bij het melken).	Hij is kort aangebonden; kort ge- bakerd.	He is quick-tempered.

LIST OF CAPE IDIOMS.

Koerantdrukken.	1. Kourantdrukken; 2. Hij is een krantdrukker.	2. He is a tale-bearer.
Kousband.	Konsband.	
Kraal.	Kraal (in de La Plata republiek "corral").	Small, many-coloured snake. Kraal (enclosed space for keeping cattle over night) also Kafir village.
Krans.	Kleine, bonte slang. Omheinde plaats, waarin het vee 's nachts bewaard wordt, (ook Kaffergehucht). Steilopgaand rotsachtig bovenstuk eens bergs.	Rocky ridge crowning a hill.
Kreef.	1. Kreeft; 2. Jij is een kreef.	1. Crab; 2. You begin your work at the wrong end.
Kruidje.	Kruidje-roer-mij-niet.	Touch-me-not (name for a pretty-looking plant that gives out a very unpleasant smell when injured).
Kruipmol. Kwipper.	Kruipmol. Kwipper (kwippers).	Fraaie stinkplant, die men niet ongestraft kan aanraken. Small kind of mole; a plough. Quince (quince).
	Kleine soort mol; een ploeg. Kweepeer (kweeperen).	
Lammerschaap. Lat.	Een troep lammerschaap. 1. Lat; 2. Hij slaan ver mijn met een kwipperlat saam.	A flock of ewes and lambs. 1. Lath, stick, twig; 2. He beats me with the twig of a quince-tree.
	Een troep ooien met lammeren. 1. Lat; ook stokje en takje; 2. Hij slaat mij met een kweepeertakje.	
Leeg.	1. Leeg; 2. Die toon iste leeg; 3. Taaiboschleegte (naam eener plaats in het Colesberg-distr.).	1. Low; 2. That tone is too deep; 3. Name of a farm in the Colesberg district.
	1. Laag; 2. Die toon is te laag; 3. Taaiboschlaagte.	

LIST OF IDIOMS—continued.

Words in Alphabetic Order.	Cape Idioms.	Dutch for the Idioms.	English for the Idioms.
Lek.	1. Lek; 2. Ik zal ver jou lek (van 't Eng.).	1. Lekken of likken; 2. Ik zal je een pak geven.	1. To lick; 2. I'll give you a licking.
Likkewaan.	Likkewaan.	Leguaan (kleine alligator).	Alligator.
Lijf.	1. Lijf; 2. Hij is lekkerlijf.	1. Lijf; 2. Hij is halfdronken.	1. Body; 2. He is half seas over (drunk).
Lol.	Lol (door fatsoenlijke lieden gebruik).	Plat Holl. kletsen, zeuren.	To chatter (bother).
Lunsriem.	1. Lunsriem; 2. Hij is een lunsriem.	1. Lensriem (riempje door de as gestoken om het afloopen van het wiel te beletten); 2. Hij deugt voor niets.	1. Strap which prevents the wheel from slipping off the axle; 2. He is a good-for-nothing.
Maneschijn.	1. Maneschijn; 2. Ik gaat ver jou rol' in die maneschijn.	2. Ik moet verschrikkelijk om je lachen.	2. You make me split with laughter.
Manuel.	1. Manuel; 2. Manuel het zijn vel al bespreek al.	1. Geïmproviseerde naam voor een huidenkoopman; 2. Die man lijt op sterven.	1. Fancy name for a dealer in skins; 2. That man is on the point of death.
Mater.	1. Mater; 2. Zijn maters is morsdood.	1. Maat; 2. Hij heeft zijns gelijke niet.	1. Mate; 2. There's no one like him.
Matraskop.	Matraskop.	Krullebol.	Curly-headed person.
Meebos.	Meebos.	Zoet-zout konfijt van abrikozen gemaakt.	Apricots preserved with salt and sugar.

LIST OF CAPE IDIOMS.

Mensch.	1. Een mensch; 2. Waar kan een mensch brood koop?	1. Altijd gebruikt voor het voornw. men; 2. Waar kan men hier brood koopen?	1. A person (used for the indef. Pers. Pron. *one*); 2. Where can one buy bread here?
Middel.	1. Middels: 2. Ik is in die middel (wellicht van 't Eng. "muddle").	1. Midden; 2. Ik weet niet hoe te beslissen.	1. Middle; 2. I am in a fix (in a muddle).
Moeg.	1. Moeg; 2. Hij is baing moeg; 3. Hij gaat die moegmaak in.	1. Moede; 2. Hij is dronken; 3. Hij houdt te lang aan met het een of ander.	1. Tired; 2. He is drunk; 3. He doesn't know when to stop.
Moeker.	1. Moeker; 2. Ik moeker ver jou.	1. Moker; 2. Ik zal je een goed pak geven.	1. Sledge-hammer; 2. I shall give it you.
Mossie.		*Musch.*	Sparrow.
Mot.	1. Mot; 2. Ik is een mot (onder de bruinen).	2. Mot; 2. Heb ik dat niet knap gedaan?	1. Moth; 2. Wasn't that a clever trick?
Muis.	1. Muis; 2. Hij zit net zoo gerus as een muis op een brood.	2. Hij zit vast in den zadel.	1. Mouse; 2. He sits well on his horse.
Mukstok.	1. Mukstok; 2. Hij is een mukstok.	1. Gaffelvormige stok onder den disselboom van een afgespannen kar geplaatst, om die in balans te houden; 2. Hij heeft korte beenen.	1. A forked piece of wood placed as a support under the shaft of a cart to balance it; 2. He is short-legged.
Muziek.	1. Muziek (een muziek).	*Harmonium of piano.*	Harmonium or piano.
Na'al.	1. Na'al; 2. Hij het na'als gescherp.	1. *Nagel;* 2. *Hij heeft hard geloopen.*	1. Nail; 2. He has been running fast.

371

LIST OF IDIOMS—continued.

Words in Alphabetic Order.	Cape Idioms.	Dutch for the Idioms.	English for the Idioms.
Na'als.	1. Na'als; 2. Hij het 't achter die na'als.	1. Nagels; 2. Hij is er klaar mee.	1. Nails; 2. He is finished.
Nam.	Nam (naam). Hoe'snam?	Hoe heet het ook weêr?	Name; What's the name again?
Nas.	Nas-eergisteren.	Voor-eergisteren.	Three days ago.
Nek.	1. Nek; 2. Hij het ver hom in die nek laat kijk.	1. Hals; 2. Hij heeft zich laten beetnemen.	1. Neck; 2. He has been taken in.
Net. *Non.*	Net-nou-maar(tjes). 1. Non; 2. Hij is met die non gepla' (geplaagd); 3. Hij's met die non.	Op 't oogenblik, dadelijk. 1. Non; 2. Er loopt een streepje door bij hem; 3. Hij is dronken.	Presently. 1. Nun; 2. There's a screw loose in him; 3 He is drunk.
Noy.	1. Noy (Portugeesch); 2. Een gawe noy.	1. Juffer; 2. Een flink ontwikkeld meisje.	1. Lady (married or unmarried); 2. A clever, accomplished lady.
Onderduims.	Onderduims.	Onder'shands.	Underhand.
Oolijk.	1. Oolijk; 2. Na vroolijkheid komt oolijkheid.	1. Ziekerig, kurig; 2. Eerst lachen dan huilen.	1. Indisposed, put out; 2. Merry-making ends in heaviness.
Orrelstrijk.	Orrelstrijk (orgelstrijk) [misschien verbastering van het Eng. "all right"].	Antwoord op de vraag: hoe gaat het? (bet. goed).	Answer to the question: How do you do? (meaning: all right).

LIST OF CAPE IDIOMS.

Ouderwets.	1. Ouderwets; 2. Een ouderwetse dingetje.	1. Precocious; 2. A precocious child.
Ou'ma.	Ou'ma.	Grandmother.
Ou'pa.	Ou'pa.	Grandfather.
Ou'tata.	Ou'tata (Sanskrit) [Boheemsch tata = oude vader].	Name for an old coloured man.
Ou'tijs.	1. Ou'tijs (oudtijds); 2. Ou'tijse mensch.	1. Ontwikkeld boven leeftijd; 2. Een voordeelig ontwikkeld kindje. Grootmoeder. Grootvader. Benaming van een ouden bruinen man. 1. Ouderwetsch; 2. Oudmodische mensch.	1. Old-fashioned; 2. An old-fashioned person.
Paadje.	Paadje.	Scheiding in het haar.	Parting (in the hair).
Padda.	Padda.	Pad (vorsch).	Toad.
Palilie.	Hij palilie (onder de bruinen).	Hij loopt rechtop, trotsch, te pronken.	He holds himself straight, is proud.
Pappelellekoorts.	Papelellekoorts hebben.	Zeurig (somtijds ingebeeld ziek) zijn.	To have imaginary ailments.
Parrak.	Parrak.	Kikvorsch.	Frog.
Pasganger.	Pasganger.	Paard, dat een gemakkelijken trippelgang heeft.	A horse that has a nimble walk.
Patat.	1. Patat (Spaansch batata); 2. Hij het van-dang patats in die kis'.	1. Yam; 2. Hij heeft nieuwe schoenen aan.	1. Sweet-potato; 2. He is wearing new boots.
Pen.	1. Pen; 2. Hij hou' zijn lijf pen.	1. Pen; 2. Hij loopt zoo recht als een kaars.	1. Pen; 2. He holds himself erect.
Pepen.	1. Peper; 2. Mijn peper is zoo goed als jou saffraan.	1. Peper; 2. Ik ben even goed als jij.	1. Pepper; 2. I am as good as you.

List of Idioms—continued.

Words in Alphabetic Order.	Cape Idioms.	Dutch for the Idioms.	English for the Idioms.
Peperkorrel.	1. Peperkorrol; 2. Peperkorrelkop.	2. *Hoofd van een Bosjesman* (*wegens de eigenaardige alleenstaande pruikjes haar*).	1. Pepper-corn; 2. Head of a Bushman (on account of the peculiar hair-stubbles with which his head is covered).
Perd.	1. Perd; 2. Hij is gauw op zijn perdje.	1. *Paard*; 2. *Hij is gauw kwaad.*	1. Horse; 2. He rides a high horse (is easily offended).
Perske.	Perske (meervoud perskes).	*Perzik* (*perziken*).	Peach (peaches).
Pienangvleesch.	Pienangvleesch.	*Kerrievleesch.*	Curried meat.
Poort.	Poort.	*Nauwe doortocht in eene bergketen.*	Narrow pass between (not over) mountains.
Priëel.	Priëel.	*Ongeleide wijngaardstok.*	A vine-trellis.
Pronken.	Pronken, (gebruikt van wilde bokken).	*Zich statig en bevallig bewegen.*	To move majestically and gracefully (said of wild goats).
Raai.	Raai!	*Denk eens aan!*	Only think!
Reg'.	1. Reg' (recht); 2. Reg' maak'.	1. *Recht*; 2. *Eene rekening vereffenen;* (*ook mores leeren*).	1. Right, straight; 2. To settle an account; (also to take anyone to task).
Renosterbos.	Renosterbos.	*Rhenocerosstruik.*	Rhinoceros-shrub.
Rinkals.	Rinkals (ringhals).	*Zwarte slang met witten ring om den hals.*	Black snake with a white collar round the neck.

LIST OF CAPE IDIOMS.

Rissies.	Spaansche peper.	Cayenne pepper.
Roepen.	1. Roepen; 2. Hoe noemt men dat?	1. To call; 2. How do you call that?
1. Roepen; 2. Hoe roep je dat? (Anglicisme).		
Ronddawel.	Rondgebouwd huis met puntvormig stroodak, naast het woonhuis (dienende als keuken).	Circular building with a pointed thatched roof, next to a farmer's dwelling-house (used as kitchen).
Roosterkoek (ook Aschkoek en Oliekoek).	Slaperige jongen.	Drowsy fellow.
Rijs.	1. Tak of stok; 2. Ik zal hem een pak geven.	1. Twig or stick; 2. I shall give him a thrashing.
1. Rijs; 2. Ik zal ver hom rijs*.		
Saam.	1. Te zamen; 2. Wat zanik je aan mijne ooren; 3. Hij eet met zijne hand.	1. Together; 2. Don't stand there chattering; 3. He eats with his hands.
1. Saam; 2. Wat lol' jij met mij saam; 3. Ilij eet met zijn hand saam.		
Saffraan.	Saffraan (zie Peper).	Saffron (see Pepper).
Sambal.	Mengsel van fijngehakte komkommers, kweeperen, Spaansche peper enz. (dienende tot specerij).	Mixture of finely chopped cucumbers, quinces, Cayenne-pepper, etc. (used as a pickle).
Sambalbroek.	Korte broek over de knie vast.	Knickerbockers.
Sambok.	Zweep aan één stuk uit een rhenoceroshuid gesneden.	Whip in one piece cut out of a Rhinoceros-hide.
Saroet.	Saroet (van het Eng. cheroot).	Cigar.
Sausati.	Gekruide stukjes vleesch aan ijzeren pinnen geroosterd.	Spiced bits of meat, roasted on small iron spits.
Sausati; (Javaansch gerecht).		

LIST OF IDIOMS—continued.

Words in Alphabetic Order.	Cape Idioms.	Dutch for the Idioms.	English for the Idioms.
Schaam.	1. Schaam; 2. Ik is schaam ver hom; 3. Schaam vang jou!	1. Beschaamd; 2. Ik ben beschaamd voor hem; 3. Schaam je wat! (als iemand bij 't werken achterblijft).	1. Ashamed; 2. I am ashamed to meet him; 3. Shame upon you!
Schaapsteker. Schateren.	Schaapsteker. 1. Schateren; 2. Ik schater ver jou.	Giftige slang. 1. Uitschateren; 2. Ik lach je uit.	Venomous serpent. 1. To burst out laughing; 2. I shall laugh at you.
Scheppen.	1. Scheppen; 2. Hij is een flukse vent, jammer hij schep zoo baign.	1. Scheppen; 2. Hij is een goede kerel, 't is maar jammer, dat hij zoo drinkt.	1. To dip up; 2. He is a good fellow, 't is a pity that he drinks too much.
Scherm.	Scherm.	Afdak of strooien hutje, bij eene tent geplaatst (dienstdoende als keuken).	A shed or straw hut next to a tent (serving as a kitchen).
Schoenlapper.	1. Schoenlapper; 2. Jij praat net of een in je mond zit schoen' te lap'.	1. Schoenmaker en vlinder; 2. Je spreekt onduidelijk.	1. Cobbler and butterfly; 2. You speak indistinctly.
Schoonmaken.	1. Schoonmaken; 2. Maak schoon!	2. Uit elkaar! (tegen twee vechtenden).	To clear, clean; 2. Hold off! (said to part two people fighting).
Schoor.	Hij zoek' schoor.	Hij zoekt twist.	He is looking for an occasion to quarrel.
Schoot.	1. Schoot; 2. Kom hier zoo'n schoot.	1. Maal; 2. Kom even hier.	Time, turn; 2. Just come here a moment.

LIST OF CAPE IDIOMS.

Schraapblok.	Schraapblok.	A flat-bottomed instrument drawn by oxen, used for cleaning the kraals.
Sies!	Sies!	Fy! bah!
Sif.	1. Sif; 2. Die perd sif.	1. To sieve; 2. That horse has an easy rocking step.
Slap.	1. Slap; 2. Kerels, moet toch niet laat slap kom nie (uitdrukking ontleend aan den ossenwagen).	1. Slack; 2. Fellows, don't slacken the rope (used as an encouragement to keep up the spirit of a game).
Smous.	Smous; (zie Tochtganger).	Itinerant merchant, Jew or Christian, but always a buitenlander.
Snaaks.	1. Snaaks; 2. 't Is een snaakse patroon.	1. Grappig, niet alledaagsch; 2. 't Is een wonderlijke kerel.
Soetriet.	Soetriet.	Suikerriet. Sugar-cane.
Sop.	1. Sop; 2. Sopemmer.	1. Soep; 2. Een te groote hoed. 1. Soup; 2. A hat that is too large.
Spaansch spek.	Spaansch spekken (meervoud).	Meloen. Sugar-melon.
Spek.	1. Spek; 2. Hij kan goed spek schiet.	1. Spek; 2. Hij kan knap liegen. 1. Bacon; 2. He is a famous liar.
Spochter.	Spochter.	Pocher. Boaster.
Spoor.	1. Spoor; 2. Pas op trap in jou spoor, (uitdrukking ontleend aan den ossenwagen).	1. Spoor; 2. Gedraag u fatsoenlijk. 1. Track; 2. Behave properly.

LIST OF IDIOMS—continued.

Words in Alphabetic Order.	Cape Idioms.	Dutch for the Idioms.	English for the Idioms.
Spul.	1. Spul; 2. moe' nie' spulletjes maak nie'.	1. Spel; 2. Gekscheer niet (spreek in ernst).	1. Game, play; 2. Don't talk nonsense (talk seriously).
Stap.	1. Sap; 2. Hij het laat' stap'.	1. Stappen; 2. Hij is gestorven.	1. To step; 2. He has died.
Stadig.	Stadig.	Langzaam.	Slowly.
Statie.	Statie.	Spoorwegstation.	Railway-station.
Steeks.	1. Steeks; 2. Hij is steeks.	1. Eigenschap van zich niet te willen verroeren (bij paarden); 2. Hij is zoo dronken, dat hij niet voort kan.	1. Stubborn, jibbing (said of horses that won't move); 2. He is as drunk as a door-post.
Stenga.	Stenga.	Onder elkaar (met elkander smoezen).	Having a private confab.
Stert.	1. Stort; 2. Zijn stert val' af.	1. Staart; 2. Hij is erg kwaad.	1. Tail; 2. He is mad with rage.
	(De overlevering wil, dat een zeker hagelisje (het geitje) zich zoo kwaad kan maken, dat zijn staart afvalt.)		
Slokkies.	Stokkies draai'?	Stukjes draaien (uit de school wegblijven).	To stay away from school.
Stootwagen.	Stootwagen.	Duwwagen.	Perambulator.
Struis.	Struis.	Strooien huis (contractie) [pondok]. Kaffer	Straw hut, Kafir-hut.
Suikerbos.	Suikerbos.	Struikgewas met lichtroode, kelkvormige bloemen, die een zoet vocht bevatten, waarvan stroop gekookt wordt.	Sugar-bush.

Tamaai.	Tamaai.	Zeer groot. Large.
Tamboer.	Tamboer.	Trommel. Drum.
Tandentrekker.	1. Tandentrekker; 2. Hijlieg' als een tandentrekker.	1. Dentist; 2. He lies like anything. 2. Hij liegt alsof het gedrukt staat.
Tannie.	Tannie.	Tante. Auntie.
Thee.	1. Thee; 2. Die thee trek' in hom.	1. Tea; 2. The wine is going to his head. 2. De wijn begint te werken in hem.
Tjurang.	Tjurang.	Valsch spelen. To play false.
Tochtganger.	Tochtganger (zie Smous).	Geboren Afrikaander, die in het bovenland allerlei artikelen opkoopt en ze in de binnenlanden uitvent. Africander, who buys up all sorts of articles in the neighbourhood of Cape-Town and sells them inland.
Toe.	1. Toe; 2. Ga zoo'n toe; 3. Ik ga Kaap toe.	1. Toe (gebruikt als eenig voorzetsel ter aanduiding van de richting); 2. Ga dien kant uit (ook — schrijf wat op); 3. Ik ga naar Kaapstad. 1. Towards; 2. Go up that way; 3. I am going to Cape-Town.
Touw.	1. Touw; 2. Nee jonk, jij kan maar gerust touw wergooi; 3. Hij het o'er die touw getrap (beide uitdrukkingen ontleend aan den ossenwagen).	1. Touw; 2. Doe geene moeite meer, dat meisje wil u niet hebben; 3. Hij heeft zich misdragen. 1. Rope; 2. Don't trouble yourself any more, the girl won't have you; 3. He has misbehaved.
Trappen.	1. Trappen; 2. Hij het goed vastgetrap.	1. Trappen; 2. Hij is zwaar ziek geweest. 1. To stamp; 2. He has been dangerously ill.
Tree.	1. Tree; 2. Hij tree' af.	1. Treden, stappen; 2. Hij neemt grooter passen dan zijn metgezel. 1. To step, walk; 2. He takes longer steps than his companion.

List of Idioms—continued.

Words in Alphabetic Order.	Cape Idioms.	Dutch for the Idioms.	English for the Idioms.
Trek.	1. Trek; 2. Jij kan maar trek'.	1. Vertrekken; 2. Ga maar heen.	1. To depart; 2. You are at liberty to go.
Tronk.	Tronk.	Gevangenis.	Prison.
Tros.	1. Tros; 2. Trossieskop.	1. Tros; 2. Krullekop.	1. Bunch; 2. Curly head.
Tsa.	1. Tsa; 2. Hij is een tsa-maker.	1. Tsa (tot aanhitsing van honden); 2. Hij is een kwaadstoker.	1. Tsa (for setting on dogs); 2. He is a mischief-maker.
Twak.	Twak.	Tabak.	Tobacco.
Uilespie'l.	1. Uilespie'l (spiegel); 2. Hij is een uilespie'l; 3. Uilespie'l in die maneschijn.	2. Hij maakt een zot figuur; 3. Iemand met eene paraplu bij helder weer.	2. He makes a ridiculous figure; 3. Someone who goes out with an umbrella in fair weather.
Uitgegroeid.	Uitgegroeid.	Volwassen.	Full-grown.
Uitklop'.	Uitkloppen.	Een pak geven.	To give a beating.
Uitkochel'.	1. Uitkochelen; 2. Hij het ver mij uitgekochel; 3. Een kocher.	1. Bespotten; 2. Hij heeft mij nageaapt; 3. Een plauyyeest.	1. To ape; 2. He has aped me; 3. A tease.
Uitplak'.	1. Uitplakken; 2. Plakpampier.	1. Behangen; 2. Behangselpapier.	1. To paper (a room); 2. Wall-paper.
Vaalpensen. Vaconta.	Vaalpensen. Vaconta (see Kasta).	Transvalers.	Transvaal-people.

LIST OF CAPE IDIOMS.

Vark.	1. Vark; 2. Hij kan niet vark vang'.	1. Pig ; 2. He is bow-leegged.
Varkblom.	Varkblom.	Arum-lily.
Vat.	1. Vat' (vatten); 2. Vat jon hoed; 3. Hij zeg' ik het an hom gevat; 4. Laat vat.	1. To take hold of; 2. Take your hat; 3. He says I laid hands on him; 4. Get off.
Veldschoen.	Veldschoen.	A rough kind of shoe of brown leather, mostly home-made; also a plant with two large leathery leaves (lying close on the ground) and a soft underground stalk.
	1. Varken; 2. Zijne beenen zijn krom. Aronskelk. 1. Nemen of aanraken; 2. Neem uwen hoed; 3. Hij zegt, dat ik hem aan 't lijf geraakt heb; 4. Vertrek. Ruwe soort schoen van bruin leder, meestal eigengemaakt; ook plant met twee groote lederachtige bladeren (die dicht op den grond liggen) en een weeken stengel onder den grond.	
Vorlieste.	Verlieste en verlorens.	Manifold losses.
Verkleurmannetje.	(See Jantje-trap-zuutjes).	
Verspot.	1. Verspot; 2. Jij is verspot; 3. Zoo'n verspotte kind; 4. Hij raak verspot bij die baas.	1. Ridiculous; 2. You make yourself a laughing-stock; 3. Such a foolish child; 4. He makes himself ridiculous before his master.
	Menigvuldige verliezen.	
	1. Belachelijk; 2. Gij zijt belachelijk; 3. Zulk een dwaas kind; 4. Hij maakt zich belachelijk bij zijnen meester.	
Verzondig.	1. Verzondig; 2. Die klonk verzondig mij al te danig.	1. To give offence; 2. That little boy causes me much annoyance.
	1. Laten zondigen, ergernis geven; 2. Die kleine jongen geeft mij heel wat ergernis.	
Vieselijk.	1. Vieselijk; 2. Een vieselijke ding.	1. Disgusting; 2. A disgusting thing.
	1. Afstootelijk; 2. Een afstootelijk iets.	

LIST OF IDIOMS—continued.

Words in Alphabetic Order.	Cape Idioms.	Dutch for the Idioms.	English for the Idioms.
Vinnig.	1. Vinnig; 2. Hardloop vinnig mijn kind.	1. *Vlug*; 2. *Loop hard, mijn kind.*	1. Quick; 2. Run fast, my child.
Visch.	1. Visch; 2. Hij vang visch.	1. *Visch*; 2. *Gezegd van iemand, die in de kerk zit te slapen.*	1. Fish; 2. Said of anyone who falls asleep in church.
Vischblikkies.	Voor: blikjes visch.		Tinned fish.
Vlieg.	1. Vlieg; 2. Een vlieg wat in de karnomelk gevallen is.	1. *Vlieg*; 2. *Een wit aangekleede Kaffer.*	1. Fly; 2. A Kafir who is dressed up.
Vliegen.	Hij vang vliegen.	*Gezegd van iemand, die altijd met open mond loopt.*	He is a patent fly-catcher (has his mouth open).
Vo'olstruis.	Vo'olstruis.	*Struisvogel.*	Ostrich.
Vrek'.	Vrekken (van dieren).	*Sterven.*	To die (of animals).
Vuurhoutjes.	Vuurhoutjes.	*Lucifers.*	Matches.
Vuur.	1. Vuur; 2. Die ding was al lank in die vuur al.	2. *Ik heb het al lang in 't neusje gehad.*	1. Fire; 2. I have had wind of it for a long time.
Vijftien.	Vijftien dagen (van 't l'ransch).	*Veertien dagen.*	A fortnight.
Wa'.	1. Wa'; 2. Zijn wa' is gesmeer.	1. *Wagen*; 2. *Hij heeft een klap gehad.*	1. Wagon; 2. He has had a slap.
Waai.	Laat waai'!	*Pak je weg!*	Be off!
Wals..	1. Wals; 2. Hij wals'.	1. *Walsen*; 2. *Hij slingert over den weg.*	1. To waltz; 2. He staggers.

LIST OF CAPE IDIOMS. 383

Warm.	1. Warm; 2. Ik zal ver jou warm maak.	1. Warm; 2. I'll give you a beating.
Watlemoen.	Watlemoen (Waterlemoen).	Water-melon.
Wat.	Al is 't nou wat!	Let it be what it may.
Wa'wielooren.	(Wagenwielooren).	Ears that stand out.
Wereld.	1. Wereld; 2. Die wereld draai'.	1. World (also used for district); 2. He is giddy (said of a drunken person).
Wind.	1. Hij 's deur die wind; 2. Hij schep wind.	1. Hij is half gek; 2. Hij loopt zijn schoen scheef.
		1. He is half a fool; 2. He wears his shoes on one side.
Woltoonen.	Woltoonen.	Kolonisten.	Colonists.
Wijs.	Wijs.	Bij de hand.	Forward.
IJs'lijk.	1. Een ijs'lijke ding; 2. Een ijslijke stuk koek.	1. Een bijzonder groot ding, stuk koek.	A very large thing, piece of cake.
Zens.	1. Zens; 2. Hij werk met die zens, (hij maai').	1. Zeis; 2. Hij liegt.	1. Scythe; 2. He tells stories.
Zouten.	1. Zouten; 2. Die perd is al gezout.	2. Dat paard heeft de paardenziekte reeds gehad.	1. To salt; 2. That horse has had horse-sickness.

VOCABULARY. WOORDENLIJST.

Note.—The letters affixed to the nouns indicate their genders; m = (*mannelijk*) masculine, v = (*vrouwelijk*) feminine, o = (*onzijdig*) neuter, gsl = (*gemeenslachtig*) common gender.
The letters S and W, affixed to verbs when their principal parts are not given, stand for *strong* and *weak*.

A.

Able, *in staat, knap.*
Able (to be), *in staat zijn.*
Ability, *bekwaamheid, v.*
About, *van; omtrent, rond* (place).
Absent, *afwezig.*
Accede to (to), *toestaan, stond toe, toegestaan.*
Accept (to), *aannemen,* S.
Accident, *ongeluk, o.*
Accidentally, *bij ongeluk.*
Accompany (to), *vergezellen,* W.
Accusation, *beschuldiging, v.*
Accustomed, *gewoon.*
Accustomed (to get —), *gewoon worden.*
Acknowledge (to), *erkennen,* W.
Acknowledgment, *bewijs, o,*
Account (on — of), *wegens.*
Acquainted (to become—), *kennis maken.*
Acquire (to), *verkrijgen,* S.
Act (to), *handelen, handelde, gehandeld.*
Act, *daad, v.*
Activity, *werkzaamheid, v.*
Add (to), *bijvoegen,* W.
Admired, *bewonderd.*
Advise (to), *aanraden, raadde* (ried) *aan, aangeraden; raden.*
Afford (to), *verschaffen,* W.
Afraid, *bang, bevreesd.*
After, *na.*
Afternoon, *namiddag, m;* this —, *van middag.*
Afterwards, *daarna.*
Again, *weer.*
Against, *tegen.*
Age, *eeuw, v.*
Age (at the — of), *in den ouderdom van.*
Ago, *geleden.*
Agreement, *verstandhouding, v;* to make an —, *een verdrag sluiten.*
Alive, *levend.*
All, *al.*
Allow (to), *toestaan,* S.
Ally, *bondgenoot, gsl.*
Almond-tree, *amandelboom, m.*
Almost, *bijna.*

Alphabet, *alphabet, o.*
Already, *reeds,*
Also, *ook.*
Always, *altijd.*
Amazement, *verbazing, v.*
Ambiguity, *dubbelzinnigheid, v.*
Among, *onder.*
Amount, *mate, v.*
Amuse (to), *vermaken,* W.
Animal, *dier, o.*
Annoy (to), *hinderen,* W.
Annoyance, *verveling, v.*
Another, *een ander.*
Anxious, *angstig; verlangend.*
Any, *eenige, ook* (interrogative).
Anywhere, *ergens.*
Apologise (to), *excuus vragen.*
Apparent, *in het oog loopend.*
Appear, *verschijnen, verscheen, verschenen.*
Applicant, *applicant, m.*
Apply for (to), *aanzoek doen om.*
Apply (to — oneself), *zich aanpakken, toeleggen op.*
Appointment, *afspraak, v.*
Appreciated, *geschat.*
Approach, *naderen, o.*
Arrange (to — for), *toebereidselen maken voor.*
Arrangement, *schikking, v.*
Arrive (to), *aankomen,* S.; arrival, *aankomst, v.*
As, *daar.*
As . . . . as, *zoo . . . . als.*
Ascertain (to), *te weten komen.*
Ashamed (to be —), *zich schamen, schaamde, geschaamd.*
Asia, *Azië.*
Ask (to), *vragen,* vraagde (vroeg), *gevraagd.*
Asleep, *in slaap.*
Assembled, *vergaderd, bijeen.*
Assign (to), *overmaken,* W,
At, *te, om* (time).
Athens, *Athene, o,*

VOCABULARY. 385

Attack (to), *aanvallen*, S.
Attempted, *beproefden, probeerden.*
Attend (to — to), *zorgen voor*, W.
Attention, *aandacht, v.*
Attorney, *procureur, m.*
Appreciated, *geschat.*

BACK-ROOM, *achterkamer, v.*
Bad, *slecht.*
Bag, *zak, m.*
Bake (to), *bakken, bakte, gebakken.*
Balloon, *ballon, m.*
Bark (to), *blaffen, blafte, geblaft.*
Barrister, *advokaat, m.*
Battle, *slag, m.;* — field, *slagveld, o.*
Beach, *strand, o.*
Bear (to), *uithouden,* S., *verdragen,* S., *dragen,* (expense).
Beard, *baard, m.*
Bearer, *brenger dezes.*
Beautiful, *mooi.*
Because, *omdat.*
Become (has), *is geworden;* to — of, *worden van.*
Bed, *bed, o.*
Bed-room, *slaapkamer, v.*
Befall (to), *iemands deel worden, wedervaren,* S.
Before, *tevoren.*
Behalf (on my —), *van mijnentwege.*
Behind, *achter.*
Believe (to), *gelooven, geloofde, geloofd.*
Beloved, *bemind.*
Bequeath (to), *vermaken,* W
Berlin, *Berlijn, o.*
Bet (to), *wedden, wedde, gewed.*
Beware (to — of), *oppassen voor, passe op, opgepast.*
Beyond, *verder dan.*
Betting (there was...), *er werd gewed.*
Bill, *rekening, v.*
Bird, *vogel, m.*
Bit, *stuk, o.*
Blacksmith, *smid, m.*
Blessing, *zegen, m.*
Bliss, *zaligheid, v.*

Aunt, *tante, v.*
Austria, *Oostenrijk, o.*
Awake, *wakker.*
Aware (to be —), *overtuigd zijn van;* to be — of, *zich bewust zijn van, kennen.*
Awkward, *lastig.*

B.

Blossom (to), *bloeien,* W.
Blowing, (to be —), *waaien.*
Boarding-school, *kostschool, v.*
Boast, to, *grootspreken,* S.
Boldness, *brutaliteit, v.*
Bond, *band, m.*
Book, *boek, o.*
Boot, *laars, v.; schoen, m.*
Border, *rand, m.; grens, m*
Both, *beiden.*
Bottle, *flesch, v.*
Box, *doos, v.; kist, v.*
Boy, *jongen, m.*
Branch, *tak, m.;* — of instruction, *vak (o), van onderwijs.*
Breach of the peace, *vredebreuk, v.*
Bread, *brood, o.*
Breakfast, *ontbijt, o.*
Breathe (to), *ademen,* W.; — one's last, *den laatsten adem uitblazen,* S.
Breeze, *bries, m.*
Bribe (to), *omkoopen,* S.
Bride, *bruid, v.*
Bridge, *brug, v.*
Brighten (to — up), *zich verhelderen,* W.
Brightly, *helder.*
Brook, *beek, v.*
Brother, *broeder, m.*
Brown, *bruin.*
Brushwood, *kreupelhout, o.*
Bucket, *emmer, m.*
Build (to), *bouwen,* W.
Bundle of sticks, *takkebos, m.*
Burgher, *burger, m.*
Butcher, *slager, m.*
Bury (to), *begraven, begroef, begraven.*
By-and-by, *aanstonds.*
Bicycle, *tweewieler, m.*

C.

CAGE, *kooi, v.*
Cake, *koek, m.*
Call (to), *roepen, riep, geroepen;* aankomen; — upon, *opzoeken, eene visite maken;* — at, *aankomen bij iemand.*
Call (to wake), *oproepen, riep op, opgeroepen.*
Calm (noun), *kalmte, v.*
Calmness, *kalmte, v.*
Camel, *kameel, m.*
Camp, *kamp, o.*
Capable (to be — of), *in staat zijn tot.*
Cape-Town, *Kaapstad.*
Capital, *hoofdstad, v.*
Captain, *kapitein, m.*
Care, (to — for), *lust hebben in;* to take —of, *passen op.*

Careful (ly), *voorzichtig, zorgvuldig.*
Carelessness, *achteloosheid, v.*
Carpet, *tapijt, o.*
Cart, *kar, v.*
Case, *zaak, v.*
Castle, *kasteel, o.*
Cat, *kat, v.*
Catch (to), *vangen,* S.; — up, *opvangen,* W.; — cold, *kou vatten.*
Cautious(ly), *voorzichtig.*
Cave, *hol, o.*
Celebrated, *beroemd.*
Cell, *cel, v.*
Certain, *zeker;* — ly, *zeer zeker, stellig.*
Chair, *stoel, m.*
Chance, *kans, m.;* by —, *bij toeval, toevallig.*

O

Chanced to be, *zich toevallig bevond.*
Character, *karakter, o.*
Charge, *zorg, v.*
Charge (to), *als plicht opleggen,* W.
Chariot, *wagen, m.*
Charles, *Karel, m.*
Chat, *praatje, o; to have a —, een—maken.*
Chasm, *afgrond, m.*
Cheap, *goedkoop.*
Cheese, *kaas, v.*
Child, *kind, o.*
Chinese, *Chineezen.*
Chop (to), *kappen, kapte, gekapt; — down, omhakken.*
Church, *kerk, v.*
Circumstances, *omstandigheden, v.*
Citizen, *burger, m.*
City, *stad, v.*
Civil, *civiel.*
Clean (to), *schoon maken.*
Clear, *helder, klaar.*
Clear (to — up), *opruimen.*
Clerk, *klerk, m.*
Clip (to — wings), *kortwieken, kortwiekte, gekortwickt.*
Cloak, *mantel, m.*
Clock, *klok, v.*
Close (to), *sluiten,* S.
Close by, *dicht bij.*
Cloth, *laken, o.*
Clothes, *kleederen, o.*
Coal, *steenkolen, v.*
Coat, *jas, v.*
Coffee, *koffie, v.*
Cold (bid —), *zware koude, v.*
Collar, *kraag, v.*
Colleague, *collega, m.*
Collection, *verzameling, v.*
College, *academie; — friend, academievriend.*
Colonial, *Koloniaal.*
Combined, *vereenigd.*
Come (to — in), *binnenkomen, kwam binnen, binnen-gekomen.*
Command (to), *bevelen,* S.
Common, *gemeen, gewoon; —sense, gezond verstand, o.*
Communication, *samenspreking, v.*
Companion, *kameraad, m, metgezel, m.*
Company, *maatschappij, v.; gezelschap, o.*
Comparison (in — to), *in vergelijking met.*
Compass, *kompas, o.*

Concert, *concert, o.*
Condemn (to), *veroordeelen.* W.
Conducive to, *bevorderlijk voor, goed voor.*
Confess (to), *bekennen,* W.
Confined to, *opgesloten in.*
Compel (to), *dwingen, dwong, gedwongen.*
Complain (to — of), *klagen over,* W.
Comprehension, *begrip, o.*
Conscientious, *nauwgezet.*
Consider (to), *overwegen,* S., *denken,* S., *beschouwen,* W., *houden voor,* S., *bedenken,* S., *overleggen,* W.; — *necessary, noodig oordeelen,* W.
Considerably, *aanmerkelijk.*
Consult (to), *raadplegen, raadpleegde, geraadpleegd.*
Consumption, *verbruik, o.*
Contented, *tevreden.*
Contents, *inhoud, m.*
Continually, *voortdurend.*
Continue (to — to be), *blijven,* S.
Conversation, *gesprek, o.*
Convey (to), *brengen,* S.
Conviction, *overtuiging, v.*
Convinced, *overtuigd.*
Corner, *hoek, m.*
Correct, *juist.*
Corrupt (to), *bederven,* S.
Council, *raad, m.*
Counsellor, *raadsman, m.*
Country, *land, o.*
Couple (a — of), *een paar.*
Courage, *moed, m.*
Courageous (ly), *moedig.*
Course, *loop, m.*
Course (of —), *natuurlijk.*
Cow, *koe, v.*
Creature (little —), *schepseltje, o.*
Criminal, *misdadiger, m.*
Cross (to), *oversteken, stak over, over gestoken.*
Crow, *kraai, v.*
Cruel, *wreed.*
Cry (to), *roepen, riep, geroepen.*
Cunning, *loos.*
Cup, *kop,* m., *kopje, o.*
Cure (to), *genezen, genas, genezen.*
Curios, *merkwaardigheden, v.*
Curtain, *gordijn, o.*
Customs, *gewoonten, v.*

D.

Dainties, *lekkernijen, v.*
Dance (to), *dansen, danste, gedanst.*
Danger, *gevaar, o.*
Dangerous to, *gevaarlijk voor.*
Dare (to), *durven,* W.
Dark, *donker* (noun), *o.*
Date (to), *dateeren, dateerde, gedateerd.*
Dawn (to), *aanbreken, brak aan, aangebroken.*
Day, *dag, m.*
Dead, *dood.*
Deal (a good — of), *heel wat.*

Dear, *dierbaar.*
Death, *dood, m.*
Deceive (to), *bedriegen,* S.
Decide (to), *beslissen, besliste, beslist.*
Decidedly, *beslist.*
Decisive, *afdoend.*
Decline (to), *weigeren,* W.
Deed, *daad, v.*
Deep, *diep.*
Defence, *verdedigingsrede, v.*
Defend (to), *verdedigen,* W.
Delighted, *verrukt.*

VOCABULARY. 387

Delightful, *verrukkelijk.*
Depart (to), *heengaan,* S., *vertrekken,* S.
Depth, *diepte, v.*
Departure, *vertrek, o.*
Descendant, *afstammeling, gsl.*
Desert region, *woestijn streken.*
Deserted, *verlaten.*
Desire, *begeerte, v.*
Desirous, *verlangend.*
Desk, *lessenaar, m.*
Despair (to — of), *wanhopen aan,* W.
Despise (to), *verachten,* W.
Destroy (to), *vernietigen,* W., *verwoesten,* W.
Development, *ontwikkeling, v.*
Devote (to — oneself), *zich toewijden aan,* W.
Diamond, *diamand, m.*
Dictation, *dictaat, o.*
Dictionary, *woordenboek, o.*
Differ (to), *verschillen.*
Difference, *onderscheid, o.*
Different, *anders, verschillend.*
Difficult, *moeielijk ; —y, moeite, v.*
Dig (to — up), *opgraven, groef op, opgegraven.*
Diligent, *vlijtig.*
Dim, *dof.*
Dinner, *middagmaal, o., diner, o.*
Dining-room, *eetkamer, v.*
Dirty, *vuil.*
Disagreeable, *onaangenaam.*
Disappointed, *teleurgesteld.*
Discharge (to), *ontslaan, ontsloeg. ontslagen.*
Discover (to), *ontdekken, ontdekte, ontdekt.*
Discuss (to), *verhandelen, verhandelde, verhandeld.*
Disgrace (to bring — to), *schande brengen over.*
Disheartening, *ontmoedigend.*
Dismiss (to), *wegsturen, ontslaan.*
Dismount (to), *van een paard stijgen.*
Disobey (to), *ongehoorzaam zijn aan.*
Disperse (to), *overwaaien, uiteengaan.*

Disrespectfully, *oneerbiedig.*
Distance, *afstand, m.*
Distinction, *onderscheiding, v.*
Distress, *nood, m.*
Distressed, *beangstigd.*
Distribution of justice, *rechtsbedeeling, v.*
District, *distrikt, o.*
Dive (to), *duiken,* S.
Divide (to), *verdeelen, verdeelde, verdeeld.*
Doctor, *dokter, m.*
Doctrine, *leerstelling, v.*
Document, *stuk, o.*
Dog, *hond, m.*
Doll, *pop, v.*
Dominion, *gebied, o.*
Done, *op.*
Donkey, *ezel, m.*
Doom, *doem, m.*
Door, *deur, v.*
Doubt (to), *betwijfelen.*
Dove, *duif, v.*
Down, *dons, o.*
Drag (to), *slepen,* W.
Draught, *drank, m.*
Draw (to), *trekken,* S. ; — near, *naderen,* W.
Drawing, *teekening, v.*
Dress, *japon, v.*
Dress (to — oneself), *zich aankleeden, kleedde zich aan, aangekleed.*
Drift (to — about), *ronddrijven, dreef rond, rondgedreven.*
Drill, *boor, v.*
Drink (to), *drinken, dronk, gedronken.*
Drive (to), *rijden, reed, gereden.*
Driver, *koetsier, m.*
Drop (to), *laten, vallen,* S. ; — asleep, *in slaap vallen; —* down, *neervallen.*
Due west, *vlak west.*
Due (time), *bepaald.*
Duke, *hertog, m.*
Duly, *naar waarde.*
During, *gedurende.*
Dutiful, *oppassend.*
Duty, *plicht, m.*
Dwelling-house *woonhuis, o.*

E.

EARLY MORNING, *den vroegen morgen, 's morgens vroeg; —* this —, *van morgen vroeg.*
Earn (to), *verdienen.*
Earth, *aarde, v.*
Eastern, *oostelijk.*
Eat (to), *eten,* S.
Edge, *rand, m.*
Edition, *uitgave, v.*
Effort, *poging, v.*
Elaborate, *zorgvuldig bewerkt.*
Eldest, *oudste.*
Elephant, *olifant, m.*
Elsewhere, *ergens anders.*
Embitter (to), *verbitteren,* W.
Embrace (to), *omhelzen, omhelsde, omhelsd.*
Emotion, *aandoening, v.*
Employer, *baas, m.*

Empire, *rijk, o.*
End, *eind .*
Enemy, *vijand, m.*
Enjoy (to), *genieten van,* S.
English, *Engelsch.*
Enter (to), *binnenkomen,* S.
Entertainment, *voorstelling, v.*
Entirely, *volkomen.*
Entreat (to), *smeeken,* W.
Entrust (to), *toevertrouwen,* W.
Escape (to), *ontkomen,* S.
Especially, *voornamelijk.*
Equal, *gelijk; —ly, even.*
Equanimity, *gelijkmoedigheid, v.*
Esteemed, *geacht.*
Eternal, *eeuwig.*
Europe, *Europa.*
Even, *zelfs.*
Ever, *ooit.*

o 2

Events (at all —), in alle geval.
Everyone, iedereen.
Exactly, juist, precies.
Exaggerated, overdreven.
Examination, examen, o.
Exclaim (to), uitroepen, riep uit, uitgeroepen.
Execution, voltrekking (v) van het vonnis.
Exercise, oefening, v.
Exist, bestaan, bestond, bestaan.
Existence, bestaan, o.

Expect (to), verwachten, verwachtte, verwacht.
Expense, onkosten.
Expensive, duur.
Expert, deskundige, gsl.
Explain (to), verklaren, W.
Explanation, uitlegging, v., verklaring, v.
Explosion, ontploffing, v.
Exquisite, uitgezocht.
Extend (to), uitbreiden, W.

F.

FACE, gezicht, o.
Fact (in —), inderdaad.
Fail (to), niet slagen, W., druipen, S. (examination).
Failed in business, is bankroet gegaan.
Faint (to), in zwijm (flauw) vallen, S.
Faithful, trouw.
Fall (to), (of prices), dalen, W.
Family, familie, v.
Falsehood, leugen, v.
Fancy (to), zich voorstellen, W.
Farmer, boer, m.
Far-off, verafgelegen.
Fat, vet.
Fatal, noodlottig, doodelijk.
Fate, lot, o.
Fatigue, moeheid, v.
Faultless, zonder fouten.
Fear, vrees; —ful, vreeselijk.
Fear (to), vreezen, W.
Feathery coat, veeren kleed.
Feeble, zwak.
Feel sure (to), ervan overtuigd zijn.
Fellow-citizen, medeburger, m; — man, medemensch, m.
Fertile, vruchtbaar.
Fetter (to), boeien, W.
Fever, koorts, v.
Field, veld, o.
Fierce (of dogs), kwaad.
Find (to), bevinden, S.
Find fault with (to), aanmerkingmaken op.
Find out (to), ontdekken, W., bevinden, S.. uitvinden, vond uit, uitgevonden.
Finished, af, klaar.
Fire, brand, m.
Firm, vastberaden.
First, het erst, eerst.
Fit, geschikt.
Five, vijf.
Flatter (to), vleien, W.,—(vanity) streelen.

Flee (to), vluchten, W.
Flight, vlucht, v.
Floor, vloer, m.
Flower, blo-m, v.
Fold, kraal, m.
Follower, volgeling, gsl.
Following, volgend.
Fond (to be — of), houden van.
For, voor; —asmuch, aangezien.
Forage, voeder, o.
Forbid (to), verhoeden, W.
Force, kracht, v.
Foreign, vreemd, uitlandsch.
Forget (to), vergeten, S.
Forgive (to), vergeven, vergaf, vergeven.
Former, oud;. in — times, in vroegere tijden.
Fortnight (a), een veertien dagen.
Forward, voorwaarts.
Fought, geleverd.
Found (to), oprichten, W.
Fountain, fontein, v.
Four, vier; —footed, viervoetig.
Fowler, vogelaar, m.
Fowls, hoenders.
Fox, vos, m.
France, Frankrijk.
Frankly, openhartig.
Frankness, vrijmoedigheid, v.
Free-State, Vrijstaat, m.
French, Fransch.
Fresh, frisch, versch.
Frighten (to), verschrikken, verschrikte, verschrikt.
Frightfully, verschrikkelijk.
Front-door, voordeur, v.
Frost-bitten, doodgerijpt.
Frozen over, bevroren.
Fruit, vruchten; — tree, vruchtboom, m.
Full subjection, algeheele onderworpenheid, v.

G.

GAIN LAURELS (to), lauweren behalen, W.
Galleys, galleien, v.
Game, spel, o.
Games (to play —), spelletjes doen.
Garden, tuin, m.
Gardener, tuinier, m.
General, algemeen.
Generation, geslacht, o.
Get (to), worden, S., krijgen, S.; — on, vooruit komen, kwam vooruit, vooruit gekomen; — into trouble, in moeielijkheid raken, W (conj. with zijn).

German, Duitsch.
Germany, Duitschland.
Give (to), geven, gaf, gegeven.
Girl, meisje, o.
Glimmer, schijnsel, o.
Glitter (to), glinsteren, W.
Globe, aardbol, m.
Glorious, roemrijk, luisterijk, verrukkelijk.
Glove, handschoen, m.
Go out (to), uitgaan, ging uit, uitgegaan; — with, medegaan met; — to war, ten

strijde uittrekken, S. ; — on repeating, *gedurig herhalen*, W.
Goes (by the name of), *men hem . . . noemt*.
Gone, *weg*.
Good, *goed*; the —, *welzijn, o.* ;—hearted, *goedhartig*; —looking, *knap*.
Gorge, *kloof, v.*
Government, *regeering, v.*
Gradually, *langzamerhand.*
Grand, *grootsch.*
Grandfather, *grootvader, m.*
Grant (to), *schenken, geven*, S., *toestaan* S.
Grasp (to), *grijpen, greep, gegrepen.*
Grass, *gras, o*, — border, *grasrand, m.*

Gratitude, *dankbaarheid, v.*
Grave, *ernstig.*
Greatest quantity possible, *grootst mogelijke hoeveelheid, v.*
Greece, *Griekenland, o*
Greek, *Grieksch.*
Green, *groen.*
Grey, *grijs.*
Grieve (to), *verdriet doen.*
Ground, *grond, m.*
Grown to manhood, *man geworden.*
Guard (of a train), *conducteur, m.*
Guess (to), *raden, raadde, geraden;* (to surmise) *gissen, giste, gegist.*
Guest, *gast, gst.*
Guide, *gids, gsl.*

H.

Hairy, *harig.*
Hall, *zaal, v.*
Hand (to), *overgeven, gaf over, overgegeven;* — back, *teruggeven;* — over, *overhandigen, overhandigde, overhandigd.*
Hand (at —), *bij de hand.*
Handsome, *mooi.*
Happen (to), *gebeuren*, W.
Happiness, *geluk, o.*
Happy, *gelukkig.*
Hardly, *bezwaarlijk.*
Hardship, *ontbering, v.*
Harness (to — to), *voorspannen*, W.
Harvest, *oogst, m.*
Hastily, *haastig.*
Hat, *hoed, m.*
Hatchet, *bijl, v.*
Hazardous, *gewaagd.*
Health, *gezondheid, v.*
Hear (to), *hooren, hoorde, gehoord.*
Heart, *hart, o.*
Heavy, *zwaar.*
Heed (to), *luisteren naar*, W.
Height, *hoogte, v.*
Hellas, *Hellas, o.*
Help, *hulp, v.*

Hereupon, *hierop.*
Hesitate (to), *aarzelen*, W.
Hewn, *gehouwen.*
Hex River Pass, *Hex Rivier pas, m.*
Hiding-place, *schuilplaats, v.*
Hill, *heuvel, m.*
Hind-leg, *achterpoot, m.*
Hoarse, *schor.*
Hole, *gat, o.*
Home, *huis, tehuis*; — (noun), *tehuis, o.*; at —, *t'huis.*
Honesty, *eerlijkheid, v.*
Horrible, *gruwelijk.*
Hospital, *hospitaal, o.*
Hour (an — and a half), *underhalf uur.*
House, *huis, o.*
How, *hoe.* However, *hee . . . ook.*
Human being, *mensch, m.*
Humility, *nederigheid. v.*
Hundred, *honderd.*
Hunger, *honger, m*
Hungry, *hongerig.*
Hurry (to), *zich haasten*, W.
Hurt (to), *bezeeren*, W.
Hut, *hut, v.*

I.

Idea, *idée, o., denkbeeld, o.*
Idle away (to), *verluiren*, W.
Ill, *ziek*; — (noun), *kwaad.*
Image, *beeld, o.*
Imitate (to), *navolgen*, W.
Impartial, *onpartijdig.*
Impatient (—ly), *ongeduldig.*
Important, *belangrijk.*
Imposing, *indrukwekkend.*
Improve (to), *ontwikkelen, ontwikkelde, ontwikkeld*; *verbeteren*. W.
Incessantly, *onophoudelijk.*
Inclination, *neiging, v.*
Indeed, *inderdaad.*
India, *Indië.*
Indignant, *verontwaardigd, gebelgd.*
Induce (to), *bewegen*, S.; *er toe brengen.*
Inferior (to be — to), *achterstaan bij*, S.
Inform (to), *mededeelen, deelde mede, medegedeeld.*

Inhabitant, *inwoner, m.*
Injury, *kwaad, o., beschadiging, v.*
Inkpot, *inktpot, m.*
Inn, *herberg, v.*
Inquire (to), *vragen*, W,
Inquiring (noun), *onderzoeken, o.*
Instance (for —), *bij voorbeeld.*
Instead of, *in plaats van.*
Instruct (to), *bevelen*, S.
Instructed, *opgedragen.*
Instructive, *leerzaam.*
Instrument, *instrument, o.*
Intelligent, *verstandig.*
Intend (to). *van plan zijn.*
Interest (to), *interesseeren, interesseerde, geïnteresseerd*; *belang inboezemen*, W.
Interpreter, *tolk, m.*
Introduce (to), *invoeren*, W.
Inward, *innerlijk.*
Irishman, *Ier, m.*

J.

Jailer, *cipier, m.*
Jane, *Jans (je).*
Jewel, *juweel, o.*
John, *Jan, m.*
Joy, *vreugde, v., blijdschap, v.*
Journey, *reis, v.*

Judge, *rechter, m.*
Jump (to), *springen, sprong, gesprongen.*
June, *Juni.*
Just, *rechtvaardig.*
Just, *juist.*

K.

Kafir war, *Kaffer oorlog, m.*
Keep (to), *bewaren,* W.
Keep (to — down), *bedwingen, bedwong, bedwongen.*
Key, *sleutel, m.*
Kill (to), *dooden,* W
Kind, *soort, v.*
Kind, *vriendelijk.*

Kindness, *vriendelijkheid, v. ; vriendschap, v.*
Kitchen, *keuken, v.*
Knee, *knie, v.*
Kneel down (to), *neerknielen, knielde neer, neergeknield.*
Knock (to), *kloppen,* W.
Know (to), *kennen,* W., *weten,* S.

L.

Ladel (to), *adresseeren,* W.
Lace (boot—), *veter, m.*
Lady, *dame, v.*
Lamp, *lamp, v.*
Lap-dog, *schoothondje, o.*
Lapse, *verloop, o.*
Large, *groot ;* at —, *in het algemeen.*
Last, *laatst ; —* (adv.), *'t laatst ; — night, gisteren avond.*
Late, *te laat, laat ;* of — years, *in de laatste jaren ; —* at night, *den laten avond, s' avonds laat.*
Lately, *in den laatsten tijd, onlangs.*
Latter (the), *laatstgenoemde.*
Laugh (to), *lachen,* W
Law, *wet, v.*
Lay out (to), *aanleggen,* W.
Lay to rest (to), *te rusten neerleggen,* W.
Learned, *geleerd.*
Learn (to), *leeren,* W.
Leaf, *blad, o.*
Least, *minst.*
Leave (to), *nalaten,* S. ; — for, *vertrekken naar,* S.
Lend (to), *leenen,* W.
Less, *minder,*
Lesson, *les, v.*
Lest, *opdat . . . . niet.*
Let, *laten,* S.
Letter, *brief, m.*
Level at (to), *aanleggen op, legde aan, aangelegd.*
Library, *bibliotheek, v.*
Lick (to), *likken,* W.

Lie down (to). *zich neerleggen,* W.
Lifeless, *levenloos.*
Lift (to), *oplichten,* W.
Lightning, *bliksem, m.*
Like (to), *lust hebben in; —* best, *het liefst willen.*
Likely, *waarschijnlijk.*
Likewise, *ook.*
Linnet, *vlasvink, m.*
Lion, *leeuw, m.*
Listen (to), *luisteren naar,* W.
Lit, *aanstak.*
Little, *weinig.*
Live (to), *leven.*
Lively, *levendig, speelsch.*
Load, *vracht, v.*
Loadstone, *magneet, m.*
Lofty, *verheven.*
Lonely, *eenzaam.*
Long, *lang ;* as — as, *zoolang ; —* since, *reeds lang.*
Look (to), er . . . *uitzien, zag eruit, eruit gezien ; —* up, *opzoeken,* W. ; — for, *zoeken naar.*
Looked on, *schouwden aan.*
Loose (to), *los maken,* W. ; *bevrijden,* W.
Lose (to), *verliezen, verloor, verloren.*
Lot, *hoop, m.*
Loud, *luid.*
Louis, *Lodewijk.*
Love of truth, *waarheidsliefde, v.*
Low, *laag.*
Lydian, *Lydisch.*
Lyons, *Lyon.*

M.

Madam, *Mevrouw.*
Main road, *hoofdweg, m.*
Magnanimity, *grootmoedigheid, v.*
Manage (to), *erin slagen,* W.
Manager, *direckteur, m.*
Manners, *zeden, manieren.*
Manifest, *openbaar*
Many, *veel.*
Marble, *knikker, m.*

Market-house, *markthuis, o.*
Market-place, *markt, v.*
Martyr, *slachtoffer, o.*
Mason, *metselaar, m.*
Match, *lucifer, m.*
Material, *stof, v., materiaal, o.*
Matter, *zaak, v.*
Measure (to), *meten, mat, gemeten.*
Bleat, *vleesch, o.*

VOCABULARY. 391

Medicine, *medicijn, v.*
Meet (to), *ontmoeten,* W. ; — demands, *voldoen aan de eischen.*
Merchant, *koopman, m.*
Mere, *puur* ; —ly, *slechts alleen.*
Message, *boodschap, v.*
Messenger, *gezant, m.*
Mighty, *machtig.*
Military, *militair, m.*
Milk, *melk, v.*
Mind, *geest, m.*
Mine, *mijn, v.*
Minute, *minuut, v.*
Misapplication, *verkeerde toepassing, v.*
Misdeed, *verkeerde handeling, v. ; wandaad, v.*
Miserable, *naar, ellendig.*
Misery, *ellende, v.*
Mislead (to), *misleiden, misleidde, misleid.*

Miss (to), *missen, miste, gemist; verliezen,* S.
Mistake, *fout, v.*
Mistaken (to be —), *zich vergissen, vergiste, vergist.*
Mis y, *mistig.*
Model, *toonbeeld, o.*
Modesty, *zedigheid, v.*
Money, *geld, o.*
Monk, *monnik, m.*
More, *meer.*
Moreover, *bovendien.*
Mortal, *sterveling, gsl.*
Mountain, *berg, m.*
Moved at heart, *diep geroerd.*
Murderer, *moordenaar, m.*
Music, *muziek, v.*
Must, *moet.*
My, *mijn.*

N.

NAME, *naam, m. ; by —, met name.*
Nation, *volk, o.*
Native country, *geboorteland, o.*
Naturally, *van nature.*
Nature, *natuur, v.*
Naughty, *ondeugend.*
Neared, *naderden.*
Nearly, *bijna.*
Necessary, *noodig.*
Neck, *nek, m.*
Neglect (to), *verwaarloozen,* W.
Neighbour, *naaste, gsl., buur, m.*
Nervous, *zenuwachtig.*
Never, *nooit.*
Nevertheless, *toch, niettemin.*

New, *nieuw.*
News, *nieuws, o., tijding, v.*
Next, *volgend; —* to, *naast.*
Niece, *nicht, v.*
Night (at —), *in den avond.*
Nine, *negen.*
Nobility of heart, *zielenadel, m.*
Noble, *edel.*
Noise, *geluid, o.*
North (the), *noorden, o.*
Not .... yet, *nog niet.*
Nothing, *niets.*
Notice (to), *bemerken,* W., *opletten,* W.
Number of, *aantal.*
Nurse, *kindermeid, v.*

O.

OAK-TREE, *eikeboom, m.*
Obedience, *gehoorzaamheid, v.*
Obedient, *gehoorzaam.*
Oblige (to), *dwingen,* W,
Obliged (to be —), *verplicht zijn.*
Observing, *opmerken, o.*
O'clock, *uur, o.*
Occupation, *beroep, o.*
Occur (to), *gebeuren, gebeurde, gebeurd.*
Offer (to), *aanbieden,* S.
Offended (to be—at), *zich ergeren over,*W.
Office, *kantoor, o.*
Official, *beambte, m.*
Oftener, *meer.*
Old, *oud.*
Olympian games, *Olympische spelen.*
Once, *eenmaal, eens;* —more, *nog eenmaal*
Only, *slechts.*
Open (to), *open doen.*

Openly, *openlijk.*
Opinion, *opinie, v., oordeel, o.*
Opponent, *tegenstander, m.*
Opportunity, *gelegenheid, v., kans, m.*
Oracle, *orakel, o.*
Ordinary, *gewoon.*
Originate (to), *ontstaan.*
Other, *ander.*
Ought, *behoorde.*
Outermost, *uiterst.*
Outside, *buiten.*
Oven, *oven, m.*
Overflowing, *overvloeiend.*
Overlook (to), *over het hoofd zien.*
Overtake (to), *inhalen, haalde in, ingehaald ; overvallen,* S.
Overweight, *te zwaar.*
Own, *eigen.*

P.

PACE (to), *op en neer loopen,* S.
Pack (to), *pakken,* W.
Painful, *pijnlijk.*
Paint (to), *schilderen, schilderde, geschilderd.*
Painter, *schilder, m.*

Palatable, *smakelijk.*
Paper, *papier, o.*
Paper (to), *behangen, behing, behangen.*
Parcel, *pak, o.*
Pardon (to), *vergeven.*
Parents, *ouders.*

Paris, *Parijs.*
Part, *deel, o.*
Part (to), *scheiden,* W.
Part (to take — in), *deelnemen aan,* S.
Part (to) (of clouds), *zich verdeelen,* W.
Particularly, *bijzonder.*
Parting words. *afscheidswoorden*
Party, *gezelschap, o.*
Pass (to), *voorbijkomen; overtrekken,* S.
Passage, *gang, v.*
Past, *voorbij; verleden, o.* (noun).
Path, *pad, o.*
Peace, *vrede, m.;* at —, *met vrede*
Peaceful, *vreedzaam.*
Peculiar, *eigenaardig, bijzonder.*
Pen, *pen, v.*
Pencil, *potlood, o.*
Penetrate (to), *doordringen,* S.
People, *menschen.*
Perform (to), *verrichten.* W.
Permission, *verlof, o.*
Persia, *Persië.*
Person, *persoon, gsl.*
Peruse, *doorzien,* S.
Perverted, *verkeerd.*
Philosopher, *wijsgeer,* m.
Physical strength, *lichaamskracht, v.*
Pick (to), *plukken,* W.; — up, *oprapen,* W.
Picnic, *picnic, m., buitenpartij, v.*
Picture, *portret, o., prent, v., schilderij, v.*
Piece, *stuk, o.;* — of poetry, *gedicht, o.*
Pine-wood, *pijnbosch, o.*
Pioneer, *voortrekker, m.*
Pipe, *pijp, v.*
Pistol, *pistool, o.*
Pity (to have — on), *medelijden hebben met.*
Place (to), *plaatsen, plaatste, geplaatst.*
Place, *plaats, v.;* — of worship, *plaats der aanbidding.*
Plant, *plant, v.*
Play (to), *spelen, speelde, gespeeld.*
Pleasant, *aangenaam, plezierig.*
Please, *als 't u blieft.*
Please (to), *bevallen, beviel, bevallen.*
Pleasure, *plezier, o., genot, o.*
Plenty of, *ruim, een overvloed van.*
Plough (to), *ploegen,* W.
Pocket, *zak,* m
Poetry, *poesie, v.*
Point, *punt, o.*
Poisoned cup, *giftbeker, m.*
Political, *politiek.*
Pond, *dam, m.*
Poor, *arm;* — (of animals), *mager.*

Poor (noun), *armen.*
Positively, *beslist.*
Possession, *bezit, o.*
Possible, *mogelijk.*
Post, *post, m.*
Postman, *brievenbode, m.*
Post-office, *postkantoor, o.*
Potato, *aardappel, m.*
Pound, *pond, o.;* — sterling, *pond sterling.*
Poverty, *armoede, v.*
Powder, *kruit, o.*
Power, *macht, v.*
Practice, *beoefening, v.; praktijk, v.*
Practise (to), *zich oefenen,* W.
Praise (to), *prijzen, prees, geprezen.*
Precious, *kostbaar.*
Prefer (to), *voortrekken,* S.; — to, *verkiezen boven,* S.
Present, *tegenwoordig;* at —, *op het oogenblik;* — day, *huidige dag, tegenwoordige tijd.*
Preserve, *konfijt, o.*
Pretty, *mooi.*
Prevent (to), *voorkómen, voorkwam, voorkomen.*
Price, *prijs, m.*
Pride, *hoogmoed, m.*
Priest, *priester, m.*
Priestess, *priesteres, v.*
Prison, *gevangenis, v.*
Private house, *woonhuis, o.*
Prize, *prijs, m., buit, m.*
Profit, *winst, v.*
Profitable, *nuttig.*
Profound, *diep.*
Promise, *belofte, v.*
Promise (to), *beloven, beloofde, beloofd.*
Promoting (in), *met het bevorderen.*
Proof, *bewijs, o.*
Properly, *behoorlijk.*
Property. *eigenschap.*
Protect (to), *beschutten,* W.
Provide (to — for), *zorgen voor,* W.
Province, *provincie, v.*
Prudent, *voorzichtig.*
Public, *openbaar, publiek, o.* (n u).
Pull (to), *trekken,* S.
Punish (to), *straffen, strafte, gestraft.*
Punished (to be —), *gestraft worden.*
Purity, *reinheid, v.*
Purpose, *doel, o.*
Purse, *beurs, v.*
Put down (to), *opschrijven,* S.
Put right (to), *in orde maken.*

Q.

Quarter (of an hour), *kwartier, o.*
Quench (to) (thirst), *lesschen,* W.
Question, *vraag, v.*
Quickly, *gauw, vlug.*

Quick-tempered, *opvliegend, van aard.*
Quiet, *rustig, stil.*
Quite, *heel; geheel en al.*

R.

Race, *wedren, m.*
Rail (by), *per spoor.*
Railway accident, *spoorwegongeluk, o.*

Rain, *regen, m.;* —clouds, *regenwolken, v.;* —water, *regenwater.*
Raise (to — an army), *een leger op de been brengen.*

VOCABULARY. 393

Raise (to — wheat), *graan verbouwen*.
Rarely, *zelden*.
Rather, *liever*.
Reach (to), *bereiken*, W.; — home, *t'huis komen*, S.
Read (to), *lezen, las, gelezen*; — out, *voorlezen, las voor, voorgelezen*.
Reading-room, *leeskamer, v.*
Ready, *klaar*.
Really, *waarlijk*.
Reason, *reden, v.*
Reassemble (to), *zich hereenigen*, W.
Reassuringly, *geruststellend*.
Rebel (to), *in opstand komen*.
Receive (to), *ontvangen, ontving, ontvangen*.
Recite (to), *reciteeren*, W.
Reckless, *roekeloos*.
Recognise, *herkennen*, W.
Recollect (to), *zich herinneren*, W.
Reflect (to — great credit on), *veel eer aandoen*. S.
Refuse (to), *weigeren*, W.
Rein, *teugel, m.*
Relapse, *instorting, v.*
Relative, *verwante, v.*
Relieve (to), *verlossen*, W.
Religion, *godsdienst, m.*
Remarkable, *merkwaardig*.
Remind (to — of), *herinneren aan*, W.
Renowned, *beroemd*.
Repent (to — of), *berouw hebben van*.
Reply, *antwoord, o.*
Reply (to), *antwoorden, antwoordde, geantwoord; hernemen, hernam, hernomen*.
Report, *bericht, o.*

Report (to), *berichten*, W.
Request, *verzoek, o.*
Require (to), *noodig hebben*; —d, *noodig*.
Rescue, *verlossing, v.*; for the —, *tot ontzet*.
Resemble (to), *gelijken op*.
Resolve (to), *besluiten*, S.
It source, *toevlucht, v.*
Responsible, *verantwoordelijk*.
Rest, *rust, v.*
Result, *uitslag, m., gevolg, o.*
Return (to), *teruggeven, gaf terug, teruggegeven, terugkeeren*. W.
Revise (to), *nazien, zag na, nagezien*.
Revolver, *revolver, o.*
Reward (to), *beloonen*. W.; n, *belooning, v.*
Rich, *rijk*.
Riches, *rijkdommen*.
Riddle, *raadsel, o.*
Ride, *rit, m.*; to take a —, *eenen rit maken*.
Right, *recht*; to do —, *recht handelen*; to be —, *gelijk hebben*; —minded, *rechtgeaard, weldenkend*.
Rising, *opstaan, o.*; — generation, *opkomend geslacht, o.*
Risky, *gewaagd*.
Room, *ruimte, v., plaats, v., kamer, v.*
Rotation, *wenteling, v.*
Round about, *in den omtrek, in de rondte*.
Rouse (to), *wakker maken*.
Rubbish, *vuilnis, o., vuil, o.*
Rumbling, *rommelend*.
Rumour, *gerucht, o.*
Run (to), *loopen, liep, geloopen*; — up to, *toeloopen naar*, S; — off, *wegloopen*.
Rush (to), *springen*, S.
Rusty, *verroest*.

S.

Sad, *treurig*.
Saddle (to), *zadelen*, W.
Safely, *veilig*.
Sage, *wijze, gsl.*
Sake (for the — of), *om, ten einde*.
Salary, *salaris, o.*
Sample, *monster, o.*
Sandal, *sandaal, v.*
Sand-hill, *zandheuvel, m.*
Satisfied, *tevreden, voldaan*.
Save (to), *redden, redde, gered*; — oneself trouble, *zich moeite besparen*.
Scan (to), *aandachtig bekijken*, S.
Scene of the fire, *plaats (v.) van den brand*.
Scenery, *landschap, o., natuur, v.*
S hool, *school, v.*
Schoolmaster, *schoolmeester, m.*
Scissors, *schaar, v.*
Scold (to), *berispen*, W.
Scream (to), *gillen*, W.
Sculptor, *beeldhouwer, m*
Seal (to), *bezegelen*, W.
Season (to), *kruiden*, W.
Search (to), *doorzoeken*, W.
Secretary, *secretaris, m.*

See (to — to), *nazien*, S.
See (to), *zien, zag, gezien*.
Seed, *zaad, o.*
Seeing that, *aangezien*.
Seem (to), *schijnen*, S.
Seize (to), *grijpen*, S.
Self-possessed, *zich zelven gelijk*.
Send (to), *zenden, zond, gezonden*.
Serious, *ernstig, gevaarlijk*.
Servant, *bediende, m.*
Several, *verscheiden*.
Severe, *hevig*.
Service, *dienst, m.*
Shackle, *boei, v.*
Shame, *schande, v.*
Share, *deelen*, W.
Snare (to), *verdeelen, verdeelde, verdeeld*.
Shavings, *krullen*.
Shawl, *shawl, m., onslagdoek, m.*
Sheep, *schapen*.
Shelter (to), *schuilen*, S.
Shell, *schelp, v.*
Shield (to — from), *beschutten voor*, W.
Shine (to), *stralen*, W.
Shop, *winkel, m.*; — keeper, *winkelier, m.*
Shore, *oever, m.*

394 THE COMMERCIAL DUTCH GRAMMAR.

Shortly after, *kort daarna*.
Should, *zou ; moest ; behoorde*.
Shoulder, *schouder, m*.
Show (to), *toonen,* W. ; *laten zien ; wijzen,* S.
Shower, *bui, v*.
Sick-bed. *ziekbed, o*.
Sickly, *ziekelijk*.
Side, *kant. m*.
Sideboard, *buffet, o*.
Sight, *gezicht, o*.
Simply, *eenvoudig*.
Since, *aangezien ; sedert ;* — then, *sedert dien tijd*.
Sir, *Mijnheer*.
Sister, *zuster, v*.
Situation, *betrekking, v*.
Sixteenth, *zestiende*.
Skill, *bekwaamheid, v*.
Skin, *vel, o*.
Sleep, *slaap, m*.
Sleep (to), *slapen, sliep, geslapen*.
Slipper, *pantoffel, v*.
Smile, *glimlach, m*.
Sniff (to — at), *ruiken aan,* S.
Snow-white, *sneeuwit*.
Soap manufactory, *zeepfabriek, v*.
Sober, *nuchter*.
Soberness, *matigheid, v*.
Society, *maatschappij, v*.
Soil, *grond, m*.
Soldier, *soldaat, m*.
Solomon, *Salomo*.
Some, *een paar ; wat ; eenig ;* — or other, *de eene of andere*.
Soon, *weldra*.
Sore, *zeer*.
Sorrow, *verdriet, o*.
Sorry (to be —), *spijten,* S.
Sound wisdom, *diepe wijsheid, v*.
South (the), *zuiden ;* — Africa, *zuid-Afrika*.
Southerly wind, *zuidenwind, m*.
Sow (to), *zaaien,* W.
Spacious, *ruim*.
Spade, *graaf, v*.
Spare (to), *missen,* W.
Speech, *woorden, rede, v*.
Spelling, *spelles, v*.
Spend (to), *doorbrengen,* S. ; *besteden,* W. ; — one's life, *zijn leven slijten,* S.
Spirit, *geest, m*.
Splendour, *pracht, v*.
Spoil, *roof, m*.

Spot, *plek, v. ; plaats, v*.
Spout, *goot, v*.
Sprung from, *ontstaan uit*.
Stable, *stal, m*.
Stake, *paal, m*.
Stamp, *postzegel, m*.
Standing (of long —), *oud*.
Start on (to), *beginnen,* S.
Start for (to), *vertrekken naar,* S.
Startle (to), *opschrikken,* W.
State (to), *verklaren,* W.
State, *toestand, m. ; staat, m*.
Stately, *statig*.
Statement, *bewering, v. ; gezegde, o*.
Station, *station, o*.
Stay (to), *blijven,* S. ; — away, *wegblijven,* S.
Steal (to), *stelen, stal, gestolen ;* — away, *kruipen naar,* S.
Steamer, *stoomboot, v. ; boot, v*.
Stick, *stok, m*.
Stiff, *stijf*.
Still, *nog*.
Sting (to), *steken ;* — by pride, *prikkelen,* W.
Stop (to), *ophouden,* S.
Story, *verhaal, o. ; geschiedenis, v*.
Straightway, *regelrecht*.
Strand, *strand, o*.
Stranger, *vreemdeling, gsl*.
Street, *straat, v*.
Strict, *stipt*.
Strike (to), *opvallen,* S.
Strong, *sterk*.
Study, *studeerkamer, v. ; studie, v*.
Study (to — on), *doorgaan met studeeren*.
Stung, *aangezet*.
Succeed (to), *slagen, slaagde, geslaagd*.
Such, *zulk*.
Suddenly, *eensklaps*.
Suffer (to), *lijden,* S.
Sufficiently, *voldoemda*.
Sugar, *suiker, v*.
Suit (to), *bevallen,* S.
Sum, *som, v*.
Sunrise, *zonsopgang, m*.
Support (to), *onderhouden,* S.
Suppose (to), *veronderstellen,* W.
Surprised, *verwonderd*.
Surely, *waarlijk, voorzeker*.
Surpass (to), *overtreffen,* S.
Sustain (to), *onderhouden,* S.
Sweep (to), *vegen,* W.
Syllable, *lettergreep, v. ;* (here), *woord, o*.

T.

Table, *tafel, v*.
Tail, *staart, m*.
Take back (to), *terugbrengen,* S.
Take care (to), *zorgen* (*zorg dragen*) *voor*.
Take into consideration (to), *in aanmerking nemen*.
Take down (to), *afnemen,* S.

Take food (to), *voedsel gebruiken,* W.
Take leave (to), *afscheid nemen van*.
Take a ride (to), *eenen rit te maken*.
Take shelter (to), *schuilen,* S.
Take up (to), *opnemen,* S.
Tale, *verhaal, o*.
Talk, *gesprek, o*.
Tasted, *geproefd*.

Tea, *thee, v.*
Teacher, *onderwijzer, m.*
Tell (to), *vertellen, vertelde, verteld.*
Temper, *humeur, o.*
Temple, *tempel, m.*
Tent, *tent, v.*
Terms (on good —), *op goeden voet.*
Terrific, *vreeselijk.*
Test (to), *onderzoeken,* W.
Thank-offering, *dank offer, o.*
That, *die, dat.*
Thereupon, *daarop.*
Thief, *dief, m.*
Thin, *mager, dun.*
Think (to) (to consider), *het houden voor.*
Think (to — it an honour), *het zich eene eer rekenen,* W.
Third, *derde.*
Thirsty (to be —), *dorst hebben.*
Thistle-finch, *putter, m.*
Those, *die.*
Three, *drie.*
Throw (to), *werpen, wierp, geworpen ; gooien, gooide, gegooid.*
Thrush, *lijster, v.*
Thunder, *onweer, o.*
Thunderstorm, *onweer, o., onweersbui, v.*
Tide of war, *krijgsgeluk, o.*
Till, *totdat.*
Time, *tijd, m. ;* at the —, *destijds ;* in —, *bijtijds ;* for some —, *een tijdlang.*
Tired, *vermoeid, moe.*
Tobacco, *tabak, v.*
To-day, *vandaag.*
Together, *bij elkaar, samen.*

To-morrow, *morgen.*
To-night, *van avond.*
Too, *ook, te.*
Tool, *werktuig, o.*
Top, *tol, m.*
Touching, *aandoenlijk.*
Towards, *naar. . . . toe.*
Town, *stad, v. ;* — hall, *stadhuis, o.*
Tradition, *overlevering, v.*
Tram-fare, *tramgeld, o.*
Translate (to), *vertalen,* W.; *overbrengen,* S.
Translation, *vertaling, v.*
Travel (to), *reizen, reisde, gereisd.*
Traveller, *reiziger, m.*
Treasure, *schat, m.*
Treat (to), *behandelen,* W.
Treatment, *behandeling, v.*
Tree, *boom, m.*
Tremble (to), *beven,* W.
Terrific, *vreeselijk.*
Trip, *reis, v.*
Trouble, *moeite, v.*
True, *waar ;* to remain —, *trou blijven*
Trust (to), *vertrouwen,* W.
Truth, *waarheid, v.*
Try (to), *probeeren,* W. ; *beproeven,* W. — one's hand, *de hand leggen aan.*
Turn (to), *zich keeren,* W.
Twelve, *twaalf.*
Twenty, *twintig.*
Twice, *tweemaal.*
Twig, *twijg, v.*
Two, *twee.*

U.

Uncle, *oom, m.*
Underground, *onderaardsch.*
Undertake, *ondernemen,* S.
Undisturbed, *onverstoord.*
Undo (to), *ongedaan maken.*
Undoubtedly, *ongetwijfeld.*
Unexpected, *onverwacht.*
Unfailingly, *onfeilbaar.*
Unfortunate, *ongelukkig.*
Ungrateful, *ondankbaar.*
United, *vereenigd.*

Uninterrupted, *onverstoord.*
Unless, *tenzij.*
Unmanly, *onmannelijk.*
Unshaken, *onwrikbaar.*
Up and down, *op en neer.*
Upright, *oprecht.*
Upset (to), *omgooien.*
Urgent, *dringend.*
Use, *nut, o. ; gebruik, o.*
Used to say, *placht te zeggen.*
Utter in reply (to), *antwoorden,* W.

V.

Vain (in —), *tevergeefs.*
Value, *waarde, v*
Vanity, *ijdelheid, v.*
Various, *verscheiden ;* — kinds, *allerlei.*
Vehicle, *voertuig, o.*
Veil, *sluier, m., voile (Fr.), v.*
Venetian, *Venetiaansch.*
Venture (to), *wagen,* W. ; — out, *zich buiten wagen.*
Verse, *vers, o.*
Very, *zeer.*
Victory, *overwinning, v.*

View, *photographie, v.*
Vile, *laag.*
Village, *dorp, o.*
Vine, *wijnstok, m.*
Violent, *hevig.*
Virtue, *deugd, v.*
Visit, *bezoek, o.*
Visit (to), *bezoeken, besocht, bezocht.*
Viz., *n.l. (namelijk).*
Voice, *stem, v.*
Vocabulary, *woordenlijst, v.*

W.

Waggon-house, *wagenhuis, o.*
Waiter, *bediende, m.*
Wake up (to), *wakker maken, wekken,* W.
Walk, *wandeling, v.*
Walk (to), *wandelen,* W.
Walk about (to), *rondloopen, liep rond, rondgeloopen; — off, heenloopen,* S.
Wall, *muur, m.*
Want, *behoefte, v.; — of, gebrek aan.*
Want (to), *willen; noodig hebben; hebben willen.* [*doen.*
War (to make — with), *den oorlog aan-*
Warn (to), *waarschuwen, waarschuwde, gewaarschuwd.*
Warning, *waarschuwing, v.*
Watch, *horloge, o.*
Weapon, *wapen, o.*
Wearily, *moe.*
Weather, *weder, o.*
Weigh (to), *wegen, woog, gewogen.*
Well, *bron, v.*
Well, *goed, wel;* as — as, *evengoed.*
Were, *waren.*
Whatever, *wat . . . ook.*
Wheat, *koorn, o.*
When, *wanneer, als, toen.*
Whenever, *wanneer.*
Whereby, *waardoor.*
Whether, *of; —* or, *of — of.*
While (a), *tijd, m.;* for —, *een poosje.*

Whisper (to), *fluisteren,* W.
Whistle (to — to a bird), *eenen vogel toefluiten.*
Whither, *waarheen.*
Whole (on the —), *over het geheel.*
Wholesome, *gezond.*
Whose, *welks.*
Why, *waarom.*
Wild, *wild, in het wild.*
Will, *testament, o.*
Will, *zullen.*
Will (to), *willen, wilde, gewild.*
Windy, *winderig.*
Wing, *vleugel, m.*
Winter, *winter, m.*
Wisdom, *wijsheid, v.*
Wise, *wijs.*
Witnessed, *bijgewoond.*
Woman, *vrouw, v.*
Wonder, *wonder, o.*
Wood, *bosch, o.*
Wood-pigeon, *woudduif, v.*
Word, *woord, o.*
Work, *werk.*
Work (to), *bewerken,* W.
Worked (to have —), *laten bewerken.*
Workshop, *werkplaats, v.*
Worn out, *versleten.*
Would, *zou.*
Wrong, *verkeerd;* (noun), *kwaad, o.*

Y.

Yard, *achterplaats v.*
Year, *jaar, o.*
Yesterday, *gisteren.*
Yonder, *gindsch.*

Young, *jong.*
Your, *uw.*
Youth, *jongeling, m.*

Z.

Zeal, *ijver, m.*

www.ingramcontent.com/pod-product-compliance
Lightning Source LLC
Chambersburg PA
CBHW020101020526
44112CB00032B/772